For LABOR'S Sake

Gains and Pains as Told by 28 Creative Inside Reformers

Edited by
Arthur B. Shostak

University Press of America, Inc.
Lanham • New York • London

Library of Congress Cataloging-in-Publication Data

For labor's sake: gains and pains as told by 28 creative inside
reformers/
edited by Arthur B. Shostak
P. cm.
Includes Index.
1. Trade-unions--United States.
I. Shostak, Arthur B.
HD6508.F58   1995   331.88'0973--dc20   94-38272 CIP

ISBN 0-8191-9775-0 (pbk. : alk. paper)

Excerpts from the 28 Essays:

1.) "Instead of just hanging on by our fingernails, we should just open our hearts and minds to others, especially those we froze out, good people with whom we can soon build coalitions to turn this country around." **Terrell Nicolodis, Painters Union (IBPAT).**

2.) "Hell, if the labor movement is sinking...which I do *not* think is happening...at least we're trying to bail out some of the water." **Tom O'Donnell, International Brotherhood of Electrical Workers (IBEW).**

3.) "We're constantly making improvements...in getting better working conditions, or a safer airplane...many of which gains remind me of what my mother tried and failed to get for her co-workers so many years ago." **Mary Kay Hanke, Association of Flight Attendants (AFA).**

4.) "...if you don't keep visiting out there [with your members where they work], keep picking up *new* things, you become stagnant." **Javier M. Perez, Jr., Amalgamated Transportation Union (ATU).**

5.) "People who are hurting have a big need to talk about it, to mull on it, to turn it around...and we help them work through all of it. We share the pain and lighten their load, mostly by being there, by bringing our UAW local to their side...A lotta families of our members have gotten a lotta help they probably never expected to get for their union dues dollars." **L. Max Schmitt, United Auto Workers (UAW).**

6.) "I took the opportunity recently to go to a weekend-long men's retreat. It turned out there were five other men from my local there...It was pretty cool, pretty interesting...I learned a lot." **Paul Blaski, Roofers Union (URWAW).**

7.) "That's the thing about union work...you take your victories where you can find 'em!...it's something to keep you going." **Paul Finn, Painters Union (IBPAT).**

8.) "The new Labor Studies course I developed is titled 'Labor and Community, Race and Ethnicity'...it includes every question you are NOT supposed to talk about in the labor move-ment...The class scares some people, but most seem to think it is wonderful to have a class which deals with these issues directly." **Deborah Moy, Labor Educator (SEIU; AFT).**

9.) "Cooperation, participation, and determination have now replaced futility and frustration. New management teams meet with labor to discuss market share rather than termination hearings...Had it not been for the unions, TWA would fail to exist today." **Robert Langro, International Association of Machinists (IAM).**

10.) "In us the *good* employers have an ally they never had before - if they are willing to work with us...." **John Dalrymple, Service Employees International Union (SEIU).**

11.) "...we need to play the game at more than one level! We'll fight like hell to stop them taking away merit increases *and* at the same time we'll attempt to establish what could be a Total Quality environment....These struggles can co-exist, but only for people who can see two things at once." **Susan Pacult Foregard, Service Employees International Union (SEIU).**

12.) "Union leaders must be able to speak the language of the investor and the financier...and bring to their respective industries a powerful and a beneficial knowledge of how to save money and boost production." **Wendell W. Young. 3rd, United Food and Commercial Workers (UFCW).**

13.) "We in labor must model the kinds of behavior that we expect those we deal with to begin to demonstrate." **David Cracium, International Union of Electricians (IUE).**

14.) "The company is a 'customer' of the union. And the union is a 'customer' of the company. *W e* will survive, or *w e* will fail...jointly!...there's cold nights coming, and we're gonna' have to lay down by the fire together to survive. We can't keep scratching each others' eyeballs out all the time." **William Franklin, United Mineworkers Union (UMW).**

15.) "...history has shown that if management is left to run things by itself it always screws it up! Management is just too important to be left to the managers alone...and that's a *fact!*" **Daniel Bailey, United Rubber Workers (URW).**

16.) "We had to confront the fact that we were in a different industry than the one we would like to have...we had better find some innovative ways to deal with this, or we were going to get crushed." **Ike Gittlen, United Steelworkers Union (USW).**

17.) "...what I've done is try to explain the TQC program to my local union officials, and try to get them to see it as the opportunity it is to revive labor, change management, help the people in the plant, and just maybe, rescue the entire nation." **John Alexander, United Rubber Workers Union (URW).**

18.) "What my role became - as a unionist - was to figure out what in hell they [the telephone companies] were saying?! ... I went into it as if I was trying to make sense of a foreign language." **Karen Hart, Communication Workers of America (CWA).**

19.) "...we created a coalition of local presidents who just won't roll over and be nice...the company had better think twice or the 'wild people' out in the field - all of us - will *really* make trouble! We're betting this will work: They need our cooperation!" **Rhonda Bailey Maddex, Communication Workers of America (CWA).**

20.) "...we have a formal progressive caucus now within our union, and we kibbitz with similar guys who have won control of two other railroad brotherhoods." **James Teague, Brotherhood of Maintenance of Way Employees (BMWE).**

21.) "I started talking with other UTU Legislative Reps in the state, and with higher-ups in the union who were legislatively-inclined. And I found out what their secrets were. This enabled me to know what to say and what to do, and, all of a sudden, I began to get some respect." **Richard A. Finamore, United Transportation Union (UTU).**

22.) "Having been branded a dissident, and assigned a seat in the back of the class, having been labeled a 'radical' and put 'off limits' to brothers and sisters who might otherwise talk with me, I continue to challenge the system that has made me an outcast." **Paul Plaganis, Transportation Communications Union (TCU).**

23.) "When I first proposed a mail survey I had no one on my side. People said it was stupid, a waste of time. No one would take it seriously...we got back over 32% of our mailing list...It was really great! As a result of survey feedback we changed a lot of things in our platform." **John Murphy, International Brotherhood of Electrical Workers (IBEW).**

24.) "I don't know if there is any precaution that can be taken once the government has determined it will go forward with a civil, or perhaps criminal RICO suit, as it has in the case of other unions in this country." **Roy Silbert, Hotel Employees and Restaurant Employees Union (HERE).**

25.) "If there is a message in this terrible tragedy it is that no one union can do it alone. It takes the power of many unions working together to fight an onslaught such as Local 675 has experienced." **Dennis Walton, International Union of Operating Engineers (IUOE).**

26.) "This is a fertile field to cultivate, this matter of graduate student unionization....This is a chance to influence them before they leave the university, to teach them how important and valuable are labor organizations, how important is collective action." **Diane DeYoung Rau, American Federation of Teachers (AFT).**

27.) "Unions, you know, are the worst employers around. Sorry about that! I've negotiated with many, many employers, and I've never met one as bad as the one I work for!...I'll just keep pluggin' away, confident that the good in unionism will win out." **John Scally, Communications Workers of America (CWA).**

28.) "Unions will continue to be the social conscience. I believe our charge will carry us well into the 21st century, 'cause there's nobody around who can protect people and be the social conscience any better." **Paul Anderson, Communication Workers of America (CWA).**

Table of Contents

Preface

"A diamond is a chunk of coal
that made good under pressure."
Anon

Having spent nearly 40 years studying trade unionism here and abroad I believe one of the most important stories that can be told about organized labor is too rarely shared. As the men and women involved, a special type of union activist I call *inside reformers*, are a colorful lot on whom hinges much of the fate of organized labor, I have worked for four years (1990-'93) to get them to tell their own story.

Intrinsically interesting, their account of on-going improvements in their local or international union offers valuable advice for unionists eager to help labor boost its prospects. As well, academics trying to better understand the current labor scene will find much of value in their wry behind-the-scene perspective. Finally, all who wonder what contribution unheralded citizens can make to the renewal of vital social movements will find inspiration in these "battle reports."

Although as diverse as are the nation's 16-million trade unionists, inside reformers are set apart by their belief that the rank-and-file wants labor leadership ready , eager, and adroit in grappling with change: Just saying "No!" to the employer does not cut it anymore. As well, they stand out in their willingness to give their all, an effort known in earlier times as a Calling or personal mission.

A few are paid staffers (AFL-CIO employees or international reps or business agents). Many are full-time local union officers. A small percent are unpaid rank-and-filers, the kind who work the tools all day and then volunteer several nights a month to run their local's evening school apprentice or safety education program. Regardless of their particular role all approach the travails and rewards of the activist's life with wry fortitude.

Over recent decades I have come to know scores of inside reformers while teaching at various union education centers, conducting research on or for unions, attending meetings of relevant groups (conferences run by the AFL-CIO, FMCS, Association for Union Democracy, etc.), serving as a consultant to locals or international unions, and most especially, while teaching since 1976 at the AFL-CIO's George Meany Center for Labor Studies in Silver Spring, Maryland. In my twice-yearly week-long Meany Center classes, and after class at the Center's high-spirited bar I have listened with fascination to talented change-agents explain the strengths and weaknesses of an on-going social invention of theirs, a bright new tactic or strategy paying off so handsomely that other listeners began thinking out loud about how they might adapt the innovation to their particular union circumstance.

What I especially like about these gutsy change-agents is their insistence that "business as usual" will not suffice. They do not believe innovations are too risky to try. Or leaders are too busy to undertake anything new. Or if it has not been invented here it cannot be worth trying. Long ago persuaded this obsolete idea system invites only decline, inside reformers insist instead on trying this and that, on taking calculated risks with social inventions (their own or those of others), and demonstrating to everyone organized labor is *not* behind the curve.

Highly individualistic, the inside reformers I know mix improvisation and vision so adroitly that admirers and detractors alike wonder what will come next. Highly opinionated, their conviction labor can do a lot better is fairly contagious. Highly motivated, they are energized, even driven, by their reform "Cause." And highly outgoing and personable, they energize others with their belief a few committed dues-payers with a sound strategy and a compelling vision , a few "ordinary" people capable of extraordinary things, can make one helluva good difference.

Naturally, these men and women share certain shortcomings, which make them a lot less saintly and far more human. Many rue the time they have lost from family, childrearing, and homelife pleasures, time lost to endless union-related phonecalls, meetings, and the hectic like, all at real cost to edgy, loving marriages. Many wish they had known more about relevant reforms underway elsewhere in the labor movement, reforms that might have spared them "rediscovering the wheel."[1] And nearly all have had occasional doubts about their own capabilities, and even about labor's recovery prospects. Challenged, however, rather than debilitated by such misgivings, they generally take a "count of nine" and come up swinging.

Why this book? First, because far too little attention has been paid to reformers working *inside* unions, an over-looked group the media, most pundits, and many academics under value to no one's benefit or credit. Second, because these change-agents are an inspiring lot, a colorful bunch with whom a reader can profitably spend time. Third, because their lives are lived in the service of a remarkable contention, one with powerful implications for the fate of us all: They believe a finer America and a finer labor movement go better *together*, and cannot be secured, either one, without the other. If so, gains...and losses...of labor's inside reformers are meaningful far beyond the union hall, a conclusion I've long ago come to share with the men and women in this volume.

Why Tales of Pain? Because if locals and unions are not experiencing setbacks, they are probably not taking enough risks. Leaders who try must occassionally stumble. But those too timid or unimaginative, too frightened or prosaic to even try provide only costly (non) leadership.

Jonathan Tasini, president of the National Writers Union, contends that the *highest* priority in promoting labor's recovery should be "engaging in a serious debate, without recriminations, about the weaknesses inside the labor movement. The common argument that an honest discussion will help the corporations is the last refuge of scoundrels and cowards. The corporations are strong enough without our help."[2]

Inside reformers in this volume do us the compliment of sharing bruising experiences of theirs from which we can all grow...provided we do not flinch from troubling accounts of favored plans and projects gone awry, and work very hard instead to wring every last valuable lesson from the tale.

Summary: Tales of Gains! As the stakes then are *very* high, it is well-nigh time union change-agents told their own story. Should their words and example inspire fresh confidence in their type of union reforms, a major goal of this volume will have been achieved. If other unionists sit up and take notice, if the volume's *many* reform ideas are widely adapted coast-to-coast, America may soon profit from a high quality of trade unionism labor's remarkable inside reformers can best help us secure.

Arthur B. Shostak
Drexel University
Philadelphia, PA

---

1   Shostak, Arthur B. *Robust Unionism: Innovations in the Labor Movement*. Ithaca, NY: ILR Press, 1991.
2   Tasini, Jonathan, "Establishing an Independent Organizing Arm," in *The Future of Labor*, edited by Greg Tarpinian. New York: Labor Research Association, Inc., 1992; 72.

Introduction:
Inside Reformers

> There are ...companies, political parties, and unions in this country
> that are like dinosaurs waiting for the weather to change.
> The very ground is shifting beneath us. And what is called for is nothing
> less than all of us reconceptualizing our roles."
>
> John Naisbitt, *Megatrends*,
> 1984;100.

Nearly four decades of reading labor history, teaching industrial sociology, and learning from union students of mine has me persuaded organized labor takes second to no other social movement in its resolve to adapt and survive. Little wonder, accordingly, that Lane Kirkland, president of the AFL-CIO, contends "the sole reason men and women organize unions is to bring about change."[1]

Inside Reformers. Much to labor's benefit its 16-million members include several thousand unsung heroes and heroines...grass-roots types dedicated to serving as internal change-agents. Opponents often bad-mouth them as back-breakers, ball-busters, malcontents, trouble-makers, and self-serving egotists. Supporters, however, salute them as morale builders, natural leaders, and self-effacing "can-do" achievers.

In this volume 22 men and six women from 20 international unions stand in for several thousand counterparts and explain what being an *inside reformer* means today in the American labor movement. All but four are volunteers from nearly 1,200 students I have known over 15 years of adjunct teaching at the AFL-CIO George Meany Center for Labor Studies (Silver Spring, MD) where for two weeks a year I meet with two classes daily of 15 to 25 unionists per class. (Two others, L. Max Schmitt and Richard Finamore, are from a student body I addressed at the 1992 Cornell School summer session for trade unionists; a third, Dennis Walton, I met doing research for *Robust Unionism*; and a fourth, Wendell Young, Sr., is a union friend of mine many years standing). Together the 28 unionists cover a very broad range, one that stretches from unpaid rank-and-filers to a full-time highly influential union staffer in charge of his union's personnel program. In-between are business agents, international union reps, staffers of large locals, and local union officers, this last type the most frequent among all internal reformers.

What They are Up Against. To begin to understand the men and women who speak through this volume, a type I call *inside reformers*, is to appreciate that over 90 percent of local union officers are part-time voluntary representatives.[2] This means most have received little or no formal education or training for their union post. Their learning is not abstracted from the work-place and union hall, but directly draws on years thoughtfully spent in both.

Many are vulnerable to loss of their job or a mandated transfer, as they have no special protection from their union role against these hazards. Most are not paid for evening and weekend hours spent on union business, a time when much is conducted. To make matters even worse, more and more employers are tightening up their interpretation of the contract clause that permits local union officers to devote "a reasonable amount of paid work time" to handle work-related problems during regular working hours.

All of which understandably gives would-be inside reformers pause. Before opting to take on this controversial role they must get very enthusiastic about specific reform ideas they pick up in labor education courses, union-sponsored conferences, or directly from other activists. They must think through these reforms, often devoting scores of hours to complex discussions with close supporters. They must feel assured of support from their spouse, "significant other," and children. And they must seek mentoring from more experienced co-unionists.

Still more fundamental yet is an ability to keep immediate crises at work or in the local from consuming all of one's energy and attention: Unless a reformer has a compelling vision of what could and should be, a vision powerful enough to extend beyond today's emergencies, he or she may get sidetracked or even suffer burnout during a prolonged reform campaign.

Range of Reforms. More interested in correcting labor's shortcomings and helping to chart a course for the future than in finger-pointing and blame-assigning, the change-agents who "speak" through these pages promote such improvements as replacing authoritarian styles of leadership with participative modes. They reject prejudices, such as sexism and racism, long ago in need of replacement. They create a reward system to encourage innovative projects. They assure an adequate supply of scarce and valued resources for innovative projects. They take a union of staffers into a "win-win" cooperative relationship with their employer, a very large labor union. They utilize the best of modern personnel practices to upgrade work inside union bureaucracies.

Pragmatic and rewarding, their reforms help broaden the limits of what other unionists see as achievable and begin to desire for their own situation. Intent on proving to themselves and everybody else that labor is not behind the curve, and that there is life beyond pain, they promote the kind of creativity without which organized labor cannot long survive. And they have learned how to rebound from disappointments to try a second and third time, improving their effort with each successive attempt. They do so without rancor, finger-pointing, or self-disparagement. Instead, each is preoccupied with uncovering *lessons*, uncovering pointers and guidelines well-worth calling to the attention of fellow unionists and supportive students of labor alike.

Reform Constraints. Unlike more militant dissidents with whom they cooperate the contributors to this volume seek an "engineered" evolution rather than sweeping overnight change. Most have little interest in soaring ideological perspectives, and prefer a "down home" focus instead on what is right under their nose. Almost all disassociate themselves from fiery calls to "smash" company or union "bosses," convinced as they are this is disproportionate in cost to any possible gain. Aware their reform agenda is far less colorful than that of fiery militants, they content themselves with the belief their blueprint is far more attainable and likely of success.

Willing to give as good as they get if need be, most prefer the art of verbal negotiations to the clash of verbal armor. Disinclined, however, to back off when "called out," they search for face-saving "win-win" options of benefit to all sides, in preference to "winner-take-all" resolutions that perpetuate divisiveness and secure at best only a Pyrrhic victory.

All of which helps explain why inside reformers generally have the respect, albeit sometimes begrudgingly, of current leaders of a local or a union. Much like the "Loyal Opposition" in parliamentary democracies whose role it is to shake things up, inside reformers accept the legitimacy of the incumbents even while challenging much about the situation. Most have learned from years of experience to reject the naive belief that "all high-minded participation impulses are found in the membership, only to be frustrated by the rascality and deviousness of union leadership."[3]

Unconvinced by fervid calls for an immediate top-to-bottom overhaul, for an overnight transformation of the entire situation, inside reformers judge this both unattainable in fact and unclear in purpose: Theirs is the mid-course, the path of incremental reforms won steadily and sensitively over time, by the rules, and without vendetta-provoking harm to any decent folk with whom they have honest differences of opinion.

In this way most of these change-agents proudly define themselves as *moderates*. They bristle at, or shrug off condemnations of themselves as punch-shy class collaborators, spineless cowards, or bloodless wimps. Fully aware of the limitations of certain elitist power-holders, certain business and union officials with whom they warily co-exist, aware as *only* those behind the scenes can be, inside reformers believe their chances of winning *some* reforms *some* of the time are far better through accommodation than through antagonism...far better through cutting deals (via the art of negotiation, at which they excel) than through (figuratively) cutting throats. Their brand of union militancy favors unity over factionalism, and compromise with, rather than the forced capitulation of an embittered opposition..

An uneasy truce-of-sorts commonly links moderates with other far less moderate activists. Anchored in a workplace neither has the latitude to easily leave (thanks to accumulated seniority and pension rights), both types generally give the other breathing space, maneuvering room, and a wary sort of mutual respect. Joined together by their shared conviction things should and can be better, albeit seeing very different ways of achieving this, the rival change-agents learn much from their "odd couple" situation, a little-noticed development that helps minimize the shortcomings for organized labor of *both* empowering approaches to union reform.

Methodology. I was able to secure research cooperation thanks to the trust I earned in my teacher-student relations with these low-profile individuals. With four exceptions previously noted I tape-recorded their unrehearsed spontaneous answers to my questions at either January or July week-long Meany Center sessions in 1990, '91, '92, and '93. After I transcribed and lightly edited the tapes for readability I added section headings and sent a copy to each for their final "signed off" approval: Given the high stakes in reputation and careers involved I allowed any last changes and asked each contributor to assume responsibility for the version printed hereafter.

Happily, as I suspected from my prior knowledge of these men and women, few felt obliged to pretty up or otherwise mince their words. While one or two removed vulgarities they had long ago stopped hearing in their spoken language, little else was changed. Instead, they chose to tell it as it is, at least as they have lived the experience and want to share selected aspects of it.

This collection, of course, does not purport to represent *all* types of inside reformers, as the necessary research to outline the type has still not been done. As well, I had access to only 20 of the 87 unions in the AFL-CIO, and that further limits the generalizability of my observations.

How reliable is this material? How much confidence can be placed in it? None of the material has been authenticated by cross-checking interviews with everybody involved, as I had neither the time, funds, or desire to undertake such an enormous task. Instead, having intently listened to and even scrutinized each respondent up close, having challenged some with sharp questions any time something gave me pause, I now believe (almost) everything I was told. Having known all but the three non-Antioch Program activists for over three years, and having seen 25 of them interact with other unionists for week-long sessions at six month intervals, I feel I know them well-enough to trust to the presence of a truth-telling bond between us.

Listening to the Speakers. To get the most from all of this you might imagine yourself in a booth at the back of a "no-frills"diner, alone with a union activist who has one helluva good story to share, his or her own story of an on-going inside reform effort. Listen carefully to the language used; the choice of adjectives can reveal much, as do points of emphasis (noted by underlining). Listen especially to misgivings, as the self-criticism of the reformer tells much about them. Finally, relax and enjoy their considerable story-telling craft of these individuals, for as writer William Zinsser has observed, "the eloquence of the so-called ordinary man or woman is the most extraordinary resource waiting for any writer who goes looking for America."[4]

Outline of Case Studies. Each participant was asked to answer five revealing questions, any and all of which they were free to treat as they preferred -

1) **Background**: What about your personal history helps explain why you now find yourself a "wave-maker"?
2) **Work/Career Impact**: What about your entire work life helps explain your present role?
3) **Focus**: What particular internal problems of unions preoccupy you?
4) **Dynamics**: Who is helping your reform effort? Hindering it? And what are you doing in turn?
5) **Transferable Lessons**: What can other would-be internal union reformers learn from your example? What mistakes of yours can they possibly avoid making?

Far more attention was paid to the last three of these five matters, as these activists - their detractors to the contrary - dwell more readily on programmatics than on personalities (their own or that of anyone else).

Outline of the Volume. While one can dip into the book at any point it does have an underlying logic that explains its arrangement and invites a front-to-back reading.

The volume's opening section, **With Open Arms,** groups two case studies that demonstrate strategies and tools for "organizing the organized." A familiar local union problem, such as self-defeating rivalry among skill levels or hostility to non-whites, is countered by a successful exercise in personal and organizational recuperation. Less familiar matters, such as the potential of a health-promotion campaign or a unique school for apprentices, help move a local toward a finer state of affairs.

Part II, **Offering More Care,** employs three cases to highlight sensitive approaches to such trying matters as the AIDS epidemic, or a member's loss of a loved one, or the corrosive racism of certain members. Taken together the cases demonstrate some of the very personal rewards membership in a union "family" can actually entail.

In the third section, **Better Use of Better Information,** attention turns to the significance for labor of the popular notion that information is power. Three cases explore the importance of a local helping members stay abreast of the latest developments in work safety and product changes, in the use of computers, and in their grasp of both labor history and the changing world around them.

Part IV, **Shaping Stronger Structures,** focuses on form and how it helps shape content and meaning. The first case offers sound advice for uniting previously rival locals into a larger and more cost-efficient organization. The second puts the spotlight on privatization. It offers a unique, creative, and field-proven response through which a besieged local can finesse its hazards and make far more of this fast-spreading policy option than either admirers or detractors may suspect.

The third raises questions about the "shotgun weddings" that have an international union order two locals together in a resented merger. While often necessary for financial reasons and sometimes even advantageous for all concerned, forced mergers can be done well or poorly, the latter causing much unnecessary pain. The last case explores the pros and cons of employee ownership. An inside reformer explains the plight of a union leader who finds himself in the "Alice-in-Wonderland" position of bargaining with himself, as he represents the (unionized) employee-owners with whom he must negotiate.

Two case studies in Part V, **On "Walking the Talk,"** call attention to the centrality of integrity and persistence in modern union-management relations. Both inside reformers detail the hardships commonly experienced by unionists who learned long ago management is too important to be left exclusively to the managers. Both are committed to a "continuous bargaining" approach, one that artfully combines vigilant policing of a contract with cautious cooperation with progressive supervisors.

Part VI, **Twists-and-Turns,** offers four case studies in the uncertainties introduced in Part V. This time the focus is on hostile overseas ownership of a plant, on erratic company leadership in a depressed industry, and on company mis-management of the most costly sort...all major sources of pain where local unions are concerned.

Part VII, **Downsizing's Toll,** explores the trauma associated with endless churning in the job market, especially the toll taken by large-scale loss of jobs. Particularly helpful are leads offered for alleviating the pain of prospective pink slip targets, along with advice for how to transfer some pain to corporate higher-ups.

The next section, Part VIII, **Potent Political Action**, extends the book's focus to the complex and dramatic matter of political struggle. Two case studies explore ways in which efforts to register and inform the voting behavior of members can help turn labor's large numbers to the greatest advantage.

Part IX, **Union Democracy at Bay**, raises the lid on a proverbial Pandora's Box. Consistent with their 19th century origins certain unions still operate as top-down tightly-controlled single-party operations. Opposition to incumbents is frowned upon (to put it mildly!), and opponents are often dealt with harshly. Loyalty from all on the payroll is a cardinal rule, and dissidents are treated much as if contagious heretics. Accordingly, two case studies explore this particularly painful matter, both bloodied and bruised inside reformers noting in closing their resolve to stay in the fight until the culture inside every local and union nutures authentic democracy.

Part X, **Unionists at Bay**, may prove the most controversial part of the entire volume. These inside reformers, in a special type of nightmarish situation, have had to surrender local union office at the insistence of the federal government (albeit with no acceptance of the allegations by the "defrocked" unionists). Both raise substantial questions about the role of RICO and DoL in the policing of internal union affairs and of pension investments, the source of their respective problems. While allegations of Mafia infiltration and reckless endangerment of pension funds are very serious matters, the two targets of these charges merit a fair hearing.

Part XI, **More Unionism**, dares to go where few book-length discussions of organized labor ever venture. Widely regarded as a taboo topic, one far too explosive to discuss except discretely within the House of Labor, the subject of union employees unionizing themselves earns overdue attention. Three case studies help us understand why and how union administrations can profit from the overdue inclusion of those on the payroll in the ranks of organized labor. These cases are offered by dyed-in-the-wool trade unionists who take second to none in their commitment to organized labor. Each helps conceptualize the unionization of unionists as a "win-win" situation, a subject that belonged "out of the closet" long ago.

Finally, in an effort to maximize the general applicability of the volume's 28 cases I close with a brief Epilogue that outlines what a recruit should expect if he or she is drawn to try this role. The Epilogue reminds us there is much unionists *are* now doing, and *can* do to promote organized labor's remarkable self-renewal.

Summary. According to no less an authority than Secretary of Labor Robert B. Reich, the nation's labor movement is "the most articulate, indeed the only voice of the front-line worker in America."[5] All the more telling, then, is the instance of Professor Thomas A. Kochan, a labor expert, that "American society cannot afford another decade of a declining labor movement."[6] Given the state of siege with which the American labor movement struggles it is vital that its every component - from the AFL-CIO through to the thousands of locals of its 87 affiliates - be as sound as possible: Each should be member-centered, effective, and future-oriented.

Each should operate with open arms, more caring ways, better use of better information, stronger structures, finer TQC programs, smarter job loss responses, more potent political action, sounder internal democracy, fairer and more unionism than ever before.

An extraordinary effort on this behalf is now well underway, one for which the volume's contributors are owed much credit... and one that needs all the new recruits it can muster.

---

1   Lane Kirkland, "It Has All Been Said Before," in Seymour Lipset, *ed. Unions in Transition* (San Francisco: Institute for Contemporary Studies, 1986), 394.

2   I draw for this statistic and for many of the ideas through to the next footnote on an unpublished research report, "The Local Union in Transition: A United States Perspective," by Ralph A. Johnson and Higdon C. Roberts, Jr. (Center for Labor Education and Research, School of Business, University of Alabama at Birmingham, 1992).

3   Paul Sultan. *The Disenchanted Unionist* (New York: Harper and Row, 1963), 13.

4   William Zinsser. *American Places: A Writer's Pilgrimage to 15 of this Country's Most Visited and Cherished Sites* (New York: Harper Collins, 1992), 6.

5   As quoted in Peter T. Kilborn, "Labor Secretary Sees a Vital Role for Unions Economic Growth," *N.Y. Times*, February 17, 1993; A-13.

6   As quoted in promotional material for *Unions and Economic Competitiveness*, edited by Lawrence Mishel and Paula B. Voos, New York: M.E. Sharpe, Inc., 1992.

Part I

With Open Arms

"We believe that the labor movement draws its life from many thousands
of committed persons who work, day in and day out for years,
to bring unions into being, to resist their bureaucratization,
and to better the lives of others, not just themselves."

Alice and Staughton Lynd,
Rank and File: Personal Histories of Working-Class Organizers; 1973; 5.

Topping every list of challenges labor confronts is its need to rapidly
grow substantially larger, its urgent need to reach out and attract into
membership hundreds of thousands of workers with whom it has had a very
uneven history.

To put it mildly, unions have a checkered organizing and servicing
record where people of color, women workers, and young workers are
concerned (albeit labor has a very proud record in the political struggle to
advance civil rights, feminist issues, and the concerns of young adults).
The good news is that labor has been very busy making amends here in
recent years, and remarkable gains in building diversity are increasingly on
record.

All the more welcome, therefore, are the two cases with which this
volume opens, as each details overdue creativity in outreach to workers
under-represented in union ranks.

Terrell Nicoludis, for example, uses a bizarrely-painted training site to
illustrate how young union apprentices might be drawn further into trade
unionism. He also explains how health and safety issues can be leveraged
to everyone's advantage, worker and union organizer alike.

Similarly, Thomas O'Donnell highlights field-tested "win-win"
responses to labor's pressing need to extend beyond the "old boy" network
of yesteryear. He offers fresh views of the challenge posed by non-union
workers and takes appropriate pride in the many civic accomplishments of
his assertive local.

Taken together, these two upbeat accounts give cause for new
confidence labor may soon score big gains in the organizing
area...provided, that is, that these bright examples of inside reformer
ingenuity soon earn widespread imitation.

Apprentice Training and Health Screening
Terry Nicolodis
(IBPAT)

Part of the special appeal of this narrative by Terry Nicoludis, formerly an officer with Local 6 (Pittsburgh, PA.) of the Painters and Allied Trades Union, and now on the staff of the International Union, is its two-pronged nature: Comparable attention is paid to current as well as to prospective members. A crisis in skyrocketing health care costs and related health risks at work receives very bold reform response, even as unusually sensitive and imaginative attention is paid to the needs of young pre-apprentice and apprentice types.

Six questions in particular are highlighted by the narrative; e.g.,-

How can an inside reformer turn a major national dilemma, the need to contain rising health care costs, to a local's advantage?

How can workplace health hazards be turned to re-organizing advantage?

How can a lackluster apprenticeship program be modernized and effused with fresh morale?

How can a building trades local turn societal pressure to accept minorities to re-organizing advantage?

How can the values, vision, and ideas of a gathering of labor radicals be utilized by a labor moderate?

Finally, and linking all of these policy questions, what part does one's personal life, one's family life, have in this matrix? How deep must unionism course for the efforts of an inside reformer to bear fruit?

I work at painting numerous of the 1,100 bridges that are in Allegheny County, Pennsylvania. In 1986 I was elected Recording Secretary of my local. I have no idea why, except that one of my best friends with whom I worked on the bridges wanted somebody he felt he could trust on the local's staff. He appointed me a full-time organizer in 1987, and I took on the job of Apprenticeship Coordinator in January 1990...not because I am a superman, but because the economics of unions these days requires that you do more than one job.

In 1986 no existing officer or E-board member (except one) survived a sweep made by a reform slate of which I was a part. We took over a local that had a failing health and welfare system. Membership was declining. We had a debt of about $11,000 with no end in sight. And our health care costs were skyrocketing.

Taking Charge. Right away we learned that our guys had the highest experience of health care increases of any other group in the building trades. There are several reasons: One is the exposure we have to hazardous materials. Second, we have a high rate of alcoholism. And third, we have a high rate of drug abuse. As I'll explain later we now think these last two problems may be linked to solvents our guys continue to have to work with, even after countries overseas have banned them as killers.

We knew we had to contain costs. We brought in some advisors, and everyone had good ideas. We found we could spend money to save money, as in instituting a program that provides a free physical every year to every member of our health care plan...which, over the long run will save us a lot of money in early detection. We took charge of the mess, and have been on a roll ever since!

Turning to Self-Insure. When I became a trustee for our local's Health and Welfare Fund I saw the funds of other locals around us folding right and left. Costs were going through the ceiling, and many were in pretty bad shape.

Naturally, we listened carefully when an outside firm that specialized in managing self-funded plans came to talk. We chose to go this way, and have now converted our reserve fund into something like an insurance fund: It has to remain untouched so as to keep our people insured.

We now keep contributions and costs down by not having to deal with the large insurance companies all the time. Our reserve when we took over five years ago was only about a half million dollars: Now we've built it up to over 4 million for about 450 participants, thanks to our decision to self-fund most of our health care costs.

We started with our Eye and Dental Plan, because costs here were going out of sight, and it was where Blue Cross was always banging us. The second place we did self-funding was life insurance. We used to go to Lincoln Life. But we found they were never paying out, because our retirees had given it up and only kept their health insurance. Our members who were covered for life insurance were too young to commonly die. And, when a guy did die, we found delays in meeting claims. So we took it over, and we not only did that but we also doubled the death benefit - from $7,500 up now to $15,000. Because we knew if we did have to pay it out, let's pay it out!

Just recently in Washington, D.C., we lost a member. He had his head blown off by a faulty compressor. A 29-year old guy...and we delivered $15,000 to his wife in a week. We delivered the double-indemnity after the accidental death was verified by the coroner two weeks later. So here was a widow with two children, 7 and 9, she's 30 years old, and we *delivered!* That's the important thing...being able to deliver!

Our local is pretty unique in having our own life insurance and doing our own major-medical plan: I don't think there are a whole lotta people who are doing this. Our switch to being self-insured has given members something they're really proud of, even though a lot of them originally objected to the idea.

Hell, every other local is cutting benefits, while we've increased them! Its worked *real* well...and other locals are now looking enviously at us and asking how can they get in it.

Preventive Healthcare. Another bonus we've gotten out of self-insuring involves affordable health exams. In our negotiations last year our contractors asked for health testing to meet a new OSHA reg calling for pulmonary function testing and respirator fit testing. We got them to cover its costs by giving us two more cents to put into our Health and Welfare Fund.

Now our members get a physical worth about $300, one that includes an EKG, chest x-rays, a cardiopulmonary function test, all kinds of blood work...a *complete* workup! We get charged only $110 per member, so long as they are participating in our Health Insurance Plan.

Medical Research. A year or so ago I ran into somebody at a State Painters Union Conference, and he told me about a specialist in Occupational Medicine at the University of Pittsburgh who is really interested in solvent dementia. That's the accumulation of damage to your nervous system, your cardiovascular system, and your brain over a period of time because of sensitization to solvents. It reaches you through your eyes, the pores of your skin, your respiratory system, and wherever it can get it. It doesn't happen immediately: The acute cases are easy, because then they're quickly over. But it generally occurs over a long period of time as sensitivity builds up.

A high rate of alcoholism and drug abuse among painters *might* be due to a *solvent* addiction. Because there are effects that solvents give you: You are high, you have a buzz all day! So, instead of alcoholism preceding work problems, we're finding that apprentices who come in with no drinking history, within a year they're starting to develop one. It's not only peer pressure, but it's actually a chemical reaction we're isolating through university-based research.

This was something painters always knew, but nobody ever wanted to admit. It was just easy enough to go out and get a few beers and not worry about it.

Now, the university researchers are using a new battery of tests designed to measure our brain, heart, and respiratory activity. They have begun to isolate the effects of solvents versus drugs and alcohol. It's just the tip of the iceberg...and our apprentices are all signed up and participating in the project. They report to the researchers whenever work exposes them to a certain solvent, and then go in to take this battery of tests.

We're starting with our newest members. After a year of testing them we'll bring in 30 journeymen who have at least 10 years in the trade. Then they'll find another control group of 30 people who have little or no exposure to solvents, and test them. Right now the researchers have a four-year grant, with an extension that should take them to eight.

We're the only local involved at this time, and we're in it because I took my Business Manager with me when I went over to the University Research Unit to see what this was all about. It hasn't cost us a penny, and our members who participate get paid for showing up for the tests. We plug it at our meetings and in our newsletter.

It feels good when members come up to us and say with pride, "We seem to be on the leading edge, the cutting-edge of all of this." And I really believe we are! We haven't gone far enough: There's a whole lot more that can be done, but I don't believe a whole lot of locals have gone as far at this time.

As for myself, I personally think we should look to Scandinavia, where they have banned solvent paints because they were killing people, just like we've banned asbestos. But we're always 50 or 60 years behind those people.

Lead Exposure. Just as with solvents, the new leadership of our local has moved to help our guys with lead problems.

For one thing, we just filed a class action suit on behalf of painters who feel their health has been hurt by lead-based paints. For another, over the past three years I've trained over 300 members in lead-abatement techniques. As well, I've just finished making two videos on this subject for the international, which will distribute them nationwide.

Lead is *very* dangerous. When we teach our guys how to work with lead and lead dust we use almost all of the asbestos training to a "T." We just tell them you're in just as hazardous an environment and you have to protect yourself in the same way.

By the way, our local will assist our employers in keeping costs down through our apprenticeship and journeyman upgrade program. We will train any of their employees who they send to us - at no charge - in hazard abatement and safety efforts. Lead abatement is the same thing, as is our solvent and our asbestos containment efforts.

Asbestos Response. We didn't think we worked with this stuff. Now we know different. We've learned it comes at us from the material we sand-blast or remove with power tools. For instance, there is a coal-tar epoxy that is used for lining of tanks, and it turns out it has about 30% asbestos fibers in it that break up into small enough particles to be breathed in.

Now we have a medical van that provides our people with real asbestos four-way x-rays. And we found 30% of our painters had related diseases, like plural thickening, in addition to other asbestos problems.

Thanks in part to the availability of funds to meet claims of health damage, we got 120 or 130 to come out, and some of the guys have since collected on their claims against the asbestos companies. One guy collected as much as $5,000. And another, who got $3,000, wrote a great letter thanking the local for caring enough about the people to have this screening.

We see this campaign as a way of mobilizing our members, looking toward any litigation or pressure we may eventually want to build for legislation - like the Black Lung bill to help miners - that we may want to help solvent or lead or asbestos victims.

All in all, health care has become a big feature! We hang our hat on it everyday!

Apprentice Training Revision. Its kinda weird to find myself directing our apprentice program as I backed into this line of work and never had an apprenticeship myself. My father said "O.K., you're not smart enough to be a doctor. So you might as well be a painter." Those were the only two options he thought were available to anyone. My apprenticeship consisted of somebody saying "Here's your union book. Now get out there and start paintin' that bridge." And that was that.

Our local's program is run through the Community College of Allegheny County. I've taken it over and changed it. What we used to have was a bunch of kids sitting around in school and reading books. I said you don't learn painting from books. (This is not a slight to painters, but if we were academically oriented we wouldn't be painters. We are oriented toward doing something with our hands.)

The trade school itself, while not dilapidated, was rundown quite a bit. So what I did was tell my instructors - "Let's paint this school!" Its a 10-story school, and it will take us about 15 years to do it, so we've started the job.

After a visit to the site the School Board has concluded they like what we're doing, dressing up their rundown building. I've got to admit, its rather colorful, since we rely on canceled colors and remnant paints we find on sale at 50 cents a gallon. So we have some *very* strange-looking rooms...but, they're freshly painted!

Apprentice Outreach. I know we've got to bring in more minorities and women. I can recall a few years leaving City Council chambers when some "level playing field" legislation the building trades wanted had been tabled. There was a large crowd of black protesters there. They said this was a *white* union legislative thing, and it would shut out blacks.

I was standing there, and a guy was in my face. Thank God, a TV camera was at my back, and I said "We're gonna get this passed, as it will help everybody!" And he said "We're gonna stop it!" I asked "Who *are* you?!" And he answered "Me, and my black army!"

I was left asking what had made this guy so angry? Why did he hate unions?! I had to think about it, and I have.

What I want to do is leverage our local's apprentice program to make a difference. I have an idea for a new approach I call "two-plus-two." It has not yet won anybody's support, not my Business Manager or E-Board or the School Board, but I'm going to continue to work on it.

What I propose to do is create a branch of our apprenticeship program exclusively for the city school system. Instead of waiting until inner-city kids are out of high school and have had some jobless time to get hooked on crack and get disgusted, why not reach out to them earlier? We could take them two nights a week in their junior year in high school and bring them into our trade school and teach them painting. Then, in the summer they can work full-time for the School Board painting schools under the direction of one or two of our union journeymen who can supervise and teach them.

I'm proposing this not only because we like to do the right thing and know we should be cutting these kids a break: I'm also proposing it because this way we can deny some work to our non-union competition! Every school building in the city of Pittsburgh and the entire state, when it's being painted, that's considered "maintenance." It isn't covered by our "prevailing wage" requirement, so about 90 percent of the schools in Pittsburgh are painted by non-union contractors.

So, I do have an ulterior motive; I want my members in there. But at the end of these students' high-school careers these youngsters would still be in our union, and their whole lives could have been turned around for the better...which is why I'm *very* committed to this crazy idea of mine.

Opposition to Outreach. I get resistance inside my local from guys who do *not* want me to organize and bring in new members because they feel new painters will rob them of the way they live. So I'm looked at as "the enemy within" for my organizing successes. It took me three years to win my first NLRB election, because bottom-up organizing like I do is so hard in the building trades. Employers use the excuse of "lack of work" to lay off my key people just before an election, and the Board upholds them.

Opposition to my apprentice "paint-the-schools-at-night" idea asks "Do we *really* want *these* kids?" I added drug testing to the enrollment criteria and I'm boosting the criteria to stay in over the three-year period. I've made the idea a little more palatable, and I'm about ready to spring it one more time.

Enriching Apprenticeship. In the Winter I'll introduce a new course for my apprentices, one I call "Unionism," and one I'll teach myself. Sounds like a real broad subject and it is! I want to use some movies in it, like "Out of Darkness," the Mine Workers' 100th anniversary movie. And, one of the greatest labor movies I've seen in a long time, "The Babe," about Babe Ruth. I want the apprentices to watch it together, and then I'll ask them what is it about this guy? How did he manage to rescue baseball and what can we learn from his story?

Women: A Special Challenge. When we started interviewing women for our apprenticeship program, I told my committee -

"Every woman who applies *must* be accepted!" They asked why? I said "Well, because we have goals that we have never hit. I think we should start because I don't want the Labor Department to come down on us." Basically, I bull-shitted them, because I *didn't* have to hit any goals.

Actually, I have the pleasure of working very closely with the Department of Labor in Pittsburgh. I'm not afraid of them. These people have come in and shown me how to comply with the targets, how to get into areas where we were historically not getting in to talk to inner-city people or talk with women considering our work.

What I *have* done is get one woman through who is so good that I now have her come in and nurture the new ones following behind her. Because someone has to go in and say "It's gonna be tough on you. You are gonna have to be tougher than the men!" Because that is true.

Employer Prejudice. Contractors call me up and say "I need an apprentice sent tomorrow morning." I say "O.K., she will be there." They say, "Oh no! Not *she*! She is not gonna be there! I don't want a 'she'!" This is illegal, of course, but they can say it if you are not recording it or making some kind of record of it.

What I am going to do is take this to arbitration, though I don't even know if I can get the support of my side on this. Everyone of my apprentices - black, white, yellow, male, female, or whatever - is going to have a written record. When there is a call for an apprentice I want to refer directly off of their record. If they are refused, the contractor will have to give a reason to the agent that he was refused for, like "I had him before. He was very lazy." That's okay. I want an evaluation of every apprentice, and I want it available.

Nowadays my instructors evaluate our students. I evaluate them. but we only get *very* informal evaluations from our employers, not systematic at all. I want to change this. But contractors fear entanglement: They don't want to say something even that they believe, since they fear retaliation in lawsuits.

I want to propose to my committee that we set up this written record system. Even if we have to use a number system, 1 through 5, "How would you rate this apprentice?" So when there is a refusal, the contractor better damn well have a good reason. It's very frustrating when I get a call and I say I've got an available apprentice, and I'm asked - "Is he black? Does he have short hair? Does he have an earring?" They're concerned about the way a guy looks to their customers, and I can understand that: But I ask myself, "What difference does that make to his painting?"

Seeking New Ideas. I'm always looking for stimulation, for fresh ideas about how our local could do things better. Last year I took to heart an article that announced a national meeting of union activists, people who were very different than anybody I have known in the labor movement. As a matter of fact when I went to my international and asked them if they would fund my trip to this *Labor Notes* conference they said "Why do you want to go to be with those communists?!" But I went anyhow: I sold my Telecaster guitar to fund the flight and the hotel.

I found myself in the first day *very* timid, because the ideas were *so* left. It was *very* left! But then I realized it was that it was all so new to me, and that I just had to "translate" it. There was something there, and I just had to recognize it was in a different language, one I *could* translate. The ideas were too good to lose...provided I toned them down and adapted them to my own situation.

Political Outreach. One direct product of my attendance at the 1991 *Labor Notes* Conference was greater-than-ever commitment to getting members into politics.

My father had been a union contractor for 35 years, a rather large painting contractor. Corruption in the construction industry was *very* real to me as a youngster. My father would go out to lunch with a customer, and I would have to go and cash a $5,000 check in $20 bills and give it to him in an envelope. I knew exactly what was going on: he was paying for the job that he wanted.

That is something that happens in a lot of school districts, and that is what our local members, when elected to school boards, are now trying to expose. That's one of the places where we are trying to make a *real* difference! We now have three people that sit on school boards. We have a few people that sit on area boards that run townships and stuff. These are *winnable* elections, and we are going to go after more of them...as unionists and citizens who give a damn!

Changing Direction. I found that through my organizing I came to have different ideas and feelings about "outsiders." Those non-union painters we call "scabs," and everyone hated...I now feel that was the *wrong* attitude. When I was talking to my guys on the picket line I told them we've got to learn to be friends with these people. We can't fight them any more because that's why they ran away in the first place.

I want my guys to understand they have the responsibility to *live* unionism! I went through a period of Christian fundamentalism where I used to go out every Saturday to win souls, because that was what I thought I had to do as a Christian. I was Twice-Born, and continue to be everyday. I still believe in the same things. But I have found that you win a lot more people through your life than through your words. A lot of people want to walk the talk, but I think it's time for people to walk the walk!

Carrying the Message. The Boy Scouts called me recently and asked me to speak to high school students, sophomores to seniors, on their Career-Awareness Day. This usually involved a speaker twice a year, but I called and arranged to speak *every* month. So, in the last 24 months, I think I've talked to over 5,000 high-schoolers who had never before gotten the labor perspective. They had never heard about our culture and other aspects of unionism. We *must* educate this new generation.

Sometimes my sort of unionism can lead to embarrassment. I know I embarrass my children when I tell them we are not going to *that* store because they don't do business with me, as a unionist, and we're going to drive another five miles to another store, a unionized store. I believe we must internally organize not only our locals, but our families as well.

That's what I teach my apprentices. That's what I teach the men and women who stand with me on the picket line and on the handbill line. *That's* what you have to do: Don't only come here and serve this union for eight hours a day when you are at work. You have to go home and serve your union during the time when you are with your family. You have to let them know what you are about and where you came from. For that's that only way we'll bring about the revitalization of the union movement: Its not going to happen any other way!

We are one-on-one "evangelists," who have to preach a message of truth, justice, and dignity. We often lose focus on what we really are...the social conscience of this country, the last remaining portion of it in a lot of cases. Instead of hanging on by our fingernails, we should just open our hearts and minds to others, especially to those we froze out, good people with whom we can soon build coalitions to turn this country around.

Reaching Out to Minorities, Employers, and Voters
Tom O'Donnell
(IBEW)

Re-organizing, at least as recounted in the preceding case study, can be a slow and uncertain matter. All the more vital, therefore, is the support offered by this more buoyant and encouraging tale of a once-staid local now definitely on the move! Cogently told by an assistant Business Agent, Tom O'Donnell, of Local 481, IBEW (Indianapolis, In.) the story fairly crackles with the excitement of a local unafraid to take chances and pioneer fresh approaches.

Tom draws on his years as a semi-pro football player to take no-nonsense positions on several challenges confronting locals everywhere. His case study helps answer such questions as-

How can an inside reformer regain control of a rowdy meeting and earn appreciation for this?

How can an affirmative action program be turned to local reform advantage?

What strategy especially assures "win-win" relations with progressive employers?

Why should a dynamic local with a full agenda bother with C.O.P.E. political activities?

How can a local help allied employers outbid non-union competition and win valuable jobs for the rank-and-file?

Intent on enlarging labor's share of the job market, Tom offers an innovative strategy for reaching this goal, and, as with the actual accomplishment of his dynamic local, thereby leaves a reader much to ponder and or adapt.

I guess the earliest contact I can recall with unionism came through my father. Although he was in the fireman's union he was so poorly paid as a city fireman that on his days off he worked a union job as a stagehand. He never hid the fact he was union on this job and I think he was even proud of it. I think he attended local meetings pretty regular, but I don't think he was ever an officer. He made my brothers, my sister, and me conscious of the fact that those people bargained a good wage for him, and that's why he made good money at it. He valued a wonderful retirement plan and pretty good health insurance his union had gotten for him, but the city just didn't pay a decent wage.

It was a helluva note, 'cause he had to work two jobs just to make it. He wasn't around much, what with 24 hours at the firehouse and shows to work in the evening: So he spent most of his time working.

My folks sent their three sons to Cathedral High School run by the Brothers of the Holy Cross from Notre Dame. Dad knew he couldn't keep a finger on us, but he knew the Brothers would...and they did!

When I graduated from high school a friend of ours who lived down the street was serving on the apprenticeship committee for the electrical workers. He talked to me about how good it had become since its 1938 startup, and about the possibility of me signing up. My brother, who is three years older, had already gotten in (after trying out a year at college and another year in a foundry). Since the Vietnam War was going on it was an excellent time for me to join up, what with a serious shortage of electricians then in the country.

So I signed up and was accepted into IBEW Local 481, as I heard there was a lot of money to be made, and I've always liked to have money in my pocket...heck, since I was a little kid I've always had a job of some kind. It also helped that I knew somebody, the man down the street, who was on the apprenticeship selection committee. It may be regrettable, but nepotism at that time was part of the scene. They only took 75 of 400 applicants, and I felt damned lucky. Last year, about 60 of over 400 made it, and they were *very* lucky, 'cause its a damn fine way to make a living.

Becoming a Craftsman. It wasn't easy. I had to work 40 hours, go to school every Saturday for five hours, and do homework for another 10 - 15 hours every week. It's no wonder our local's apprentice program continues to rank among the top 5% in the whole country.

As a raw beginner I learned quickly how to uncrate a light fixture, cut a piece of flexible conduit, push the wire into it, put connectors on the flex, mount it on the fixture, make proper terminations to the ballast, and close the fixture. Today, all a kid has to do is pull the fixture out, stick it into the drop ceiling, and plug the end of it into the next one, and so on and so on...as the kind of simple stuff apprentices used to do is now done in a factory, probably in Mexico somewhere.

Well, I got lucky and went through the apprenticeship in four years, no problems. Since then I've worked 18 years steady in the field, have been president of my local, have served on the Executive Board, and now they've brought me on board as a full-time assistant Business Agent.

Getting Active. As a new kid I became a steward in my local because somebody asked me to: They said "Hey, we need somebody out here whom we feel we can trust, who is not a company suck-ass. And, not too radical, on the other hand. Just check to see the guys all have paid up dues receipts and, if anything gets out of whack, just give us a call."

After a period of time of being a steward, and people asking you questions, you kinda school yourself and you get them answers. And the more you get, the more natural it feels to be a steward.

Later I ran for a three-year term on the local's Executive Board, and won. In the next election I decided to challenge a friend of mine, the president, who was trying to ramrod everything through the "E" Board. I wound up beating him, though he had been in office for six years. The job, you've got to understand, is not full-time: You just run the local meeting and the "E" Board meeting, while continuing to do regular electrical work.

Taking Charge. To do the job better I went to a nearby college and took a course in parliamentary procedure, and I started running our local meetings a lot differently from how they had been in the past. I took the "E" board to one side and said "Look fellows, we can't run a good union meeting. Because we've got people standing up, we've got people yelling out." I said I'd entertain a motion if one of you guys make a motion that we make everybody sit down. So we did that in the Executive Board, and we read it on the union floor.

There's always one guy who is going to challenge you. So I said "Either take a seat or get out!" He got mad and left. After that I was thanked by a lot of people. Other people said "Oh, you're gonna be the 'big guy' now. You're gonna rule the roost. You're gonna tell everybody what to do." But I said "No, it's not that at all. It's just chaotic as hell. People want to come to meetings and talk about the important issues, not listen to a bunch of B.S. from everybody else."

Today we still run our union meetings pretty much the same way. And I feel I had a part in that. I was an E-Board member, then President, and now I am full-time as a Business Representative.

Moving On. I saw some things that I wanted to do differently, and could only reach them from my new spot, things like stopping some layoffs that shouldn't have occurred. And keeping some people from getting walked on at the job. I saw contractors give union work away, and watched the company-sucks say, "That's okay, I'll turn my head away." But somebody has to stand up to that shit!

Basically, what my job now involves is taking care of scores of little shops we have under contract. And you may get to bargaining just as hard for a contract that has 900 people under it as for twelve people in some little shop over here. I take care of the Convention Center, Star News, 3 sign shops, 3 motor shops, 8 communication shops, 1 lighting manufacturer, 2 High Voltage Shops and the Residential Electrical Shops. Each has a separate contract, and it's my job to administer them.

Job Expectations. We've made a lot of changes recently, all to the good...and we're goddamn proud of what we're accomplishing. I've been a member of Local 481 now for 23 years. We have excellent training. We produce some of the best workers out there. We're civic-minded. We're aware of affirmative action and we react constructively to it.

Hell, if the labor movement is sinking, if the goddamn ship is sinking... which I do *not* think is happening...at least we're trying to bail out some of the water: Other unions in the building trades, they're just re-arranging deck chairs on the Titanic, to use an expression I've heard somewhere.

I like talking about some of the changes I'm proudest of, but it won't make sense unless you understand the work we do is *hard*, its goddamn hard! It's manual labor. And we do it in some of the worse damn conditions you can ever have. Because if you're doing construction you're either out on a remodel, where they're tearing half the building down while you're trying to build it. Or you're on a new project where the sun is boiling. Or you're freezing your fanny off...or a lot of those things. By the nature of the creature conditions are that way, and our work therefore demands a helluva lot from us: So we expect *a lot* from one another!

Affirmative Action. We've gotten a lot of help here from our involvement in the Indianapolis Plan, our hometown plan. We hire non-whites and women from the Plan's sponsor as "job site trainees," which is not a classification that we ordinarily recognize in our IBEW local. But we hire them on as help so we can meet all of the race and sex quotas we have to...we have been conscientious enough to try and meet all of these new standards.

This is a valuable filter system for us, in a way. We can go through several people and pick the better of them. By virtue of the fact that you've got 100 non-whites working on several job sites you're going to find the group of them that does the best job, that's punctual, that seems to apply themselves and want to learn...you're going to find that out. We get the *best* of those minorities.

What's really good all around is that we get a period of time to look over the trainees. So if you get a guy that's a load, and he isn't gonna come to work, you don't invite him in to your apprentice training program and have to deal with getting him out of there. Instead, we get to pick the best of the best. We look at the whites and minorities who become unindentured apprentices the same way.

The guy that runs the entire Indianapolis Plan is in our IBEW local, though he runs it for all of the building trades in the area . He supplies us with people, and he provides schooling and training for them. And his staff seems to weed out the ones that ain't going to hold their weight. We get some good new members; some non-whites and some women get to be *good* electricians; the contractors, our international union, and the feds get their quota numbers; and everybody comes out ahead!

LMCC-B.E.S.T. (Better Electrical Service Thru Teamwork). We started a new B.E.S.T. program in '85, part of our on-going Labor-Management Cooperative Committee (LMCC) Program, that relies on a tight alliance between us and our unionized contractors (NCEA, the National Electrical Contractors Association). We use VCR promo films and radio ads to boast that both sides now work together to meet tight deadlines within every project, no matter how complex the job may be. Funded by an employer contribution equal to *10 cents per* hour of our wages, the program had about $425,000 to work with in '91.

Heck, thanks to our apprenticeship program, in their first five years our Journeyman Wiremen receive over 800 classroom hours and

10,000-plus hours of instruction on the job. In their first two years our Residential Wiremen get nearly 300 hours in our classrooms and about 4,000 hours of teachin' at the job site...none of which non-union guys come even close to!

We also boast that our guys have lower accident rates, better problem-solving skills, and less overruns in time and materials...we're reliable people with a "proven history of meeting time and cost requirements." Hell, our people can even get advanced schooling in fiber optics technology, computer training, and programmable controllers, along with a lot of other state-of-the art technology.

Above all, B.E.S.T. promo material tells the world we really work *together* with management. We haven't had a strike against a B.E.S.T. contractor in over 60 years! Instead, when we have a grievance we go to the Labor-Management Committee (three from each side). And if we can't settle it there, we go to the Council of Industrial Relations for the Electrical Industry, which is another full-board, located in Washington, that meets quarterly. They have six NECA and six IBEW reps on it, and the Council decides the outcome of our grievances. Instead of third-party arbitration we have Council language in most of our contracts.

LMCC. We also have a LMCC to help guide the many different civic things we do in Indianapolis, a jointly-funded project. We created it for several reasons: We wanted to make users more aware of what we had to offer. We wanted to bring management and the union together to talk about some of our problems, and maybe work them out before they happen. And we wanted to promote activities like our charity drives, and that sort of thing.

Most of all, however, we wanted to improve our lousy PR. We'd go downtown and put up Christmas lights in the Circle, cables of over 4,600 lights on a 300-ft. tall monument. If you read about us in the newspaper you'd see us referred to as "a volunteer worker from the Downtown Commission..." The story wouldn't identify Local Union 481 and explain we were out there, giving up our personal hours. So, when we got this money in the LMCC Fund we started honking our *own* horn, so to speak.

Now we have a helluva lot of solid PR material and damn good coverage. Our full-time LMCC directors, in combination with our use of the best PR agency in the state, gets us the kind of positive media attention we've always wanted...the kind that helps area people finally know and maybe appreciate the fact that our people have given up two Saturdays every Christmas season for the past 30 years so the city could enjoy what we call the world's largest Christmas "tree".

The LMCC language is part of our B.E.S.T. arrangement. It's a contractual matter, and not a volunteer thing. If you're in the inside journeyman contract it's not an option. It has been contributed on your behalf by the employer, as a matter of fact.

Overall, we've had such good returns on this investment that the IBEW intends to create a statewide version. Everybody agrees it's really helped put us back in the ballgame!

Committee on Political Education (C.O.P.E.). Unlike our B.E.S.T. situation, with its mandatory contribution, all of our C.O.P.E. monies come in voluntarily, and we ask only a nickel an hour worked. We're particularly proud that we got the language into our contract for a C.O.P.E. deduction, and we push it hard.

With 66 percent our local is *the* best in the entire Sixth District as far as participation! Last year alone we raised over $100,000. We think its *very* important to bargain this into the contract, rather than rely on selling raffle tickets, or some other such approach.

We've got a C.O.P.E. deduction authorization card that we hand out when a guy comes into the referral hall. If he kind of questions signing off on the C.O.P.E. card, that's O.K. with us though we try to explain its importance.

Unless we get voluntary C.O.P.E. donations we can't put the finances out there to have "the best Senator money can buy"...you know what I mean? I don't agree that that's the way you should have to play, necessarily, but if that *is* how the game is being played and you want to participate, you better get in line.

We've gone now in Indiana from a totally Republican state, where the House and Senate were both controlled by the Republican Party, to where we have a Democratic Governor, the House is 52-48 Democrat, the Senate is 26-24 Republican. A lot of our legislation gets stopped in the Senate, but we are working very hard to help get a Democratic majority in the Senate.

We boast that to our membership, and tell them of the success of candidates we backed: We even put some of our money into Republicans! If we've got a Republican who votes "labor" we'll put money into his campaign...and on occasion that happens.

When we show our members C.O.P.E. has had some effect they're not half as reluctant as before to see a nickel an hour of theirs go into it.

Market Recovery Program. Our basic dues used to include a one and a half percent assessment. We decided nearly three years ago to go to the body and tell them we wanted to start funding a new target program. We wanted an additional one-half percent to pay for a new business agent, and an additional one percent to go directly into a targeting fund. We would use that money to subsidize a union guy to beat a non-union guy out of a job, and thereby gain new work for our people...far too many of whom were jobless far too long.

At the meeting for the vote we had the largest turnout we'd ever had in the history of the local. The motion was highly debated, and, as a previous request for a dues increase had been turned down twice, we assumed the same thing would happen. Our presentation, however, made enough sense to everybody that they wanted to try it, and our target program won the vote.

Now, if one of our contractors finds himself up against a low-ball bid from non-union bastards he can phone NECA's area office, and indicate how much of a financial subsidy he'll need from our local in order to under-bid and win the job. NECA calls us and explains the situation while not identifying the requesting Contractor. We'll say "yay" or "nay," and when we say "yay" we figure out the details and arrange subsidy payment terms. When our man wins the job, our people get the work.

The main thing about the market recovery program that I think is *very* important is a difference between our plan and the approach in other areas of the country. Where locals are under tough economic conditions, and the work's not there, the way they target is to say - "O.K., guys, we're going to take concessions on this job. And if you want to work it, you've got to go out there and work for $14 an hour, even though brother Bill's going to be over on the big job at $20."

The good thing about our plan, the way it is set up, is that it is a "share-and-share alike." I personally would morally have a problem saying "O.K., I need ten guys over here on this job. But because we wanted to get that job from the non-union guy over there, we told them they could do that for $15 an hour. We haven't built a fund to subsidize that, so in fact you have to go to work over there for $15." And there's areas in the country where that's how they do their market targeting program.

Because we all put our 20 cents an hour into our targeting fund, and we have money to go to a contractor, we can pay *everyone* the *same* as it says in the contract: A "share-and-share alike" affair, as opposed to the alternative, an unfunded program where you are trying to scramble to get the jobs back, so you have to go out there and throw something out.

Because everybody puts an equal amount in, when we subsidize a job the burdens not on any small group in the union: It's everybody sharing the cost, because of the way the market recovery program is set up.

If you had it any other way you'd be leaving yourself suspect. Because, you know, Joe is going to come down the street, and he is going to get a job. And he is going to say, "Oh, I see, I gotta go over here and work on this job," while his friend Bill, he's over there on a *good* job.

If we generated enough work through our targeting program last year to work 28 journeyman the entire year, to me *that's* the value of that program: Dollars and sense! And not only that - we had 28 people working who wouldn't have been.

We earmarked a $100,000 from our General Fund to start our targeting program. At that time I had just come into the hall. And it became my job. I was the guy who looked over the jobs. NECA would deal with me and I would ask how many journeyman hours and how much of a subsidy was involved to get us the job. And I'd say, "O.K.," and it was a done deal.

Later I make them verify that we actually got all the hours promised. The contractor sends me back their time reports, and occasionally we'll do a spot audit and we'll talk to the men who are on that job and verify its being done as agreed.

After we did it for a year we figured out how many jobs our $100,000 investment had gained us. And I think this was *the* thing that put it over the line and got the Bylaws changed and the one percent assessment passed [one percent of the local's base rate of $20 an hour].

Recently the assessment was challenged. We were going from $20.05 to $20.70, but because of health care cost increases we had to take the entire 65 cents scheduled to go on the check and put it into that. And this pissed the membership off. They thought the negotiating committee had deceived them, because we had gone from 94 cents employee contribution to almost $1.80, in only 2 1/2 years, on an hourly basis, paid the same by everyone.

A group on the floor said "O.K. fine! You're taking that 65 cents - I want my targeting money back! I make a motion we do away with the targeting funding." It didn't carry! The majority of the members responded, and said "No! I've worked on those targeted jobs, and I'm glad that they were there. That was work for me!"

It stood a big test here recently, and when you had everybody mad: They were expecting 65 cents on the check, the biggest raise we would have had in probably six, seven, or eight years. And they were ready to shoot the messenger when the 65 cents was taken away - but they still wouldn't kill the targeting program.

Look to Smaller Jobs. Now, it wouldn't be fair or honest to give the impression that everything is coming up roses, that everything is going along just fine. Because that ain't true. When I started in this trade in 1969 we were doing about 60 to 65 percent of all the electrical work in the Indianapolis area: Today we are lucky if we've got about 40 percent, and it is hard as hell to hold onto even that.

We've made a lot of mistakes. We got complacent. We behaved like we were a goddamn country club and let the non-union guys crawl all over us. We sat on our ass too long and didn't organize people.

We'd better wake up and smell the roses. Or we're all gonna' be making goddamn hamburger-flippin wages...and not have unions as good as the IBEW to force up the level of even those lousy wages.

The biggest problem we have is the non-union element, and it is gettin' bigger. We've got to do everything we can to combat this. We've got to stop sitting on our hands and get out there and organize 'em. There are some non-union contractors that are getting very large, O.K.?! If I'm a big union contractor, and I'm sitting there and I can see that this guy can operate unmolested, so to speak, by the union, because we can't gain control of him, and he's making money...why can't they?! And I'm afraid if we don't continue to pound on them and try to do something with them, we'll lose support with the builders we presently have, and we'll fall farther and farther behind.

My heart aches when I see the non-union element coming on as strong as it is. And nobody really actually knowing where to turn. We're pullin buttons and pushing levers, and doing a lotta things. But sometimes you feel like your spinning your wheels.

We've got studies that show the union craftsman does the work faster and better the first time. That one union electrician can do a job that it may take three unskilled workers to do. And those kind of statistics somewhat justify the extra money we earn over non-union types. When we are serenading a guy to get him to operate "union" we naturally make a lot of this.

But I think we've got to go beyond PR and stuff to try a new slant. Where I think we're missing the boat in the building trades is that all we give a good goddamn about is this great big job down here, 'cause that's the big piece of the pie for the employer. It's not necessarily the union that wants that: It's the employer. He doesn't want to fool around with the little job when he can make the big money off of the big job.

We've even created a special residential wage classification, and expanded it to include strip shopping centers, to help them bid on these small jobs. But they don't want to mess with it unless there is a 'K'Mart in it. Or a Target Department Store. They want the *big* work.

To me, the only way you're ever gonna beat the non-union contractor is to go out there and take those *little* jobs away from them, 'cause that is where they breed. It's just like mesquites. You got to go after them down by the creek, where they breed. And that's how I feel about the non-union element in the electric industry.

I just feel like until we're doing all the McDonalds, all the Burger Kings, all the houses, until we're controlling all that kinda work, we're not gonna get back to where we hold a majority of the market. Because it's in those little jobs that the non-union people train their people to do the work - and then later they come in and start taking the bigger work away from us. Let that guy get to the point where he can do that piddley-shit work and do it well, and he's gonna go from there to bigger pieces of the pie. And then he's gonna be bigger and tougher competition than he is right now.

Don't get me wrong! I'm not ready to be any kind of goddamn pallbearer for labor. Mistakes of management and its tendency to get greedy will *always* cause suffering, and that will *always* lead people to unionism. As well, there will be mountains of work for qualified persons on increasingly technical jobs, the kind of persons only our union apprenticeships turn out. It's just that we, as union leaders, must stop clinging to outmoded approaches, to outmoded ways, and get with it! There's so much more we can and must do...if we're not to go down like the Titanic did.

Part II

Offering More Care

"...by a labor movement I mean an association of trade unions - more important, of trade unionists - who...have some vision of more than routine service and efficiency; who feel that in some sense they are committed to a vision of life; who serve as a source of hope and identification for many persons outside the labor movement; who may ever seem, as once they did, models of a more selfless and devoted life than can usually be provided by our commercial society."

Frank Marquart. "New Problems for the Unions."
Dissent (Autumn, 1959), 388.

Old-timers tell me Walter Reuther urged labor leaders in the 1940s to recognize it was as important to "organize the organized," to keep members enthusiastic about labor's vision, as it was to organize the unorganized. Reuther understood the danger to labor's spirit posed, on the one hand, by the "soft fog which is the uniform of the labor relations man's language."[1] And, on the other, by the "barnacled social vision and the soggy prose" of archly-conservative labor chieftains, the crowd that fears to dare, figures small angles incompetently, and makes the least best of life's chances.[2]

To counter both dangers, to foster the identity without which the rank-and-file cannot become a social movement, Reuther and his brothers spoke on behalf of labor's wider destiny, on behalf of a model of social unionism with profound connections to America's utopian impulse.

Forty years later, labor journalist Abe Raskin advised that "reorganizing the organized must transcend all other union priorities if those inside, but divorced from any sense of genuine involvement, are to become bona fide trade unionists."[3] Unless and until locals, their international union sponsors, and the AFL-CIO itself took up this challenge, Raskin warned, labor's good intentions would probably falter and the movement quite possibly fail.

With this in mind three case studies below recount on-going efforts by inside reformers to reduce apathy, improve morale, and enliven unionism as never before. Their goal is to get dues-payers to perceive themselves as thoroughgoing trade unionists, as proud members of revamped caring "families" that happen to be labor organizations.

Mary Kay Hanke explains the life-shaping connection of a birthday of hers, an industry age quota on employment, and the power of her union of flight attendants. She draws a convincing picture of a remarkably caring union, and uses its response to the AIDS crisis to underline the value of sensitive outreach.

Similarly, Javier M. Perez, Jr., discusses his tireless efforts to help rank-and-filers feel better about themselves and one another. His use of a film of early workers to promote better inter-racial relations is noteworthy, as is also his shirtsleeve "walk around" style of leadership.

Finally, L.Max Schmitt defines his unusual role as a union-sanctioned lay "chaplain" in the workplace. This role, fully as emotional demanding as any in all of labor, requires a rare combination of empathy, caring ways, and the capacity to listen. While few of us can measure up to its demands, any local that can fill the role will profit immeasurably from that achievement.

Today, in nearly every sector of American life extraordinary efforts are underway to humanize organizational forms thought starkly out-of-touch with our modern appetite for participative democracy, for open and affable organiza-tional cultures. Likewise, labor's inside reformers are attempting to get rank-and-filers to think "family" when they think union, and to identify labor as *their* social movement...two indispensable achievements if organized labor is to make a desirable difference in the years ahead.

References

1   Murray Kempton. *Part of Our Time: Some Monuments and Ruins of the Thirties* (New York: Delta ed., 1967), 296.
2   *Ibid.*, 294.
3   A.H. Raskin. "New Directions for the AFL-CIO." *New Management* (Winter, 1986), 12-13.

Taking Flight - and Fighting Back
Mary Kay Hanke
(AFA)

Like many of the activists you will meet in this volume Mary
Kay Hanke was deeply moved by a childhood experience. Her
mother fought to unionize her workplace, and paid a price that
shaped the lives of everyone she touched, a price that left her
daughter sensitive ever since to employee rights only secured by a
successful organizing campaign.

Mary Kay's history as an inside reformer is also typical in its
wide range of posts, its steady gain in skill and significance, and
its fundamental concern with helping others. Energetic and a "fast
learn," she demonstrates the versatility expected by unions of
their key people, an expectation that helps explain the zest and
"can do!" aspects of many such activists.

Answers in the case below to five questions help explain the
optimism of Mary Kay and her counterparts who believe labor is
on the rebound:

How do strikes promote the learning and bonding from which
a union can grow and thrive?

How can a union turn its political action and safety and health
concerns to best advantage?

Can a union operate as a thorough-going democracy?

Can a union keep its paid staff to a minimum, and rely on
volunteers to get the job done?

How can the AIDS challenge and that of other critical or
disab-ling illnesses be used to promote a caring form of
solidarity?

Coursing through all of this is still an even more basic question -
How can a small, but spirited labor organization keep up with
rapid changes in one of the world's most turbulent industries?

Mary Kay Hanke's responses to all of these questions "take
wing" and apply far beyond the bounds of her lifelong concern,
the well-being of fellow employees in the commercial aviation
industry. Cogent and yet still compelling, her insights help show
the way to the sort of empowering unionism her mother sought
and failed to secure, the kind her mother's daughter has spent a
lifetime helping to extend to others in need.

I was born the youngest of six children and raised in a small town
in Nebraska. I would describe my family background as somewhere
between the rich and the poor—basically a middle-class family by the
1960's standards. My father was employed by the city and my mother
worked. Neither were unionists, in the true sense of the word.
However, when I was in the sixth grade, my mother started working in
a new factory located in the community. As I look back on it now, I
recognize my mother as a unionist she was one of the in-house

organizers for a union. I remember the secrecy of the initial organizing efforts and getting co-workers to support the union effort and I remember her talking about the consequences if the company found out.

My mother was one of the earliest employees hired in this factory, and she tried to help unionize her workplace. However, they weren't successful. They lost the election, and thereafter, my mother's job seemed to change. For as long as I can remember, my mother worked the midnight or swing shift.

I don't recall her specific reaction to the lost election, but I do remember her being very upset. She recognized the consequences of a "no union" plant, without the benefits of plant wide seniority system. If the union had been successful, the employees would have benefited from plant wide seniority and the other benefits associated with collective bargaining. Instead, the company used the department seniority system. Just when she was about to reach the top in the seniority list of the department, there would be cutbacks. My mother never got off the midnight or swing shift. She identified it as a punitive action for her involvement in trying to bring a union into her workplace.

I also recognized it as such. If my mother had the benefits of a union in her life, my life would have been different. I missed her as a mother, because as I was going to school in the morning she was coming home from work. When I was coming home from school, she was sleeping. Because she never seemed to work the day shift, I missed years with her.

The family lived with this. If my mother's efforts had been successful, her rights as an employee would have been protected. She would have had some rights. Our life would have been different.

When I think about my background—union, non-union—that's what I relate to. I'm not from a union family per se, although I *am* from a union family. Although neither parent was a member of a union, they recognized the benefits of a union, and attempted to get a union...but were unsuccessful.

Going To Work. I began my working career at the age of 20 with United Airlines in 1969. There were major changes taking place in this country with regards to Civil Rights. Prior to this, a flight attendant (stewardess) could not be married, have children, or be pregnant. Also, you had to be female and sign a paper agreeing to quit at the age of 32. I signed that piece of paper—to quit at 32—I didn't have a choice in 1969 if I wanted the job. The average seniority of a "stewardess" in 1969 was eighteen months—not a long working career.

Hearing The Call. Because of my family background and the experiences my mother had endured, I became involved. I appreciated the benefits my union had brought about. The Association of Flight Attendants (AFA) had fought the discriminatory practices—no marriage, no children, only female, age requirements of quitting at 32. AFA was successful in their battles. Now we can be male or female, married, have children, be pregnant and work while pregnant, and work beyond the age of 32.

From the beginning, I was a participant in my union—attended meetings, voted in elections and contract ratifications. I became more active in 1975 when I attended my first grievance training. I had a conversation on an airplane with one of AFA's attorneys, and he suggested that I would be good in grievances. That's where it started.

For personal reasons, I didn't pursue a high degree of AFA activity in the grievance area. I remained involved by volunteering for the phone tree and membership education and communication efforts. I was always there to assist the local leadership on union projects, but I didn't pursue an activist role within the union as an officer or committee person.

Union Maid, Union Made. When I turned 32, I thought "I'm 32, and if it had not been for the AFA I'd be out of the flight attendant profession—forced out for no other reason than my birthdate. What would I do? I didn't have a college degree. What would I be doing?" I concluded it was time to *really* become involved and give back to the organization that had made this all possible. That was the turning point in my level of activity within my union, AFA.

The first position I volunteered for was as a member of the Safety and Health Committee. There is always room for improvements in this area, and I viewed it as a positive, non-adversarial way to improve the working conditions for flight attendants. The changes can be presented in a "win-win" way: If the flight attendants benefit by a safer and healthier work environment, the company can also benefit.

In 1985, our brothers and sisters at ALPA (Air Line Pilots Association) went out on strike against the company. AFA supported the pilots and honored the picket lines. It was during this time that I became even *more active* and *more committed* to AFA and the union movement. As anyone who has been through a strike knows, it's a very trying and stressful period. But it can also be a very learning and bonding experience. For me, the 1985 strike gave new meaning to the word "solidarity".

The airline industry was deregulated in 1978, and during those seven years I had seen many changes. CEOs like Frank Lorenzo, Carl Icahn, and Richard Ferris had come into it...with union-busting tactics. The PATCO strike and the firing of the air traffic controllers by President Reagan sent out a loud and clear message to the CEOs and they heard it and acted accordingly.

United Airlines was a big company when I started, but suddenly with deregulation, the whole atmosphere within the company seemed to change. Even though United was large, in the early years you had a sense of being part of the company. With deregulation, and the management style that came with it, the employees became nothing more than a number on the bottom line.

During the 1985 ALPA strike, I served in a very visible capacity...organizing and being part of the Strike Preparation Committee of my local in Denver, Colorado...making sure we had shifts of pickets everyday at six different locations where we picketed. After the 29 day strike, we found ourselves in very divisive time within the local. We had the people who worked, and the people who honored the picket lines and didn't work. We had the "B" Scale, we had the "A" Scale, there were many factions among the flight attendant group. I had been in Denver for twelve years, so I knew many of my flying partners there. Because of my experience within AFA, several people approached me and urged me to run for local officer. I agreed and ran for local vice-president and was elected. I did not seek reelection after the completion of the two-year term.

While serving as vice-president of my local, I was elected to serve on the Executive Board of the Colorado State AFL-CIO. During this time, I became very interested in politics. I saw the political process as one of the ways to make change and improvements. My involvement with the AFL-CIO made me aware of not just flight attendant issues and concerns, but broadened my interest in the labor movement. Now it was not just the AFA, or the 10 locals we had at United, but how does this impact on the building trades, or the government employees, or the musicians? And on the Movement itself?

When I completed my term as vice-president, I served on the AFA Legislative Committee, and became the Legislative Affairs/PAC Chairperson for my local. Throughout this time, I continued to serve as a member of the AFL-CIO Executive Board and an active participant in the AFL-CIO's "COPE" efforts.

In 1990, a position became available at AFA's National Office in Washington, DC in the Air Safety and Health Department. The area of safety and health had always been of great interest to me, and the time seemed right for a change. I applied for the position, got it, and soon joined the national staff of my union.

Spreading The Word. I worked as the Assistant to the Director of the Air Safety and Health Department for fifteen months. At the national level of AFA, I worked on behalf of all the members of AFA from the 22 different airlines represented. The majority of the efforts required seeking changes at the federal government level, in both the administrative and legislative branches. I also updated the training program for the Air Safety and Health Representatives working the field within their locals. The program provided information on how to be a vocal and active advocate on behalf of the flight attendants at their individual carrier. It also provided information needed to participate in accident investigations.

Moving Up. In November of 1991, the National President of AFA asked me to become her Assistant. This position is a political appointment and requires confirmation by AFA's Executive Board. I accepted the position knowing the current term of office ends in

December, 1994. I viewed the new position as a real opportunity to assist the National President in taking our union forward and meeting the challenges of this changing aviation industry. Ours is a *very* democratic union, and we do have changeover...so I could be back to flying and volunteering at my local in 1995. There is always a lot of work to be done out there, and I could certainly use many of the skills I've learned while working at the National Office.

Critical Illness Awareness Resource and Education. One of my favorite projects currently underway at AFA is the C.A.R.E. Project. A member and AFA activist in Denver identified the real need to educate our members about the myths, rumors, and misinformation associated with many serious illnesses. Jon suffered from AIDS and experienced it personally. We had been flying partners and supportive friends in Denver, so he called me to discuss the issue and the ways to address the need. We're an aging workforce, with our members being diagnosed with illnesses or perhaps dealing with a parent or loved one who has been diagnosed. The need was there for such a program, so I encouraged him to proceed with it.

At AFA, many of our programs are initiated by grassroots efforts at the local level and move up for approval by AFA's highest governing body, the Board of Directors (BOD). The decision to develop such a program would require BOD approval, and I encouraged Jon to discuss the project with his local president. Together they devised the framework for the agenda item and presented it to the Board of Directors in November, 1991. Jon personally lobbied the members of the Board, and they gave approval for a pilot program in 1992. Jon's efforts paid off.

The initial project designated October, 1992, as C.A.R.E. month, during which the local C.A.R.E. coordinator would provide information on a variety of illnesses to the members. At the national level, we provided information and wrote articles in the national publication on estate planning, wills, resources available, and personal experiences.

The national office designated a National Coordinator for the project, another AFA volunteer, who oversees the project. I serve as the liaison to the National President and the Board of Directors on the project and keep it moving. I give full credit for the project to Jon, who passed away last December, another "Unionist Improving Unions." He recognized a need and a way to meet that need for our members.

The project has been well-received by our members. Although it is barely two years old, it has been a success. Flight attendants have become more aware, they have written or phoned for additional information, and they have expressed an interest in developing a Buddy Program to build membership interest and involvement.

This October, [1993] AFA will, for the second year, provide our members with additional information on the issue. We have developed a Community Resources Guide containing information on the variety of programs available in their community for assistance. We have also joined with the American Cancer Society and will provide information on the "Look Good--Feel Good" program which they support and sponsor.

Reaching Even Farther Out. At the 1992 Board of Directors meeting, the Board took the project one step farther, and directed us to establish a relief fund for our members in need of financial assistance due to a critical or disabling illness. Papers to establish the fund as a tax-exempt program have been filed in Washington, DC, and the relief fund, titled the Pegasus Project, is off the ground and progressing.

Like many unions, times are financially tough for such discretionary programs. There will be a grassroots effort by volunteers in the field to involve the entire membership in fundraising and contributing to the fund. We have written the brochure which will explain the Pegasus Project to potential contributors.

As flight attendants, it is possible to work with someone different on every single trip. Quite often we don't have the benefits of working with the same people every day and the feelings of support that go along with that. However, we want to create a system of support, because there may be members out there who don't have family or other support in their lives.

AFA has an excellent Employee Assistance Program in operation, one other unions have studied. The C.A.R.E. Project and the relief fund are similar to the EAP program, but also different. The EAP program provides peer assistance for flying partners in need. The program offers counseling and help in specific areas such as substance abuse, stress, post-accident trauma, and family issues. The Pegasus Project relief fund will focus on our members' financial needs.

AFA Democracy. Our structure is different from most other unions. We don't have business agents, but rather we depend on volunteer activism. There is a paid staff at the National level to assist the local officers and committee members, however, the people out in the field are *all* volunteers. They really work two full-time jobs--one as a flight attendant and the other as a union leader and activist. Because of this, we have a high rate of burnout. People get actively involved in leadership positions for two years, four years, or maybe even six years. But, when you're working two full-time jobs, one as a union volunteer and the other as a flight attendant, it doesn't leave a lot of time off.

Why Bother?? If you ask a flight attendant "Why do they fly?" I'm sure one of the reasons will be the amount of time off. It is one of the benefits of the job. So, if you're going to choose the flight attendant career to begin with, why would you volunteer and work at a second job without pay? Because it is something you *really* believe in!!

People who *do* get involved from the 22 carriers represented by AFA cite personal values, commitment, a need to give back.... We *do* make a difference!! If we didn't , I would have had to leave my chosen profession 12 years ago. There is a need, and AFA activists continue to identify those needs and address them. We continue to educate the public, the press, and the politicians about the true role of flight attendants as safety professionals on board the aircraft. We're constantly making improvements...in getting better working conditions, or a safer airplane, or a healthier work environment, and all those good things... many of which remind me of what my mother tried and failed to get for her co-workers so many years ago.

Healing Rifts and Using Information
Javier M. Perez, Jr.
(ATU)

Cultural diversity is no stranger to the labor movement, however novel the concept seems to white male power-holders in supervisory, managerial, and executive ranks. Which is not to say that labor has an unblemished record in this account: Labor has fallen victim to more prejudice and discrimination than any but its worst enemies might ever have wished on it.

At present, however, inside reformers like Javier M. Perez, Jr., the president of Local 1287 of the Amalgamated Transit Union (Kansas City, MO.), are pioneering new methods of helping members discover the common humanity that can reduce mutual unease and help build solidarity. His narrative explores such vexing questions as-

How does an indifferent member change into an activist? What sparks such a substantial transformation?

How can a change-agent survive a campaign against him or her by powerful incumbents?

How can a local split by feuds among skill levels be united?

What is the importance of union democracy to a local's well-being?

How can an inside reformer use a personal computer to advantage?

What might a progressive policy resemble on substance-abuse testing?

How can a struggle with management over health care cost-containment be turned to reform advantage?

Coursing through the entire narrative is Javier's insistence on ceaselessly finding and trying out new things so as not to become stagnant. He challenges readers to stay in close touch with the membership, retain a sense of mission, and be wary of getting spread too thin...a difficult agenda his example helps make clearer and thereby more achievable.

I was raised by my mother, along with a sister four years younger than me. My mother raised us by herself. My father - I didn't see him after I was four, until three years ago. A lady who became my Godmother became like a second mother for me: She became a part of my family and I loved her. She was involved in Democratic politics, and had a strong influence on my values. She took me to Democratic Party events and the store front party office. She taught me that Democrats were the Party of the workingman, and she thought Nixon was a snake in the grass! A lot of that discussion - when I was just a kid - heavily influence my values and thoughts today.

My mother was a member of the ILGWU, and she belonged to it for as long as it was possible for her to belong to that union. As long as there was a union shop in Kansas City she worked in a union shop...until finally, one day, they were there no more. Since that time she has worked in a variety of places as a seamstress. Her current job she's held for about eleven years is as a seamstress in a department store.

I can remember at night hearing her complain by phone to her friends of things that went on on the shop floor. She would tell my sister and I of things that were unfair. Sometimes she would be very frustrated by these things. At other times she would tell us about comical things that went on in the shop, like how some of the women did some things to the supervisor without the supervisor knowing. They did them to sorta get back at supervisors who treated them unfairly.

She also told me about her union representatives: What they did and what they didn't do. She thought at some times they were fair. But at other times they were working in concert with the company...more than they should have. I can remember her saying that certain union representatives forgot where they came from: When they got to be reps and they weren't sewing any more, they forgot where they came from! And that sometimes when she or the other women did not think their position was being dealt with fairly, they had shouting matches. And they would remind the reps where they came from!

I think that has always stuck in my mind. And even today, though I don't get out there as much as I should, I do try to spend a considerable amount of time on the company's property - not just between 9 to 5, but also on weekends and holidays I'll pop in. When I'm traveling around at night I'll drop by and see what's going on. When I get home I return calls. Things that nowadays are probably considered to be good politics, I do because I genuinely enjoy dealing with the members.

To me, when I'm having a bad day at the office, and management is kicking me around on an issue, and I've got problems of that nature, sometimes its a source of comfort to go back out and talk to the membership. It kinda recharges my battery and refreshes me.

Getting Involved. My earliest recollection of filing a grievance form, and this is kinda strange when I think back, but I actually helped my mother when I was still in grade school and in my early years in high school. Now, my mother speaks English, choppy English: I understand her, and people who have been around her understand her. And she reads English well. But she doesn't write English well. She would come home and try to explain some situation in which she felt she was grieved. And she would ask me to write it out on the grievance form for her. At times it was real pain in the backside, not knowing the situation, not knowing what was going on. Not sure of my own wri-ting skills in the latter part of grade school I was not sure what I was doing.

But anyway I would write out these grievance forms for her. And, to the best of my recollection she would come home and say she had finally won her point! That her position was taken! That she got her fair share of the overtime. Or was being dealt with in a fairer manner.

Schooling (Lower Grades). I was taught for many years by nuns. I cannot recall if they were pro-union or not. They would tell us stories about Holy men and women, and teach us Church values of compassion, forgiveness, and selfless work for others...the need for caring for other people...that the Church was something more than just bricks and mortar. And I know that has had a profound effect on my life. Those are precepts I still hold today, and still believe.

The Christian Brothers at the all-male high school I attended taught about the service of St. John the Baptist De La Salle, that we have a role to play in serving others and not just ourselves. They worked hard to awaken us to the world and what goes on. We were young teen-age males, and they wanted to make sure we spent *some* time studying , and not just running around, partying, as some of the people wanted to do.

Becoming a Worker. Well, right after high school I went to college. I could have gone to a Jesuit College, but I decided instead I wanted to go to one that had just recently turned co-ed. Somehow I felt that I wanted to do something different. I was one of six males in an all-female situation. I had several platonic friendships, but I never really dated anyone there.

College was harder than high school. I think what happened in high school was that I was tracked into one of the lower tracks and given easier classes. I finally got into a high track and graduated 35 out of over 100, and I finally was assigned some classes in a higher track than the one I was originally scheduled in. You miss out in so much of the education aspects when you are in a lower track: Not so much in the basics, but some of the stuff that is beyond the basics. I kinda missed that... but maybe it was best for me at the time.

Well, anyway, when I went to college it was hard! I didn't study as much as I should have because at that point in time I started dating. And I didn't do well at all: I received an academic dismissal. Later I got married at age 21. And I was determined I would go back to school someday on a part-time basis.

Work and Discontents. All of which connects to my transit work history. During high school I worked part-time for a sporting goods store in their warehouse. I was laid-off around Christmas time every year. And though I could never prove it I felt it was a case of racial bias by the head of the department. It seemed to me that no matter how hard I worked, I was the guy picked on for being laid off.

That may be a biased perspective of mine. But, in a sense, it was also an incentive to unionism, because I guess in my own mind I was exploring the unfairness of it: "Why wasn't lay-off done on a rotation basis?" (Which later on I understood was called the seniority system).

After that I worked for a clothing manufacturer. I started as a trim and demin expediter who would make phone calls. It was my first taste of office work: I would make calls to locate where denim was, and get shipments away from our competitors (people were buying jeans like crazy!). I did very well in that job, and I was asked if I would be the foreman in a mini-trim warehouse.

We had another warehouse, and it was unionized. I don't remember, but I think it was the Teamsters. The workers were not making oodles of dollars, but they were making $2 an hour or so more than I was. They were doing the *same* kind of work, manual, but not paper work, and I was making *less*! So, it kinda got to rub me the wrong way!

When raise time came around I got a pretty good verbal annual review. I had access to the figures and knew how much my new warehouse was saving the company - compared to what they were spending before. At least in my mind, the increase that was awarded me was not a fair share of the pie! I did not know what share anyone else was getting. But I did not think mine was big enough, because I was still going to be well below the unionized workers who did not have anywhere near the responsibilities that I had.

I was married and I was looking to make some good money. And we did not have any benefits. So this became a point of contention. It enraged me enough that I became determined to find another job.

Going into Transit Work. I looked in the newspapers and found an ad for a metro operator for a city bus. I was pretty naive: I thought, "That sounds like a nice job! I'll go out and pick a Country-Club route, through a fairly nice part of town. And I'll work 8 to 5, driving up and down nice streets. It's no big deal!"

Well, I didn't fully understand the the way it works, like - there's seniority! You have to start at the bottom and work your way up. And you've got to accept what's left at the bottom. You are not going to get that Country-Club route; And you're not gonna have Saturdays off for a long time. But, I applied as the job could more than *double* my salary!

When I was tested I scored 100, and I think they wanted me because of that, and also because I was Hispanic. I thought this greased the wheels a bit, and someone said, "We've got to get this guy in here!" But, for whatever reason, I was glad I was hired.

Working 'Union.' In August of '73 or '74, when I just turned 21, I started as a transit driver: I trained for a month, got my badge, and started driving a bus.

I knew this was a union shop and I knew that I'd be required to join it. It was a closed shop. I knew what the initiation fee was, $135, I believe. "Boy," I thought, "that's a chunk out of my money!" And I'm like anybody else: I thought that's a lot of money all of sudden! But I was making much more money than in my other job, and I now had health insurance benefits. Being married, the new job satisfied a lot of our needs and immediate concerns for our family.

I even had a retirement plan - though it was very, very poor: It's one of the things I'm working on now.

So, overall, it was a good deal! It more than doubled my salary! There *is* a difference between union shops and non-union places! After I was there 2 1/2 months the contract expired and they negotiated a new contract. I received another increase in excess of a dollar an hour! And so I was *extremely* happy: It was "Seventh Heaven!" I said, "This is all right ! This is an all-right place to work for!"

Which was probably the mood of most people. A lot of people my age were starting there because there had been a lot of people die or retire. The service was expanding, and so things went well, for quite awhile.

Becoming a Unionist. I worked for the bus company, enjoyed life, and never was too much involved with the union.

The reps were okay, and some were even fire-and-brimstone. One in particular, some people thought he was crazy! He would fan the fire, and say emphatically "By God, this...!" and "By God, that...!" It seemed like some of the union reps didn't care for him a whole lot, but he did what he had to do in order to get elected steward. People knew he would look after your situation. And he was eventually elected president of our local.

I rarely attended union meetings. One of my best buddies down there, a kinda idealistic guy, said, "Why don't you go to union meetings?" I said "What do we want to do that for? I've got to much to do!" And he kinda got on my case and said "That's your job! That's your money! That's where things go on and they control what goes on down there! And they've got a large say! And we've got a large number of us in the same age range, and we've got our own needs and concerns! You've *got* to get involved!"

It's kinda like my buddy took me down there, and that started a long process that brought me to where I am today. I *did* get involved! And he was right: There were a lot of young guys like myself down there, by no means a majority, but we were starting to be a growing number.

Becoming an Activist. What I found there was a local union president - I never did get to know him personally - but everyone has told me he was a very good man. Seemed very gracious and nice when you talked to him. A very tall and presentable figure. A lot of people in our local say he was *the* best president our local ever had! And that's probably true.

Things were going well. After the Urban Mass Transit Administration was formed they started funding mass transit properties in the mid-'60's: They passed laws and statutes that provided for matching funds or even better than matching funds for local communities for transit. In our area a half-cent sales tax was passed that Kansas City could charge specifically for buses. So the money was rolling in!

Funding was not a problem: We wanted to take good care of transit. So it was easy to go after wages, since the money was coming in. The environment was right. Before the wages and the fringe benefits had not been good. Now, we were able to make significant progress in these areas because the money was coming in.

That's a luxury - as you can guess - I'd like to have today. I'd like to have the luxury of lots of money coming in and continuing to grow, and a future of still more money, more revenue, just keep coming in. But that's not a luxury that I have: The environment has changed. I have the *reverse* problem. So, it may have been very easy to have been looked at as a good president back at that time.

The local's president had a good relationship with the Executive Board members and stewards that worked with him. They were all just a little younger than he was, and they had a thing together: They knew what they wanted to do, and that's what they did!

Resenting Tight Control. One thing that kinda struck me when I went to the meetings was that it was that it was kinda like a railroad: The president would say "We want to do this," and there was *no* dissent from the Board members. And ironically, the Board people wouldn't push it on the floor before the union meetings. You never hear about the things that were coming up. I mean, this stuff would just come up, and it would get voted in.

And it was almost like the Board people...well, they revered the president: He was an intelligent person. He was a political person, active in politics. A friend of the Mayor. Active in the Central Labor Council and actually president of it for a while. They revered him, and had a lotta respect for the man. And I'm not downgrading the man. The man did a lotta good things and was progressive for our local for the time.

But, my view, from sitting out on the floor was, gosh, we'd raise things, and we were told "we'll look into it." Or "we'll discuss that later." There were things younger people like me were starting to ask. And it's not that we wouldn't take "no" for an answer. It was that sometimes there wasn't even a "yes" or a "no." We were not a large enough constituency to have anyone afraid of our voting bloc, though we did start asking some of these questions.

Choosing a New Leader. The man who was president when I came into the local was elected for a third term: No one ran against him. It was a "done deal." Everyone he wanted in, they were in! With the exception of one guy, who raised a lot of hell! He got elected 'cause sometimes people just want a hell-raiser. When the president decided not to run for a fourth term, but to retire instead, he had a hand-picked successor, a gentleman from the Maintenance Department, who ran for his office. But all this time the hell-raiser had been actively campaigning.

The maintenance seniority unit was a minority group, and the incumbent had come out of the operator's division, a larger bloc. I think the Executive Board could have pushed and gotten his choice elected. But what happened was they didn't have the oomph the president had had, and he was sick at the time. He did not get out and vote for his candidate, and so that maintenance man lost by a very, very few votes. And this kinda gave me a clue that he (the president) was the glue that held things together.

The winner was a transportation man. The knock against him was that "he's crazy! He'll get us out on strike," and the whole bit. And he sees "right as right," and "wrong as wrong," and there's no gray! If he was to find out the company was over-paying a guy, or calculating the pay wrong, or giving a guy too much for whatever reason, he was just as apt to go and tell the company! "Right is right," and "wrong is wrong!"

And some of the guys would tell him - "Hell, when it's in our favor, keep your mouth shut! Let'em find out. And if they do you know they can do it right. They certainly wouldn't do it if they was payin' us wrong!" But he would say "Right is right!" So he won by only four votes.

Union Dissonance. A lot of the Executive Board members were not in awe of the new president as they had been of the retiring president. There were a few holdovers, board members, but not many. And some minorities got elected, for the first time. And so there was conflict and turmoil on the Board itself. There is some lost pay time when you get elected, some time off the bus. And I think some people got elected because they wanted to be off... maybe some were more interested in that than in serving the membership: To some extent that might have been true.

The new man did not have cooperation on his Board, and I do not know if he had a good battle plan. He took notes and kept detailed records, but I don't know if he had a good battle plan. It soon came to where the Board really ruled him, and did as they wanted. There was talk that if the Board wanted to get off a day early, you know, when they had Executive Board business, what they'd do was pick a fight with him. And get him so mad he couldn't think straight. And he'd get so mad and frustrated he'd say This meeting's over! And they'd be out, if it started at 9AM, by noon! At one time the Board even wanted him to resign, and he refused.

Taking a Stand. All of this time I was attending meetings, and becoming eligible in this way to run for office. No one had run for a steward's position in transportation, and I was appointed to it. I got some training, and had some classes: I wouldn't consider it adequate by the standards we hold today, but I got involved.

The next time I ran and was elected for a term. Meanwhile the fire brand president ran for a second term and lost: He was just creamed by the man he had earlier beaten: Hundreds and hundreds of votes compared to only 21!

I ran next for the Executive Board, and was elected. I wanted some changes, and I made a genuine effort to work out my differences with the new president. It was clear I did not have a majority support on the board, and I got frustrated over my 3-year term. I decided to run for vice-president, though some people wanted me to challenge for the presidency. I didn't think I could win that election at that time, and I was still willing to try and work within the existing framework.

The president could see I was becoming a threat to him, as our differences were starting to become wider. So he backed my opposition, and would actively steer lost-time cases to this guy so that he could deal with the membership and spend a lotta time with them: You know, you've got to do *a lotta* politics to get elected.

I was able to continue to spend my own time with the membership, and this other guy and I got into a pretty rough election. I ended up winning by several votes, since the president over-did his support for my opponent: It was clear what was going on, and it ended up hurting my friend, and I got elected.

Had I lost, I intended to appeal to the International that the president had used union funds to back my opponent (he had released a one-sided newsletter in support). And I think I would have won that battle - so this kinda broke the camel's back between the president and myself.

Fighting Back. From the outset I was told I'd never sit a day in the president's chair when he was absent. I was not invited or even asked, and was more or less directed not to go down to the Maintenance Department on any issues. Well, I didn't listen, and dropped by instead to say "Hi" to different people, you know, just to kinda get a feel.

Sometimes, though, the local's directors would tell me they didn't want me wandering around, for safety reasons, etc. It wasn't really super obnoxious. But it was made clear to me that somehow "the word" had gotten around: The "word" was to minimize my influence within the department... at least that was my perspective.

At any rate I decided to run for union president because I was putting in so much time on my own. I was interested. I thought I had something to contribute to the membership. I thought we needed a change. There were times when I thought the present policies compromised our membership. I did not see us, as did the local president, as a dying organization. A dying union. That the best we could do was to minimize the hurt while we died. And we *had* to make concessions in the transportation department because we were not as highly skilled as the mechanics.

Now, it is true the maintenance mechanics are *highly* skilled people. And there were cuts made in transportation, and concessions were made. But I thought they went too far, way too far. I felt a lotta times the grievances were compromised - "You give me this one and I'll give you that one" - and I understand there is give-and-take. But does the grievant*have* a case? Or *not*?! The facts should speak for themselves.

I decided to challenge six months before the election, fairly early in the matter, and I let it be known. And it was kinda interesting. My opponent took the position that the people knew him and his record: They knew what he had and could do for them. He never really got out and campaigned. He had a good group of people working for him and on his behalf. So I just out-hustled him.

Winning Office. I did away with the concept that you just pass out a business card and get votes this way. I had been very active in United Way and had done a TV commercial for them. I had served on the Central Labor Council. I printed all that up, and told a little about my background on a brochure or campaign flyer. I passed these out and went out and got people to vote for me.

And I was able to assemble a good group of supportive people, because I knew from looking around that there was a group of lower-rated people, less skilled people, in the mechanics group that were not sure they were getting fair treatment... particularly minorities. You see, even to this day, there is social stratification on the property. It's not overt, and it is not done a whole lot. But you can still see it in different people. So, I put together a coalition of those people, plus progressive Caucasians and females.

The Maintenance Department did a lot of campaigning for me. And I talked to a lot of people! Constantly! And some in office/clerical. Well, I won the election... by a little bit better than a 2 to 1 margin. And then I started anew. I liken it to the move, "The Candidate," with Robert Redford: "Okay, you've won. Now what happens after you've won?!"

I wanted to make some changes in our union, in some things we had done from the past. People in transportation, my co-workers, had a lotta hope I would do some good things for them. They were glad to have an operator back as president. People in my age group said "Our needs will be addressed, 'cause he is one of us!" People in the Maintenance Department - some felt I was green and didn't know what I was doing: If they had been the whole election unit I'd have lost. There was also an attitude about my having won because there were so many minorities on the property. But I could not have gotten better than 2 to 1 with only minorities!

Taking Charge. Where to start?! To me, we had a fractured union. We had new Executive Board people and stewards come on who were like me in being new to the job. I relied heavily on a maintenance rep to help me understand their portion of the contract: He didn't trust me much at the outset, since he had campaigned for my opponent. But in time he assured me we could work together and he would not be an obstructionist.

That was good, because that was what I wanted. I did not want people to be "yes, yes!" because I do *not* know all the answers. And I want people to work with me to find the right answers and the right path to do some things.

Our international went into educational reforms, and began having seminars - every three months a regional seminar for the locals, and we also got heavily involved in that one. And then there is a regional seminar the locals are involved in, and we got heavily involved in that. And there is a legislative seminar. And then we have classes at the Meany Center.

As a new local president I was sent by the international to three or four leadership classes right away. Not to have fun! There's work to be done, and work expected to be done! I think my international has done a really good job with these. It really helps us out a lot!

Making Change. Since then we've started a newsletter. We changed its whole format. You have to make it readable. You can't use old mimeograph equipment that sometimes fades and you don't get a good copy; you've got to make it readable.

It shouldn't be solely a "bully pulpit," where you get out what you want to hear and nothing else. To get people to read it you need to put in different perspectives, different views. We allow people to write opposing "letters to the editor." Not many have done that, but it is a standing open opportunity, just as long as you do not curse or swear.

We also do spotlights on people. And for a period of time we did birthdays. And we still do a variety of human interest stories to try and get people to read the newsletter. It is hard to get articles to continue to come in , as the volunteers running it have got lives to lead... but they continue to try.

Diversity Focus. I got it into my mind to use my local paper to tell a little about our pioneers, you know, the first women we had as bus drivers or mechanics, the first blacks, and so on.

The general perception of the first women was that they were big and tough. Fifteen years ago, on my first day on the job, one of them leaned across the table and said - "I mean to have you, little man!" And all the old-timers laughed, but I got kinda upset. I didn't know what in hell she meant, and she was *big*!

I wrote up the history of the first blacks in our local, and put it in our paper. The company *really* liked it, and they turned it into a videotape! Some of the members, however, especially the young guys in what we call "the Gun Club,".... you know, "the NRA gun-loving"' Archie Bunker types....were pissed. I was actually told not to send the local paper to a guy's home anymore, as he didn't want "that kinda garbage in his home."

Making Democracy Work in the Local. In running things nowadays I first read over the minutes of the previous meetings and those of recent executive board meetings. I then place the issues to be discussed into an outline of "The Order of Business." I study the issues, and prepare notes for what I want to say and how I want to say it. I put emphasis on the items I need to change depending upon the audience.

Our first meeting, usually at 8 p.m., involves the transportation department...and I consciously spend a noticeable amount of time on *their* issues. I try to convey the message - "I am not just the locals' president. I *also* understand your issues: I am a driver! I operate a bus! It *has* happened to *me*! I *am* one of you; I have not forgotten the department I came from!"

The next day at 4 p.m. I meet with the maintenance members. We usually discuss things only someone intimately involved in that department would know - like who is having babies, whose children won a scholarship, and so on. The message here is - "I am not just the local's president. I *also* know the inner-workings of your department. I know the gossip: Yes, I even know that one of you, as a practical joke, recently put old cheese into supervisors' phone, but I'll never say who: I *am* one of you!"

Computer Aid. One of my goals for the local was to help computerize it because when I was vice-president I set up files, but I couldn't keep up with it as a volunteer on my own time. So one of the first things I did as president was set up a file for every member. And they are hard to keep up: We need more office staff. I try to keep it up myself now, and use some members to help me (and pay them lost time).

So now we've got a good data base: I have catalogued every grievance that we've filed; who handled the first, second stage; and third what the resolve was; and who the arbitrators were if the issue was arbitrated, and what the results were.

Our training has continued, and we've sent two people to the Meany Center to learn arbitration, and another two to local arbitration classes. We're starting to do them ourselves, and save the membership some money. And it will pay off in the long run - that's one thing we're using our computer for... along with keeping up addresses.

Finding Our Voice Again. We've been 2 1/2 years without a contract, and we're suing the company to go to binding arbitration. We've gone without a dues increase for the past twelve years, one that has gone specifically for the local.

So we've had to cut down on the regularity of putting out a newsletter. Within the last three months, however, we've been able to convince the membership to increase their dues by $8 a month. And we've now begun to publish the newsletter again...with help from ads from our HMO, our Blue Cross-Blue Shield, and the bank that handles our pension fund we should be able to get out three or four issues a year.

New Venture. Years ago we wouldn't have tried to do any of our arbitrations ourselves. Now, however, as part of an economy move, a cost-saving measure, we do...and comparing '87 with '90 we've saved $22,000 in legal fees. We are winning over 50%, a pretty good win-loss record.

And we're no longer taking poor cases, as in the past, just to keep up our popularity. The attorney used to say "I don't want to take your money to arbitrate this case; it's a bad one, a loser." But we'd do it to please the membership, whereas today we try and convince our people not to waste *their* dues money on cases without a chance. We try now to explain *better* why there's no merit in the case.

Arbitration and Drugs. We've had an Employee Assistance Plan (EAP) on our property since 1974, but it mainly focused on alcohol, not on drugs. As we got into the late '70's we began to have some problems with drug abuse. In the 1974 agreement our union negotiated an EAP clause for the entire membership, and later expanded coverage from solely alcohol to drugs and alcohol.

As hysteria grew over drug use, particularly after the big train accidents, which brought about all the calls for random testing, other transit companies started doing what we were already doing. As we were faced with this, unions began to ask - "What should unions do? Do they sit back and just take the word of management that a person is positive on a test? How do you provide a member with protection against misdiagnosis?"

The other side of the issue, which was probably equally as important for us, was that when we take a drug case to arbitration in our local our membership gets assessed our share of the costs of the arbitration. It's not covered in the dues. So, we've got to keep this in mind as we are a *collective* organization.

We were faced with either having to let a guy go out the door or having to spend many dollars on arbitrations that we were not going to win. We didn't have enough facts. We didn't have the basic "who, what, when, where, and why?," while chemical data would win cases. The bottom line was we would spend a lot on a losing cause.

We decided we needed to be able to check out the facts, to have the facts front and center. We developed a plan to secure a split sample so we could see what was going on. It wasn't a matter we felt we had to ask the company for: We *demanded* a split sample; we said we had a right to it! And our members, for his or her own protection, were more than happy to comply, because they were seeking protection from us as an organization.

What that did was help us *win*! As in a case where we proved to the arbitrator that the "chain of custody," the way in which the specimen jar from one of our members had been handled, was not good enough. Mind you, an arbitrator does not want to put anybody even remotely associated with drugs back to work. Our case was so compelling the arbitrator found the evidence inconclusive, and put the person back.

We had a lot to learn before we got good at this. Initially we had chemists come over from the labs that we hired to talk to us about the process. We toured labs, and we developed a base of information. The important thing was we were no longer just taking management's word or depending on them to give us the information. Not everybody was pleased, of course. Some members thought our new behavior, our insistence on getting our own test results from a split sample, was not the way a union should go. They urged us to remember we're not a business; we're a union! That we were for the little guy no matter what, and shouldn't be swayed by test results: That sorta stuff was best left to management, where labor could fight against it, fair and simple.

I do not see it that way. My perception of the issue was your heart belongs with the members, but you still need the power of new information. Our split sample program provided us with a base of information we needed to 1) get at least one individual back to work; 2) convince management not to challenge us because we now had facts; and 3) force management to become more "enlightened," and take a half step back in their approach.

The more we do to enlighten ourselves, it forces them to become more enlightened. It's not only at the upper echelons, but at the lower as well, and it gets day-to-day dealings more in tune with reality.

We not only protected members required to take tests - with our union-certified chemical lab results - but we also protected those not required to do so, the members who would have been required to pay for any drug use arbitration case. Instead, they shared the cost of the split test, which was under $100, versus $2,500 to $3,000 cost per arbitration. Finally, when our results agreed with those of the company we insisted a guy go into treatment, and we refused to take his case to arbitration - so we saved money there also.

Now, in the last year, we've been able to drop our split test demand since new government regulations require management to give us the safeguards we had sought. When we were using it we had maybe ten cases a year, with only three or so men required to go into treatment. They were all rehabilitated and returned to driving buses, but two later turned up positive and were dismissed.

Health Care Cost Containment. Our health care costs keep going up, and our members hate it. Part of the reason is our costs for drug and alcohol EAP rehabilitation procedures. Some members say "We never use these drugs or alcohol: Why should we pay for it?" So we've negotiated a new contract clause that says there will be no random testing unless required by the government for our industry. As well, we rely on the AFL-CIO Department of Community Services to train some of our people in referring members constructively to rehab programs. We're particularly alert to a record of poor attendance. We're trying to be pro-active, to save a person's job or keep them out of jeopardy, so we reach out, in the spirit of what we think we should do...and help them help themselves.

We're also looking at the possibility of contracting directly with health care providers as an organization. It could be a royal pain-in-the-ass, but we would be assured we could select the health care plan the majority of our members want. The Executive Board of the local is studying this, with an economist from Washington, D.C. we've contracted to help us evaluate the idea.

We know the company is evaluating other plans. We'll compare ours and theirs, and try and make the best decision. Initially we were very confrontational; we didn't like what the company was doing with our health care plan and felt they were imposing an inferior plan on us. Our members clearly wanted a better one, and were willing to pay for it out of their pockets.

We got angry at the bargaining table, and it got pretty steamy for awhile. We got the vast majority to refuse to renew their health care coverage at open enrollment time - until the last day, that is. We don't want to be caught in a position that because of our policy the members didn't have any health coverage. And so we told them at the last moment to go in and sign up for the health care plan; that we would continue to pursue new options during the following year.

It's not earth-shattering or earth-shaking like a new idea that nobody ever thought of before, but its a stretch of an idea used by other locals. Membership nowadays will not sit long for anybody that sits still forever.

Assessing Change. We're not saints. I'm not a saint. But we've tried. And I think our membership understands that and they feel they're gettin' a fair deal. It may not always be the answer they like, but it is the answer that is realistic and would be given to anybody in the same situation.

What happens in a local union is that when you want to bring in a whole lot of these changes, the perception of the membership as a whole changes. There is the notion the union will *do* somethin'! And there is more request for activity.

Well, when you have a limited budget...when you haven't had any dues increase for three years, and the members are still reluctant to raise their dues, (it's human nature...they want somethin' for nothin'), what happens is you get more and more requests. Expectations get raised. Demands for improvements and changes are made. Not only within the local union structure, but within the local union committees.

"Why can't we do this?" Well, what happens is there are areas you want to explore where you think you can do things better. Computerization is one good example. For a long time it saved us from having to hire somebody else to come in and do a lotta work. But it also provided a tool with which we can categorize the membership, and keep records for our collective bargaining needs. It creates more work, because you have more information, and you have the ability to do more cause you have more information.

The membership comes to have more expectations. At a point in time you either have to add more staff or reduce the membership expectations. And if you do that, that is when the revolution starts!

So you've got to find a way to satisfy the need, to channel it. To me, the concern in the future is not to spread ourselves too thin to do an effective job and not satisfy what people *really* want, desire and need. That's a balance we're gonna have to strike. How we're going to do that, I'm not entirely sure yet. I'm still working on that.

"With a little Help from my Friends." My international listens, though they don't always agree, and we get help from them. They were using slides for educational purposes, but have responded to a suggestion to convert to VCR format. That's what people prefer. They're now bringing out a Spanish-language version, in response to an issue raised by members.

I do talk on a regular basis with local union presidents from other transit unions to find out what are they doing. How are they addressing the needs of their membership? What projects have they started? We copy, borrow, and steal...we try to improve on projects that are appropriate. I've seen methods that I use borrowed by them, and it is good. We pick each other's brains.

The international sends us to a lotta training seminars for local union presidents. And a lotta training goes on in class, and also when we're just sitting around. You can have a beer, or soda pop, or whatever, with your contemporaries from across the country, and find out what is going on.

I'd like the AFL-CIO to take more seriously the computerized bulletin board that's run by the Meany Center: I've logged on, but I don't think ideas are shared on that as much as they could be or should be.... I don't know that that's a high priority, because older union leaders are not into that yet.

Perhaps their secretaries do that type of work. I don't have a secretary and I do my own. To me, the computer was something I learned by accident, and I finally got into it: I was able to adapt to it. Maybe others are not into it yet. So, these kinds of things need to be explored.

As for the future, I expect our locals overall to be better-managed, better run, because of what I see as emerging younger leadership availing themselves of the opportunities the internationals are providing. And because they have ideas.

One thing that is important is that we'll have to have a sense of mission. We'll have to develop the ability of not spreading ourselves too thin. And not let international political struggles hold us back from trying things, trying new ideas.

It's one thing to stay in office, keep your support, and keep everybody happy. But if you don't keep visiting out there, keep picking up *new* things, you become stagnant. You become ineffective. For me, that's a big challenge for labor. And that's a big challenge for myself. I hope for all of us that labor is successful. I hope for me that I'm successful...in learning how to do that. And I think its an on-going process.

Caring and a Lay Chaplaincy
L. *Max Schmitt*
(UAW Chaplaincy)

Much to their credit a steadily-growing group within the United Auto Workers Union attracted 256 registrants (a record!) to their 1992 Fifth Annual National UAW Chaplaincy Conference. Attendees from 21 states, including L. Max Schmitt, author of the case study below, joined hands across 34 different denominations to learn in workshops how as lay persons with a special gift, a special capacity for helping hurting co-workers, they could make a critically needed difference to anguished UAW members and dependents.

Thanks to my chance encounter with Max at the 1992 Cornell ILR School Summer Session he offers below some cogent answers to four critical questions:

How can a secular organization help meet religious counseling needs without stirring a hornet's nest?

What are the risks revealed by five years of UAW experience with a lay chaplaincy, and how can they be overcome?

How is it best to relate a local's Employee Assistance Plan and a Chaplaincy Program?

Finally, what is the unique value, the special message that only a Chaplaincy Program can send? And, how critical might it be in demonstrating to an increasingly fragile and vulnerable membership that organized labor can really be *there* for them?!

I've always given a hand by being involved in our plant UAW apprenticeship program for the past eleven years. In the last two years, however, I've added something new, something I like to think has helped Local 1097 in a very special way. It's helped me a heckova lot. And it's even helped bring some troubled souls to the Lord. What I mean is I've become involved in a chaplaincy program within my UAW local, along with Herman Daily, an ordained minister who has been a UAW Employee Assistance Program rep for the past 20 years.

I spend a lot of evening and weekend hours visiting members or their loved ones in nearby hospitals. I go to funerals and funeral homes to do what I can to console people. I sit by the bedside of a sick or even dying brother or sister. And I pray with them, or I joke with them, or I even sometimes cry with them...whatever seems to make it a little more bearable, a little easier to take, a little easier to put up with.

All of this is on my own time, after I complete my turn on the third shift. I've enough seniority after 15 years in the plant to pull a better shift. But I asked for this late one because it lets me get to the hospital before surgery begins: A lot of people want someone to kinda hold their hand and assure them it will be okay...before they go under the knife.

I pay all of my expenses, from parking fees through gasoline and what have you. None of us, and there are a lot of us across the entire UAW who volunteer as chaplains, none of us take a cent in expenses. Heck, I get more out of this than anyone could ever pay me!

Hospital visits, and funeral parlors, and rides out to the cemetery, and one wake after another...it sounds kinda gloomy to a lot of people. But it gives me a real lift because it means so *much* to the grieving people who are left behind. Many do not know how to thank me enough...after they get over their surprise that a UAW local cares enough to have someone actually show up and show some concern.

While we don't make a fuss about it, or talk about it very often, we like the idea that being a chaplain for the local is helping show we're "family," that we *do* care in the UAW about one another! I feel we are taking my local *and* the Lord to people who need *both*.

Coming Together. When we get asked what a labor union chaplaincy is all about, we like to repeat an answer we first heard at our 1992 Annual Meeting - "We're caring people helping hurting people."

Over 256 auto union rank-and-filers, good sound ordinary folk, came together in April '92 in Detroit for the fifth regular gathering of UAW Chaplains, the largest such gathering ever! Half were women, and many of the gals and guys were taking evening college courses in counseling, social work, or, like me, in preparation for becoming a licensed minister.

Our union president, Owen Bieber, spoke to our meeting for the first time, and this formal recognition meant an awful lot to us. He gave our organization his blessings and pledged his continued support by saying "I know who you are and I support what you do." He even invited us to give the benedictions at the '92 UAW Convention. Our officers assured him we would not compete with UAW EAP [Employment Assistance Program] reps, but would respect their role and cooperate fully with them - a policy question president Bieber had previously raised with us.

We really got a lot out of the speakers we heard and the workshops we attended. You could choose to learn about the grieving process. Or how to console. Or how to refer people to community social services. Or how to be a better listener. It was all high-quality stuff, and it felt good, *real* good to be part of it.

Our organization is now working up standards so that a member can know if they are really ready to assume the role. We're going to set educational standards, and fellowship standards. We also have written forms to help chaplains keep records of their expenses: In this way we can deduct some of them, and wind up spending a little less out of our pocket - not that anybody begrudges a cent of what doing this service costs us!

Becoming a Chaplain. I got "Called" to this only a few years ago when I took some heavy blows in my own life. I had to reconsider how I was living, and I've since become born-again in Christ. I've never felt better, never been more in touch with life, never been more on top of my own life.

So I've got a lot to share and a need to share it. I began two years ago by volunteering to serve as a Chaplain for my American Legion Post. Our members are pretty well along in years, and when winter is on us we can have one or two veterans die in a month. I go to the funerals and hospitals and homes to try to console the family. Sometimes I'm even able to help bring someone back to the Lord, or at least to the comfort you can find in his Word.

Non-Denomination Emphasis. Mind you, our work as UAW Chaplains is *strictly* non-denominational. We go out of our way to respect everybody's beliefs. We've got guidelines we have to respect or we'll get removed from our post by the local president who appointed us. And the strictest guideline of all demands that we stay non-denominational.

Nobody should promote his own brand of religion...nobody! We believe any of us can be right - You can be right. And I can be right. And we can both have very different religious beliefs. That's our right...and a UAW Chaplain respects it to the hilt! Chaplaincy does not ask that we compromise any of our beliefs. It does ask that we respect the beliefs of others. Everybody is entitled to his own way of relating to the Lord.

What we are especially opposed to is anyone using the chaplaincy to create their own ministry: That is not what chaplaincy is about! We're always on the lookout for it and we'll stop it just as soon as we get a whiff! We don't want anyone to get it into his head that "I have the Word!" "I am a Minister!" And "This is my flock!" We're on guard against this temptation, and we just won't permit it.

Relieving Some Hurt. Since petitioning our local president to appoint us Chaplains we've made arrangements with the UAW benefits rep in our plant to tell us when a member is hurting. We learn right away about someone going out on extended sick leave. Or sent by an accident to a hospital. Or maybe even dead or dying. I also pass out little wooden coins throughout the plant with my beeper and phone number inked on them: Whenever I hear the sound of that phone ring I know somebody is in trouble...and I drop whatever I'm doing and hurry to help.

Much of the time I just listen. That's probably the biggest part of the job, just listening. People who are hurting have a big need to talk about it, to mull on it, to turn it around...and we help them work through all of it. We share the pain and lighten their load, mostly by being there, by bringing our UAW local to their side, in their time of need.

When referrals are needed we guide a brother or sister to turn to our EAP rep in the plant for proper subject counseling. As for problems with alcohol or drugs, we also refer these to our UAW-EAP Partner in Christ in the plant. We work closely together, and make one heck of a fine team: A lotta families of our members have gotten a lotta help they probably never expected to get for their union dues dollars.

Looking Ahead. We got started five years ago when a few UAW reps, now retired, but still active in chaplaincy, began to promote this idea of theirs. They put their own money and time to get it going, and they are still boosting our organization.

I first learned about it at a local meeting when our president read a request for a volunteer to go to an annual meeting of UAW Chaplains. Since I was already doing this sort of thing for my Legion Post I asked to go, and I've been 100% involved ever since. I guess you might say it's become my Calling, my *labor* Calling.

Every year for the past five we've gotten larger and larger at our annual meeting. I can only see this continuing because we meet *real* needs! We're just ordinary union folk helping one another...guided by the Lord, and His chaplaincy movement in labor is going to spread, I just know it, because its "caring people helping hurting people in the work place."

Part III

Better Use of Better Information

"The winds and waves are always on the side of the ablest of navigators."
Edward Gibbon

"The great end of life is not Knowledge but Action."
Thomas H. Huxley

A visit to the office of a robust local union reveals considerable reliance on high-tech information-enhancing equipment (modem, PC, fax, teleconferen-cing systems, etc.). Staffers explain that it helps assure parity for unionists who go one-on-one with comparably equipped corporate types. As well, staff specialists can better handle the myriad details of arbitration and grievance research, organizing campaigns, political election efforts, and the complex like. The good news, in short, is that many locals are making the most of powerful new "infobahn" equipment. Better still, this enables inside reformers to experiment with bold imaginative approaches to the information needs of the rank-and-file.

Three case studies below illustrate several information utilization options promoted by inside reformers, both of the non-computer and the computer-reliant type.

Paul Blaski, for example, explains how he helps meet the need his members have for good information about on-site safety issue and for the details of new roofing materials. The better to meet his own need for current information about the lives of his members Paul shares his thoughts about a weekend he spent with a Men's Movement group in his area, an example of personal outreach more such union leaders might attempt.

Paul Finn, in turn, uses his union office and home computers to facilitate a far-ranging corporate campaign, as well as help celebrate the birthdays of members. He polices Davis-Bacon enforcement matters, a major communication task, and also employs the art of persuasion to try and get his members to reconsider their wage level politics, a frustrating matter for even the most adroit of inside reformers.

Finally, labor educator Deborah Moy traces the personal evolution of her bold pioneering approach to curriculum that helps blend labor history and ethnic studies, an approach that offers unionists more empowering information and insights than previously true. Deeply troubled by racism, sexism, and other irrational divisions among rank-and-filers, she draws on new models of ethnic history and her considerable knowledge of labor history to show how inside reformers can promote fresh intellectual, emotional, and spiritual gains for everyone in this critical matter.

Accident-Prevention and Product Updates
Paul Blaski
(UURWAW)

Two-term Business Manager of a small local of the Roofers Union in Seattle, WA, Paul Blaski is typical of many inside reformers in believing the choice his local faced recently was quite stark: Either it would rapidly and substantially revive. Or it would die (No ifs, ands, or buts about it!). His cogent tale below highlights the potential of workplace safety regulations, new product education, and personal outreach in securing fresh momentum for a local on the comeback trail...provided, that is, that a change agent with vision is there to guide the entire scenario.

Paul's case study calls attention to four questions of value to all prospective reformers; i.e.,

How can an inside reformer turn accident-prevention options to a local's advantage?

How can the eagerness of members to stay up with fast-breaking industry improvements be turned to reform advantage?

What can candor about one's own drinking history, along with curiosity about the Men's Movement, contribute to improving the culture of a once-staid local?

Above all, what part does self-confidence play in helping to revive a local on the edge and giving it a new lease on life?

Paul's tale has relevance in and outside of the building trades, regardless of the size, location, and culture of a local: All that is required to profit from its lessons are determination and diplomatic ingenuity.

Like so many of my local's members I come from a union family, though I've gone farther and gotten more involved than anyone else in the family.

My father was an Auto Union member who worked in an auto factory in Buffalo for 32 years, or something like that. He's retired now, but he's still pretty active in the union. He and my mother go once or twice a year to the UAW Education Center in Michigan for week-long seminars, or whatever.

I remember one instance, back in 1956 or so, when I was about six years old. I came home from church and I said something like "The unions are really bad for this country!" My mom and dad sat me down and said "We've got to tell you something." They went on to explain to me how the union put food on our table, and a number of other items in the house. (Years later I came to figure out that it was at the height of McCarthyism, and the Church was real anti-union at this time. I didn't realize it then.)

Renewing Building-Trades Unionism. Our leadership in all the trades has gotten at least 25 years *younger* in the last few years. A lot of the older guys who were still around in the '50s, '60s, and '70s, when they could put their feet up on the desk and everybody listened to them...they've retired or passed away. A new generation of business agents, leaders, and presidents have taken over. And they're pushing a lot of *new* stuff. Many have actually gone to the Meany Center, and they serve as a lightning rod for their internationals.

Razor-thin Margin. Promoting change is *not* always popular: The last election for full-time office I won by only four votes out of about 50 cast. We just ratified a contract recently by only two votes - so I'm always one vote away from disaster. But I look at it this way: As long as I win, I just move on from there. I feel now that as I've won these two very close votes I've almost turned the corner. People have said: "O.K., he's for real. He's marching along. Let's get behind him!"

Taking My Own Stand on Workplace Safety. I've been in the roofing industry since 1971, or over 20 years. Some ideas here are very backward as far as safety is concerned, a kind of machismo sort of thing. But in the nation as a whole, and in my state of Washington in particular, over the last two years there has been dramatic improvement in "fall protection," thanks to new legislation and administrative rules.

I sit on a statewide Advisory Committee, and I've taken a lot of flack from my members for the stand I've taken in this matter. Almost two years ago some very rigorous regs, very rigorous safety measures, were proposed in an attack on "business-as-usual." All of our contractors and many of my members fought tooth-and-nail against them. Which I thought was crazy, because they really made a lot of sense. The proposed regs meant contractors would have to put up warning lines and safety protections on edges of roofs over 10' or higher (it used to be 16').

I supported these regs. Most of organized labor wanted more stringent rules. I helped negotiate a little bit of leeway, because I knew that if we would have said "No!" we would have gotten an even harder set of administrative rules dumped on us.

My position is that the administrators, the architects, and the builders of the projects have to share responsibility with my members for safety. They have to engineer safety *into* a building. If it stands for 100 years you're going to have 5, 6, or 7 roofs put on up there. And this means dangerous construction going on every time you do that...and so this danger to my people should be factored into the original design of the building.

Since the new regs have passed I've had to change our local's education program to take account of them. In our apprenticeship program we're actually running classes on work site safety to insure we have what they're calling a "fully competent person" on the roof, in other words someone who is responsible for fall protection. Contractors now have to have a safety plan for every job site. As the average duration of a roofing job may be a week they must have a whole stringent schedule for the entire job...and our local helps them out with this.

Protecting Our Competitive Edge. Our industry has changed so dramatically in the last five years. With the use of space-age materials, the roofers can no longer assume they automatically know how to put the roof system down. So what we've been doing is getting the manufacturers and some of the members who do know the new systems to help train our journeymen. At least expose them to the new systems so that they will be able to teach the younger guys as well as produce. If we had offered these classes five years ago, nobody would have shown up. Today, people are beating the doors down! They know its going to keep them working.

Helping One Another. Naturally, I offer referrals to AA and the like to our members who need help with their personal problems. I'm a recovering alcoholic myself. I don't try to hide that fact. I try to help my people out in that way, in being that open about it.

My international used to have a substance-abuse program, but it was so successful it bankrupted itself. It got such use that it eventually went broke! Its a *great* idea...so we rely now on an informal referral system. I try and get sober and recovering drinkers to talk to somebody else...those who know who we are, so to speak, reach out when we hear so-and-so is having a problem and try and get him to accept some help.

It's interesting because when I first came to the local in '80 there were a lot of hard-core drunks, a lot! *Unbelievable!* There are still some, but I think people now have more of a handle on it. I've helped a bit, as much as I can, though it is not my major concern.

Trying This and That. I try to keep an open mind about things that might appeal to different types of members. I've got one guy, for example, who has been going to men's workshops for the last seven years. So, I took the opportunity recently to go to a weekend-long men's retreat. It turned out there were five other men from my local there, including my seven-year friend. It was pretty cool, pretty interesting: There were even some guys out there barking at the moon! Crazy! But I learned a lot.

Summary. Just a few years back we were at a level where we were just surviving. We had no energy to go out and organize or do anything. We were either going to crash and disappear, or go the other way.

Now, we've been able to push it up over that threshold. Today we have about 30% of the roofing business in our area. In five years we should have it up to 45% - and in the mid-1980's we were down to about 20%. We're on a comeback, with many new younger members (I'm recruiting women and minorities, and we have several). A lot of people are coming in from the non-union sector, because they're slow on work and we've got the work. People are seeing that we've gotten a better name out there the last couple of years: We're more active and more visible than ever before.

All humility aside, it's helped that I had a vision to see that this is where we have had to go, and these are the things we've had to do to get there. We still need more members. And we need to start putting more pressure on the industry to do the things we want! We haven't reached that yet, but at least we're finally heading in that direction.

Afterword (July, 1993). In June, 1993, I was nominated on a "white ballot" [an unopposed ballot] for another term, and with my re-election I will serve as Business Manager until 1996. Local 54 has more members than ever before!

Computers, Corporate Campaigns, and Structure
Paul Finn
(IBPAT)

Soft-spoken and thoughtful, Paul Finn, Financial-Secretary of Local Union 333 of the Painters and Allied Trades Union (San Diego, CA.), may be *the* reformer in this volume with the greatest outreach: No one else I know of regularly spends evening hours in computer-based contact with unionists all over America. After arriving home from his union office Paul scans several sources of fast-breaking news on his home computer. Then, on his own initiative, at his own expense, and out of his own sense of what other reformers might find useful, he faxes items hither and yon to help unionists from coast-to-coast.

Convinced years ago organized labor was both indispensable and yet also inadequate, Paul shares his responses to such vexing questions as-

What part can a computer, a modem, and a fax play in promoting revitalization?

How can enforcing Davis-Bacon terms help vitalize the membership?

What part can a corporate campaign by a single local officer play in securing new gains?

What compromises must a reformer expect to make with small-minded union politics?

How can the case for rollbacks be made without stirring a hornet's nest?

What sort of approach should an enlightened local take to non-union workers with whom its members compete?

How meaningful are current union mailings, and how might they earn a more attentive readership?

Especially revealing are Paul's misgivings about his union-management situation, and the attitude he employs to keep up his spirit and resolve.

A graduate of both the Antioch College Degree Program at the Meany Center and the Harvard Trade Union Seminar (a 10-week program), Paul has sufficient reason to doubt whether reform can come quickly and substantially enough. Typical, however, of such reformers throughout the labor movement, he does not let this slow or sidetrack him, but persists instead in doing his part - and then some!

I graduated from a junior college in 1972, and got a degree in Civil Engineering Technology. But as there were no jobs in San Diego in that profession, I decided to go into building painting. And found I was

soon making more money in it than I would have in the trade I had wanted to go into.

My father had been a painting contractor, and I'd worked with him. He got out of the union in '59, as a contractor, because the rule at the time was that if you were a small contractor, and you only had work for one man, then the contractor stayed home, and sent the one man out to do it. My dad couldn't afford that, so he had to get out of the union in order to continue working. And back in '58 and '59 they lost quite a few contractors for that reason.

My father never held any animosity toward the union that I know of. I was elected to office while he was still alive (he's dead now three or four years). My mom tells me he thought there were some funny things going on with the union when he first got out - and apparently there were! I've talked to some old-timers, and there were some shenanigans back in '59 that kind of turned him off to the process. But he was always a pro-union guy.

My mother's father was a union lather who joined when he was 12 years old, and was a charter member in some local in Spokane. I guess he got in around 1902...or something like that. So, I don't *really* have a union background, even though I've got people in the family who were in a union.

Meanwhile...at Work. I started out in new construction, in housing. Later I switched over to painting for a hospital, about 13 or 14 years ago. They were regarded as *the* "gravy" job in town! We had about 3 to 15 guys there at various times. And I worked my way up into a *good* job; I started making signs for the hospital.

I also became kind of the point man there for all of the guys' problems. I was usually the guy they came to when something wasn't right.

About six years ago we were going to have a strike sanction vote, which is standard procedure in negotiations, and the foreman at the hospital said, "Well, if you guys go on strike, I want each one of you to come back singularly and see me, and we'll see if you've got a job or not." I know now that this was grounds for an unfair labor practice charge. Well, that angered me! We voted the sanction, but we didn't go out: That doesn't work anymore. But I was still angry. So, about six months later I quit! I had no other job to go to, and I quit over some little thing not worth quitting over. But it was the other thing that bothered me so much.

Doing It Differently. Now, in some of our building trades unions, we don't have what I've seen in some other unions - the association between worker and the union - that I think there should be. And the Financial Secretary would say things like, "Aw, don't worry about it. It's no big deal. You don't need to come to the meetings." Over the years this kind of set up an attitude where the guys aren't involved with the union. There's no social networking. There's no interaction among our members, hardly.

We don't really have strict grievance procedures. We don't have seniority. The boss can lay you off whenever he wants. He can hire his buddies. What the union does for us is guarantee our wage rate. And that's all anybody has ever asked of the building trades unions. In the 16 or 17 years I've been in I've never seen a grievance filed against an employer, unless it was over an incorrect wage rate or travel pay.

We're to make sure there's some work. Or get some work. Sign the contractors up. And make sure everyone gets paid the right wages. And that's been the extent of involvement with our members.

Moving Up. I had been working non-union until back in '74 when the contractor I worked for had to sign a union agreement to work on a particular job: When he joined the union, I joined the union. And I was happy to.

Now, from the time I joined in '74 I've been one of the few regular attendees at the meetings. Very few people do as I've done. The Financial Secretary in our local, (that's who runs the local pretty much...and that is what I am now) discouraged attendance at the meetings.

I continued to go to the meetings, and wanted to get involved. I put the word out - after five years of watching this - that I'd like to be involved on the "E" Board [Executive Board] at some low level. I didn't push it, 'cause I was still a young guy, and not aware of everything.

Other guys kept getting put onto different positions. They had no interest in the union. They were kind of buddies, hanger-ons. And at the time I wondered why these guys were being put in. But I know now! I've seen it happen in lots of unions. They're "Yes" men. They were wanted on the "E" Board, because they would agree with whoever appointed them. And that's kind of how it went.

We don't have our "E" Board like that now...and, it's tougher! We've got a bunch of *individuals*, but it's better for the union.

Taking Over. About 6 or 7 years ago I worked up some other people who came regular to the meetings. We got involved. And we ran a kind of mini-slate for some of the smaller positions, and I got in as a trustee. I kind of sat back and watched what went on, watched a little too long, and didn't like it.

When the Financial Secretary finally resigned, I ran - against some pretty stiff opposition - and won. And I've held the job now about four years.

Our local president is paid a monthly expense, is not a full-time employee, and chairs the local meetings, that's all. I'm the only full-time officer of the Local and I have a lot of latitude regarding job duties. The level of work in the office varies during the month and I am able to spend time on Davis-Bacon enforcement.

I started doing some things a little bit differently. I was trying to figure out what to do to get the members involved again - because when you are in the office it's a lot easier than trying to fight it from the outside.

I bought a computer for the office, and it has changed my life! I had used somebody else's for about a half-hour on a word-processing program, and I thought that was really a tool that would be nice to have. Convinced the "E" Board, maybe five years ago, to buy a computer. And it has turned out to be a tool that has made *all* the difference in the world...as far as communications with our members.

I have a regular daily routine. As a computer fanatic I'm trying to make it so that everyone will check in every morning for messages and such. Everyday when I walk into my house I kind of grin at my wife, then I walk into my study where my computer is. I check my "mail": I've got a route. I hit the local computer bulletin boards first until 6PM; I hit the Meany Center board, then the Department of Labor; then the AFSCME board in Washington, DC; I hit NABET or National Association of Broadcasting Engineering Technicians board in Chicago; then I hit a legal board in Seattle for Supreme Court decisions; then I relax abit. This keeps me up-to-date, especially concerning all the Department of Labor press releases...which, by just hitting a button I fax to unions I think might be interested. And it costs only $50 a month for 60 hours of data-transmission phone service.

No one has begun sending me any faxes back, but people do stop me and say "Oh yeah, I got your fax. Thanks!" I think it helps, and I'll continue doing it. It's a hobby that kind of turned into a job, but is still really a hobby.

My job is supposed to be managing the local's fiscal affairs. It used to have about 1,500 members when I joined, and is down to about 650 now. You do what you need to do to get the thing together or keep it together: The definition of the job isn't there anymore - so I'm involved doing a variety of tasks.

Learning the Ropes. One of the things I did was to go back to the Meany Center about three years ago to take a class in "Working with the Media." I thought that was one subject I could use help with - I'd never had any experience with the media. I felt *nothing* we were doing was newsworthy, and I needed to know what to see what we could do.

Well, I learned *alot!* In a one-week class I got sold on education. What happens in our trade, if you run for office and beat somebody, that guy's not going to help you. Most of our business agents have been around for a long time. And the rules have changed - especially in the building trades - in the last 10 years. So, we're kind of all new at this game, even the guys who've been in for a long time.

I've been Financial-Secretary in a full-time capacity for four years, I guess, and just got elected to a new 3-year term. And there's a three-year apprenticeship to be a painter. So I feel I'm just now coming out of *my* local leader apprenticeship! I don't have the answers. But I feel I'm starting to gather enough information so that I can help, and make some difference...hopefully.

In the media class, for example, I learned how to put out press releases. I learned how to do public service messages on the radio, and public access TV on the cable networks. And I've done all three since leaving the course. A week after I got back from the Meany Center in the summer of '87 I decided to write a public service announcement from our local regarding what Labor Day *really* meant - and it got played over the three-day holiday on radio. It didn't cost me anything. It took me a little while to do it. And it worked out really nice!

Tactics. One thing I'm getting notorious about is that I won't let go! I just won't give up: I'll just get hammering things. And sometimes its a fault. And sometimes its a benefit.

It came into play recently over the Davis-Bacon Act, the prevailing-rate law in construction work. The prevailing rate is close enough to the union rate in San Diego that we should be getting all the work. San Diego is a Navy town: Millions of dollars worth of work here every year is in Navy construction. But work here has gone 90% *non*-union! Our unionized contractors will bid the work, and lose it, by 50%! There is *no* way this should be: Except that it has turned out the Navy has literally quit enforcing Davis-Bacon. I've talked to Navy personnel, and they say "Well, that's about on the bottom of our list of priorities...enforcing prevailing wage."

So, I wrote a letter to one of our local congressmen, a *Republican* Congressman, I should have known better! But he's on the Military Construction Committee, and I live in his district. And I thought he'd be the guy to write to but I never heard back from the guy! I never got a form letter, or so much as "Thanks for your letter. I'll get back to you some year."

I wrote him another letter...because I just won't let go! Never got a response to this one, either. So I called his office, and explained that I wanted him to target some jobs for strict enforcement of Davis-Bacon standards--some paint contracts on Navy work here in San Diego. They said they'd look into it. And I never heard back from them.

Now, having learned at the Meany Center how to do it, I put out a press release on this Congressman. I never expected anyone to pick it up. Very few people care about prevailing rate. Our wages - and my members get angry when they hear this - have been too high for the market in our area. So, nobody cares if a painter is only making $11 an hour when he should be making $20, because they think $11 is pretty hot too...so its not a big topic in the news.

I did put out a press release. It didn't go anywhere...but the Congressman heard about it. And I got a response from him. He *did* what we requested, and we were able to start a case - three years ago - that I'm still working on today. So, when it comes to Davis-Bacon, I think I've *made* a difference, at least here in San Diego.

Later on I got a call about Davis-Bacon from a TV station in L.A., and I just unloaded on the guy! I said, "Jesus Christ! You don't know the half of it!" And I went into it. And they came down and interviewed me for a TV story. I would never have had the nerve to do that: I'm not a public speaker kind of guy. I'm not the kind of guy who would get up front like that. It's not my way. It's the Meany Center media class that gave me some understanding of how the system works that enabled me to do something!

So, we've gotten two or three *good* news stories on Davis-Bacon. And *that's* what's gotten the Navy's attention...its a *fear* of bad publicity. That's the thing about union work...you take the victories where you can find 'em! Things are *so* damn tough that it's hard to keep at it, hard to keep going. And if you get a victory every now and then, it's something to keep you going.

Looking for Leads. I've gotten into the Meany Center College Degree Program because my International pays the tuition, room and board, and the books.... And that has made a *big* difference for me, 'cause I don't fully understand union attitudes. I've got to intermix with other unions, and find out what *they're* going through...because what's worked for us in the past - hitting the contractor over the head and saying "You *will* be union! And get your guys in here and sign our contract!" - won't work. And strikes won't work anymore.

We had a big carpenters strike here about a year ago. And I feel the building trades are finally realizing that strikes *won't* do it! You've got to have your men behind you in order to win a strike...if there is such a thing as winning a strike.

In San Diego we've got *severe* labor problems. The Mexican border is 16 miles south of downtown. And I've got about 40 members who live in Tijuana, and they can use a trolley we've got from downtown to the Tijuana border. So, there's a lot of available cheap labor here in San Diego! A guy can work in Tijuana for $7 or $10 a day, or he can come up here. And in the dry wall trades, he can make $7 an hour *non*-union and think he is doing *fantastic*! Now, our union scale is $16.74 plus $5 in fringes...we've got various scales, but that's roughly it...and there's too many people here looking for work. So, a strike *won't* work. We need to do *other* things!

We need to do *new* things! I have *real* problems, for example, in one area dealing with unions that I haven't sorted out entirely. Unions in the past, their strength has been in their ability to cause trouble. And I'm not the kind of guy who likes to cause trouble, and I don't know if its always been good. It's gotten bad press, and the negative image of the unions is what makes it so easy for the Republican Administration to ignore the labor laws that help us. If half the people thought unions were great the Administration would *not* be able to do what they are doing now.

So, I'm torn right now between what got unions strong - which was involving the members *and* the ability to cause trouble - and trying to work it from a strictly business point of view. I haven't figured that part out yet.

Corporate Campaign: Crossing the Pacific. I had a case here about two or three years ago, of a large job being built downtown...a 30-story high-rise building with a hotel complex. And one of our contractors bid it and lost it. It was about an $800,000 paint job, which is a *large* paint job. We also represent drywall tapers, and there was a lot of drywall in that job.

I feel our bid was "shopped," which means somebody took the low union price, and said "Well, hey, I'll beat it!" I can't prove that, but that's what I feel happened.

I talked to the Union General Contractor - there is no contractual requirement to subcontract union - a multi-national construction company, and I also called his Labor Rep *before* the bids were open, and said "You've got a *non*-union contractor in there bidding, and I just want to let you know ahead of time." And he said, "O.K., thanks! We didn't know that." The bids were opened - and, whatever happened, they beat our contractors.

I called them up and I said, "I want this thing to go union, because you're a good union company - and I want it to go union with the subcontractors!" And they told me there was nothing they could do.

Well, it came down that we didn't get the job. Now the one thing building trades unions do is that they guarantee a guy's wages and they get guys work. We're loosing work big time, so I got on my little campaign here...I knew the contractor was owned 40% by the Shimizu Corporations of Japan, so I started my own little corporate campaign.

I went down to the library, and got the corporate profile of the contractor, and the corporate profile of Shimizu Corporation. I wrote to 40 or 50 of the officers of Shimizu in Japan. I explained to them that the labor movement in America was different from that in Japan - where a guy goes to work for a company and stays there all of his life. His benefits are taken care of. In our country its a little bit different: The men belong to a union, and their benefits are paid into funds, and they work for different contractors. And the union is here to maintain their benefits - and act something like a Japanese company would to the members.

I wrote that the contractor here in San Diego - owned 40% by Shimizu - was doing something other than what they would normally do: They were subcontracting to a non-union painting company, one that did not have the same quality of benefits or workers we had.

We could have thrown up a picket line down there. Walked the picket line for two days. Walked away, and slapped ourselves on the back and said, "Jeez, wasn't that neat!" I thought, "No, I'll try something different!" So I wrote these letters to Shimizu. And I wrote about 20 more letters to the corporate executives all over the country of the contracting firm. I explained that something was going on different here in San Diego than normal - because normally they use all unions subs.

Part of our strength in this corporate campaign, by the way, was the help I got from our computer. I could enter a data base, put in corporate names, and I'd type one letter. Then I'd say "Type this to all 50 of the corporate directors!" It was a letter-writing campaign. And the only thing I had in it - other than my soul - was postage!

I got a lot of heat on this. The guy here locally who had let the contract got *extremely* angry. He wrote me a nasty letter. And he wrote the painting contractor a nasty letter. This kind of nasty stuff, which I don't like, went around. We lost the job, eventually. But it got to the point where the CEO of the contracting firm called me up and said - "If you've got any problems, you come talk up in San Francisco to me about them!"

I don't know if the next time this contractor comes into San Diego he'll say specifically "We're not going to go union because you're an asshole." Or maybe think "Gee, it will be easier to go union than to go through this grief again." So, we'll see what happens.... I probably aged a couple of years in the six months it took to run that campaign!

I actually flew up to San Francisco and met with the CEO who called me. We spent a pleasant two hours talking: He understood what I was doing, I guess. We battered around how tough times were.

It's left me a lot to think about. We can be nice guys to our grave. Or we can try to figure out the best way to handle this stuff. I still don't know. Maybe that's part of being in office only four years...though I don't think anybody knows. We've got to do something: I just haven't figured out what.

Union Politics. What angered me to no end was that two or three months later, when the Painters Union District Council 48 met to okay paying bills, some guy whose I.Q. may approach that of room temperature asked "Why in hell are we paying that guy's airfare to Oakland for?" Nobody even said "Well, gee, this guy's been doing a lot here trying to straighten this thing up." Nobody questioned what I had been doing: They all thought I had been doing the right thing! Instead, somebody questions paying my air fare! That kind of union politics is *always* going to be there, but it makes me mad!

No matter what happens - I've found out - if you stick your head up, and do something, somebody's gonna take a shot at it! The higher your profile, the more somebody's going to pick at you. And that's just the nature of union politics, or maybe any politics, for that matter. But that's the way that goes.

The unions live or die by politics. I think it's probably what runs this country. And it's something we can't live without. But I think that in the union movement politics has killed a lot of good stuff.

A lot of stuff goes on behind the scene. Like when I tried to get a waiver of our $450 initiation fee to bring in a contractor with 15 new members. And I couldn't get an agreement quietly. So I had to bring it up on the floor at a District Council. And some guys opposed the idea, not for any real up-front reason, but for politics. And we went round and round on this.

So the issue was voted down, and we had to walk away from it. The issue was not the $450 waiver. The issue was "Where are the members going? To what local?" And "Gee, we don't think this is quite right."

We've all seen this in union politics: There's one guy whose got good ideas...I'm *not* talking about myself...but because he goes against the grain or says something somebody doesn't like - it doesn't matter what he does: He could come up with the *best* motions, the best ideas - he's cut off! Nobody will listen to him.

We've got a guy like that in our District Council. And I've often said, "If that guy made a motion to adjourn, we'd never get out of there. Because no one would second it!" No matter what idea he'd have, no one would like it.

I don't really care that I'm on the right track as far as the 'in crowd" or not. But if you want to get anything done you got to work on that method.

Politics can make or break unions. We've seen administrations surround themselves with people who are "Yes men," people who are not there because they're better than anybody else, but because they'll agree. When the guy who put them all there dies or retires, you've got an administration able to say "Yes!," but it can't do anything else. I think we've all seen a lot of that.

Painter's Blues. I've often thought that one of these days I'm going to run away and join the Peace Corps. Because there its *all* good! One of the problems with being a union leader - and I've told this to quite a few people - is that in the position we are in, we used to represent people only in contract negotiations. But now it seems like we're trying to save the entire trade! The training in it has gone to hell! Holding back non-union has gone to hell! And sometimes, if we do a good job as union leaders, *both* sides, workers and contractors are pissed!

We often talk about "win-win" bargaining and "win-win" negotiations. But sometimes its still a mess. It's a pressure-cooker kind of job! It sure does have its own rewards, but every now and then the "big hammer" will come and get you. And you'll get totally pissed off about the politics, or somebody will try to take a piece of your hide. You win some, and you lose some: I've lost a couple of big ones, and it hurts...a lot. And it has a tendency to bug you out. But I know that overall, even though sometimes it doesn't seem like you're making any progress, you're helping people.

Perspective: Tough Times Ahead. It's kind of funny. I get members coming in...we *know* what's gonna happen. The trade, the quality of the work, the living standards of the building trades...are all going down. We were at the top of the heap when it came to union workers: We were really proud of the fact we were making the big bucks!

Now, we're in for a repositioning of our whole economics. And the building trades are going to be repositioned more than most! You ask any building trades guy: If somebody is working for $9 an hour in a factory, that's pretty good money, they think. But if a painter is making $13 an hour, they think he's getting ripped off. $13, plus fringes. We just got a new contract for $16.75 an hour, plus about $5 in fringes. And our guys are mad! Because we had a *higher* rate than that before!

My guys are getting *too* much for our market! I'm up front with this opinion, and I've been telling everybody this for years. They think I'm full of it. For over 10 years I've been warning that we're pricing ourselves out of the market and *must* take a cut, me too, of course. They say, "You're full of it! We've been going forward 100 years! Why would we want to take a cut?!" Hell, I'm proposing to have my own compensation cut! No one wants to take a cut, but the fact that our contractors are not getting work is based mostly on the wage differential between union and non-union.

I'm aware that many out there speak of the dangers of the "low wage strategy," but we are competing in a tight market. Efficiency and training will overcome only a portion of our wage differential. We will always be the best qualified and highest paid workers, but it will be at a slightly lower level.

They'll come into the office...angry! And I don't know if I'd call it justified or not. The union leadership for the last 30 years has said "O.K., guys, let's see how much we can get for you this time!" Now, in the last two or three contracts, over the last six or eight years, it's been eroding. The top rates have always been there, but we've been adding additional rates. And the trade has been eroding, the wages have been eroding, and its been getting tougher.

I have lots of guys come into the office and ask - "When is this ever gonna' turn around?" And once, I answered - "It's going turn around, but when it does, you won't recognize it." And it wasn't a play on words; it just came out that way. But I think that's the way it's going to be.

The paint trades, and the construction trades, evolve...and cut back. It will be like it was 30 years ago: We're going to step back. Because that's going to be part of a readjustment period. We're too few people who are too far ahead of the majority of the craft, right now. And we can't bring everybody up to our level: I don't think that can happen.

We're in for some different attitudes. And the guy's who've been in the trades for some 30 years, and have seen the increases every year, some say of the current union leadership - "They're a bunch of assholes!" They don't realize it's going to hell all over the country. And I believe it is...I *know* it is out here in the western states.

Looking back to the 1950s, our union negotiated the first health insurance for painters here in San Diego. They had no retirement: Pensions weren't won until '58 or '59. So, ever since then we've elevated everybody to a point where they can all afford to be Republicans! And their politics have changed, especially when a construction worker can make $45,000 a year and own rental property: We've got to involve them in *more* politics, but in *our* kind.

Labor's Role? The unions are the only thing standing between what we've got now and...and nothing! When guys working outside want to get into the union I ask 'em how much they're making? Two or three years ago I got lots of guys saying $14 or $15 an hour: These days I'm getting lots of people saying "I'm makin' $9 an hour." I get people coming to work under our shipyard agreements at low, low wages...and they're just tickled to be getting it: Because they're getting health insurance.

So, I think we're in for some *really* tough times. And I don't know what the answer is. We've got that basic core of membership that says "Hey, look, I've made good money all my life: I'm not about to change this now!" So, it's going to be *tough!*

I question what it's going take to get people believing in the union. I believe in it, and there's a lot of guys who do. But we need a majority! Everybody who is a union member is not necessarily a union believer. So, we've been working on our 650 current members to make them feel like they're part of a *group*.

I've gotten a computer program that will print out everything that happened on a guy's birthday - what famous people were born that day - a whole page printout. So I pull out of the data base everyone who has a birthday coming up in the month. And for each guy I print it out, with a cover letter, and send it to each one. I send out about 50 a month, I guess. And, hopefully, over a period of time, some attitudes are going to be changed. And somebody's going to say, "Gee, I'm really part of the group!"

Getting Heard. I've said this for years, and I don't know if it's just the building trades unions - maybe some of the other unions feel this way - we would put out a letter to some 650 members and say - "We're going to come over and take your first-born child!" Or "We're going to come over and steal your TV." Or we could say any crazy off-the-wall stuff. We've never done it, but I get this feeling that we could! And I say, out of 650 such letters we might get 2 or 3 phone calls that say "What are you talkin' about?"

It's hard to keep hammering at it, because sometimes it seems there's nobody out there. I got to hammer at it. I mean, we have no choice. We keep at it. We put out a lot more mailings than we used to. It used to be, all our local ever did was send out dues notices. So, I'm starting a newsletter...it's kind of sporadic, but it's something we need to do.

Wrap Up. One of the things I've found very important about this job is that you've got to maintain your level of interest. Union leadership has a tendency to either burn people out or eat 'em up: I'm not sure which! So if you gain a small victory every now and then, you keep on plugging! You know you're doing something right!

My remarks have kind of honed in on some of the negative things: Like ten years ago we had maybe 40 to 50% of the work hereabouts, while today we have only 10 to 15%. I didn't mean to do that. I've got great hopes! I think that the building trades in particular - and I'm not going to speak for the East Coast - we're in for a big shakeup! I've told all my members this: When you hit bottom, things have a tendency to level off. And that's a warped view, but I think that's kind of where we are right now. It's going to take a lot of work...but our effect on the trade *will* continue! Our members, the ones we have trained well, even the ones we have lost, are the *better* guys out there... even in the non-union shops.

For years we have been degrading the non-union workers in the construction industry. The idea that every non-union construction worker is a "rat bastard" is asinine. They are just another guy/girl trying to make a living and they by far are a majority of the workers. We can't continue to alienate these workers and then someday hope to organize them.

I'm still trying to figure out how to get the names and addresses of non-union painters, so I can get a newsletter to them. I'd help them as much as anybody: In fact, they probably need help more than anybody. We've got to stop the decline in our standards, and try to bring these other guys up to *our* stand-ards. We've got to be bulldogs about this...if you win one in ten, it's enough to keep you going.

Afterword (July, 1993): Many of the disputes mentioned in my article have been between me and District Council 48. As of July 1, 1993, it was merged into District Council 36 in Los Angeles. This particular Council is very progressive, and I now have great hopes things will be better.

A Multi-Cultural Approach to Building the Labor Movement
Deborah Moy
(SEIU; AFT)

Some serve on the shop floor. Some out of a union office in the plant. Others travel far and wide as international reps or business agents. Debbie Moy, however, serves on and off a university campus as the lone labor educator in the volume, a role of strategic importance if organized labor is to regain momentum in the 1990s.

Raised in a Chinese-American family fairly removed from union concerns, Debbie achieved her union consciousness through a wide variety of field experiences with cannery workers, farm workers, garment workers, and others. Coursing through all of these challenges was a question that came to perplex her more and more: "Why did a strange, non-productive relationship between unions and the Asian community exist, and what could be done about it?"

A close student of Asian American history, and a strong believer in unity among nationalities, Debbie has pioneered in developing fresh educational approaches to union-Asian relations. Her essay below helps answer such questions as —

How can organized labor substantially improve its ties to Asian American workers?

How can labor educators modernize courses dealing with labor and community, race and ethnicity?

What can organized labor hope to win, concretely, for Asian American workers?

Above all, Debbie provides sensitive advice about how to create a culture of union readiness, advice applicable far beyond the Asian-American scene. Encouraged by the 1992 formation of the AFL-CIO's Asian Pacific American Labor Alliance, a group whose very existence attests to the soundness of strategies she champions, Debbie offers readers a field-tested and proven prescription for new labor studies success.

On the one hand, I'm not your typical "labor person" as defined by the established labor movement. None of my immediate family members worked in union shops. Nor did I grow up in a union community or company town. I never even really knew what a union was until I got into college.

On the other hand, I grew up in a typical working class Chinese-American family. My grandparents immigrated from Southern China, and my parents were born and raised in Chinatowns from Chicago to Sacramento to San Francisco. My extended family did what they could to succeed—mainly in the grocery and butcher trades.

When I was small, I remember some family members complaining about a union coming and picketing in front of their grocery store because they sold non-union grapes. I couldn't understand why anyone would want to put us out of business. Also, I remember whispered stories about a relative who tried to bring a union into his workplace and was fired.

So my family's outlook on unions (which impacted my own view) was basically that unions were something dangerous - something to avoid.

Furthermore, unions seemed anti-Chinese. This impression came from an incident when another relative was fired from the Post Office. Although many other carriers had participated in the same incident as my relative, only he (the Chinese carrier) was fired. Whether true or not, it left us with the impression that the union let the Chinese carrier be the scapegoat.

The only person I knew who had a positive impression of belonging to a union was my uncle, who worked as a machinist at United Air Lines. He would often talk about going out on strike for higher wages, as if it were a planned vacation that union members took every contract period. He was probably one of the first Chinese Americans in that IAM local.

Are Unions Good or Bad for the Chinese Community?
I was in high school in the late 1960's when students at San Francisco State College went on strike for ethnic studies. It was a time for ethnic identity and awareness, and a time to realize that there was both a reason and a way to deal with prejudice and discrimination in society.

My high school district also experienced racial tension and incidents. Schools were closed for several days, and special assemblies held to air out the problems. Later I participated in a multi-ethnic in-service training for district high school teachers about the Asian American experience in the U.S.

Through my high school history teacher, a Japanese American raised in the World War II internment camps, I studied Asian American history for the first time. He also put the Asian students at my high school in touch with the Stanford Asian American Student Alliance. It was a very exciting time, which left me with a life-long commitment to fight for racial equality and justice. It also made me a strong believer in unity among all nationalities.

I attended college at the University of California, Davis, and became actively involved in the Asian American Studies Department. One of the strong points of this program was its belief that education and Asian American studies should serve the community (not just use it for research studies!). I began to work in the Sacramento Asian community on the southside of town.

There were a lot of interesting programs being organized - legal aid, elderly assistance, etc. All of the people we were working with were "working class." Many belonged to the Teamsters Union through their work in the canneries. Yet as far as I could tell, there were no union programs which involved these folks.

I ran an after-school program for the children of these cannery workers called "Yellow House." Their parents were mainly Chinese immigrants who lived in the Sacramento housing projects. During the canning season, these parents worked seven days a week for 8-10 hours at a time. During the rest of the year, they were on unemployment. I remember them wondering why many of the English-speaking workers got to work for more weeks than they did. But they never once mentioned the union or that the union would help with their problems. (Later on, a group of cannery workers began organizing a rank-and-file caucus in Sacramento. I learned that many workers were critical of the union for treating them as a "dues mill" — all money and no service.)

Meanwhile, back at Asian American Studies, unionization should have been, but was not a big factor in the overall picture of fighting for equality. Ironically, the main union program I remember was the United Farm Workers. Hundreds of Asian American Studies students traveled to Delano, California, to help build a retirement village for elderly Pilipino farmworkers. "Agbayani Village" was a hands-on, serve the people project with left me with a deep respect for the lives and working conditions of farmworkers. Maybe unions weren't so bad, after all....

I left college after two years to continue my work in the Asian community. I was still curious about Asian Americans' role (or lack of role) in unions. So, I moved to San Francisco's Chinatown and got a job working at Koret of California, one of the biggest and oldest unionized San Francisco garment manufacturers. (Koret of California moved its operations overseas and closed its San Francisco plants in the 1980s).

This job was a real eye-opener. First of all, the shop work was divided by nationality. The lowest paying work - single needle stitching - was done by the Chinese immigrant women. The faster, high-paying triple needle sewing was done by a combination of Eastern Europe and Chinese immigrants who spoke better English. The trimmers were all Pilipinas, the pressers mainly African American, and so on.

The second surprise was at the union meetings. While many Chinese immigrants attended the meetings, the translation left much to be desired. It was very difficult for the women to participate in the union's business. Also, there were no Chinese-speaking business agents to help the women out with their day-to-day problems.

While there was some grumbling about this situation, in the main the women were happy to be working in a union shop. It meant better conditions than the Chinatown sweat shops: an eight-hour day, decent hourly wage, and most importantly, health benefits. This was the extent of their understanding of what a union could do for workers.

On the other hand, the union also did not appreciate the resources it had in these women. Many of the women had a much higher level of education and job experiences than anyone realized. Some people think that garment workers and immigrants generally are stupid. In reality, former teachers, agency heads, and union officials are working as room cleaners and at other low-paying jobs in the United States because they cannot get their licenses recognized or don't speak English well enough.

Why did this strange, non-productive relationship between union and the Asian community exist, and what could be done about it?

Overcoming Labor's Exclusionary Past. Since the 1800s, Asian American workers have the same proud traditions as workers everywhere. They work hard, stand up against exploitation, and fight for their rights. They were often killed for their efforts.

Unfortunately, the American labor movement often saw Asian workers more as the enemy rather than as brothers and sisters. Asian workers were most often used as a cheap labor source for expanding industries, be they railroad or agriculture. This often placed them in a convenient position for scapegoating, by the general public and by unions, during times of economic downturn.

Indeed, the first union label in America was an anti-Chinese symbol used by cigar workers, to show that their product was made by Caucasian workers and not by "heathen Chinese." Ever since, "Look for the Union Label" has been a hallmark of the labor movement - but it makes many of us cringe with remembrance of its history.

It's no wonder, then, that such a strange relationship existed between unions and Asian Americans. This is not to say that everyone in the labor movement was and remains prejudiced. But there is always that ambivalence just under the surface: "They couldn't really be loyal union members - when push comes to shove, they will end up siding with their own kind instead of with the union."

There is also justifiable hesitation remaining in some sectors of the Chinese community. For many years, notably during the McCarthy era, anyone associated with unions or workers' associations was presumed to be communist. Since Chinese in particular were already under suspicion, union involvement was not something one wanted to advertise publicly.

Since the mid-1960s, the influx of Chinese immigrants from mainland China has positively impacted views towards unionization. Many of these immigrants were union members in China and have a culture of unionism.

Finally, unions themselves have many strong Chinese members who have not been brought forward to participate. If a union actively draws in these members, provides translation, and promotes activities and ideas with which Chinese members feel comfortable, they are just as hardworking and active as any other union member. They only need the opportunity and the means to do so.

Chinese Americans in the labor movement like myself are faced with a daily barrage of conflicting messages. On the one hand, many

Chinatown community activists wonder why we are so active in our unions (with their less-than-welcome history). This is especially true among some sectors such as construction, who feel that unions hurt minority small businesses by continually pushing for a prevailing wage which they claim they cannot afford to pay.

On the other hand, we are viewed with suspicion by many in the labor movement. I remember vividly the first labor council meeting which I attended as a guest speaker. I was particularly nervous because it was during the mid-1980s, when it was popular to blame Japan for America's economic woes.

The labor movement was actively promoting "Japan-bashing," which had a direct effect on the safety of the Asian American community. The murder of Vincent Chin at the hands of two Detroit unemployed auto workers (who thought he was Japanese) was a blunt reminder of just how little it took to become "the enemy." "What am I doing at this meeting — I could be killed!" was the main thought running through my mind.

Nevertheless, I was too committed to building understanding and alliances between the labor and the Chinese community to give up so easily. I began to organize Asian workers through the Asian American Federation of Union Members (AAFUM) in San Francisco, and later at the Hotel and Restaurant Employees Union Local 2.

My work at Local 2 was an exciting and humbling experience. I was the organizer in charge of running a picket line for the Commercial Club workers - a group of 34 men, mainly Chinese immigrants, who went on strike to preserve the health and pension benefits. The average worker was in his 50s, and had been a union member with more than 18 years of service at the Commercial Club and in Local 2.

The workers elected their own leadership and took charge of the picket line. They met weekly, and made day-to-day tactical as well as strategic decisions for their strike. They worked actively to involve the Chinese community in their labor dispute, with much success. Most importantly, they showed how the Chinese workers were the backbone of the strike. They had a deep understanding of the importance of unionization, balanced against the politics of the union and how it treated the strikers.

Bringing These Lessons into Labor Studies. How did I end up at City College? I was organizing for Local 2 in Chinatown, and running the labor/ community support coalition for the mainly Latina cannery workers in Watsonville at the same time. I began talking about organizing issues with the Chair of the CCSF Labor Studies Program, Barbara Byrd. In particular, I was concerned with changing the whole culture of how unions function, and bringing more women and minorities into active and leading roles in their unions.

I didn't know it then, but Barbara wanted to change the character of her program, and was looking for a way to accomplish this. Both of us realized that what had been a traditional trade union leadership program needed to expand to meet the needs of a growing non-white work force, especially for new immigrants.

Somehow, Barbara talked me into teaching the Union Organizing class for the Labor Studies Program in January, 1989. This was quite a courageous and innovative thing for an educator to do — bringing a field worker (me!) onto her teaching staff.

It also puts me through a lot of changes. I felt confident in my work. But I didn't think I had the ability to teach what I did to anyone, or that I belonged in an academic setting. I didn't even have a college degree (although I did have years of experience in community and labor organizing).

Most of all, I did not think of myself as a role model. I've always felt (and still do) that I always learn more from other people than they do from me. Barbara worked hard to encourage me to teach and to have confidence in my knowledge and abilities. Still, it was quite a shock to find myself standing in front of a classroom.

Much to my surprise, both the students and I loved the class! In addition to the usual organizing techniques, I focussed the class on current and unique organizing efforts taking place in California. One of the most inspiring guest speakers was an organizer from the victorious Watsonville cannery workers strike. This organizer later went on to become the mayor of Watsonville.

I learned a valuable lesson — that adults learn best by hearing each other's experiences and having a chance to fully discuss the issues. My role as a teacher was to facilitate that learning and discussion - "critical thinking" as the education folks like to call it. And the students really appreciated having a place where they could step back and take an objective, analytical look at the labor movement's organizing efforts.

Creating a Multi-Cultural Labor Curriculum. I became more involved in the Labor Studies Program and became more concerned about three areas. First, the materials were very standard, "labor-y" type of topics, and did not reflect the rich diversity of work experience in California or the United States.

Second, the student body reflected a certain sector of the unionized workforce, but did not include the diversity of either the unionized or non-unionized sectors. In particular, very few immigrants were taking classes, in a city which is almost one-half immigrants.

Finally, instructors were not clear on the availability of mutli-cultural resources, nor of others in their fields who could provide diverse perspectives. For example, the labor history and grievance handling classes could be enriched by having speakers from different cultures and backgrounds discussing their unique relationships within the workforce and the union movement.

What began as an unconscious thing became a conscious effort to broaden and deepen the scope of the overall Labor Studies program. In the organizing, grievance handling, and history classes, I make it a point to always include Latino and Chinese immigrants among the guest speakers and points of view. I work with local unions to develop trainings which helps them reach out to their diverse memberships, organize internally, and build community alliances. I have also worked with the other instructors to update their course materials.

An "American Cultures" Approach to Labor Studies. It was not enough to just revise existing course materials. There was too much material that could stand alone as a separate course. Fortunately, the University of California at Berkeley came along with their "American Cultures" fellowship program, which served as a focal point for a brand-new class.

The American Cultures graduation requirement says that any discipline should look at the multi-cultural contributions made by non-Caucasian groups. Furthermore, it should look at the interrelationships between different groups (including European immigrants), and compare and contrast their experiences. So, you can have American Cultures courses in architecture, music, literature, geography - it is a fascinating approach.

The new Labor Studies course I developed for the American Cultures requirement is titled "Labor and Community, Race and Ethnicity." It includes every question you are NOT supposed to talk about in the labor movement - such as, why didn't union organize Chinese workers in the 1800s? Was it a good or bad thing that Henry Ford used churches to recruit African American workers into his assembly plant? How do you handle inter-ethnic conflicts between union members? How can union locals do a better job of reflecting their diverse memberships?

The class scares some people, but most seem to think it is wonderful to have a class which deals with these issues directly. However, it is not easy to have a group of 20 strangers discuss these very sensitive topics, no matter how sympathetic they are.

After teaching the class twice, I found that using exercises and techniques adapted from multi-cultural awareness trainings helps students adjust to the new experience of discussing race and ethnicity issues in an open classroom. For example, an exercise called the "Power Shuffle" enables students to play both the roles of those in power, and those without power; as well as to appreciate how quickly their fate can change with the change in power categories.

From here, we go into an historical examination of African American, Asian American, and Latin American workers. A new textbook titled *A Different Mirror*, by Ron Takaki, does an excellent job of laying out historical backgrounds of a number of groups (including Irish and Russian immigrants). It contains more labor history than most general or ethnic studies texts.

Finally, we examine contemporary issues facing unions, communities, and the United States as a whole. Topics such as labor's involvement in environmental racism issues have attracted a lot of attention. Immigration reform and resulting implications have also been hotly debated.

Students come from all unions and ethnic backgrounds. The universal feedback at the end of class semesters has been, "We need to have two semesters to cover all this material!" It is wonderful to provide a safe setting and then observe, while workers explore tough issues like race relations without fear of reprisal. Furthermore, students left the class with a desire to learn more about ethnic studies and how it applied to labor unions and union/community coalition building.

Reaching Out to the Unorganized Sectors. All of these changes made a significant contribution to the Labor Studies Program. However, they still did not address directly the needs of unorganized workers. I was particularly motivated in this area, because of the increasing number of wage and hour violation charges which were being filed in the Chinese community.

For example, when the Cloissonne Restaurant closed in 1989, it left more than 40 workers without a job and without their last two months' pay. As we investigated the case more closely, we found that many people were owed minimum wage and overtime pay in excess of several thousand dollars! They didn't know that they were entitled to overtime pay, nor how to calculate it correctly. They were also misinformed on the correct minimum wage scale. Finally, we found a prevalent view that since it was a Chinese owner and they were Chinese immigrants, that it wasn't right to file for back pay.

Ultimately, we ended up winning more than $40,000 in back pay for 16 of these workers. More importantly, we established the principle that if you work in America, you are entitled to all your benefits under American law, whether or not you are a citizen or immigrant.

The case attracted a lot of attention in the Chinese press. In fact, the state and federal governments have turned their attention to Chinatown wage and hour violations as more people come forward with their stories.

It was important for Labor Studies to offer a class which met the needs of these workers. With the willing assistance of the department chair, we hired more bilingual, experienced union staff to develop and teach Worker's Rights classes. They created a trilingual *Workers Rights Manual* (English, Chinese, Spanish).

The Chinese bilingual instructor did a tremendous job in integrating the real-life experiences of immigrant workers into the teaching materials. We were all nervous as we waited for the first class to begin in Chinatown (taught in Chinese). We were elated when more than 50 people turned out - standing room only! There was a good combination of garment workers and restaurant workers. Yes - this was the right track!

Topics include wage and hours laws (including the existence of a minimum wage!), disability, unemployment, workers compensation, unionization, and health and safety issues. The workbook exercises include questions such as "How do you calculate your hourly wage?" The class is very practical - for example, we tell people that they are not supposed to wait three months before getting paid.

It is a very fundamental course, but essential for securing even the most basic rights for workers. There are many people who feel that if they are not citizens, they are not covered by American laws. It's important to break down these myths and help people get what they are due.

We also explain to undocumented workers that if they work in the United States, they *are* covered by American laws. The government is not supposed to check immigrant status if it is a wage and hour violation, or a health and safety violation. You may not be here with papers. But once you are here, you'd better be paid correctly, or else!

Another innovation in the Labor Studies Program has been the introduction of Vocational English as a Second Language (VESL) classes. These classes are co-sponsored with particular unions, such as the ILGWU and SEIU. These classes enable unions to reach out to the community, fulfill a pressing need, and establish a union presence.

The labor movement benefits in very basic ways from these types of programs. First, having classes such as these demonstrates to unions that these are the kinds of activities you need in order to reach out to unorganized workers and bring them unto the culture of unionism. Second, we serve as an important resource for unions who need our materials. Third, the course has been used to actually help people get into union jobs or to help with ongoing union campaigns.

The Labor Studies program also tries to combine direct community outreach with ongoing educational needs. For instance, we ran a conference on Chinese immigrant workers. We brought a lot of different union people together with community activists to discuss why we needed to deal with the issue of organizing unions in Chinatown.

We also try to consciously work with Chinese immigrant workers (like the Cloissonne workers) and provide back-up and assistance to their efforts. We brought together community activists and the Hotel and Restaurant Workers Local 2 to run a workshop on how to get a job in a union hotel. "This is what you do. This is how you dress. This is the terminology you need." Workshops such as these go a long way to getting your foot in the door of a union hotel.

Creating a Culture of Union Readiness. Organizing in Chinatown has always been somewhat of a challenge to unions. Only 8% of garment workers in Chinatown are organized, and none of the Chinese restaurant workers. It's important to recognize that efforts such as the workers' rights and VESL classes and job preparation workshops are part of creating a new pro-union culture.

Unionizing Chinatown must be an integrated, community-based campaign. It cannot be the standard "target a big house, find out if there are union people, roll in, get the cards, do your campaign, etc."

Community people must be given an opportunity to solve for themselves some of the contradictions between Asians and organized labor which have been going on for the last 100 years. To do this, unions need a consistent, stable union presence.

This is *very* patient work. It is a different approach than what most unions are accustomed to, even of they already have a "culture of organizing." But the work is definitely worth it. Chinese workers, through all phases of labor history, have always been willing to be an active part of labor unions. The question has been, were they given the opportunities they needed to join and fully participate in making decisions about the direction of their shop and their local union?

While this is a different approach than most unions are used to, it is not unproven. The successful Watsonville cannery strike in 1987 showed how important it was to closely integrate community and labor organizing. It also showed the willingness and ability of Latino immigrants to fight for justice and respect through a union contract.

Similarly, organizing efforts at Delta Pride catfish company in Mississippi relied heavily on community involvement in the campaign.

The Asian Pacific American Labor Alliance. My individual experiences as an Asian American trying to bridge the gap between labor and community are not unique. The exciting new development is that I can now share my experiences with hundreds of other Asian American trade unionists across the country in a united *organization.*

The formation of the Asian Pacific American Labor Alliance (APALA) in 1992 was a historic event in the labor movement. First and foremost, it means that the AFL-CIO has finally recognized Asian Americans as a significant part of the American workforce, and is willing to devote some resources to us.

Secondly, it provides each of us with a support network. It's not easy being out there in a union as the lone Asian staff person, putting up with "misconceptions," and worrying about your personal safety in case someone mistakes you for the "enemy."

Thirdly, it gives us a voice to speak out on important civil rights issues, and a vehicle to organize our communities. The theme of our first annual convention held in August, 1993, was "We Are One - Labor and Community Working Together."

It is significant that in its first year, APALA was able to spearhead efforts to successfully introduce and pass a major resolution regarding immigration rights at the national AFL-CIO Biennial Convention in October, 1993. It is a measure of the maturity of Asian Americans in the labor movement.

Our time has come!

Part IV

Shaping Stronger Structures

"What needs to be understood, and what needs to be changed,
is not first this and then that detail of some institution or policy.
...what needs to be analyzed is the *structure* of institutions, the
foundation of policies.   In this sense, both in its criticism and in
its proposals our work is necessarily structural...."

C. Wright Mills. In *The End of Ideology Debate*,
edited by Chaim Waxman (New York: Simon and Schuster, 1969),
134.

Structural reforms of labor can include a dizzying array of issues, such as the forced merging of reluctant locals, the unnerving challenge posed by the threat of privatization, and a local's need to adapt to employee ownership. Four case studies below explore these increasingly common challenges, the writers taking care to underline smart and foolish choices available to those who recognize in structural turmoil an opportunity to swiftly achieve internal reforms long on hold.

The forced merger of seemingly compatible locals, a straight-forward administrative matter, is often anything but clear-cut and readily accomplished. Instead, as the first and third cases reveal, it can involve troublesome complexities that would try the wisdom and patience of a Solomon, better yet busy and stressed local union officers. All the more helpful, therefore, are Robert Langro's and Susan Pacult Foregard's guides to how to do it all better - next time around. Sensitive and inventive, they persist when weaker types would have folded, and they demonstrate the indispensability of artful persistence in longterm reform campaigns.

Privatization, the bane of locals within the public sector (or with many members employed as public "servants"), takes center stage in the second case study. Rare attention is paid to its structural ramifications, and John Dalrymple, an especially creative inside reformer, lays out a fascinating plan for turning the privatization threat into something far more promising.   Capable of making significant players of a local's membership, this plan details a major structural overhaul likely to reward labor, employers, and other stakeholders as well.

Employee ownership, whether through outright purchase, an Employee Stock Ownership Plan (ESOP), or some other device, poses an extraordinary challenge to trade unionism: How is a local to help its unionized worker-owners bargain with themselves? The final contributor to this section, Wendell Young, Sr., has had extensive experience with this increasingly popular alternative to shutdowns and job loss. His frank and revealing account makes clear how much care and clear-headed thinking is required if labor is to truly gain from this complicated structural reform option.

Turning Amalgamation to Advantage
Robert Langro
(IAM)

As companies downsize, "rightsize," and struggle to make the most of major changes in their size, structure, and format, a vital set of opportunities becomes available to labor's inside reformers. When what anthropologists call "the cake of custom" is broken, reformers may find themselves - sometimes overnight, as in the account below - able to help introduce a superior culture, albeit one whose very unfamiliarity is bound to provoke considerable resistance.

Committeeman Robert Langro offers an increasingly common tale below of a situation much like a "shotgun wedding," a forced merger of two union bodies (in this instance, former bitter rivals), the members of which would just as soon the deal had never been made necessary by corporate wheeling-and-dealing far removed from their influence or control.

Three questions of far-reaching consequence are addressed:

What can an inside reformer do to heal rifts of ancient and deep-reaching nature, rifts carried with vengeance into a forced merger?

How can establishment of a local's own medical program and EAP help build interest and unity?

What help, if any, can a local rely on from management?

Especially valuable is the emphasis placed on resourcefulness, on a local's never-ending search for novel and promising supports for blending the mutually-suspicious halves of a new "odd couple." As this phenomenon will probably increase in frequency for years to come, the advice offered in the case below warrants careful attention...even from those naive enough to believe it cannot possibly happen to them.

My dad worked in air-conditioning refrigeration and as a kid, I worked alongside him. He insisted I get an apprentice card from his union, and we were often the only two card-carrying unionists in the non-union shops where he got work.

My wife was a shop steward working with New York Telephone when we first met, and her father was an officer with the International Typographers Union, a part of the 'Big Six' unions in the printing trades in the "Big Apple." He brought a devout union ethic with him when the ITU merged with the CWA You can see I've been involved with unionism one way or another for a *very* long time. Unionism was routinely discussed at the dinner table.

Upon graduating from high school I did a brief stint at a local university, but left soon to go to work in 1972 for Trans-World Airlines (TWA). Within two years I became a shop steward representing members at the carrier. I held this post for 12 years. I learned a lot, as I was working with some *really* talented people, I mean, some *really* talented trade unionists!

I came to TWA in St. Louis in '85, and got elected to my current job as a full-time Committeeman, a post I've been elected to every two years for the past six years. I also hold other titles: Chairman of the Health and Welfare Committee, and, Trustee for my local. I'm only the second person in the history of St. Louis to be elected three times...and I consider myself *very* lucky!

When I run I use literature, but I find that personal reputation is far more significant. People know we've started a lot of *new* plans since I arrived in St. Louis. Like our Health and Welfare Plan. And the Health Plus Plan that we put together. We now make more use of Workmen's Compensation...we run seminars to help people learn what they are entitled to. And we're making progress getting the word out.

Post-Merger Blues. Our biggest problem has not been of our own making...and it's a doozy!

In 1985 TWA was taken over by investor Carl Icahn. The choice was between him and Frank Lorenzo. At that time we chose to take a $2 an hour pay cut for a period of three years rather than fall into the hands of Lorenzo. The company would stop its contribution to the "B" (pension) plan, in order to pay for the Icahn takeover.

Immediately afterwards TWA purchased Ozark Airlines. It was a regional airline, with its largest station in St. Louis. It had approximately 500 mechanics, and about 600 ramp service people. We took the Ozark employees in with <u>full</u> seniority and *full* benefits, despite the fact that the Ozark mechanics belonged to a rival union.

And then our problems began...and as time went on these problems became worse and worse.

TWA refused to give any consideration to the fact that Ozark people had never been notified what TWA policy and procedures was. One problem involved the attendance program. The Ozark people raised this...and they were right! If you worked for GM and quit and went to work for Ford, would you expect Ford to hold your GM attendance record against you? No, they wouldn't! Well, that is exactly what happened! From day one, TWA charged some Ozark people with "excessive absenteeism" while they were with Ozark. And that got to be a big thing!

People were forced to work on different kinds of equipment they had never worked on before. A whole different type of operation, TWA vs. Ozark. It was difficult for people to understand: Plus Ozark had a different philosophy about how that did their maintenance. Everybody's got their *own* procedures, how they do maintenance. Regardless of whether another company did a great job, you now want their people to fit under a single program. Continuity and consistency are important to operations.

So we set up a special dispensation for the Ozark mechanics. They had previously worked on small aircraft, DC-9's and MB-80's. They had no knowledge or experience on L-10's, 747's, or 767's. So we intermeshed them in with TWA people.

The company, on the other hand, created a wall between the Ozark employees and the TWA employees. The company tried to polarize the groups.

By forcing the company to intermesh the groups our TWA people actually *taught* the Ozark employees about widebody equipment , while the Ozark mechanics *taught* us about DC-9's. And we felt that by doing that, the Ozark people would feel like they actually belonged, because we needed them. And would see that they were getting cooperation from the TWA people.

It worked well for awhile. It was tumultuous, but it worked well.

Rival Unionism. But then things got progressively worse. A rival union was on the property and now was becoming a constant pain-in-the-neck. They were always trying to tender their philosophy, which is not to organize the unorganized. They like to raid, because if you win you take over the contract that is in existence until a new one is negotiated. All you need to do is hope to God that you can get another contract!

We had no knowledge of a lot of things they had done. We got their contract book: Much of the language came directly out of ours...as they were at one time IAM. And that helped. But there were many things that caused problems. It would have helped if we had sat down with the company before everybody signed on the dotted line and said "Now, let's look at this stuff...."

We now had three distinct groups...the Ozark employees, the TWA people, and the "B" scalers (the new hires). "B" scalers were being wooed by the rival union, which promised to get them more money...so there was an undercurrent of rivalry between us, the IAM-TWA types, and the rival mechanic group from Ozark.

Reaching Out. We decided to run meetings to get the Ozark people in touch with what was happening. There was a lot that we needed to teach them, as well as a lot we had to learn from them. We focused on the basics of TWA policies and procedures - the shift and days off; the bidding for your vacation; the attendance program; stuff like that.

Then we moved on to hold "Lead" meetings. The majority of the leads were TWA, because they had been here prior to the merger. As we knew that the Ozark people would start to get the lead positions we wanted to make sure everyone was going in one direction. It was as much to our benefit as to the company's to have everyone following the same line, operationally.

As the equivalent of foremen the leads are critical to the operation. Back in the 1970's the leads did everything; there was little supervision out there. Today, we are attempting to go to our roots. We're trying to get everybody back into the idea that a lead has a responsibility towards his crew. And towards the company. It is hard to get people to go back to this. Because as society has progressed we've come to worry about ourselves, and we think of ourselves as individuals. For some reason we ignore the benefits of collectivism. We're trying to get the idea going that if you take care of everybody else, they'll take care of you...this will benefit everyone.

We held our lead meetings at 8 AM, 3:30 PM, and at 11 PM for the twilight shift. We did this just about every other week...in addition to regular union meetings, which were twice a month, and along with a regular Shop Steward's *Newsletter*, which we circulated every other week to keep the Stewards informed, because if they're not in tune with what is going on you're really in trouble. (You have to remember that the Icahn era was tumultuous not only to the employees but to their families also).

We also sent our lodge newspaper four times a month, and three times a month the back page is strictly filled with our local's news. Plus, we run a phone hotline...and our Committee office is *on* the property, so there is quick and immediate access. We did all of these things to *assure* our lines of communication were open.

Moving On. After awhile the leads stopped showing up. So we con-verted it to an informational meeting. And they began showing up again, at least for awhile. We have between 2,300 and 4,000 in the group: We were lucky sometimes to get 10 people. Of course, if there was a hot issue you have a lot more than that, but essentially, that was what it was.

We have since given up the meetings, because essentially it was eating up all of our time - and only two people were showing up. We needed to try other things.

TWA is self-insured in Missouri. So I started our own medical program. We knew we weren't getting a raise; we knew that would not happen. We knew the contract was going to be difficult. Medical bills were killing us. I went to different hospitals and was able to establish our own benefit plan to help our members.

It's been seven years since we've had a raise, and, with the Reservations people, it's been longer. The company took away vacations, all sorts of things, and there has never been a cost-of-living adjustment,...nothing. Seven years...no raise, and of the seven, three involved a giveback of $2 an hour, plus no pension money going in.

So, we keep trying to put more things on, like the new health coverage plan, and our EAP effort. I started it and found myself with the two guys I work with running around from hospital to hospital to see our people. And not only them, but also their wives and their kids. Stress, alcohol, marital problems...they are incredible (drugs are *very* rare).

We'd get referrals, we would go down and grab somebody. One good thing about our IAM local office is that we have contacts all over.

For a good period of time, management, if they had somebody at work that they had questions about, they'd call us up. We would go down into the workplace and we would check out the problem. We would be there if he needed help. We would let them know that they would be hurting themselves and their family if they didn't seek treatment.

And I've got to say - a lot of people in the company, they were great! They really were! And that was the first time in years that I had seen both sides working together, for the good of the employees. And it worked really well.

Once the EAP was established it actually got too big to handle. Today a joint committee of union and company people provide help to those that need it.

Union "Blend." We were lucky in that both the TWA and the Ozark people were in the same local. So all the people who held office prior to the merger had been elected by both groups. What we did with non-members was to look for guys who were stewards with the other union. Their knowledge and skill was considerable, and a lot of them were good union people. We went to them, spoke to them, and we ended up getting many of them to come become shop stewards, chairmen of committees...and they are *outstanding.*

We run a lot of social events to help mix the two groups, to help bring them together. We raise charity, run a Christmas Party, run a food bank, and we hold a "Night at the Races," "Las Vegas" Night, and joint events with the St. Louis Labor Council. We put on Health Fairs, and we keep everything free: These people haven't had raises in seven years, so it has been *very* tough on them.

Race is not significant. We've had a mixed labor force as long as I can remember. People are more concerned about whether a person can carry the weight than what color they are. As far as socialization and interaction I really don't see any problem, though it is possible it is out there.

Since 1975 TWA has been actively employing women as ramp service workers. This involves baggage handlers, cargo movers, and air freight movers, all of whom can handle a considerable amount of weight. The females have been excellent workers, excellent! Ozark hired a lot of women, so when we merged the two workforces we did not have many problems with this at all. When you're in the belly of a DC-9, crouched down, passing bags, your co-workers are more interested in whether you can handle your weight than in who or what you are. Because if you can't do it, it means I'll have to do it, and I don't want to do it.

Colors that Count! If you look to see who is running the local, you can see it's not all TWA. And it's not all Ozark. It's a good conglomeration of people. A lot of *hard*-working people!

But, when push comes to shove, the problem is if you said to somebody "Why is it you can't work with 'X' or 'Y?'" the old thing will still come out: "Well, he's a 'green' [Ozark]. Or he's a 'red' [TWA]." And you still get that!

The groups are inter-mingled, and have been for over seven years now. The TWA guys welcomed the Ozark people with open arms. And yet, somehow the bottom line always seem to be who is "Red" or who is "Green"! Whether it be the workers or management, that distinction still exists. It's not just the workforce; it's management itself. It's the collective...and it is striking. Our people identify with the culture and colors of the particular company they work for, and this counts for *a lot*!

Much of the inter-group resentment has been diluted, thanks to the strenuous effort we've made to bring the "Greens" and the "Reds" together...but occasionally it's still there. They are increasingly available to respond as one to a threat or opportunity, but, at some very deep level, some still cling to being "Green" or "Red."

Going It Alone. When a merger forces a "shotgun wedding," when it forces two separate work groups into one, a local union has to expect to shoulder all the problems by itself. To do it alone! We did it as a union; the company did absolutely nothing to help. They were too busy trying to make money. And they didn't care where they got it from. They stripped the employees and then they stripped the company of anything with value.

We want the company to make money: The more money it makes, theoretically, the more we're going to make. So our doing it, that's fine. That's good for the membership, and that's what a union should do. But the company - it's kind of like, the merger: "We did it. It's done. We signed the papers. We handed over the check. We did the loans. Let's just forget about it, O.K.?"

It's beneficial for *both* sides, for the union and the company, to work together. But it was something the company was not willing to do. They didn't have time. Nor were they willing to spend any money to do so. And earlier I didn't see Pan Am do it either. Still, if the new post-merger company does not make money it is a union person who is to go out the door. So, it is best if the two sides can cooperate, rather than have it all done by the union...though I wouldn't count on the company to recognize this and do anything different to get it going. Union members should be prepared to shoulder it all alone.

Looking Back...and Forward. Most of the things we did we would do again. But now, after going through all of it we pretty much know that when you go through negotiations it goes *very* quickly - so you must have a check-list ready, like a pilot taking off. There's a lot of things you can mark on it. As well, you will want to spend more effort in putting things in writing with the companies. A lot of this stuff, it just comes up at you and you do your best at the time, but some of it can be expected. During the merger management is more concerned with jockeying for position between the two management groups than running the operation. Unfortunately, when the operation fails it is the low line employees that suffer the brunt of management's infighting.

We need to reflect on the whole process and refine it. The way this airline industry is set up, there's going to be more buyouts, more mergers more acquisitions, and more airlines going into bankruptcy and totally destroyed. So with everything we've gone through we're going to be confronted again...and again...and again...which means we've got to get better and better at it.

Afterword (July,1993): After seven years without raises and after three and a half years of protracted contract negotiations a contract was finally signed. It came about because of the perseverance of the membership and the dedication of the IAM leadership. With the signing of a new agreement a semblance of order will come to the employees of TWA. Or will it? Rumors of other mergers and other bankruptcies abound within the industry. Here we go again!

Years of leveraged buyouts, mergers, and asset stripping have taken their toll on American industry. After everyone's greed was satisfied the unions and the employees have to deal with the aftermath. After the money mongers and the power brokers are gone we are the only ones left to rebuild what they left behind.

In January, 1992, TWA announced its intent to seek protection in the bankruptcy courts. After months of haggling, the unions at TWA and the company's creditors announced a buyout of the company. The employees received a 45% stake in the company. The creditors received a 55% share.

Today we now deal with a new TWA. This partnership has brought into the present a new relationship between labor and management. Emphasis now lies with customer satisfaction rather than the traditional power struggle. Cooperation, participation, and determination have now replaced futility and frustration. New management teams meet with labor to discuss market share rather than termination hearings.

In 1993 there is a future for this company, as well as its employees. A new beginning! With all sincerity and with total conviction, I can say that if not for the perseverance of these employees, if not for the hard work of the unions, the lives of 24,000 TWA employees and their families would have been destroyed. Had it not been for the unions TWA would fail to exist today.

Turning Privatization to Advantage
John Dalrymple
(SEIU)

Few ideas are as contentious nowadays in union-management relations as the notion of *privatization*, a process by which a traditional public service, such as garbage collection or school teaching, is newly offered up to private-sector firms in an open-bidding process. Unions of governmental employees, such as AFSCME, or those with many public sector employees in membership, such as SEIU, are suspicious that certain calls for privatization, once stripped to their hidden ideological core, are treacherous efforts to replace and destroy unionism. Proponents, however, insist nothing so insidious need be involved, and focus their advocacy instead on alleged savings attainable in tax revenues and cost reductions.

SEIU field representative John Dalrymple asked fellow staffers and rank-and-filers he services if together they couldn't devise a plan to finesse the matter, to defang the threat and turn it to reform advantage. His material helps raise five vital questions:

How can the current holders of jobs become significant players in the privitization process?

What sort of detailed process can an energetic local pursue to shape a desirable privatization outcome?

How can a democratic ethos be protected and even enhanced?

Why might politicians prefer a pro-local routine when privatizing a public service?

Above all, how can an inside reformer refrain from taking charge, and model instead reliance on the fundamental ability of average Americans to rise to the challenge? How, in short, can an inside reformer use a privatization scenario to promote a new power relationship - one that can advance the rank-and-file as do few others in modern labor-management relations?

My involvement with labor has no connection with my folks, though it does draw on my experience with a close family member. My father had been in the military, and later worked as a low-level functionary at General Dynamics. He never talked union, one way or the other, and I don't recall any influence from our neighbors in San Diego either.

I got involved in part because of the Vietnam War and its cost to me. When I was about 15 years old my older brother got *very* active in the anti-war resistance, so active that warrants went out for his arrest and the FBI would visit us every three or four months asking about his whereabouts.

I never got to see him after that, and this was very painful. I asked how was this possible? Here was a guy I thought was terrific, my brother, but I could no longer see him. I began to ask questions and develop ideas about what was right and what was wrong. I got involved myself in the anti-war movement after high school and continued to ask these sort of "deep" questions.

From that I got a little into the counter-culture, which led me next to the alternative health care field...because I felt it was one way to help people. I got tired of that real quick, however, because its political impact was very limited.

Going Union. I became more politically involved as a result of my anti-war and civil rights interests, and I wanted to make a difference. I self-consciously went into the labor movement.

First I went to work and then I organized the factory I was working at and brought it into ILWU [International Longshoremen and Warehousemen's Union] Local 6 in Oakland, CA. It took me two years, and I was fired a couple of times for my activities, but eventually we organized it.

I was active in that local six or seven years and helped build an opposition caucus to democratize the local. After a couple of years, I was elected to the local's Executive Board. And, just as we were prepared to capture the leadership with a good coalition of rank-and-file activists our candidate for president was assassinated, and another executive board member was murdered. It was a *very* tough time. I was blacklisted and forced out of the local and the industry.

Joining the Staff. I bounced back by getting a staff job with a state employees' union, the California State Employees Association, which was a non-AFL-CIO independent association at the time. When I left that job I worked with the CWA and the California School Employees Association for short stints, and have ever since been with a northern California group, Local 250 of the Service Employees International Union, as a field representative.

Now, after about ten years as a union staffer I continue to see organized labor as a key to empowering working men and women, a key to their having an impact on this country. When I started I was lucky enough to get into the ILWU in the warehouse division, where I met a lot of great trade unionists - in the tradition of their legendry president, Harry Bridges - older people who shared a lot of their wisdom and gave me a great orientation. Theirs was a *very* different culture from most unions...a culture of empowerment that continues to inspire and influence me.

Getting on with It. Happily, my SEIU local has now come through some dark times and been reborn. We have about 31,000 health care workers of all types as members, including many new members in emergency medical services (EMS) in 13 counties who serve over 5-million Californians...a group I personally service. In the last few years we emerged from a calcified 25 year leadership clique, and a politically gut-wrenching two-year trusteeship, to develop a revitalized, stable local.

Just three years after a devastating strike loss involving 10,000 Kaiser workers, we negotiated the best health care agreement in the country for these same workers. We eradicated two-tier contracts in the 1989 hospital negotiations with the former affiliated employer group. (These hospitals started two-tier in the health-care industry). At the end of trusteeship we were losing $70,000 a month. We are now in the black and have close to a million dollars in our strike fund. And we have grown by a 1000 members a year over the last four years.

EMS as "Something Else"! Consistent with these gains is a break-through I've kinda promoted since 1990 among the EMS people in our ranks. (S.E.I.U. staff members Steve Wolinsky and Greg Lim played key roles in developing our vision for this work).

We have a new section of paramedics and emergency medical technicians, organized only four years ago, the only one in the entire labor movement made up entirely of EMS personnel working in the private sector. Mostly white (95 percent) and male (60 percent), they routinely "do the impossible:" They save lives. They prevent deaths and deliver babies. They rescue accident victims and rush patients to emergency wards. They do the impossible...but not without a lot of stress and heartache in the doing of it.

When we started signing EMS people up we were able to quickly boost their earnings from a top rate of about $26,000 in '88 to an average top rate in '92 of more than $42,000. Even more impressive we've established industry standards for total employer-paid dependent medical coverage, despite the current crisis in health care. Our bargaining power was largely the result of the success of our organizing drive. We won 25 out of 26 elections and we gained hegemony in the industry.

But we learned just as quickly that more than lousy compensation was bothering EMS people. It became clear we would have to address their extreme sense of loss of control over their work. Many also felt the job lacked respect. They said to us - "We are life savers! We assist in childbirths! We do all these incredible things. But nobody seems to notice and we have no control over the tools we need to be effective. Emergency room doctors and nurses, they make all the decisions, just as if we were nobodies."

Moving In on the Bidding Process. After thinking hard about this problem it occurred to me we might have some leverage we hadn't ever recognized or used, leverage in the form of a role we could play in the contract-bidding process.

Our people in Northern California commonly work for a private em-ployer who is contracted to provide "911" services in an exclusive jurisdiction. In some cities, such as New York or San Francisco, the Emergency Medical System (EMS) is in the public sector. We've organized those workers where it has remained in the private sector. We bargain with 23 such businesses, that vary from "mom and pop" organizations to $100 million-plus companies.

In the past whenever a service contract lapsed and a county government published an RFP (Request for Proposals) our people held their breath and waited anxiously to learn which private sector bidder had won the new service contract. These contracts covered what type of ambulances would be used. What type of emergency gear was in the ambulance. What type of training and who pays for that training for our members, etc., etc. All vital areas of concern to these highly motivated workers.

Sometimes the business that had held the old contract beat out its rivals, sometimes not. Sometimes it looked like a deal had been cut along political lines. Or in favor of a bid so low as to assure a real loss in service quality...and much pain for EMS people deeply committed to doing the best possible job. In every case those most effected, those most at risk, had no input, and only waited and worried on the sidelines.

At a strategy session with union activists in one county the decision was made not to be a passive player. Instead we decided to carve out a role for ourselves! We would interview and rate the bidders, and tell the county supervisors our preference among the EMS management firms bidding on the new contract - and since deciding this we've been off and running!

Creating a Method. The idea of selecting their own boss - and deter-mining the level of EMS service they would provide - created a lot of excitement in the local. An interview committee was elected by the members, not of the local's officers, but of natural leaders who came out of our organizing drive...people free to go all out to make a success of something nobody we knew of had ever tried before.

Guided by this new body, one we called the Provider Selection Committee, certain rank-and-filers focused directly on the key decision-makers, the county Board of Supervisors. They did some PR work designed to influence them, such as having politicians ride with the EMS ambulances with our shop stewards.

Other activists focused on area newspapers and developed personal relationships with people we wanted to "reach." First, however, they agreed that if they were going to go to the press they had better have something for them. So I developed an "Incident Report" form that was placed in every EMS ambulance. We used it for a couple of months to document abuses like ambulance maintenance problems, late response times that were totally the fault of the current system, and EMS people responding to cardiac response cases without having the proper equipment to save the patient. We then educated the media about such matters, and developed a level of respect, of credibility, with the newspaper staffers.

Focusing on the Bidders. As things developed it became clear that our people wanted to seize control of the bidding process - and that's where most of their energy went.

Members of the Provider Selection Committee surveyed other EMS workers and got almost 30 questions they wanted asked of the bidders, the management companies that might win the contract and be their future boss. Questions like -

What sort of communication systems do you favor for EMS unit-to-base contact. And why?

What is your quality control program?

What is your history of dealing with labor unions? And why?

Describe your affirmative action program.

What improvements do you expect to make in EMS working conditions? When? How? And why?

Invitations were sent to all the bidders, and every last one agreed to appear and answer our questions...even though the questions come from a source never before heard from in the bidding wars - EMS workers themselves!

We used a union hall, and on the date we had designated, the paramedics on the selection committee sat on one side of a long table, and one by one we invited the bidders to sit across from us and answer our 30 or so questions. The interview sessions were conducted by the workers themselves. No union staff was present. This created a different power relationship from the start. These potential employers were required to recognize the authority these elected representatives had. Respect for these rank-and-file leaders started before they were their employees!

Checking Out the Bidders. When it was all over, the Committee reviewed all the answers. They looked them up and down and sideways. It was understood from the beginning that the panel would not take its final rank-ings of bidders to a vote of the rank-and-file: When panel members were elected it was understood they were being given the ability to make a final determination for the local. It would have been very difficult to do this by a popular vote, but we might look at it in the future. The panel members, however, were *very* "plugged in" and spoke for the great majority: There was no question about that.

Once the rank order of bidders was determined, the Committee used a mailing to be certain the Commissions knew which bidders EMS workers preferred, and which we opposed, and why.

I've probably gone too fast here if I've given the impression that our ranking was based only on the 30-question interview. Not so! Members of our Committee also made site visits to EMS operations run by various bidders. They talked to past and present employees. They saw rank-and-file leaders wherever the sites were unionized. They read and discussed the proposals submitted by the bidders. They did a *very* thorough job. They probably spent 100 hours on this...and they worked *hard*, very hard, before they decided the local's favorite and less-favored bidders.

Changing Perspective. When I get asked if all this running around, all of this extra effort, has been worth it, I like to think we have structured the content of what the bidders are going to provide our members, the public, *and* the community. We pushed the bidders not in our own narrow self-interest, but in terms of the wellbeing of the entire community. For example, when one successful bidder proposed to close a unit, our selection committee successfully led a fight to keep it open. In other counties our SEIU local committee has successfully fought to upgrade communication systems and the equipment on the EMS ambulance.

Our people have come to believe they are special, that they can make things change. Many of them had had a very narrow sense of what a union meant beforehand - that it's for "problem employees," and so on - and this bidding process has helped them see a union could be *much* broader than just concerned with contract negotiations.

I believe the amazing success of our organizing effort has been the result of promoting this vision of worker empowerment. By giving these workers concrete tools to control their worklife the word spreads that the organization is *the* route to changing power relationships in the industry.

With the movement to privatize public services going national, to take over prisons, to take over house-keeping services in public sector hos-pitals...we can input into the process! And bidders will have to defend their record. This could really help change the nature of employee-employer relationships for the better.

Gains All Around. While our local obviously gains power it never had before, we cut the issues in a way to allow for others to gain from our program.

Our EMS industry in California used to have over 500 ambulance companies. It is down now to about 200, and will probably be less than 100 in seven or eight years from now. Very few companies can meet ever-higher level of expectations put on all of them. So the question becomes for an employer - "Do I want to be one of the few left?" And we reply - "If you want to be, then here is the process we've constructed to help sort you all out. We prefer to have you in business *if* you measure up - to *our* expectations - as set them forth in the bidding process by our members!"

People are living now who would not because our process has helped raise the quality of emergency health care service. They pay more for it, but I think it is worth their lives. And that's an absolute truth - that people are surviving who could not have. So that's a win for the County Board of Supervisors, who can say to the public they now have a system that is truly accountable. In us the *good* employers have an ally they never had before - if they are willing to work with us and treat their EMS workers the way they should.

Scorecard. As of this point, January 1992, all three times we've gotten into the bidding process we've come out ahead!

In San Mateo county, where a $130-million contract was at stake, the empowerment that started during the bidding process has continued under the new agreement. Our stewards now help select front-line supervisors. They help select new employees. And we provide seven of the eight members of the systems' Status Management Committee, which controls how ambulance service is provided, what are the relationships to the hospital, and so on.

Decisions made by this Committee are made by majority vote (the eighth person is a management rep). So, the most immediate day-to-day working conditions of the EMS personnel are controlled by rank-and-filers themselves. In terms of participatory democracy, ours are the most advanced bargaining units I have ever seen. These workers also have the best labor agreement in the country for private sector EMS.

Bargaining a New Contract. Once the Supervisors have made their choice we sit down with the successful bidder months before their management contract takes effect and hammer out a new contract with them.

We interact with the CEO in these matters, and he/she soon develops a fundamentally different view of his/her new employees...one based on *much* more respect. And it opens these executives up to more ideas and questions about EMS work: They now ask - "Just what *is* the role here of a manager? Of the EMS workers?" Our members deal with the industry in ways often more sophisticated than those of some middle managers...and many CEO's come to recognize and even value this.

Our process establishes - from the first day of contract negotiations - a very different set of relationships than I have in other places with more conventional bargaining ways. At one of my "process" locations in the last year we have not had a single grievance go unresolved at the first step by the stewards. And it's not because we're not very effective there: It's because management does not mess up as much! And this would not have happened without our whole prior process of interviewing bidders, supporting our preferred bidder, and so on.

The people at these sites are left by our new process with more self-confidence than ever. They tend to see the bigger picture. At one site people are calling me to ask if we could begin thinking about how the cost of their service to the public can be kept from going up even while we look to make gains in negotiations a year and a half away. Now, usually as a paid negotiator for a local you're often in a position of trying to educate your bargaining committee about the harsh realities of the bargaining environment right up to the day when they're trying to come up with a defensible recom-mendation on the employer's "last best" offer.

So, to have members call me with questions that urge *early* preparation for negotiations is pretty astounding! Especially as this industry is only newly organized. So these are not workers with 30 or so years of experience thinking about the political economy of their industry, as in the auto or steel industry.

Transferring the Process. I don't see why this model couldn't be used to confront privatization throughout the country. Clearly this strategy becomes significant when the union makes the assessment that the political fight to stop privatization is not a winnable one. The scenario appears somewhat similar everywhere: You have a request for a proposal. That proposal generally has to be approved by somebody. It is done in public, so unions can interact at that level. And when it goes out for bids, who bids on it is all public information. Accordingly it should be possible for other unions to capture the process much as we have in the EMS scene.

If this works correctly it should take the advantage out of sub-contracting. Subbing will not wind up being that much cheaper, because in the end a union will have earlier shaped the terms of the RFP and the final contract. If we can politicize the process we can take it out from behind closed doors. Politicians who see privatization as a shortcut to union- busting will no longer see it the same way.

Sacramento - Our Current Test. We have contracts with two of the five EMS providers already working in the Sacramento area, so this one has been a little hard. The paramedics on the Selection Committee decided that these two - even though they had union contracts - did not serve the interests of our members or the community best. So after considering the bidders they chose to support an outside provider who has a more sophisticated operation ability to meet higher standards in the delivery of emergency medical services. The other two were essentially "Mom-and-Pop" operations that grew, but were still developing their operations.

Naturally, our rank-and-file is not 100% behind the choice we're backing in Sacramento. There's a lot of people for whom the idea of a new employer is *very* scary. Now at least you *know* the boss for whom you are now working.

We change everybody's expectations. In the other three areas where we have gone through the entire process we now have the best private-sector EMS labor contracts in the United States. Any new provider here can expect they are going to have to produce substantially better than current Sacramento conditions. They understand they are going to have to deliver! They are going to face a very sophisticated leadership and a rank-and-file with high expectations of them.

If we're successful the new provider will know the principal reason they got the $140-million five-year Sacramento EMS contract was because of *us*! The only reason it went out to bid was because of us. And the principal reason they may get it has to do with our influence...on behalf of moral issues and the need for improvement in EMS quality in this community.

Its a *very* long process - and it has been going on in this case, Sacramento, for three-and-a-half years. The results of this will be that instead of having seven companies, as we did four years ago, most of which were non-union, we'll have one or two contracts for the whole region. And it should be the provider(s) we have publicly endorsed, one for whom we have actually gone quite out on a limb. It will be a close vote, and it may not finally work out in our favor.

If we lose it will be a setback. But our unionized paramedics are still going to be there. And the RFP we helped shape, the one that's already been approved, is *already* a significant win for us - since whoever gets the contract will have to go by its terms. We'll monitor everything over the five-year term of the contract, and then repeat our process when it comes up next for bid...with fresh questions about whether the incumbent was the best choice for the job. Our process is one continuous loop.

Summing Up. In a very important way we gain, regardless of the final vote of the Sacramento County Board of Supervisors, regardless of whether our choice wins among the bidders. Clearly our EMS workers have come to feel they are playing on a level that they've never had an opportunity to do so before, a level of real consequence.

The fact that they are now seen by the Board of Supervisors and the Medical Associations as *significant* players, the fact that their local union president is called by the editorial board of the *Sacramento Bee* to find out what is going on - these are things that would never have happened before we began our process.

Our response to the privatization threat resonates with a lot of basic union themes and values. It's a populist idea. It's an empowering idea. It activates and energizes members. It gives them useful, meaningful things to do. And they take charge of the conditions of their lives, especially of their work lives.

We've turned the competitive-bidding process from a frightening and far-removed matter into a source of influence for the people who actually do the work. And we've done it overnight. Without any high-faluting planning process. No reliance on expensive consultants. No enormous use of scarce union resources. Just the dedication, hard work, and real "smarts" of people hungry to gain more self-respect, increased wages and benefits, better service for the public, and far more control over their way of work... which is much of what unionism is about all.

Challenging Amalgamation
Susan Pacult Foregard
(SEIU)

Reared in war-torn England, and here only 26 years (as of 1992 when the material below was prepared), this urbane change-agent has been at one and the same time a County Management Analyst, a local union officer, an activist in state politics, and a former President of the Las Vegas Friends of Carl Jung Society. She recently sought to divide her SEIU local into two separate and equal parts, a task that tried her every skill as a reformer...and led in '93 to a compromise (trusteeship) that will enable a local election soon to resolve the matter (Susan will run for the presidency).

Three questions earn discussion: -

What are the "fault lines" in a heterogeneous local? And what part might attitudes toward labor-management relations play in this?

How can local leaders reach out to both high status and low status members in the same local?

When division of a local seems desirable, what private and public maneuvers seem most advisable?

Above all, Susan's case underlines how difficult it can be to force together rival rank-and-file cultures. And it can alert readers to desirable and undesirable options in the matter...one organized labor may increasingly experience in the pro-amalgamation and pro-merger years ahead.

I'm not representative of what most people think union people are about. It would seem that I'm the very last person who would ever be involved in the type of union business I'm involved in now. For example, I don't come from a labor background at all, and so I don't have any of the kind of roots that would be considered normal for a working person.

I was working on my degree in management and, being a history buff, I took a course called "The American Worker on Film," a fascinating course, and one of the turning points in my life, certainly. A book that was the reading material for this course, *The World of the Worker*, by James Green, helped me realize I didn't have the whole story from my management courses: I only had one side of the story.

At the same time an iron worker friend of mine told me about the Antioch College-Degree Program at the George Meany Center, and I became involved in that. And it felt right.

About four years ago our Public Employees Association affiliated with the Service Employees International Union (SEIU), and I became a shop steward. (It still sends shudders up and down the spine of many members to hear the word "union;" they prefer to still think of themselves as "Association" members. I can see where they are coming from, and I don't have a problem with that).

I ran unsuccessfully for the office of Treasurer, and then, two years ago, ran unopposed for Vice-President. The president was a man with tremendous union background and know-how from Boston, where he had organized cops about 20 years ago...very successfully. As a team we made a lot of progress, not only in our local but within the state. Things began to happen!

I am now employed as a management analyst, poised on the ladder of management, with excellent advancement prospects. At the same time I am an officer of a large and growing union local with prospects within the state which have tremendous potential. So, for me, it's a balancing act, but maintaining a very strong stance in both camps is doable. I'm able to see both sides of the picture, and I've found that to be very helpful at the negotiating table. I'm trying to help bring about a synthesis that works.

We are now in three-year terms, and I ran recently unopposed again for Vice-President. My team-up with my Boston friend, however, is not in existence anymore. I'm having to deal instead with an unwanted local president, a lady who may have some good intentions for our local, but surely lacks all the necessary background, even as do I, though we have each put together very different approaches to union-management relations.

As an elected vice-president under our contract I can use 20 hours a week to spend on union business, the rest going into my job as a Management Analyst for our county government. For the last two sets of negotiations over the past six years I've been the Chairperson for all of the county employees under one of five contracts our local handles: I've bargained for the 65 to 70% of our 6,000 members, the rest of whom work for the county hospital, our other major unit.

Now, however, the president of my local sees me as a management spy, and she is attempting to have me taken out of office, claiming I am acting for some unnamed management person. I have no fear of her succeeding, and expect instead to defeat her soundly in a September '92 showdown. Better yet, I expect to take over two-thirds of the local away with me, and leave her in our wake, a move entirely in the best interest of everyone involved, her followers and mine!

Trouble from the Outset. Our county-wide unit was established over 20 years ago. But it wasn't until our international, the SEIU, came along and organized the County Hospital that we were anything other than a well-paid "knitting club." Things went smoothly for the most part. But some of our members began to ask "Why do we need them, the Hospital workers, with all of their troubles? They're costing us money, and we're not where we need to be!" So a level of resentment began to grow.

We have, as president of our local now, an employee of the County Hospital, and she organized it against very difficult opposition. She is still in militant mode, and that is quite understandable. Those of us, however, who have in fact been organized a longer time, and hold different positions in county employ, see that the need to work *with* management in a non-militant way will become necessary...number one, to safeguard our job security, which we can only secure by offering something new in exchange, and number two, to promote worker input, and see to it that it is valued by people at the top.

Naturally, we have the usual adversarial-style relationships that accompany government employ. We have fights right now about the evaluation and appraisal process, in terms of how management wants to cut down on merit raises...but we need to play the game at more than one level! We'll fight like hell to stop them taking away merit increases *and* at the same time we'll attempt to establish what could be a Total Quality environment, one where I think a worker could have a greater sense of self-worth. These struggles *can* co-exist, but only for people who can see two things at once.

Our president, unfortunately, is not willing at this time to admit to different levels of relationship. The problem we have with her resolute militancy was recognized and rejected by many members almost from the outset. I'll never forget the major meeting we had after she had been in office one month, and was being challenged by the person she had defeated (the candidate I had backed and run with). We had about 500 turn out, along with a court reporter and two attorneys. I was called upon to chair it, and the atmosphere was electric! There was <u>so</u> much friction flying.

The vote was very close on the challenge. And the ridiculous thing was that if I had voted I could have made the difference, but as chair, I did not have a vote. The final vote was 6 to 5 in support of the leader I am now challenging. So, you can see we do have a history of difficulties with maintaining presidents and having dissatisfaction with them. That, unfortunately, is our inheritance.

A Division of the House. Employment in our ranks, that is, in the county part of our local, not the hospital part, is becoming more and more technical - and that means we are getting a type of member for whom a different type of unionism is needed.

County government is hiring more civil engineers and the like. Even the Sanitation Department is taking on more technicians to do more kinds of chemical testing and analysis, and so on. In fact, the whole technical/professional field is expanding greater than is the field of entry-level positions...a vast change from ten or so years ago, and an index of the future in public employment. We are hoping to address this future by planning *now* for its emergence.

One of our talked-about plans - at this stage - is to organize a new bargaining unit, one comprised primarily of technical/professional county workers. These people would include District Attorneys, chemists, and planners...some of whom are now mixed in with our bargaining unit, our 6,000-person general membership, one that combines those of us in county employ with everyone in our county hospital. About 1,000 of the fast-growing technical/professional types are under one or another of our five county contracts now, and when we create a unit especially attuned to their needs we could easily pick up 1,000 or so more!

A Special Agenda. At present in our very heterogeneous local, we have a mix of hospital and non-hospital county employees, the technical/ professional types. These people have not had a representative voice, and they are beginning to need one. Their needs are different from those of a hospital worker.

Probation officers, for example, are very concerned about not being able to carry guns, as they have to go into gang-infested areas...and apparently there is a "contract" out on them. (I'm not sure if that is true, but they perceive it as a distinct danger). As well, the people at the Sanitation Department are dealing with a high-risk of contracting Hepatitis B, and it could be epidemic (I don't think it is, but it could be!). So, we have different types of hazards experienced by people who are not police officers or firemen, people whom you normally associate with risks built into their jobs.

A second distinction concerns proposals being made by county managers for creating a Total Quality Program, an idea likely to appeal to many technical/professional types. If in fact, the county hierarchy is flattened out, if teams are formed where employee input is meaningful, our people will definitely be interested - though this concept will have to be tested out in the workplace before any of us can actually endorse it. If it is ever to be effective, it will have to have the cooperation of a representative bargaining agent...and management, even though it does like to downplay the usefulness of unions, sees the need for a union representative.

Breaking Free. What all of this comes down to is the need many feel to go back to the situation *before* the hospital unit was forced on us, a situation that allowed us room to operate a union local far more to our liking.

I've now had some conversations with SEIU international staff, and anticipate some direct meetings later this month. I gather we petition the International for division of the local, but only after we secure a declaratory judgment from the Employee Management Relations Bureau, which administers public sector problems in Nevada. We could form a new unit based upon a stipulation approved by the EMRB...if it were also agreed to by our existing local.

Our president will probably not agree to any such thing, and this is where the fight threatens to get heated. She knows I opposed her candidacy and ran on another slate. She knows I'll head the new unit after its creation, and, as there are no secrets in county work, she knows what is afoot and she is marshaling her forces to fight us.

I'm hoping cooler heads prevail and the appropriateness of dividing up is acknowledged. I'm hoping for the best, but, quite frankly, I'm planning for the worse.

Battle Plan. We're preparing a multi-faceted platform, part of which is the truly logical argument that this is in the best interest of everyone. We shouldn't be "married" to each other. We should be separate and distinct. We should be or-ganized in separate ways.

I'm also preparing a message for the membership which may bring out the worst in people and cause a fight. It will say the current president is *not* acting in the interest of the county workers, who are getting the shaft in terms of union resources, energy, and time...and that you need to do something about it! I feel such a motion may be part of what it takes to get people working for our cause.

Were the matter to go to a secret ballot vote of all 6,000 in the local I think our case for separation would win. We would draw on underlying resentment which has always been there in terms of having taken on the hospital (the only one organized in all of Nevada). Also, we'd emphasize the logic of allowing us to concentrate energies differently: This way the hospital local could have its own particular staff, which could concentrate its efforts on just hospital and health care issues. And the rest of us, who are in a more diversified environment in county employment, with its "A" to "Z" range of jobs and careers, would focus differently...and this would be a better all-around use of resources.

We'll get the word out, in either a soft or hard sell, in the way my slate deems most appropriate, and seek a clean-cut victory. We'll have a major meeting in the Fall and debate the whole matter in front of a very large turnout. Then the Executive Board will vote on it, and I generally carry seven out of 12 votes.

Personal Reflection. It's all very exciting...and scary. I didn't want to do it; I had to be forced by the president and her actions into doing this. I had been guilty of what I think most people do in an unhappy marriage: You give in too much, hoping this will make things better. And I gave her a lot of leeway in an effort to make the relationship work...and it didn't. And so now I must pay the price by opposing her.

There is a component in all of this of vindictiveness. But while nothing is pure, I think for the most part our cadre is concerned for the betterment of the local's members, and I do see this as a logical move. Once we have won our independence I'm hoping we can restore some stability to the scene. We'll get serious about exploring cooperation through the Total Quality approach, while our brothers and sisters in the hospital unit can stick with their more militant strategy. We'll each do our own thing.

Our international believes economies of scale are found in larger locals. That's their philosophy, and they're promoting amalgamations all across the country. So in that sense we're at cross-purposes. But my conversations with them have me persuaded they understand and I'm confident of their approval: Our fight, after all, is finally to promote gains for *every* member of the *entire* local...and we expect to soon attract many more county workers into our two better-than-ever units.

Summary. I have several aphorisms that I like to use to guide me. One of which is "It really doesn't matter if you win the game, only that you play." The burden of labor leadership is particularly important when you consider that you speak for thousands of people in many instances: What you decide or do impacts thousands of people. I try not to get oppressed by that: I take it seriously, sometimes too seriously, even to the point of questioning whether I have the right to make decisions that affect that many people: "Was I making the right decision?" Nevertheless, I am resolved to go forward and do my very best, and not feel oppressed by it.

Afterword (August, 1993): Reading my notes from early 1992, I am impressed with the dramatic differences which have impacted our local: The SEIU Trustee (Margaret Shelleda) has skillfully facilitated a compromise whereby independent, semi-autonomous chapters will be contained within the umbrella of the local's Executive Board. Revised bylaws are being voted upon which will allow officer elections, and a dissolution of the trusteeship in December.

I am now a member of the County Negotiating Team discussing TQM, pay-for-performance strategies to accompany a classification and compensation study, and other new-for-us concepts. The County Hospital is still undergoing labor-management difficulties while also at the bargaining table. It appears the International will maintain our merged and larger local, while simultaneously, the chapters will operate with sufficient independence to satisfy their constituents.

I am optimistic about our future.

Challenging Ownership
Wendell W. Young, 3rd
(UFCW)

While many labor leaders have spoken in my college classes over the past 30 years none has regularly made the positive impact of the author of the case study below. Wendell takes all the flack expected from skeptical, and often hostile questioners, only to reply in a heartfelt and engaging way, a response that draws murmurs of agreement from many in the class. He disarms critics with the breadth of his knowledge, as the courses he has, and is now taking to earn an MBA degree stand him in good stead. He draws as well on over 30 years of leadership of a large dynamic UFCW local, one widely identified with innovation, integrity, and panache.

Which is not to suggest Wendell's every venture has worked out as he had hoped. Indeed, part of the strength of his classroom appearances, and of his leadership in general, is his candor concerning the less successful of his local's major projects. Wendell practices the kind of outcome assessment too many others in labor shy from or keep entirely to themselves. He holds disappointments up for exacting study, and does so publicly in the belief colleagues can help him learn more than if he operated in protective secrecy.

Four separate, though related projects are discussed below, each a source of considerable pain to locals coast to coast. Wendell explains what he has learned from a failed ESOP ownership effort, endless threats to privatize many public sector jobs he now represents, and , in some depth, a failed worker ownership effort. Confident that mistakes need not be repeated, and utterly convinced the rank-and-file have the "smarts" to see things done better the second time around, Wendell models a method for assuaging labor pain other leaders cannot adopt soon enough.

Vocation in Labor, Human Dignity. My career as C.E.O. of United Food & Commercial Workers Local 1776 began during the civil rights era of the early 1960s. My experience in organized labor really has its roots in those ideals of peace and human dignity that were so popular in the 1960s, but I had been immersed in those ethical principles throughout my years in Catholic schools. So, as the twenty-two-year-old leader of our Union in 1962, I was filled with the ideals that Jesuit training had impressed upon me. Even though, since the 1960s, social justice issues have gone out-of-vogue, I am still as much a believer in the primacy of human dignity as I was thirty-one years ago.

I've learned that you have to think *positively*, even when the situation looks terminal. If you have a positive view of workers and their worth for their employers, for their families and for their role in society, you can motivate people to reach for excellence in their lives, in their jobs and in their relationships. For example, one of the most intriguing programs our union has been involved in was our bid in 1991 for employee ownership at the Acme supermarkets.

Bid for Employee-Owned Acme Brings Renewal! America's largest supermarket retailer, American Stores of Salt Lake City, Utah, put its East Coast subsidiary, the Acme stores, on the auction block in September, 1990. Because these 275 stores controlled over more than 30% of the area market, and because the jobs of over 22,000 members of eight U.F.C.W. Locals in six states were at stake, we had to take a positive approach. Our local unions created a network of experts on investments, securities, and employee ownership to keep the Acme team of workers and their managers together and competitive. For Acme, the moment of truth had arrived, and we put workers in a position to buy their company and to keep their jobs and their company alive.

The "Acme Multi-Union Strategy Committee" we formed was joined by a Los Angeles investment firm, Freeman Spogli. With their help, the union-sponsored ESOP [Employee Stock Ownership Plan] was able to come up with approximately $1 billion for the workers to make an offer to buy all the Acme stores across six states. It sent shock waves through the business community: A labor union was actually responding to a "for sale" sign, by seriously tendering a first-rate offer to buy. We wanted to structure a 22,000-member ESOP, and our advisers were convinced we could make it happen.

Our union-sponsored ESOP bid demanded six months of round-the-clock negotiations and was concluded in April, 1991. It provided incentives that linked workers' financial hopes and goals to the future success of their company. Our ESOP gave union members representatives on the company's Board of Directors. Opportunities were established for workers to vote on some of the key policy decisions of the company, and for workers to enjoy financial returns from the company's growth.

But, unfortunately, American Stores later withdrew their offer to sell. Many factors figured into this corporate decision. In September, 1990, American Stores stock had been low, and debt levels had been high. The aim of selling Acme was to solve debt levels by cashing in their 280-store asset. Their stock, it was predicted, would rebound. But American Stores stock levels went up during the period when Acme was on the auction block. Stock equity strengthened so much that the corporation split the stock, and Salt Lake City's debt levels subsided by April, 1991, when bids on Acme were due. So, there was not the urgency in April to turn assets into cash that there had been in September, 1990. In the last analysis, our Union-ESOP bid was the best offer tendered.

One of our attorneys felt that Sam Scaggs, the CEO of American Stores, turned down the excellent financial package rallied by our local unions because of class prejudice. Maybe he just couldn't hold his head up at the country club if he were to sell the operation to its workers.

We were disappointed as we had gone all out weaving together eight UFCW Locals, including my own, across six states, in this ESOP campaign, and we worked night and day for months to structure the Acme ESOP bid.

To make matters even harder, we had opposition from our own International Union, our own people! The top officers in Washington refused to endorse our $1 Billion ESOP bid because of the risks they said it posed to traditional collective bargaining structures. However, we had retained the nation's premier experts on employee ownership, Attorney Steve Hesyter of Arnold & Porter, as well as the dedicated and brilliant Malon Wilkus and Adam Blumenthal, respectively President and Vice President of American Capital Strategies in Bethesda, Maryland.

The eight local unions remained in the ESOP, and UFCW members employed across the easternseaboard by Acme voted at a 10 to 1 ratio to overwhelmingly approve the ESOP bid on April 1, 1991. But on April 11, 1991, when American Stores corporate headquarters in Salt Lake City, saw the positive desire of Acme workers and their managers to keep the company a vital competitor here on the East Coast, the parent company chose to forgo the sale and to run Acme themselves.

I should explain that the parent company, American Stores, was at that time the nation's largest food company with a vast network of subsidiaries involving hundreds of thousands of workers. Of course, the corporate officers devote their lives to computing bottom lines on their Lotus spreadsheets...they perceive the workers as a negative cost. However, for the first time in American Stores corporate history, the local unions were holding discussions with the top corporate decision-makers, and we were demonstrating the positive will of workers to keep their company competitive. I believe that our attempt to save the Acme jobs united the local unions in a powerful show of workers' value to their company.

This value was proven when American Stores' leadership subsequently joined local union leadership to design a plan of aggressive new investment in the Acme operation. The parent company's game plan for investment was based upon the research and the projections of the union-sponsored ESOP. That game plan gave Acme workers and managers a right to express *their* views on the operation of the company. The re-capitalizing of Acme demanded the modernizing of stores, and new computer systems, as well as an aggressive plan for expanding the operation by building new units. By way of this labor-management consultation, American Stores launched an aggressive sales and service strategy.

As a result of these negotiations with the parent company, language to guarantee jobs was guaranteed in a new four-year contract, and this from a company that just two years earlier had been up for sale. The contract also provided wage increases and continued an excellent Health & Welfare and Pension Package. Only by virtue of the union's joining with management in containing health care and insurance costs have we been able to maintain benefits necessary for our members and their families. The pension also remains protected, and we have been able to increase its benefits. In addition, we have received increases in tuition benefits and child care allowances.

Best of all, this four-year contract gives our people guaranteed jobs and no layoffs...you qualify if you have four years with the company, full or part-time.

So, we responded positively to a *really* depressing situation. The 100-year old Acme Markets had gone up for sale, with all kinds of corporate raiders and barbarians on the sidelines. Thanks to our research into the situation, we had learned the company needed to put capital into the stores. We negotiated job security guarantees into a new four-year contract, which included a guarantee for commitments from American Stores for a minimum of $200 Million in capital which they are putting into improving the Acme operation.

We took a really depressing situation and we turned it around, both for labor and management. Now, we're still going to have our problems here: There's no two ways about it. But what we accomplished proves that *all* types of problems can be solved through collective-bargaining.

We learned the union has got to offer alternatives that mean something! And union leadership must act on the strength of thorough research and information. Union leaders must be able to speak the language of the investor and the financier. The ability to know how financial analysis works is imperative. Labor's representatives must be able to analyze complex financial reports and stock reports, and also interpret bond issues. Unions and their members must be able to stay in touch with the day-to-day pulse of their companies and bring to their respective industries a powerful and a beneficial knowledge of how to save money and boost production.

All in all, you've got to send a positive message: Our ESOP bid showed workers' willingness personally to invest in Acme's century-old tradition of serving the public. Everyone knows how important employees' commitment is to any supermarket's success. Fortunately, the American Stores Corporate Officers took our lead for investment by making use of the ESOP blueprint for future expansion and re-modeling of the operation. Rather than running away from the challenge of aggressively operating this chain, they made a commitment.

The union and the managers signaled their faith in Acme and formed an agreement for a positive future for jobs and productivity. The culmination of this effort was a four-year contract guaranteeing jobs, wages, health & welfare as well as pension. This contract has also become a vehicle for management, the union, and its members to work together in making Acme a viable and aggressive entity as we look toward the Twenty-first century.

Another milestone to save jobs in our local union was our involvement with the Pennsylvania Liquor Control Board.

Protecting State Liquor Store Jobs to Protect the Community! Local 1776 has represented clerks in the Pennsylvania State (Liquor) Stores since 1970. The retail operation of the Pennsylvania Liquor Control Board is the largest volume operation of its kind in the entire country. For the past 20 years, as long as I've bargained for these men and women, almost every Pennsylvania Governor has attempted to sell off the whole system and privatize the sale of alcohol...an option we strongly oppose.

The Union's role has been to demonstrate the positive value State Store clerks represent to the voters and consumers who make up our communities. Pennsylvania enjoys one of the nation's lowest rates for highway fatalities. Experts from the State Police as well as Drug and Alcohol counselors have praised the healthy efforts of Pennsylvania liquor clerks who are trained and paid to responsibly prevent underage drinkers and intoxicated persons from purchasing alcohol.

The move to privatize the sale of liquor in Pennsylvania has mobilized our union members to know their importance to state health & safety standards that their jobs uphold. The fact that the State Liquor Stores also show excellent annual financial returns of over $200 million is another element in the UFCW Local 1776 program for pride in our State Store clerks. Of the revenues in tax and profits for which the State Stores are responsible, approximately 10% went in 1991 to State Courts and other State Agencies to support measures for the control of alcohol. Governors who have promoted the sale of stores have had to explain how private store owners would comparably protect safety and health in our communities. There is also the fact that privatization means the liquor industry, as well as print media (in pursuit of money to be made in liquor advertisements), and certain convenience store and other retail operations, would be under pressure to "push" alcohol in their efforts to stay competitive in their respective market.

Our union has had to overcome the fact that previous Pennsylvania governors who wished to sell the State Liquor Stores (for whatever reason) have tried to project a negative image of State Stores and their employees.

Our response to that initiative has been twofold: 1) We promote pride and confidence in the positive results that our workers bring to the community of consumers and citizens; and 2) we promote an active effort to support improvements in the State Store operations. This has the Union emphasizing to workers how important it is that they be positive and innovative in their daily jobs. Accordingly, our State Store union members play a significant role in improving their operation, as in creating new Wine and Spirits Shoppes, with an aesthetically pleasing ambiance.

Under the leadership of Governor Robert P. Casey, there has been a willingness to support the fine job our members are doing in the State Store system. Notably, the stores have become more pleasant and have made greater variety available to shoppers. Today, the State Store system is winning all kinds of awards. It's controlling use of the drug, alcohol, as much as you can under the circumstances...and much better than most of the other states' liquor systems.

So, hearing all the calls to privatize that challenges us in the 1970s, the 1980s, and now in the '90s, a move that could have killed our union contract, our members have responded tremendously! They took advantage of opportunities for change, for as they say, adversity creates change - and this is a lesson I really value.

Along with the pain of the Acme and State Store challenges we've also wrestled recently with perhaps our major achievement, creating Super Fresh, a new chapter in food industry history.

Super Fresh: Witness to Difficulties and Hopes. In 1982 Super Fresh food markets were designed to recreate business and jobs out of the ashes of A&P's Philadelphia Division closing which had occurred in 1981. Coincidentally, our union had been holding classes on employee ownership to educate liquor store clerks in the event they would need to make a bid to purchase a stake in a privatized liquor operation. Thankfully, the State Stores remained in tact. But we applied ideas about employee ownership to the A&P closing. We were prepared, on behalf of the workers, to buy the chain.

In the last analysis, we created a gains sharing agreement in which workers would share 1% of their individual store's gross revenues if they were able to keep the labor costs below a certain percentage of the overall operating expenses. The idea was revolutionary!

Employees *enjoyed* going to work because their ideas and their contributions were recognized. Even though they initially gave up $2-an-hour in order to bring the company back to life, they were positive. Super Fresh managers and our union members started sharing 1% of gross volumes in sales. For several years, even as the $2-an-hour was reinstated, the 1% grew and the "Win/Win" remained a "Win/Win."

So worker-friendly was the Super Fresh Concept that Japanese theorists were studying us. Super Fresh advanced its market share substantially during those initial years. Unfortunately, Super Fresh management became aware of how much money they were making and felt they could make more. Certain corporate heads decided, "Well, if we don't do this labor management cooperative stuff, we can make more money." And, unfortunately, they went basically full circle by going back to failed traditional methods.

Regrettably, the 1% gains sharing is no longer a meaningful incentive, as it is being received by only a handful of the 70 stores in the chain. Previously we joined management in figuring out better ways of getting higher sales. Today adequate equipment cannot always be found in many stores, and merchandise just sits useless in storage areas.

Ten years ago we had consultants to promote our Quality of Work Life program. Now we have far fewer and they no longer attend store-level QWL meetings. Ten years ago our union members were really excited by a new Quality of Work Life counseling program which the union pioneered with the chain. We wrote a clause into the contract that required our steward and the store director to do everything possible to solve problems at the store-level, and then explain their solution to the QWL counselor. However, about a year ago, we had to file an unfair labor practice charge just to receive responses to our "reasonable information requests" for data that the counselors used to regularly provide.

Our members have become disillusioned about the Quality Work Life system and some say it would be better not to have a QWL program at all than to have one that openly avoids its mission. Meetings have become more like company sales meetings than a forum for resolving labor and sales issues with management.

If you were to walk into Super Fresh today, and if you had been there 10 years ago when the experiment started, you would say "You might as well put the A&P sign back up again." That's how bad it has gotten.

We still have joint employer-employee meetings. We still have input. But the meetings, the input, and the business are no longer a cycle for success. The Super Fresh management blame it on the economy, but we point out the business of other food chains *has* grown. We insist the problem is that management doesn't know what Super Fresh is or wants to be - and this causes confusion to the customers and the employees.

Obviously, the Super Fresh idea is based on serving the particular neighborhoods where the stores are located. Unless stores can get the specific goods that appeal to ethnic values of customers, they simply won't have the product mix which traditionally made the chain a bell-ringer.

Unfortunately the relationship deteriorated before it became better. Just before Thanksgiving in 1989, Local 1776 members were in the process of negotiation with Super Fresh. Workers at that point were angry at the company's failure to stock the right merchandise and provide the equipment needed by each store. When negotiations began to break down, workers chose to strike, with the issue of a new warehouse as their #1 bargaining goal. Our Super Fresh people put their jobs on the line to send a message to the company that they wanted the system provided materials necessary to enable the company to compete successfully.

Truthfully though, I must point out that recently Super Fresh has made a series of new commitments toward operating more attentively on the local level. The corporation is trying to orient its buying and its distribution to the store-level needs of the operation. If Super Fresh turns its administration in the direction of giving workers the support needed to serve the consumers, the coming months and years may see a significant return of the incentives that originally made the company successful.

To put this in a larger context, it is vital to recall that unions made a "Social Compact" in the 1950's whereby they agreed to negotiate wages, hours, and working conditions. In those times, unions refrained from getting involved in business issues affecting their members. More recently, however, we have changed that by getting involved in participatory dialogue, in QWL talks , and having made significant economic advances in this way for the workers we represent, we will *not* revert to former practices. Business knowledge and research has become an important part of the union agenda. Negotiations have a new dimension. And management has to share new elements of the equation, like business data and marketing strategies.

An article this year in *Fortune* Magazine (February 8, 1993) asked, "Look What the Unions Want Now?!" I answer by saying that workers want to feel wanted, needed, and important. Workers want tools to meet standards for excellence and pride in the work. Workers today want greater effectiveness; they want to be part of motivated and well-educated work force. They want managers and as well as their fellow workers to join in programs that benefit everyone concerned. Workers want to feel as if they are accomplishing something.

For QWL programs to be successful, they have to prove they are *really* working. We must create a set of guideline for worker-participatory programs the Congress or the National Labor Relations Board can follow. Currently, management alone is running too many of the human relations programs. In order for both labor-management relations and productivity to improve, we must protect workers' opportunities to participate.

As you know, members can vote union leadership out of office. Consequently, I have to justify my programs for workers every three years. And I feel this has been a positive process for our union. I believe a greater degree of this kind of feedback and exchange would benefit management.

One example of our Union establishing a participatory scheme by which much has been learned was the 1982 founding of O&O (Owned & Operated) Markets.

Lessons of O&O (Owned & Operated) Food Stores - Model of the Human Condition. The final example I will use to illustrate that unions *can* set in motion a positive chain of events is Local 1776's all-out effort to make a success of employee-owned and operated food stores. Learning was the primary achievement amid difficulties and mistakes of O&O workers and management.

One of the things I learned in my current graduate course at Rutgers University has opened my eyes about this concept: Employee ownership has been attempted in many forms throughout American history, and has failed time and again. I researched the history of working ownership from the guilds on down through the last 300 years. I was amazed to find that what we thought was unique to our times has actually been cyclical: There have been many previous attempts at employee ownership!

All of the O&O food stores encountered the same basic problems. Today only one of the original seven stores continues to fly as a viable employee-owned entity. If I had known at their inception what I know today, our union's involvement in the process would have been structured differently. First, the union did not remain active in the everyday operation of the stores. We left them alone because we were swept up by a wave of democracy and individual determination ideas. We learned since that this system needs a structured administration.

One of the first decisions made in creating our bid for an ESOP at Acme was that management would run the operation. Employee owners would not be employee managers. A good athletic team needs a good hands-on coach...he has to keep the team concept in front of the players at all times. What was missing in O&O was the union constantly reminding employee owners of their mission.

To be successful, the collective interests in an O&O operation must supersede that of the individual. There are methods for adhering to such a mission. Unfortunately, however, the workers and their managers were left on their own, and then lost touch with the collective good. They became selfish with merchandise, and squabbled over disciplinary and scheduling matters. A more actively involved coach was needed.

The union should have played the role of the O&O's conscience. But we were not in the stores all the time, and when we reminded them of their original commitments, we became the enemy. Obviously, your friends don't always tell you what you want to hear: Friends tell you the truth. We wanted to function as a friend and as an ally in the success of the O&O's. A structure which had referees and management experts continually restating the mission and establishing timely guidelines in the daily operation would have been the best hope for O&O.

Another major disappointment in the O&O process was that Super Fresh members voted against contributing a percentage of their gains-sharing bonus to the establishment of a Special O&O Fund. It was to keep workers from being crushed by future store closings and/or corporate buyouts. It would finance and design employee-owned O&O-like stores if any of the Super Fresh markets closed down. They might have been very successful if the one percent O&O Fund had been approved by the members' vote.

Indeed, the Fund would have grown so much in the past ten years that Super Fresh workers would today have a level of job security unparalleled in the industry. But the A&P/Super Fresh administration discreetly made it known that they were against the idea. They saw worker ownership in the food industry as a potential threat, and they encouraged a shortsighted response from the workforce...a "no" vote that killed the Fund idea.

Our union was trying to give workers equity by contracts that secured the "first right of refusal" to union members in the event a Super Fresh is closed or put up for sale. And the Special O&O Fund was to work in tandem with real estate language in the labor agreements. Inadvertently or deliberately, subliminally or whatever, the company did not help us with the critical vote. When it went down, the O&O program took a fatal blow.

We had other major problems. The full-timer/part-timer issue became the program's most pervasive and lethal issue. Our first store opened with almost 70 percent full-timers. And we wanted Owner-Operators to equitably share with other workers the opportunity to invest in the stores. But the employee-owners viewed newcomers to the operation and part-timers as a threat. They tried to limit the number of owners as much as possible so that their individual stake in the company would remain high. In fact, rather than fight to increase the business and compete to enlarge the operation, the majority of the Owner-Operators tried to keep the company small.

Some, like their corporate counterparts in the junk bond era, wanted to sell out their interest in the business and take the money rather than work to make their company the most competitive, best-staffed, and best equipped. When, for example, a new PathMark opened down the street from one of the O&O's, the Owner-Operators had neither the capital nor the labor force to compete. They proved very conservative and preferred to keep the number of owners as low as possible. They also generally failed to invest in the necessary improvements which were needed.

I believe that with more extensive training and involvement of the union these problems could have been avoided. This relates to our original problem: The union wasn't in a position to do anything other than advise. If we had maintained a position on the Board of Directors, or if we had taken other roles in the administrative structure, we could have changed things for the better.

Even though the union provided the O&O workers with six-months worth of training in the practices of human relations and human resources, there was no continued cross-training within the stores. People became possessive about their work in the dairy or meat or produce departments, which they had come to think of as their own. Again, there was a need for structures to keep the common good of the store in focus.

The lessons learned by our union and others involved in the venture are many. It is my opinion that a worker's life in industry must be an extension of his or her education. There were many excellent opportunities for academics who theorize about what constitutes excellence in labor-management to become involved as umpires in seeing the O&O markets flourish, but hardly any helped out. Such a system could have played a role in getting workers to define and share their goals. It would have designated managers. Umpires were needed to design issues on which workers should vote. Some stores put too many decisions to a vote; gridlock occur.

Now, in the 1990s, as training programs are being designed and proposed, I strongly support the value of employee-owned operations run on the strength of vital education programs in which workers learn about every aspect of the operation to which they contribute. The process entails learning economics, philosophy, marketing, and responsibility.

It must be pointed out that one particular O&O store was located in a very economically depressed region of Philadelphia. Because of this, re-education was fundamental if people were to move successfully into jobs. Unless our community wakes up to this fact, we will continue in ignorance. Learning about the economics of poverty and about the discipline necessary to create opportunities should be our primary criteria. Of course, it must be learning attached to realities rather than only to theories. For the education process today is crucial. We learned this witnessing problems that emerged for O&O workers whose attitudes were limited by their educational experience in the ghetto and in ghetto schools.

Today, only one O&O store remains. It is managed by a strong personality, a person who has kept to the mission, and made some very tough decisions. He is a worker manager who has sustained our union's intent in originating the O&O's with a structure that keeps such stores viable and operational.

Labor's Position: A Spirit of Constant Renewal. Workers have the potential to bring distinct and valuable benefits to our economy: This is the theme that resonates through all of our past projects - such as our billion dollar union-ESOP bid for Acme, the renewal of the State Stores, the establishment of Super Fresh, and the trials of the O&O stores.

When workers know they have input into their destiny, they respond favorably. It means they can hope. They become motivated about their jobs. They enjoy being appreciated for the knowledge, learning, and the interest which they possess. Under these circumstances, people look forward to each day's work. When they contribute the most, they care the most about their job. They need to share in the decisions that make up their job description.

Of course, it's never easy. But people don't want the easy way out. Life is too interesting. People want to be challenged, and their jobs should become their most meaningful and rewarding challenge!

Let's not kid ourselves. This challenge pertains to me, too. That's why I'm in the union - it's a continuous challenge. The tougher it gets, the more challenging it gets.

In all of these projects we have benefited from the willingness of the membership to commit their energies and talents. When they are challenged, they have something to look forward to. When workers are empowered to save their jobs, their pensions, their health care insurance, and to provide for their families, I find them *really* responsive. The American worker, when challenged, will meet the challenge - as well as any workforce in the world!

I'm really convinced of this. And this is the principle that leaders in our churches, in our government, and in the labor movement must recognize if our nation is to grow with the historic changes of our times.

Part V

"Walking the Talk"

"In the labor movement we achieve splendid results in the transmutation
of human material because we do (we must) approach our problem
with the utmost faith and daring...."

August Claessens, *Understanding the Worker*; 1954; 21.

"The greatest use of life is to spend it for something that will outlast it."

William James

Two cases below raise a deep-reaching question that courses throughout
the book - "How are we to make progess in union-management relations
given the pain of doubt?"

Over and again, regardless of whether the topic is TQM/TQC
cooperation versus conflict (Parts VI and VII), unending job loss (VIII),
forced merger and/or employee ownership (IX), government scrutiny (X), or
internal union democracy (VI), an underlying question asks how are we to
build a reliable foundation for new trust and joint risk-taking? How are we
to provide worker security, work enrichment, and union clout along with
productivity gains, company flexibility, and stake-holder prosperity?

Seasoned union activists know part of the answer is provided by field
tests, by actual experience where the subject or strategy does or does not
come through. Some of the answer also comes from adhering to the adage -
"Follow the dollars!" - by which we are meant to unravel who stands to
benefit or lose financially from extending or violating trust. Other valuable
clues are available in reputation, in the unwritten record, and in one's gut-
feeling, one's intuition that recommends for or against extending
cooperation and trust.

A painful dilemma this, and one that goes to the core of many on-going
and proposed innovations in labor-management relations. It helps
therefore to learn below from two inside reformers how they operate in a
context rife with possibilities for misunderstanding and regression back to
raw belligerency. Both demonstrate the skills of a polished diplomat, the
creativity of an accomplished artist, and the patience of Job. Both keep the
faith even when others around them falter, and both remain committed to
helping all the parties "walk the talk," an indispensable achievement if we
are soon to improve the quality of labor-management relations.

TQC as a Renewal Aid
David C. Cracium
(IUE)

Interest in work culture reforms remains strong in progressive workplaces. Both union and management appreciate the life-and-death urgency of securing productivity gains that assure competitive advantage. Consultants and "how-to" manuals abound, undermined, however, by a lot of foot-dragging, turf-protection, game-playing, and other defensive impediments to significant risk-taking.

All the more valuable, therefore, is the case study below of success in crafting a "win-win" approach to work reforms. David C. Cracium, Training Consultant for IUE Local 717 (Warren, Ohio), raises six intriguing questions:

> How *really* blind can supervision be to major accident hazards at work?

> How *really* effective can a pro-worker activist be if he or she accepts a supervisory position?

> How can a local switch from a reactive to a proactive role at work? What sort of planning and re-structuring are entailed?

> What does it mean to negotiate a Lifetime Job and Income Security commitment? What are its strengths and weaknesses?

> Why might floor-level union reps and first-line supervisors both feel threatened by self-management gains by the workforce? What can be done to win them over?

Above all, what does it mean to a local to achieve unprecedented involvement in actually running the company with which it negotiates? What does it mean to internal reforms to have a local "literally move out of the back room into the Board room?" How far can experiments in self-management go? And, what can a local plan to gain in leverage from corporate America's urgent need to secure high-performance systems at work?

Probably my earliest recollection of unionism goes back to my father. When his family immigrated to the United States he had been left behind with a brutal uncle who was so abusive that my father would stay out in the fields all summer with the flocks. Meanwhile, his family worked and finally saved enough to bring him over. He came to America in 1919, in steerage, to look for a better life. He settled in Monroe, Michigan.

After doing a number of things he got a job at Ford's River Rouge plant during the UAW organizing drive in the 1930's. He told me many stories about the atrocities the management perpetuated against the workers...the long hours, the supervisors manhandling anyone who had anything to say about management or working conditions or needing breaks to get off of the line. When I hear people now talk about human beings as appendages of machines I can actually see that happening back in those days...being "chained" to mass-production machines, just to produce a product.

My father left Monroe, Michigan, and came to Ohio where he married. He went a long time without a job right after the Depression. And finally, around the 1940s, he was hired by a steel company that was non-union.

It began all over again. My father would take me to union meetings when I was about 6 years old, about 1949, USW organizing meetings, held in people's homes. My father would talk a lot about how bad it had gotten in the River Rouge plant, and how brutal conditions could be.

My grandfather, in turn, would show me copies of the *Daily Worker*, because both my father and his father were handing them out, trying to organize the workers. My family was always pro-union, though neither man ever actively held a position in the union movement.

My father, he had just come over. He didn't have a good education, and probably only went to 4th or 5th grade: He had trouble writing and communicating with people. But he knew what he wanted. He knew what was right! And he was willing to fight...to fight to gain those rights for the workers! He didn't want to be put in a position where he had to show people that he didn't know something: He wanted to be able to give something...and what he gave was his time. He gave his sweat. And he gave his muscle.

I remember being on the picket line as an 11-year old boy, once the unions were organized, back in the early '50s, carrying a picket sign.

My mother, in turn, had been American-born, and was raised in a very close-knit Romanian family. She went to Romanian schools in Aliquippa, Pa. Her father had also been very pro-union in the steel mills, and he was the one who had shown me copies of the *Daily Worker*.

Once my mother really got involved she was very pro-union. She worked all her life doing assembly-work at the Packard electrical plant. It was U.E. at that time, in the late '30's, and she can remember when at the Convention in Cleveland years later the UE was thrown out because of communist influence in the leadership. And the IUE was formed in '49.

My mother only had a 7th grade education. She wasn't very confident with herself, and never did run for an elective position. But she worked *very* strongly for women's rights at Packard.

And here was a case where we had a union that was supposedly democratic, but it wasn't where women were concerned: There were women's jobs and there were men's jobs. And those for women were the dehumanizing and demeaning types... the men would have the skilled trades jobs.

We would fight as hard as we could for the rights of the workers. But, within our own little structure, we had men's jobs and women's jobs.

My mother was active in opposing this, but without much success. She banded together with a group of women, and helped set up a woman's coalition in '58, '59, but the company brought in new equipment around them and everything changed.

Outside of this pro-union influence of my immediate family, there wasn't too much else of consequence. My boyhood neighborhood was *very* poor, and I don't recall any talk of unions.

At school we learned about the Rockefellers and Henry Ford, but never about the union leaders of the time and their contributions to society and the betterment of America. You just didn't hear about it. It was almost as if they were outcasts, lepers - "We don't want to talk about it. They exist. Maybe they will go away if we ignore them long enough." It was that kind of mentality.

I really didn't have any union type of training whatsoever until I went away to Ohio University in 1961 for two years. I wasn't sure what I wanted to do with my life, but I was looking at taking some business classes. I took some management classes, and we began to talk about the influence, the *negative* influence of unions... "Unions were creating problems! They were driving up wages! They were costing money, and maybe we didn't need them..." Even at that time they were starting to talk about competition and our competitive position and our labor costs. So it was a *very* negative focus as far as labor unions were concerned: Not what they could do good for us, but only what they could do bad for us. This seemed to be the MBA mentality.

I wanted to go into law, any type of law. But, even though my father tried very hard to maintain me, after two years money began to run out. So I came back to Warren, Ohio, and said "I've got to get a job!"

Going to Work. I got a job at Thomas Steel. My father had worked there more than 27 years, and he was able to help get me in. And I immediately got involved with the union...with his and with my grandfather's encouragement.

And that is when I really began to see the other side. I had heard a lot of stories up until that time, but then is when I really began to *live* it! It's something different. You read about it in a book, and you wonder - "Well, can this be the fantasy of the author? Or can this be third or fourth-generation story being changed slightly from what reality is?"

Well, then I really had an opportunity to begin to see managers and the way they really treated people and the working conditions within the plants. I was able to see first-hand a gentleman get caught up in a scrap-baler and get both of his legs taken off, because there weren't any safety precautions. (He would press a button, and begin to feed scrap metal into a machine. If he got caught he just couldn't reach the button, and hopefully somebody else would come to his aid. It took two or three men really getting injured before they decided a two-man crew was needed, one to man the button and one to feed the machine). I couldn't believe that people had to get maimed and hurt or die for management to see conditions out there weren't fit.

So, I worked at Thomas Steel for about three years. In 1965 my mother got me to switch to Packard Electric Company, a Division of GM. The steel industry was starting to wane and we had a lot of layoffs: I had already been laid-off three or four times, and it didn't look like there was a whole lot of future for the steel industry in the valley. Things were already starting to get shaky. And General Motors at that time was king! So when I had an opportunity in 1965 to go to Packard, and be part of this great General Motors family, I took it.

I lost my benefits, and had to start fresh, but the money was better, and the working conditions seemed better. I switched from the Steelworkers Union to the IUE.

I found out almost immediately that maybe the floors were cleaner and the lights were better, but basically, the way people treated people was about the same. In fact, if anything, I had a little more freedom in the steel mill, because we had one floor supervisor for an entire area. We were taught our job, though not given a whole lot of training. Sometimes another employee came over, but mostly we were left alone to do it.

I can remember on one job where I worked where they would anneal steel, these big balls of it, and the crane would come over and lift the ball out. And I would have to run over with a 10'-bar, hook the crane, and secure it on the steel ball. And I remember standing there while another employee threw a 5 gallon bucket of water on me, because the heat was so intense. In the few seconds it took me to hook the crane the heat would completely dry me. I could never understand why the hair on my arms was singed...I could never understand why it was 90 degrees in the summer and these men were wearing long sleeve flannel shirts. But I found out in a hurry why: The heat was so intense, these were annealing ovens, that it was a safety thing.

And the management of the company didn't provide any type of safety equipment: We didn't have hardhats. We didn't have safety glasses. They just weren't mandatory at the time.

Well, anyhow, when I went to Packard in 1965 I saw what was going on. Management wasn't much different. That's where I really began to feel people were just extensions of machines. In the steel mill they had been somewhat like craftsmen. There were rollers, sliders...they had men who had been on the job for years, and they trained their helpers. They literally eye-balled the steel and were able to determine the gauges. A lot of it was craft...but when I went over to Packard, a lot of it was really Taylorism.

I would think if there was any "classroom' for Taylorism, this was it! Work had been reduced to the smallest possible movement, and people performed the same task two or three thousand times a day on these machines that passed you every 18 or 19 seconds. And you would do your thing. It was bad....

Moving Up. The men's jobs were mostly manual types, like maintenance. I was hired on as a maintenance person, a janitor. The first week all I did was clean the windows of the administration building. I would go out there every single day with a bucket and a squeegee, and wash their windows, and squeegee the windows off.

Then I went into a service job. I took wire from the automatic cutting machines and fed it into the conveyor lines, where the women were building the harnesses. They would build 3,000 a day, and I was responsible for eleven leads that I had to put on. So I was responsible for hanging 33,000 leads of wire a day, plus all the components...the connectors, the metal wires, the tape, the conduit, and anything else that went along with that.

Crossing Over. I wanted to do *something*! I wanted to make an impact. In 1969 I succumbed to management, and, just like a financial secretary and a vice-president of our local, I went into supervision. I had been somewhat vocal about working conditions and they came to me and wanted to know - "If you're *really* interested in changing things, why don't you come over to *our* side? And we'll give you the opportunity to make some things different for the people you support.

I had spoken up at local union meetings and on the shop floor. While I have never been a steward or rep I *was* someone who was willing to speak up to supervisors and to the General Supervisor, and also speak up at union meetings. So, whether they perceived me to be a thorn or whatever, the opportunity was given for me to "really do something for the people on the floor" by going over to the management side...and *do* something! So, I decided to give it a shot.

I joined management in 1969, and immediately found out - "No, it doesn't work!" They tell you, upper management says, "Yeah, we'll allow you to supervise your area. We'll allow you to do some things differently." But, as soon as I *began* to do some things differently, as far as meeting with my people, building a relationship, I was immediately told - "No, that's not the thing we do. Your job is to manage; your job is not to associate with your people."

I had given my people a Christmas party the first year I was there, and that included with the fact that people liked me, *really* didn't go over well with upper management.

Within a year of being there I was supervising a line that went six months without producing a single reject. And I felt it was simply because I was treating them like human beings. Top management liked the idea my people were producing a good product. But they didn't like my methods.

I was on the job about a year-and-a-half, and I was called in one evening just before quitting time and told by management that my services were no longer needed.

Rejoining the Ranks. Because I had bargaining time, the most they could do was put me back on the floor. I went onto a molding machine, a step up in pay from what I had before going with management: It was a job you could pretty much work on your own: It wasn't a paced operation. I can remember the rate was 110 shots an hour for an eight-cavity mold, so I would produce 880 pieces an hour. It wasn't a bad job, because as long as you did your job, put in time, and produced a quality product, they didn't bother you too much.

It was not like the paced operations, where they were constantly on the women. They would get a little behind and shut the line down: God forbid! The "offender" was immediately taken off the line, sat down, and management wanted to know "What's the problem?!"

Management didn't care that you were not feeling well that day, or maybe the materials weren't very good. We were having a lot of problems with the conduit; it was too stiff. And the women were just not able to put it on the wire, and they would have to shut the line down. Management didn't want to hear that. They said - "Tape up your hands more, so you don't feel it cutting into your fingers."

We heard - "We don't care about human beings: All we care about is getting our product out!"

Paying My "Dues". As I look back on it, my experience with management was good for me. You can't learn that kind of stuff from a book...how management really treats people and how they view people.

But after losing my supervisor's job I had an uphill fight with my peers within the local, because they saw me as having betrayed the union...a *turncoat* I had taken a foreman's job and gone over to management. It took me the better part of 10 years to re-establish myself within the union hierarchy, and with some of the people with whom I worked.

In the year-and-a-half that I had been a supervisor, my area probably filed only one or two grievances: My relations with the local had been *very* good. Most of the time I sat down with the union representative and we talked the problem out. We tried to reach a solution that benefits the company and also the local.

This should have counted for something when I returned to the ranks. But you've got to understand their mentality. It was a *very* traditional union-management relationship. We were very adversarial. So you were either management *or* you were union. To actually sit down, communicate, and do something cooperatively...that just wasn't the way we did it.

The supervisors who were really climbing the ladder were those who were giving 30 or 40 grievances a week, and those who were throwing people out the door for any infraction of rules. And at that point in time we had probably 70 or 80 shop rules, anyone of which could put you out the door.

With some of the supervisors down there it was almost like a lottery: "Let's see how many people you can put out the door!" That was the mentality that was going on. When I came in they didn't appreciate my approach whatsoever. **Changing Direction.** I went back on the floor in '71. In 1980 I had finally had enough. I saw the direction the union was taking, and I knew something had to change! We were losing work. The local was taking a very militant stand. The company was taking a very militant stand. The result was that they were moving jobs out.

In '73, Packard Electric had become the first "green field" site in General Motors. We literally left work on a Friday. They brought movers in Friday night, unbolted machines, packed them on trucks, and were gone Monday morning when we came back in. No notice whatsoever! In fact, they called people at home over the weekend and told them they had been laid off. They didn't have to come back in. And they shipped out 1,000 of our 13,500 jobs that time to a non-union plant in Mississippi.

That was my first significant emotional experience that something's happening. It really hit home that they were going to start moving jobs out. And we, as a union, were either going to begin to do some things differently, approach management differently, force management into approaching us differently, or we could see more of this happening. **Coming Together.** There was a slow period when we began to evolve from our traditional adversarial relationship. And, in fact, we started doing some things together, the standard things, the blood drive, the bond drive....

But, as far as contract negotiations, they were still very adversarial. We still had to fight for a lot of the pay increases and working conditions that would improve the lot of our members.

That went on through the 1970's, and we lost another 1,500 jobs, with 2,500 in all being outsourced to Mississippi. Then, in the late '70's, we lost our Chevrolet contract with GM, which probably put another 1,000 people out on the street.

We realized something new had to happen, and a movement emerged in our local that favored a more collaborative style of leadership. I aligned myself with a very progressive union leader, a man who is currently the Shop Chairman. I remember a lot of midnight conversations, where we would sit around and talk about where we were and where we would like to be. I had always attended local meetings, and we began having a lot of conversations, this small group of us.

We looked at the local as it was, and began to talk about what could it be?! What could the future look like?! What are the forces out there to help us move in that direction? And what are the internal forces, internal to the union?

We were very reactive up to that time. We would negotiate our agreement and administrate it over three years, but we were constantly reacting to abuses by management. We weren't doing anything pro-active...as far as sitting down and strategizing: You know, "What can the organization be like, 5 and 10 years down the road?" And, as responsible union leaders, "What can we do to help you achieve *your* aim, and create a better working environment for our people?"

Work as War. There wasn't any of this going on. It was strictly "in the trenches." I can remember locking supervisors into their cages. Setting fire to the papers on their desks. It was a war, and *that's* what was going on. Management would come in: They'd get you today. Tomorrow, things would turn around, and you'd get them!

We would tear their phones out of the sockets, burn their papers...anything we could do to disrupt them. It was a war, absolutely war! There were slowdowns going on constantly. We'd find reasons not to put material on the lines, and the lines would have to be shut down. It wasn't conducive to waking up every morning to go to work. You really dreaded it.

We had a lot of people ill. The stress was unbelievable in the plants. Women were breaking down and crying on the line. Men were getting into fights in the plants. I saw quite a few of my friends revert to alcoholism. And later on in years, some actually went into the drug scene...because they just couldn't tolerate what was going on in working conditions on the floor.

Work Renewed. In 1983, Harold Nickols, a candidate I supported, was elected Shop Chairman. He came on with almost a blueprint of what he planned to do... a more cooperative environment with management. And they accepted it.

Nick had been a Sub-Chairman prior to winning election as Shop Chairman. In this capacity he had a lot of meetings with management. He understood that management knew something *had* to change. We were losing business. Most of the people in management were local people; they weren't brought in from corporate. They had some ties with Ohio, and maybe had been there for generations. And even though they were of a militant persuasion, just as the union was, they realized *something* had to change: We had to begin to approach our relationship in a different way, or five or six years down the road we may not have *any* work!

In 1981 the company moved 2,000 jobs south of the border to Mexico, to the maquiladoras. The handwriting was on the wall. In 1982 we learned there was going to be no more bricks and mortar for Warren, Ohio. There would be no more growth, and they were going to slowly phase out jobs. Perhaps only 4,500 would be left from 13,000. We were already down to 10,000 jobs.

Well, anyhow, there was enough of a discussion going on between union and management at a lower level, not necessarily at the top levels, that some things *had* to happen differently. So, Nick was elected in '83, and I was appointed Assistant Shop Chairman, something I had earned as part of about a dozen men very close to Nick.

Doing It Differently. Things began to change almost immediately. Prior to Nick's election the top manager gave an interview to the newspapers where he boasted in an off-handed way that "No one's gonna' lose their jobs because of movement to Mexico." Now, that wasn't the truth, because we *had* people losing their jobs! Why he made that statement, God only knows! But once Nick was elected Shop Chairman, he took this commitment out of the newspaper, and he blew it up, and he plastered it all over the plant.

We were just ready to go into negotiations. Management called him and said - 'Do you want to sit down and do some pre-negotiations before we go to Detroit?' And Nick's answer was - 'Well, not until we clarify the commitment.' For almost six months Nick would stand in his window, and the chief bargainer for the company would stand in his, and they would literally stare at each other across a parking lot between the union office and the plant. They wouldn't talk; they wouldn't communicate.

Finally, one day the phone call came in, and the company bargainer said "Come over, we'll talk about the commitment."

The result was, in 1984, we negotiated a Lifetime Job and Income Security Agreement at the local level. At the national level the IUE negotiated something very similar, a Jobs Bank. Nick felt it wasn't sufficient; it didn't give our people enough security. So we, at the local level, got permission to negotiate language at our level that would supersede the national. Management also got similar approval from General Motors.

What we negotiated meant that anyone hired before January 1st, 1984 could never lose their jobs because of outsourcing of jobs or movement of work to Mexico. And that was a first! It was a *big* step! At that point in time it was seen as precedent-setting language in a labor agreement.

Management, by the way, can never bring this up again. They are forbidden from talking about it. The only people that can raise the issue and renegotiate this clause are the union people. I can remember that at the Detroit negotiations as soon as the word "forever" came up - "no loss of jobs *forever*" - there were people scrambling for dictionaries. They had about a two-hour discussion over what the word "forever" means!

We said it meant just that: For as long as Packard Electric is there as an institution, and the IUE is there as the bargaining unit for the people that work there, this clause will remain in effect.

Doing My Part. From that point on some really good things began to happen.

I served as a full-time Assistant Shop Chairman for a year, and spent a lot of time getting people who had been taken off the payroll back to work. My job involved a lot of dealing and negotiating with management over workers' rights, and getting them back, and grievance settlements at the third step. And I felt real good about the fact that I got a lot of people back to work who were on suspension.

We began at that time developing a program to help people who were off the payroll due to substance abuse. We brought them back and put them into programs, through a local rehabilitation hospital, to help them either with their drug or alcohol abuse. But it was hard to keep them back at work. It was very frustrating to get them off the payroll a week or two later. We had about 3 or 4% who were habitual abusers and absentee problems, people who were always causing us a lot of difficulty.

In 1984 Nick asked me if I would deal with a pilot project on employee participation. I went in and set up a participation project in an 800-person plant.

Beforehand I went to Detroit and took the General Motors management training on employee participation, so I was able to get all the management angles on why this was good. As I recall there were two union representatives and about 28 management representatives. They treated us very well.

But all we heard all week was the great things this would do for productivity and profits: "We will make people happy. Once they are happy they are going to be willing to be controlled. We'll make them *like* being controlled. Because we'll move their benches for them. We'll paint their machines for them. And we'll give them a little bit better lighting. But still at this point in time we're *not* going to give them any meaningful say in the decision-making process! We're just going to do the menial things that make them happy."

When I took charge in '84 I immediately began to transform the process into one that would allow our people to *actually* have more say at the shop floor level. And I was really surprised at that time by the resistance from management. They didn't want to give control. But it was also coming from the union.

I became somewhat disillusioned. Here I had been involved in campaigning and helping to get a progressive unionist elected, and suddenly I was being told - "You are moving too quickly! We've got to slow down. We can't allow our people to begin to make decisions out on the floor. We have to ease into it."

When I thought about it I realized that empowerment was fine, so long as the power you have to share isn't your own. I had explained to my people that if we took employee involvement all the way out to the end, normally what it ends up with is some type of scheme around self-management. What you would be able to do, in fact, is design your own work environment, without any input coming from supervisors.

Management didn't like to hear that at all. But there wasn't a whole lot they would do: I was appointed by the Shop Chairman and they couldn't remove me from my job. So they would call me in and try to calm me down a bit.

A lot of union representatives on the floor started saying - "Hold on! If people become self-managed, there's not a great tendency to write grievances. If the grievance load goes down, maybe we'll not need one union rep for every 500 people. So, you're hurting' me too, buddy!"

Now, these people had good full-time jobs with our union: They were paid a lot better than the regular jobs, because the contract language entitled them to a lot of overtime. They did not spend a second on the machines from the time they clocked in until they went home: All they did was administer the contract and write grievances. They had their desks on the floor, and all day long they walked around and talked to the people...and filed grievances. It is no wonder they were more than a little upset by any possibility of possibly losing their role...and I had to take their fears into account.

Co-Management Packard-IUE Style. Nick's crowd wanted to get away from the militancy of the '60s and '70s. Our stand was "Let's not fight. Let's develop committees that will allow us to sit down, jointly, identify problems, and reach mutually agreeable solutions." We wanted to move into the collaborative atmosphere of the '80s and '90s, and help move toward the year 2000.

Today, we have an eight-person Jobs Board, four from each side, that actually runs the entire business. They involve themselves in strategic planning, 5-year and 10-year plans. They look at people movements changeovers on a yearly basis, manning requirements for the plants. So, they jointly run the business.

They decide what areas we are going to move into, and go out jointly to secure new business for our organization. We are moving away from GM and diversifying. In fact, our Joint Board was recently in Japan trying to get some business.

In the plants we have a similar structure called the Plant Units. They are responsible for implementing the strategy that comes down from the Jobs Board. They handle manning requirements, down time, machine utilization, overtime, and so on...in a joint fashion.

We have moved out of the back room into the Board Room. We have become really a part of running the business, and we are really concerned about maintaining Packard Electric. We want it to be profitable. We want it to make money, because if they do so the chances are they will stay in Warren, Ohio. And, as responsible union leaders, we have to be concerned about maintaining jobs for our people...and, in fact, grow, if at all possible.

Bolstering Co-Management. Ours is a jointly-managed approach, one we consider *very* progressive. We even do all training in a joint fashion.

Prior to 1984 all training was on-the-job. But we realized people had to have more, especially more skills than "how do I run my machine." If, in fact, we are going to move from an adversarial to a cooperative type relationship, one where people are actually going to get involved in decision-making, then they must have some skills and knowledge around communication and decision-making. And that we hadn't been giving them.

In 1987 I moved up to being a Training Consultant. I go into the plants and do a needs analysis. I use surveys and one-on-one interviews with both union and management representatives, all of which helps me design training...with the customer in mind.

We're working now on developing a high-performance system. We've set up a pilot experiment whereby one area is going to be totally self-managed. They will have an engineering resource person and a management resource person to work with them. But, for all practical purposes, the people will run their own department.

It is a precision-molding area. We're going to be using state-of-the-art computerized molding machines. We're going to have 60 of them with ten operators. And this has required six months of special training to prepare the folks...including classes in problem-solving, conflict management, decision-making, stress management, and so on.

Doing It Right! Our training curriculum is *very* extensive. We have a $12-million training budget. We have a stand-alone training facility, which, while only corporate at the moment, we expect to soon run jointly. And we also have access to the national training fund, which is negotiated out of the contract at 19 cents for every straight time hour worked and $2.50 for every overtime hour in excess of five percent. That's for all of GM-IUE, and that's over $46-million dollars. So any training our people are involved in at the plants, they're reimbursed for it by the national parties. Or even any tuition costs at a college; it's all covered.

Lingering Problems and Reform Responses. Our average seniority is 25 years; the average age is 47 years. And that creates a lot of problems for us. Because when you talk about change, why they look back and say - "Why should I get actively involved in change, because three years from now I'm gonna' be gone!" And change is difficult! We're having a lot of trouble, for example, getting people involved in training.

But when you sit down one-on-one and talk to them about the value of it, talk to them about "Wouldn't it be nice to feel good about yourself in the workplace?," to actually get involved and have a feeling you're part of what's going on, they...they do a lot of nodding.

So, I think what we have to do, as a democratic organization, which I hope that's what unions are supposed to be, is try to create an environment where people feel so good about themselves that they will actually want to become part of what's going on...become part of the decision-making process.

Not only relative to their workplace and the management of that organization, but to their union. We have a 9,000-member local, and we're lucky to get 200 people to local meetings. We don't get 50% of our members to vote, and we have in-plant voting! So there's something going on out there that's alienating. Members ask what good would participation do me? Candidates talk a good game, and we elect them. And yet, when they get into local union office, they forget who we are.

This is one of the contradictory things we are looking at: We have about 6,500 backlog grievances! Yet every study ever run says that as people become more satisfied there is a tendency to file fewer grievances. Yet we have this expanding grievance load. Now, my own personal feeling is that a lot of the grievances being written aren't worth the paper they're written on! So I have a feeling a lot of district committeemen, first-line committeemen, are using the grievance load for their own job security! They're filing...and the zone committeemen are saying, "Oh no, you're not going to tie me down with trying to make a decision about this one!" So they move it on to the third step. And all of a sudden we've got 6,500 grievances in back-log!

We have taken the time and energy to set up a great structure to deal with it (I think we have a *fantastic* grievance procedure... the foreman will tell you this!) But I think the foreman have more or less been told by their leadership "You don't settle a grievance at the first step." They can't tell you that, because that's in violation of the National Labor Relations Act, where it says "bargaining in good faith" and "settling grievances in a timely matter."

The supervisors and the floor representation, the local's committeemen, seems to be where the bottleneck is at...there is a lot of resistance to change there. And I think it goes back to the fact that we didn't do a real good job of defining what their role was going to be in the change. And, even consciously or unconsciously, they're still sitting back and saying "I have no job security. If this workplace becomes *really* cooperative, I might lose my job!"

We don't need a committeeman for every 200 people. And obviously, we don't need supervisors any more because we're going to be self-managed. We didn't define their job as "coaches" or maybe, "trainers" or "mentors," rather than managers, supervisors, or local union committeemen. They definitely would have a positive role in the change, but we didn't communicate that early on, and we're having problems with that now. We didn't anticipate the problem, and now, 10 years into the process, instead of things moving along smoothly, we've got to attend to this problem.

We didn't do it right, and now we're paying the price! How long will it take us to go back and re-establish trust with the first-line supervisor and the local committeeman, I'm not sure. It's gonna' take a lot of time. It's gonna' take a lot of energy. And it's going to take a lot of understanding...and testing...to get that to happen.

Everytime we try to get them together, the first-line supervisors and the committeemen in the same room, they find reasons not to be there, such as "The business dictates that I have to be on the floor" or "I have to supervise my people."

But you *don't* have to supervise your people! We've already *proven* that! You tell the people what to do, and they're capable of doing it without you standing over them.

I think there is a fear on their part of coming together and talking about what the roles are going to be...because some of them I don't think are equipped, either skills-wise or knowledge-wise, to deal with the change. They're bogged down in traditional ways - "This is the way a local committeeman reacts" or "This is the way a supervisor reacts." And, because we didn't do anything about *changing* that behavior early on its really ingrained now, and its gone to be hard to pull them out of it.

As for our backlog of 6,500 grievances, in the past what we did was to literally take the backlog to local negotiations. And management would say, "Here's so many thousands of dollars: Settle your grievances!" But that's not being done anymore, because one of the things we negotiated is that we no longer have local contract negotiations, not for the last four years. Because of the structure we've now set up, if a problem arises we deal with it today: We don't wait three years until contract negotiations. And it means we'll have to change the language before we take it to the membership and get ratification.

Before, every three years we'd wipe all grievances out prior to negotiating the local contract. Now, we don't have this option...and this is one of the things beginning to go wrong with the whole vision we set down in 1983, a vision of where we wanted to be five and ten years down the road.

We've repeated our vision exercise a couple of times since. In fact, one of the things I did here not too long ago was to bring management and union folk together for a two-day off-site exercise. We split management and the union up, drawing on a mirror-image exercise, and we asked management three questions: "How do you see yourself?" "How do you see the union?" "And how do you think the union sees you?" And we asked the reverse of the union.

Then we brought them back and processed the whole thing. We looked at similarities and differences. We have a perception of what the other party is like, and they were saying that is *not* what they were like! Why is there a gap between the way we see and the way we think they are?! And then we talked it all through in order to get a better understanding of each other.

Given the proper circumstances, the proper knowledge, proper training, and behavior modification, people can change. But you have to be willing to take the time and the energy and the money necessary, because they're not going to change on their own.

Unless, of course, they're confronted with some emotional experience that will cause them to want to change! When we began to lose jobs to Mississippi and Mexico that was a significant emotional experience for them. If those jobs had never gone from Warren, Ohio, chances are we'd have never gone from being an adversarial to a cooperative environment, because there would have been no need to change: But it was there!

Doing It MY Way. I work on carrying our story elsewhere...the training we are doing and how we've gone about changing our relationship. We have a slide presentation we put on: I have a management counter-part, and we do a lot of traveling around putting on the presentation. We are expanding the process by bringing it into the world outside.

I made contact with our area school system, and have been responsible so far for negotiating two public sector contracts, one for an AFSCME local and one for a teachers union local. This has developed from speaking and networking I've done on the outside over the past 10 years, and people are now starting to say - "Hey, look, we understand what's going on with the Packard Electric - IUE experience. Can you help *us*?" So, they're coming to me, and I'm getting permission from my organization to go ahead and do it. And I'm volunteering my time.

Now, after 26 years of involvement in unionism at Packard, and after 30 years of union activity altogether, I'm finding a need to actually get involved and run for the first time for elected office. Even though I think a lot of what we're doing is good, we'll still neglecting the *real* reason we were put in - and that's to create a better environment for our people. And that's not only better conditions of employment. It's also all those things that Maslow talked about that people need: They need *more* than security and pay, and shelter - they need a feeling of self-esteem and worth and belonging.

I don't think that type of environment is being developed. Our union has to develop it. Management is not going to do it. They're not going to go out there and say 'Hey, we want you to have a lot of self-esteem! A sense of belonging!" All management wants you to do is make a product.

What I want to do now is help spread the word about the rewards of the "win-win" approach, the good things the unions can do, and the strengths of cooperative relationships. We in organized labor must model the kinds of behavior that we expect those we deal with to begin to demonstrate. Working cooperatively - trying to achieve "win-win" - is *the* way to go! Hopefully I can win union office that will allow me to do *more* to promote this whole idea.

Addenda (July, 1993). Much has changed over the past few years. Nick, the Shop Chairman who was partly responsible for the large-scale change that took place at Packard, was defeated by 190 votes in a very hard fought election in which nearly 6000 members voted.

The bottom line was that slightly more than high of the members felt that Nick had lost touch with the membership. His preoccupation with helping to run the business and save jobs in Warren, Ohio, was not enough to win him a fourth term in office.

I guess the epilogue to Nick's nine years in office is no matter how sincere you are about improving the life of the people you represent...don't ever forget from whence you came! Never lose your visibility on the floor! The people need to touch their leaders, look them in the eye, and feel their strength, or they lose trust.

As for me, with Nick's defeat came my return to the plant. As an appointed representative who was closely aligned to Nick, my position was very threatening to a new administration.

Yet, the years I spent as Divisional Trainer for the union was a time of great growth for me, both personally and as a unionist. The education I received and the people I met had combined to give me a renewed inspiration and faith in our ability to bring about change. At Packard, the union has done a lot in moving this organization from the brink of closing, but today there is still much that needs to be accomplished, and opportunities for our union to become even more influential in charting the course of Packard's future.

I have come to realize that a union is a living thing that must be nurtured to survive. That above and beyond the ability of its leaders, in the final analysis, it is only as strong and vibrant as its membership. If allowed to become lethargic it will grow old and die. As a unionist, I must continue to look for ways to excite the membership into participation, not only participation in the workplace, but also participation in the democratic ideals that unionism is all about.

In May of 1993 I was elected to the position of District Committeeman. I represent nearly 300 people in an area that is undergoing massive social and technical change.

In the midst of my district, which is very traditional in both its technology and management style, are two high-tech, self-managed areas. Hourly people are being given the opportunity to use their talents and abilities to run the business. Although it's still too early to raise the banner of success, it would seem that given all the positive indicators the areas are highly efficient and productive. As for the people, just talking with them allows you to see the increased sense of worth that being able to make decisions has given them. They don't think of themselves as extensions to machines. They see themselves as an important part of creating a profitable and enduring organization.

But as with Nick losing touch with the floor, it will be my job to insure that the membership doesn't lose touch with their union. Through monthly newsletters and weekly meetings I am educating the membership to the importance of maintaining a strong union...one that is not only responsive to the needs of the organization, but if need be militant in its defense of union ideals.

TQC - The Jury is Still Out
William "Rusty" Franklin
(UMW)

While far too little thought is commonly given to the fact, the term *international* in the title of many American-based unions generally refers to proud Canadian locals in affiliation. A source of valuable lessons in class consciousness, class pride, militancy, nationalism, and a distinct civility rooted in a welfare capitalism more caring than our own, the Canadian sector of North American unionism is alive with internal union reforms as strategic as any underway in the United States.

Typical is the on-going effort recounted below to recast union-management relations in a government-owned coal mine, the better to heighten the chances of commercial success when the mine may soon be offered for sale to the miners. UMW staffer William Franklin helps call attention to four questions relevant on both sides of the U.S.-Canadian border:

> What arguments can a union activist offer to win a fair hearing for cooperation in place of more familiar conflict options?

> How much grass-roots involvement can a union expect of members in a sweeping re-orientation effort?

> What sorts of changes in a local's culture follow on efforts to move it from a conflict to a cooperative orientation?

> Coursing through all is an over-arching fourth question: How much reliance can be placed on the instinct to survive, in the ultimate good sense of workers threatened with the loss of everything unless they first change everything?

When I get asked now, in the summer of 1991, what I'm up to in Nova Scotia I say nothing less than helping an entire community stay alive: Unless we turn around a government-owned mining company up there and do it *soon*, the Federal government will shut it down - and a whole lotta good people will hurt something awful!

Background. It all began with a work stoppage protest they had up there in September of 1990. The company tried to do away with trucking its own coal and turn the work over to non-union independent operators. The protest of our 2,200 people in seven locals at three big mines lasted five weeks...a hard, long, and bitter work stoppage at the "Big Daddy" of all of our UMW of A Canadian mines.

After the strike was over we got word the company was coming down here to D.C. to meet with a union-busting law firm that has represented American coal companies we've fought against. We called them up and told them we heard through the grapevine they were coming (they were surprised we called them), and we said, "Why don't we get together. Let's sit down and talk."

We met with the company president and said we know why you're here in town. They said they were only meeting with this law firm to get them to represent the Nova mine in some law suits (including a $13-million law suit against us). We said we'd kinda like to see if there was any way to mend fences: "No sense in having everybody divided. And no sense in all the suffering."

They were thinking along the same lines that we were. They had hired a consultant from Toronto to do an employee survey, and they promised when they got the results back they'd be glad to give us a copy...and let us look at it.

We proceeded to have several phone conversations and a second luncheon meeting with the Nova mine management. We raised the possibility of getting a third party to kind of help us to overcome the problems we had with each other and keep us both in line. It would have full authority to press the whip on either side. We proposed two names to them, and they were interested.

Going to the Membership. We went up to Nova Scotia and met with our people to see if they were interested in participating. We were not going to force anybody to get involved in this process.

We first met with the District President, whom we had taken out of office in 1985 (due to financial irregularities). He could have been real bitter and opposed us all the way. We said "We've got a chance here to sit down with the company and work out some of our communications problems." (By this time the survey had shown the main problems were communications and lack of trust). He said "Well, I'd have to be real stupid to turn down anybody who wants to help me. I'll get the District Board together and get their feelings on this."

Which he did...and we attended and went over what we wanted to do. We explained the company knew it needed to gain some kind of trust from its employees if it was ever to regain productivity lost since the end of the work stoppage. The company knew it could not do this on its own, so the UMW was in a good position to help redo the entire relationship.

We later met one more time with our local up there and went over one more time what the possibilities were. They voted overwhelmingly in favor of going ahead, with a problem-solving process, no ifs, ands, and buts.

Hearing from the Opposition. When we met next with the District Board, one of its members said "I have an article I want to read you," and read out loud how bad quality-of-work life programs were supposed to be. They were undermining the union, and this, that, and the other thing. He said the only reason the company wanted a joint cooperation program with us was to downsize the industry, and to get out of their legal obligation to negotiate downsizing.

I said he had a valid point. We'd be certain to get the company to agree before we proceeded any farther that our discussions did not invalidate any legal obligation to negotiate downsizing...and that effectively put him in a box.

Getting Started. The first meeting drew together 26 company people and 26 union people. You could have cut the air with a knife. The company people sitting on one side; the union people on the other: Nobody saying nothing.

The first speaker, a facilitator who used to work at a UAW plant in Hagerstown, MD, got up and pissed everybody off, 'cause he talked about cash cows were coming together for mutual good, and all this mutual win-win stuff: It was too early for that conversation.

Then the other mediator-facilitator lost his patience and got up and said: "Goddammit! Either we're gonna go try to establish a cooperative program or we're not. If you don't want to go, tell us now, and we're out of here. We ain't got nothin' to gain by being here. We're tryin' to help you out. If you want to work together, fine! If you don't, we're gone!"

Some of the Nova local union guys then said, "Well, some of the questions you were asking us, about productivity and absenteeism and not really being ill - they're kinda hard things to start off with!'" The company people had to agree, these questions were hard to discuss.

Breaking the Ice. We moved to a mock bargaining session called the "Red and the Black." Both sides can lose their shirt. But if you bargain right, both sides can win.

We split up the union and the company, 50/50, into two teams. After a while everybody got the point: Either they were gonna lose their shirt or they were gonna trust what the other team was telling them. When everybody won, that really broke the ice!

We proceeded to create a Health and Safety Committee, 10 from labor, 10 from the company, all of whom were sent to the Mine Academy in Bakely, West Virginia, for a joint training program. Our union put it on, but the mine company paid to send all 20 people. We also set up an Industrial Relations Committee to look at such things as the bonus plan, and straighten out any problems people have with it.

Finally, we set up a Finance committee. Since it's a government-owned corporation they have to provide a five-year business plan to the government for approval. They are being required to take 800 workers out of the industry - and this downsizing is another reason they *had* to work with us. They were told within five years all government subsidies would be gone, and they had been living off of $31 million a year or more of such subsidies. Our Finance Committee will try to figure out how the $31 million can be replaced.

Turning to the Government. We've since gone to Ottawa twice and met with a member of Parliament representing small business. We explained we had to have about $4 or 5 million *extra*, over the life of the current five-year plan. We'll make it a profitable company, complete with downsizing, but we've got to have $4 million more dollars. It looked good for us, because we were seen as working together, as cooperating with each other. This has since been approved on condition that labor and management continue to jointly work to create a self-sufficient corporation.

Solving Early Mistakes. Our biggest of the three mines sent word it wasn't going to participate. I went over to the local meeting and asked "How come you pulled out?" They explained that the Joint Committees had no management people from *their* mine on it. Therefore they had no need to be part of these meetings. I said they had a legitimate concern.

We went to the company and got them to agree to put the Human Relations director from that mine on the committee, along with two of our local union committeemen.

At the next meeting of this local I was there 4 1/2 hours fighting with people who didn't want to participate in this program. Some were old Canadian Miners' Union people who had fought UMW of A all the way, and did not like the fact that the International was taking such an active role in their District.

We got an "old boy" to put a motion on the floor to have a special meeting of all the membership of that mine, on a Sunday afternoon, when everybody could be there (only 20 out of 500 were at this regular meeting). The District President wrote a letter to the membership explaining why we were in this program. I explained how it was for our betterment, and for the company's betterment to solve our problems and become self-sufficient. If the company was better off, we got better jobs, long term. We sent out the letter with an invitation to the special meeting, and were *really* pleased when 100 showed up.

Opponents kept stalling the voting, however, and by the time we got to it we had only 50-some people there. About 40 were active in that local, and we won the vote by 32 to 8...and this brought the local back into the cooperative process. And they had been the most volatile local up there, though now they are part of the process.

Successful Terms. After only half a year of working together we came up with a new Five-Year Business Plan that early retires 350 people at $1,700 each a month. Nobody will lose their economic security. We'll downsize over 800 people over the next four years, and none of them will lose their economic security. We'll have 200 people on a work-share scheme, where they'll work 10 weeks and be off 40 weeks, and repeat this, thereby qualifying for unemployment insurance, every one of them bringing home over $26,000 a year. We've also got a voluntary severance pay of 26 weeks pay and a $6,000 education or relocation bonus. Nobody *in*voluntarily loses their job.

In comparison with normal contract benefits the miners might have gotten in normal circumstances, this deal is 10 times better! Anyone age 54 or up can early retire with *no* reduction in their retirement benefit. If the company doesn't get enough retirees, it can go down to age 50 with no reduction in benefits. The company now pays for health care, whereas in the past the individual had to pay for it. In return, our members agreed to shut down a mine in March of '93, the oldest one, which goes seven miles out under the ocean. Its costs ran over $60 a ton, and there is no way the company could continue to operate. No way!

Disappointments. When you get people's heads screwed on right, when you get them to participate, the first little thing that goes wrong, and somebody rushes to say "I told you we couldn't trust those bastards! I told you they are lying to us, the no-good company sons of bitches!"

We reply, "Look, not everything is smooth in life. They ain't lied to us yet. We triple check, four times check their figures, and they've always been right. When they lie to us, tell us that! But until we catch 'em in a lie, you've got to assume they ain't lying. And, you know, it takes two to dance in this game. If they're doing their part, we've got to do our part."

That's been a big disappointment to me, that attitude on the part of some of our union members who are afraid to provide leadership and make decisions.

Brightest Gain. The company just took our UMW District President along on a business trip to Mexico to sell coal, and just secured a 125,000 ton order for us. And they had never before sold Canadian coal to Mexico! And its the first time Mexico has purchased foreign coal, and it's UMW of A coal! We can now go to three shifts for the rest of this year, where it looked like we were going to have to go to two shifts. Our union President played as big a part in the negotiations as did the company salesman, and the company knows this!

We had a news conference to announce this, and it made all the papers. We said "Here is what can happen when you work together! We can create win-win situations!"

I always say, "We can cooperate without capitulating." Call it climbing into bed, call it sleeping with the enemy, call it anything you want. But if we can gain better contract benefits for the membership, if we can sell coal and increase our economic security, if we can establish a "win-win" situation, aren't we better off doing it together...than fighting a war to accomplish the same goals?!

Part of the cooperative plan is that it has no interference with the standard collective-bargaining procedure. Grievances still continue. Life goes on...but what you now have is people standing up and saying, "Hey, you *don't* have a grievance here!" Or, "Yeah, you *do* have a grievance here: Let's settle it before it goes to arbitration. Let's talk about it." So, from my point of view I can't see any losses here: So far it's been a lot of advantages.

Summary. Union miners can make a difference; 50 cents, 75 cents cost-savings on a ton. *Big* contracts are being won and lost over just 10 cents difference on a ton! If we can continue to take away non-union coal supply contracts, and replace them with UMW of A contracts, we're working together...union *and* company...to produce coal at a cheaper price. That's what we're all about, anyhow, creating a future! The price we've negotiated from Mexico for our Nova coal is $44 a ton. It only costs about $27 a ton to produce it. If we can keep this production price, our Nova company should be able to sell everything it can produce.

Afterword (January, 1992): We've been successful in getting the federal government to give us an extra $10 million. We went to Ottawa and dealt with the Minister of Finance. We're closing one mine. We're downsizing the industry. We can now continue to try to solve problems. And hopefully our efforts will lead to new growth in Nova Scotia's coal industry.

We still have locals that don't want to participate: Whenever they're ready they're in. But if not, that's fine. Whoever is gonna be in, is in. Whoever wants out, is out: That's the way it is...strictly voluntary.

Their contract expires in December, 1992. Hopefully by then we'll have our people economically-educated. They'll understand that the coal market and world market have changed. That coal no longer sells for $100 a ton. Coal now sells for $55, if you get a long term agreement, and the spot market is $30 a ton: It's a different world! It's not the '70's any longer! Those people up there have been isolated, 'cause the government has always paid the check: No matter what the deficit, the government paid the check.

So we've got to be telling them, "You know, five years from now you've got to be in self-sufficiency!" That's the deal from the word "go." Last year they broke even, but breaking even meant they were losing $31 million dollars. That's $31-million in government capital. Any coal company in the United States with $31 million extra in capital could kick anyone's butt! It would be real easy to do. But that $31 million is going to stop soon. By the time it stops we have to have a contract the company can survive with, and one that will lead to the creation of jobs and a future.

Now, our membership is 1800, and it can grow a lot. We have the potential there for new mines. There's the potential there for growth. There's coal seams...there's a market there, two days closer to Europe than the American companies are. There's absolutely no reason that we can't win up there, if we're smart...*both* parties.

Source of the Problem. The company, they've mismanaged a lot of the time. They're used to the old system. At the end of the year they came out and said - "We've broke even. We had a great year!" And we had to have the head of the union go in and say "Hey, explain to these people that breaking even means *losing* $31 million dollars!" "Oh, we can't do that! We told the government we broke even." But we said, "We're telling those people we have to be self-sufficient.

That's not being honest: Be honest with them. Let them know what it is up front."

So they let us tell all the employees what "breaking even" really means. We wrote a letter from our Joint Labor-Management Cooperative Process team, explaining what "breaking even" means. It went up on all the mine bulletin boards, and copies were distributed right there at the mines.

We've now opened up the second phase of our Early Retirement effort. We're getting the last of 230-some retirements out of the way. We've been able to add shifts, and our Bridge Program - where we had 100 jobs still in jeopardy - now may be able to break even at the end of the five-year plan.

We've got to look at ways now to *add* jobs. Our people are ready for it. We can educate 'em. We can do that...by keep pounding home that the economics are reality. It's no longer a fighting thing: It's reality! Cold Economics!

Coal companies...and the union...together...have not tried economics education. That is a major, major mistake for us...for both parties. 'Cause you are competing out there, with everybody in the world. The company's employees and our membership need to know and understand the big picture.

Grassroots Education. We went to each mine recently, and explained where we were at and what we were doing. At each of the three big mines, where we have over 500 people working, only two or three questions were asked. Canadians are the kind of people, if there's something that is bothering them, they'll tell you about it *real* quick! They'll let you know real quick whether they are with you or against you. And when you go to each mine, and you only have three questions, they're with you! Absolutely!

Coal miners are a pretty honest bunch. If they think you're a no-good S.O.B. they're gonna' tell you. Mining in itself is a kinda dangerous profession. And I've always found that people who go into mining shoot pretty straight. Hell, good news or bad news, they're there to stay.

We started Year II, Phase II, in February, '92. And we've learned that we need to get more of the company's major players into the act. We've got a mixed breed of company people. We're going to a two-day summit, with all senior mine managers, all HR people, and all the Safety Reps...to ask - "Where do we go from here?" To revamp and re-look at who needs to be the players? We feel it'll be a very important meeting.

We'll get together and I'll say - "Hey, our people felt that we need more participation from senior management. We're here. Now, are there any issues we need to continue to work on? If so, what are the problem areas? And what do we see as the structure with which to identify these problem areas? Is *this* the structure? Do we incorporate it with the big committee you have had all along?

You guys, make the decision! It's *your* process! If you want us to go away, just say so, and its goodbye joint process! It's your program. You design it. You structure it. 'Cause if you don't participate it doesn't do me any good to do it."

Change Process. We're still bringing our two consultants up, and we've got them doing training. We spend about a week a month up there. We have two days set aside for the joint meetings, and three days of training.

We have the group of 56 broken down to smaller groups of 19 each, and we're training those for three days in "Communications" - how to listen to people, talk to people, deal with people...It's a mixed group of local union officers and rank-and-filers designated by the local; we've got each local union president, and one or two other people.

In the Communications class, for example, we were pretending it was a hockey game we were in (they know hockey *real* well!). One side of the table sat the management team; on the side, the players. We were negotiating for the team, and one of the roles I had was to totally distract the others so they wouldn't work out an agreement. So I got everybody talking, and that produced utter mass chaos!

Then, suddenly, the leader told everyone to sit down and get quiet. He asked - "Does that look like some of the chaotic meetings you have had here?" And then they looked at themselves, and said, "Maybe I should be listening!" In the future, they'll practice *constructive* listening! Even if it never helps the company or the union, they've gotten a new skill to help them in their lives.

Cost Sharing. We use a special section of their General Mining Building to house our meetings (they have corporate headquarters up there you wouldn't believe! In the old days, when they got their bucks from taxpayers, they really went all out!) It meets our needs. As for the consultants, the company's paying their cost entirely. The only cost the UMW of A has to bear is the cost of my expenses.

When you consider what we're getting out of it, if you can get a contract without a strike through this process, and if that $13-million law suit goes away, it's one hell of a return on the International's investment! [The law suit was settled in October, 1992.]

Nose to Nose. As for the left-over militants, you try and talk to them one on one, and hopefully something gets through.

I look at it as... it works for the membership, and it is cheaper for the union to get along. I'm not saying it s easier, 'cause it is *not* easier. It's not an easy process. In fact, a lot of times it's easier to fight, 'cause people understand fighting, 'cause they grew up fighting. If its better for the union and better for the membership...if you get more by doing this...then I'm for it.

You've got to understand coal miners. You have a hard time reinforcing the notion that you do not *have* to fight...the will to fight will *always* be there with the coal miners. If a cooperating company were to put the screws to us tomorrow I'd go back to the people and say "All bets are off." And we'd be back in the militancy business again.

We had one guy, he said we should go out and hang the president of the company. We should do this. And we should do that! And I said, "Brother, that's wonderful. That's wonderful. That's a wonderful idea you've got there. But do you know what they did to the Molly Maquires who had similar ideas? They hung 'em! I've been there! We fought! The UMWA can always fight! But when you do that - when you go to fight - understand what in hell is at stake: Your family is at stake! Your life is at stake! Your union is at stake! If we have to do it, we'll do it. But why do it if we don't have to?! If we can achieve the *same* goal without doing a knockdown fight, *why* do it? Why not solve our problems in a reasonable manner?!"

Importing the Model. Now, we're starting to bring this into the U.S. We've started a Total Quality Management process (TQM), using 3-M as the model, 3-M Corporation. The coal company, Westmoreland Coal, called and asked us to try out this "Get Along" model. We've had 3-M people come in and set up the proper problem-solving mechanisms and ask - "Who *is* your customer?" It's not the guy in the power plant. The customers for a shuttle car operation is another shuttle car operator: We're *all* each others' customers!

The company is a "customer" of the union. And the union is a "customer" of the company. *We* will survive, or *we* will fail...jointly! You have needs...I have different needs...You're a cat and I'm a dog. But there's cold nights coming and we're gonna' have to lay down by the fire together to survive. We can't keep scratching each others' eyeballs out all the time.

We're taking the 3-M TQM, and what I'm doing in Nova Scotia, and blending them together. I'm telling them our people will not listen to TQM. It doesn't make sense. But our people will listen to solving problems before they become major problems. So we're blending them together, and, in southwest Virginia and southern West Virginia where Westmoreland operates, where the Pittston strike was, we're making some progress.

This company has gone from 7,000 down to 4,000, and now, to 800 people in seven locals of ours - it's barely surviving. They're saying - "We're not going to survive under the old way of doing business." They had a choice: Either take the union on and try to bust us. Or work with the union. Senior people there concluded the old ways didn't work - and have opted for the "Get Along" approach...a new way of doing business in the coal industry.

We've now got about four other companies out there talking about doing something with us to create win-win situations. And you put all those together and you've got a pretty good-sized bargaining unit.

To help get the word out we did a teleconference recently, and beamed it to audiences at community colleges throughout southwest and southern Virginia. Retirees, coal miners, company people, and academics heard two hours on our health care crisis and one hour of how labor-management cooperation could help the coal industry and create jobs. Our president, Rich Trumpka, sat alongside the president and the secretary of the Bituminous Coal Mine Owners Association, and they took questions called in by audience members. A first step to a problem-solving process, educating our members that we need to solve our mutual problems if we are to survive.

Overall, I've learned the ideas have to come from the actual participants. The union can be more of a lightening rod, to help promote thinking - "Tell me what the problems are, you company guys!" "Tell me what the problems are, you union guys!" Nine times out of ten they're the *same* problems...and when this is understood, progress can begin solving the problems.

Afterword (July, 1992): If the Canadian politicos would only stay out of it, labor and management could come together...but they keep interfering.

We still have strong union resistance in some areas. Two weeks ago a guy made a motion at a local union meeting to get out of the cooperation program. It passed. But the local union president said "The hell with that! I'm going on with it. This is what is right. This is what is best. This is what I'm going to do." So he got some people up tight and upset with him. But the bottom line is it's coming along okay, and that local remains part of it.

We still have locals staying out, and they've been out just about all along, so we don't force them to participate. The District and International are pretty well committed to trying to work out the problems. They have to be....

The first year of our cooperation program has proven the *best* year in tonnage the company has ever had in its history. We still used $31-million of the Federal Government's money, but we used it for buildings and projects for the future. We're putting in a $14-million pier starting this summer. We paid $10-million toward an unfunded pension liability of $100-million that they'd never been able to put any money into. So, the results of our first year for the company have been great!

I'd say the results for us are even greater. Some people who have 10 years in union office up there tell us this is the first time they've ever seen the District united over anything...and working together. They've made a complete turnaround.

I continue to spend about a week every two months up there. A lot of the folks are still not used to dealing with reality. The new contract we'll negotiate in December will play a big part in whether we'll be self-sufficient three years from now. It will be interesting to see how this all works out.

In May we went through all the mines and had about 85 to 90% support from the workers for what we're doing.

Now, right in the middle of all this, the politicos have decided they want to privatize the mine. A lot of our people feel this is breaking the deal they had with us, when we agreed a year ago to push for self-sufficiency and downsize the workforce. The "big carrot" the Canadian government is offering is "We'd like to sell it to *you*, the miners, rather than to a U.S. corporation that wouldn't care about your jobs and your future."

At this time we have no worker-owned coal mines under contract. This would be the first in the Northern hemisphere for the union. I was once quite opposed to the idea, but time changes things. I'd much prefer the current management stay in charge than some total outsiders coming in.

If an American company came in up there, in about two weeks you'd have about half the people working you have now. You'd have only one of three mines producing, maybe one and a half. You'd be taking that new pier and converting it into a receiving station. You'd be shipping coal up to New Brunswick and throughout the rest of Canada, U.S. coal and U.S. scab coal, or any other kind of coal they can get their hands on. And you'd open Canada up even more to South American coal. (Right now, in New Brunswick, a new plant is becoming the first in Canadian history not to use Canadian coal.)

Our only chance to keep the management we have now is to get even more competitive. We have to get below $40 a ton, and that requires the *cultural* change we're promoting. Everyone up there opposes any loss of government ownership: They feel secure when daddy owns the farm. They like that way of doing business. But unfortunately it may change... and it is our job to bring the change that would have the least harmful effect on our membership.

New cards are being dealt, cards we hadn't expected, at least for three years from now. Back when we met the government in Ottawa I had a conversation with the Finance Minister. He asked if we could privatize. I said only after we get it to self-sufficiency, and I doubted privatization working. I thought we more or less had a deal there, and that was how it was going to be...and I was misled.

So, we're faced with a political reality that the government doesn't want to be in coal mine ownership. Twenty-eight crown corporations have been privatized in the last five years, all but one successfully.

The train is going down the tracks! It's a question of whether we get the right "deal" from this, or get run over: It's one or the other. We've met with the privatization specialists for the government, and will continue to try and influence their thinking away from privatization.

Summary. I fully expect to remain busy, *very* busy. There's always "fun and games" out there for us...'course we're coal miners.

Opponents of our cooperative approach continue to ask "Why are we doing this? It's crazy!" But then when you ask them if they've got a better game plan, if they have a better idea, nobody has an answer.

They have a lotta thoughts on why you shouldn't do it. But they don't have any thoughts on how you achieve the goal of keeping jobs and providing a future if you don't do it.

My advice to other unionists is tell management you trust 'em, but keep one eye open! They're never gonna' fully trust you, so don't you go overboard. As long as you are gaining, as long as you are adding jobs, as long as you are not compromising your own or your organization's beliefs and principles, its fine! The first time they try to get you to compromise your beliefs and principles, get out of it!

And, keep it all separate from the collective-bargaining agreement...so that the membership alone can finally decide when to get militant and over what. It's a thin line here, and there are no easy answers.

Part VI

Twists-and Turns

"...faced by increasingly intense competition, firms are more likely to succeed if they can hire and retain workers who are excited by their chosen vocations, and who are critically minded, able and eager to perceive and develop more efficient means of production...such workers are likely to insist on a greater role in the decision-making within their workplaces as well as a greater stake in the fruits of their creative labor."

John D. Wiseman. "Is There a Significant Future for Workplace Democracy?" In *Worker Empowerment*, edited by John D. Wiseman (New York: Bootstrap, 1991); 22.

"America's biggest handicap is...its inability to generate an environment where the labor force takes a direct interest in raising productivity."

Lester Thurow, *The Zero Sum Solution*; 1985

Writing in 1961 labor "insider" Solomon Barkin explained that American unions sought "to make our private enterprise society function more equitably and humanely, progressing smoothly in a stable pattern of growth, providing employable persons with jobs yielding ever-rising economic returns...They jostle and prod management, and if necessary, the community and government, toward these ends."[1]

Today, over three decades later, progressive locals and unions are continuously involved with management in various campaigns to boost quality and productivity, much as Barkin noted earlier. This time, however, it takes place against a far starker backdrop of unrelenting foreign trade competition, the outsourcing of American jobs, the loss of work to "steel collar" robots, and so on.

When the history is written of labor-management relations in the last quarter of the 20th Century much attention will be owed the effort inside reformers and progressive employers made to leverage the nation's need for productivity on behalf of unprecedented labor-management cooperation. Local unions from coast-to-coast were perplexed by many such efforts, and commonly found it difficult to know when to trust or mistrust top-down clarion calls for redoing the workplace culture.

Four case studies below explore a range of labor experience with trendy total quality control (TQC) and total quality movement (TQM) programs. While most note (partial) success, they are unsparing in documenting undeserved betrayals and unexpected setbacks. Advice is offered on how to turn these painful experiments to everyone's advantage, especially via the give-and-take with which lively locals can help boost productivity.

Taken all in all, the cases underline a paradox labor cannot help management appreciate soon enough: "Worker participation programs that do not challenge management's 'right to manage' will not succeed in achieving what management itself says it wants - a more productive and efficient work-place producing better quality products and services."[2]

References

[1] Solomon Barkin. *The Decline of the Labor Movement and What Can Be Done About It* (Santa Barbara, CA: Center for the Study of Democratic Institutions, 1961), 69.

[2] Jack Metzgar. "'Employee Involvement' Plans and the Philosophy of Labor." *Dissent* (Winter, 1992), 72.

TQC's Vulnerabilities
Daniel Bailey
(URW)

This case study is remarkable in five valuable ways: It highlights the fragility of locals to unpredictable changes in management culture. It details what it takes to secure effective labor-management cooperation. It explains how a local can go from a cooperative to a conflict mode almost overnight, provided its leadership is agile, creative, and resilient. It details what it takes to operate an "inside strike" campaign. And it relates the toll it takes on a reformer who winds up key strategist in a hellish situation not of the local's making or liking.

A careful reading of this case, the longest account in the entire volume, should help answer such questions as -

What difference to a local, if any, does it make to confront Japanese multinational management?

How can a leader win a fair trial for cooperation from a rank-and-file accustomed to an adversarial relationship?

How can this same change-agent check an effort by management to replace strikers with a permanent "scab" labor force?

Can a leader remain effective if his key policy recommendation is rejected by the rank-and-file, and he is required to take a course he opposes?

Can a divided rank-and-file mount a successful "inside strike" campaign?

Above all, this case underlines the versatility required of change-agents who find they cannot rely on management for a long-term commitment to labor-management cooperation...a vulnerability as costly as any on the work scene today.

To help set the scene, I ask you to imagine that your employer, the Bridgestone Tire Company, has just managed to gratuitously insult 1,100 of your local's members, or every last one of them, and has then stiff-armed your every attempt to bring the firm to its senses before the whole crazy situation turned ugly, like real ugly.

Now add to this the fact that your employer is a Tokyo-based Japanese international firm, Japan's largest tiremaker. Your rank-and-filers are mostly proud Tennessee country folk. And the insult involves the installation at your tire manufacturing plant of a row of six spankling new flag poles and flags - every one you might expect (the flags of Tennessee and of five countries in which the Japanese firm proudly does business), every flag, that is, except Old Glory, and all of this done in preparation for a major impending visit by overseas Japanese executives.

Daniel A. Bailey, president at the time of Local 1055, United Rubber Workers (URW), was astonished to find himself smack in the middle of this "Grade B" movie scenario one fine day in April, 1988. To be sure, Old Glory flew high on a pole around another side of the tire plant, but it was conspicuous by its absence from the new row of "Friends of Bridgestone" flags.

Almost immediately after workmen had finished the installation and hoisted the flags aloft, word spread like wildfire in the plant that another "sorta Pearl Harbor" had struck again. A workforce of "down home" hard-working types, strong in a high proportion of Vietnam, Korean, and WW II veterans, seethed with outrage over the absence in the row of six of their American flag...and the conspicuous presence of the flag of the Rising Sun.

Up until this point very little animus had surfaced toward the new foreign owners. Most rank-and-filers were actually grateful the previous "union-busting" owner, Firestone Company, was finally off the scene (especially after a bitter four-month strike in late 1979). And many had come - after some initial apprehensiveness - to admire the upbeat approach of the "deep pocket" Japanese owner. Outmoded equipment had been replaced by state-of-the-art machinery. Ergonomics had been used to make jobs less arduous and safer. New product lines had been brought in, and a new building had gone up, with 500 additional jobs coming along with it.

Best of all, the new owner had apparently resolved long before purchasing the embattled Firestone plant to earn an entirely new and far more cordial relationship with the plant's five-year old URW local. Since the previous contract between Firestone and the local had required the local's consent to the new buyer, this resolve made perfectly good sense, at least for openers: Bridgestone, however, much to the local's relief, had persisted in doing its part to deserve good union-management relations.

Until, that is, the six flags - minus Old Glory - appeared, and certain American managers in fairly high places in the Bridgestone hierarchy shrugged off local president Dan Bailey's urgent warning that a serious mistake had been made, one that could be easily rectified, but not if it lingered beyond a day or two.

Leaving the plant at the end of an utterly frustrating day, one which began with the startling appearance of the flags, and seemed likely to close without any cooperative response, Dan was urged by a fellow officer to "don't just do nothing; do something, damn it!" After his co-worker finished Dan strode across the plant's lawn and took down the Japanese flag. Careful to fold it as respectfully as he knew how, he placed it in his pickup truck and drove off to the union hall to await a phone call he knew would come next.

A furious and utterly perplexed Bridgestone executive soon rang to ask why in hell Dan had "stolen" company property, and, in the process, gratuitously insulted the firm's Japanese owners. Utterly calm and in complete command of the situation, Dan reminded the caller that the local had sought unsuccessfully all day to get plant management to pay it attention, to take seriously the local's insistence that the six flag problem be negotiated: "Well, by God, I just had to do something to get you guys to realize what a mess you had gotten into - so I took your flag. You can have it back when you agree to talk!"

Which they immediately did. A meeting was held the next day in which they agreed to put up a new pole for Old Glory higher than the rest. The pole was up two days after that meeting. A proud Rising Sun flag flew below on its one-of-six flagpoles, and a sense of symbol appropriateness would seem to have been restored.

In the manufacturing plant itself, however, where it really counts, a zillion small American flags of the toothpick-size variety suddenly appeared the day of the plant tour by visiting Japanese executives, stuck everywhere, hither and yon, silent testament to how deep the wound of Old Glory's previous omission had cut. . . a wound the local union had sought to help mend from the first, only to find plant management too callous to take notice. So slighted, the local's president stole a flag to gain a flag. . . in everyone's best interest.

Coming Closer to Date. More recently (July 1991) at my request, Dan Bailey updated the entire Bridgestone - Local 1055 story:

Shortly after we came to terms about the flags a new manager of the plant decided to implement some stringent policies. It soon came to a point where we geared up for an overtime boycott and a work-to-rule campaign. We had it set together, and everybody went and took their name off of the "available-for-overtime" list. The plant virtually became useless without overtime. We put out publicity about "management-by-intimidation," and set a deadline to arbitrate a list of our complaints. We'd already been through talking about it with several people in management.

Well, it basically came down to a meeting that went well into the night, a meeting between me and the director of management function who was over this plant manager (and several others in similar plants). They backed off, and we resolved every item on our list. So we called off our overtime boycott, and got into some *good* talks with the top man about our philosophy.

He wanted a commitment that we would jointly administer some programs to his supervisors and our stewards to help break down barriers between us. I said "Sure, I've never been opposed to that." And he said "Now you know, anytime you venture into that you always catch some political heat." And I told him, "You know, I ain't never been worried too much about political heat. If I think its right I feel like I can explain to most people who want to listen why we have everything to gain and nothing to lose from this situation."

Working Better-Together. We've been progressing ever since into the matter. We've had supervisor-steward joint training administered by a staffer from the Tennessee Learning Center, and people come out feeling like at least they've gotten a lot off of their chest. They understand the other side better, and you can see its overall effect on the climate at work.

They used to have supervisors' conferences every so often where they went over things that were strictly for supervisors. Now, union stewards are invited to go. And things that were strictly for managerial people only, now I'm invited to go. And I'm sitting in there, and they're going over cost figures and things I'd never be privy to before.

We've also got them to install five TV monitors in the cafeteria and at all the employee entrances, monitors that can continuously feed new information to our people about the rubber industry, this plant, worker issues, and news of doings of our local.

As well, we've gotten them to go back to holding crew meetings once a month. But we have laid down some new ground rules: Number one is that only one-third of the meeting can be used for the foreman talking to the employees; two-thirds is for whatever *they* want to talk about, whatever. The second rule is that notes will be taken. And the third rule is that as part of the foreman's time at the next meeting he must go over the notes and explain what has or has not been done, and why.

Finally, we've got a rule that the plant manager will make six of these meetings a month; the section manager will make all in his section - so that employees will have some access to some higher-level management. And I try to make as many of them as I can to so as to hear any bitches and see how management reacts to them. It seems to really be helping!

Doing a Better Preventive Health "Job." Naturally, this has led to a lot of new activities by our Bridgestone local.

We've begun a health screening program which has medical people come to our site and man an outfitted bus facility. Employees go through it and get a thorough health exam at no cost. We've been doing it now six or seven years, and each year we get more participation. This year in negotiations we got the company to agree to let our people go through on worktime; whereas in the past you had to go on your own hours. We wanted to assess doing it the new way.

We continually talk to the company about the benefits to them of having a healthy workforce, in terms of their longterm health policy, because if you can early detect something it is better all around. Over the years there have been several cancers found that people did not even know they had, problems they were able to get fixed and are still productive workers. Some of the guys, like last year, even learn they have a cancer from which they are going to die...a cancer they did not know about prior to going through the van.

So, the company said they would try out our idea if we would work with them. We understand the logistical problems of freeing people up, especially in an operation like ours. We scheduled one guy from one section first, and the next guy, from another section, so that no section was hurt production-wise. And so far, it has gone excellent.

While most of the rubber tire companies have some form of health inspection we are the only one so far that has gotten the company to agree to doing it on the clock at the work site.

This year we anticipate will be our best year, since you can go and get your health exam right there at work, you can do it right there while you are there. Last year we got 65 percent participation; this year I expect many more...though there are always some who do not want to know. We run a full-fledged campaign encouraging participation in our 15/20 minute exam, but some people will always avoid it.

The exam is pretty thorough. You fill out a questionnaire prior to going, and there is a hemotape type of test you do at home and bring it in. When you go into the van they measure your height, your weight, and your blood pressure. They take blood from you, and send it off to be analyzed. We do AIDS testing, and this year for the first time we also did sickle cell anemia testing (about 22 percent of our workforce is non-white). We have an eye test (you know, glaucoma), a hearing test, a body-fat ratio test, a grip-strength test, a pulmonary function test, a chest x-ray...it's all pretty efficient!

We contract with a local outside firm that specializes in curbside health testing for facilities like ours. Management is not told any results: The medical records are confidential and are not sent to us or to management. The only thing we get to know are percents of this problem or that one, like 10 percent of your workforce has high blood pressure or something like that. The data take into account our average age, and different things like that...and we track our health problems over time this year.

Rubber workers are *very* susceptible to cancer. There are several different chemicals that are used in the process, and traditionally rubber workers have had a high incidence of all types of cancer, brain cancer, especially. We're just trying to head some of that off. Our costs here are covered by a joint occupational health and safety fund that we've designated to get two cents an hour for every hour we work.

The lady, by the way, who runs the testing firm, she drove up recently to our local union hall in a Saab. And we made it quite plain to her that if she wanted to continue to work with us she would have to find another means of transportation...an American-made means! So, we're filtering some union principles off into her. Where our own members are concerned, we don't do anything to them if they buy foreign. But we point out what they are doing to hurt themselves, and we just continually try to educate them to "buy American."

Showing the Flag! Where unionism is concerned I'm trying to improve our image in the South. We've embarked on two programs here fairly recently that are kind of moving us in that direction.

One is the Adopt-a-Highway Program, which you may have seen in several states. We've adopted a two-mile heavily-traveled stretch of road in a busy section of a little community near the plant. And we promise to keep that road clean, and they've put signs on it that say "Rubber Workers Local 1055 has adopted this road."

It hasn't cost us nothing other than some time and manpower. And I've had pretty good responses from the membership on days that we decide to go out and pick up trash. It's a lot of work, especially in the summertime...but later we go back to the hall, more than ten of us, and have some beers together.

We've also gotten into what we call an "Adopt-a-Family" Program. Each year we adopt two families in the area that are truly needy (we work through several agencies to determine that, including the police department). We also want families with young children. And every family we've adopted so far has been headed by a single mother. None, however, are plant employees or related to us in anyway: They're just people in the community...some black, some white.

We've allocated $2,000 per family per year. You go and talk to them, and you kind of get to know them. Once we decide to adopt them we explain what we're doing and find out what their immediate needs are...like paying their electric bills for one or two months, or buying school clothing. In one case a little boy wanted to play Little League baseball, and his mother didn't have money for the registration fee. So we got him into the Little League baseball program. In another case we had our guys find and fix up a car that was reasonably priced, and a lady was able to use it to take a job and get out of poverty.

We ask our members, when they are cleaning out the closet, to bring clothes and food to us and we'll get it to these families...who are always shocked when we show up to help. They ask "What can we do to repay you?" And my standard response to them is "When you or your kids go into the workforce, just remember that *union* is not a bad word. That we are *good* people. That's all we ask."

Especially in the South we're still seen as a bunch of communists. A bunch of thugs. We're this; we're that. I'm just trying to let it be known that "Hey, we're just workin' people. We're no different from you."

Telling Management How It Is. All in all, we're making pretty steady progress. And we're even making a good impression on our Japanese owners, who actually still learn a thing or two from us. I've been over there twice now in 1983 and '87, and I know we've got to share with one another.

Every three to six months we get Japanese visitors. Mr. Yeiri, the functioning chief officer of the entire worldwide operation, has visited a few times, and I've talked to him on several occasions. His English is pretty good and I find him a real nice man. I've found we can talk rationally with each other, and he asks to talk with me on his plant visits. He's pretty up in age, but he's real sharp, *real* sharp.

I had an opportunity to go to Australia last summer (1990) to the Bridgestone Corporation worldwide TQC Deming Presentation. The Company's award ceremony has only gone out of Japan twice, I think, since it was set up. The first time it went overseas it was held in Tennessee. And the second time, this time, was in Australia. It was pretty interesting: I got to tour the Bridgestone plants there and meet with some of the Aussie labor leaders. On the last night the company president arrived and they held a big party to end the entire affair.

Mr. Yeiri had remained in the back of the ballroom the whole evening while different speakers from management had gotten up to say this or that. The Aussies had not planned for me to speak. Mr. Yeiri requested that I speak. When I was introduced he got up and walked to the podium, and stood there to better hear what I had to say. He knew a lot of the management stuff had been bullshit, while I emphasized that when management truly listened to working people it empowered them to change their work environment.

I explained that the presentations we had been listening to for some days now from Bridgestone plants all over the world illustrated this idea: They were excellent ideas for joint and cooperative projects that workers had come up, ideas that management had been willing to listen to, and had not just cast aside. I urged management to understand that progress here required that it look at *itself*, and set its own house in order, a task that required managers to learn the ancient art of deep listening - much like my country neighbors practiced in Tennessee.

Like Mary Walton says in her book on the Deming Method, a book I've really learned a lot from, history has shown that if management is left to run things by itself it always screws it up! Management is just too important to be left to the managers alone...and that's a *fact*!

Afterward (July '92). I've personally always believed that workers do want more of a say so in their work lives and do want to exercise their minds as well as their muscles. So we went a long way in cooperating with the company. But when I asked - "If we're really 'partners,' will you put some guarantee of jobs in our contract?" - I learned we saw things quite differently.

In 1989 Bridgestone purchased the *entire* Firestone Company. Up until that point we had been the only production plant they had owned in the U.S.A. They got into a bidding war with Pirilli Tires, and paid much too much (about $2.6 billion!), and even they recognized the price was too high. Firestone was in worse shape than they had realized, and this played into a major rift that existed then at the top of

Bridgestone. A lot of the top executives who we knew are now gone, and the attitude of Bridgestone has since changed drastically away from the old days of trying to get along.

At first, right after they bought the Firestone company, we cooperated fully. Other Firestone locals of the URW came to our plant and we explained our approach, and tried to help them get beyond the militancy they were used to aiming at Firestone and try a new approach with Bridgestone. Everybody wanted to explore developing the "partnership" we thought Bridgestone was committed to.

In April '91 the Firestone locals, negotiating as a chain, settled a contract which established the pattern agreement. Our local was not a part of this chain, so we waited next in line to negotiate. A new group of Japanese executives took charge, however, one with seemingly no grasp of our "partnership" concept. They seemed very much like a traditional American managerial group: They focused only on the bottom line and ignored their employees.

We expected at least the terms of the pattern when it came time for us to negotiate a contract. But by the deadline the pattern was not on the table. So we struck, and as soon as we went out the company sent letters to our membership saying what the last offer was on the table and urging them to contact us and tell us that they wished to ratify to this agreement.

Going to a War Footing. We held a meeting two days after we went out, and the membership told us they weren't interested in ratification at all! When the company heard this they got totally pissed off! They brought in Vance Security, a company used in the Pittston Coal miners' strikes, Caterpillar, and the like. Through channels we found out they were lining up replacement workers to come in and take our jobs.

Soon it was like a war zone. They put tractor trailers all around the plant with loaded bales of hay, as if we were going to shoot them out. We worked our asses off, however, to make sure *nothing* happened, nothing violent at all.

We met with the Police Chief right at the very beginning. I gave him my car and my beeper number, and I told him, "Look, you call me *anytime* of day or night if there are *any* problems!" (He happened to be an ex-Teamster.) And as we were leaving he said "I really appreciate you guys coming by. Because nobody from the company has called and asked me for nuthin'." I said "Well, I want you to know what's fixing to happen, what our intentions are, and all that kinda stuff."

The police were very cooperative during the strike. And later the press called and asked the Chief about us - I guess trying to dig up something - and he said "They've been a very peaceful and orderly group." He was *very* pleased...and that all looked good for us.

Bitter Ashes. What a great "partnership!" We have a little dispute, and the company moves to settle it with a "World War!" They seemed to have thought they could go around us, and use the employee-involvement groups to have direct relationships with our members. But at the same time we had improved *our* direct relationships, in part by using some of the productivity "classes" we had put on as our part of the "partnership." So their effort to go around us didn't work.

What I've learned from this is that a "partnership" between labor and management is only as good as either you can get it in contract language or you can get it through legislation. Without either one you might build a good relationship, and you may have a willing management, and it may work for awhile. But it is only as good as *that* group of management lasts...or at least as long as that attitude lasts, one or the other. Its on very fragile grounds. Without language or legislation unions are definitely left in a vulnerable position in this whole thing.

Outfoxing the Company. As the strike dragged on I could see what was getting ready to happen. The company made an announcement and sent me a letter saying they had withdrawn everything, their entire last offer, off the table.

We went to our attorney the next day and discussed the situation with him. We learned if we made an unconditional offer to return we would now confront a "clean table," rather than one cluttered with their last offer. Our old contract would still apply, we could return under its terms, and we could start negotiations all over again...as well as show a gesture of good faith by returning to our jobs.

I called an emergency meeting of my committee together at our lawyer's office that very afternoon. They had no idea of any of this until they got to his office. I didn't want them to, because we had to move quickly. If the company caught wind of what we were up to I know they would have put something impossible on the table: They would have blocked our ability to reclaim our jobs by returning to work. Ours was a countermove I don't think they ever expected of us!

We got the Bargaining Committee together and explained the situation to them. They were all in agreement: "We've got to do this!" We typed a letter right there, and my vice-president and I drove to the home of the Human Resources Manager and hand-delivered it to him. He was shocked!

The night that we delivered the unconditional offer to return we *did not* have a ratified agreement. We were simply terminating our strike with no agreement in effect or no "last offer" on the table. This allowed us to return to our jobs under the terms of the old contract, with the exception being the "no-strike" clause, arbitration procedure, and the dues check-off provisions.

Two days later the company agreed to extend all terms of the old contract for a one-month period while we negotiated. Upon returning to negotiations, the company took an unbending stand on a few issues that I think they thought would cause us to go back out on strike. However, when we took it to memberships we gave them a 3rd option on the ballot. It was to accept the contract "under protest." Which meant that they were not satisfied with the company's position on three issues, two of which were newly added proposals that the company put on the table after the strike. The vast majority of membership ratified the contract "under protest."

The message sent by this vote was not only to the company, but also to the union leadership. The message to us was that we were not to make life easy on this company and we were not to cooperate with them in any way. It was after this vote that I called the Human Resources manager and told him that he had a ratified agreement, but that he had a bunch of pissed-off people coming in there because they had ratified it "under protest!" Bottom line is we got back in there ahead of the scabs they were preparing to recruit to replace us.

Impact of Events. The strike bonded our people as a whole together. Prior to it we had about 600 or so who had been there back when our local was organized and we went through bitter strikes back in '79. We also had another 600 or so with less than five years' seniority who had not been through those battles. It was almost like we needed an initiation into an elite group, because the older workers boasted we were the founders, we were this and that, you know...and this boasting always kinda kept a division there.

This strike showed the grit of the younger employees and was a 'wake up call' for a lot of them as to what a union really is. And how what you have to do you have to do in numbers! You can't just go out and buy everything on credit cards and not think about the next contract negotiation coming up: You must be prepared for it! Don't always assume that the company and union are going always to work the problems out. I think for the younger group they absolutely learned a lesson: As a whole they did *very* well! It's almost like they wanted to prove themselves.

Three of the younger people did cross: They didn't at first, but eventually they did. But as a group, they held, and they held tight.

I learned early into our strike that many of the younger workers, and some of the older ones too, were not financially as prepared as they should have been to take on this company long and hard. I don't think they ever thought we were going to get into this position. We had been trying to educate them through our newsletters and stuff a year or so prior to negotiations, reminding them the contract was coming up, and urging them to "Save your money! Save your money!"

But what I was seeing there, after a couple of weeks of striking, was that they were holding tough, but they were getting *very* edgy, very, very nervous. I had one of my members come into the office, and be all macho and talk how "I'll hold out 'till Hell freezes over!," and this, that, and the other. And that night, maybe his wife would come in and be crying, because, you know, she was worried. So I knew somewhere something was going to give.

From Bad to Worse. With the end of our 17-day strike and our sudden return to work we went back to the negotiation table.

I soon learned why the company had cleaned the table when they submitted a totally new off-the-wall contract. It was much like - "Here it is; take it or leave it! You *will* have Employee Committees!" Well, there was no way in hell we could recommend acceptance of this to our membership.

As well, the company demanded a 12-hour seven-day work schedule. The one we had been on was what is called a six and two-thirds work schedule, with only one eight-hour down shift in the week (and that was between 8 and 4 PM on Sunday). We only worked 8-hour days five days a week, but they wanted a seven-day schedule with all hours of the day covered, in 12-hour shifts. What was so weird about this was that they had *never* brought up work schedules ever, in the earlier negotiations, in all the labor-management task force meetings we had had: They had never said work schedules were a problem, never once!

In fact, during the normal set of negotiations before we struck *we* had a work schedule proposal on the table, which we knew we wouldn't get, but it was one of those things the membership wanted brought forward...and the company consistently said throughout negotiations that our current work schedules met all needs, and the company had *no* interest in changing it...so we eventually withdrew our proposal.

But after a 17-day strike the company came in saying this was now priority #1, a 12-hour work schedule. We said, "Now wait a minute, seventeen days ago it wasn't!" But they would not move away from this.

Plus, the company resubmitted proposals that we had already signed off on, tentatively agreeing to them earlier. We had to re-negotiate them back off the table. And they called that "movement" on their part!

It was almost like they had gone to a union-busting seminar, or a class on "How to Force a Union into a Strike-busting Situation." They did everything by the book. I think they honestly thought we'd go back out on strike, and then they would hire striker replacements...who would never question or second-guess the company about anything.

Cutting Our Losses. As we were about a week or so away from the deadline we had set for reaching a new contract when we had ended our strike it was clear we were just battling about everything. I told my committee, "Look guys, its obvious their mindset is that they're going to hold onto this stuff and force our hand. So, let's take the cards that's been dealt us and see what we can do with those."

We watered down a lot of the worse shit that was on the table, and got it somewhat more acceptable. We got the right to vote on which 12-hour, seven-day schedule the members could go to, and those kind of things. Overall, we increased our pension from $23.50 times number of years service to $30 times number of years service, and we got some other good benefits...but we couldn't budge the company on its 12-

hour day demand. We tried to explain our work building tires is too physical for such a day, but they were deaf to us.

We got to the deadline, and as I figured, the company didn't budge on nothing, other than those things they had previously agreed to. We took it all to the membership.

Hard Choices. I reminded everybody that in 1979 one of the big issues we had struck for was the work schedule. We wanted to replace our seven-day 12-hour schedule with a six and two-thirds one. I told them if it was worth striking three months in 1979 for a work schedule it was worth striking again for it at least that long in 1992.

My personal opinion was we should turn this contract down and go back out on strike. But I wanted them to be aware what the company was planning to do: They were planning on bringing in permanent replacements. And we were not going to be able to be nice out there anymore. It was going to be a war, but I thought it was a war we ought to take on!

I wrestled like hell with this decision, as I knew that, intelligently thinking, that with the way things are nowadays, with a war out there on the picket line, we would be playing right into the company's hands.

It was a personal thing with me: That if we say we agree, that we ratify this agreement, and we agree to go in there and sell our labor, that we should give them 100% of our labor. We should not in any way cut them anything! If we don't, then we strike! I told them this was strictly a personal thing. My wife and I had saved our money, and I could have held out. I said "You've got to make *your* decision, but I think we should strike."

I then explained we had another option. I said I know you all have read articles about it, and about the Caterpillar situation: They're taking their company on from within. That option's out there, and you can vote on it.

The ballot gave the membership a choice between going out on strike again, accepting the company's terms, or accepting the terms under protest. 34% out of 1,100 voters said go back out on strike; 59% said "under protest, and fight it inside;" and 7% said "no problem." That's like 93% of the workforce is saying in one form or another, "Screw you, company!"

Inside Protest. That's the mode we're in right now. We're back. But we're refusing to give the company anything extra. We no longer participate in Employee Involvement Groups. We wear buttons that say "Working under Protest." We're having T-shirts being made up that say as much, and we're patrolling production in there...to try and get them to compromise.

One of the things they have now is you have to come in 15-minutes early to attend meetings of your crew (so you actually work a 12-hour and 15-minute tour). So we go in and just sit and not say a word. Or one day we'll go in and everybody will just raise hell. Its just playing mind games, and they're playing them with us. Its pitiful, that they're trying to operate this way.

Every time we meet with the company, regardless of what the issue, as when we're processing a grievance, we insist we cannot talk immediately to the issue: We must *first* work on raising morale. Only then can we legitimately turn to other problems...but we must address morale first. And to do that, we've got to negotiate the five issues that we went out on strike over. So, as a general thing, every time we meet, we ask what's your position *today* on our five items? Its an unrelenting thing that we always bring up, every chance we get.

Shutdown Risk. I've had stewards meetings and membership meetings since we began to work under protest, and I've warned everyone the company may just decide to get back at us by shutting our plant down. I wouldn't be surprised if eventually we get a distressed plant closure notification: They've got to give us a six-month notice and all of that bullshit. This statement I made at the ratification meeting when it was ratified under protest, not in a steward meeting.

This is where my membership will either mean what they said, or they didn't: The message they sent was "Take them on!" That means if we went on strike we'd be exerting economic pressure on them to try and bring them to a compromise. To me, that's exactly what we are doing now. We're "striking" inside, to try and put economic pressure on them to compromise.

Product Protection. Productivity is low. While defects have gone up, that is not due to a policy of ours. I've stated in every meeting we've had since going back is that defects is one thing I am *not* encouraging! I do not want sabotage or bad quality going out. We do not want to effect other people, like a truck driver driving on one of our tires. I said "Let's not put ahellova lot out, but let's put good things out. Because that does go into the public."

I've had arguments with my membership about this. Some say, "Now, hell, fuck 'em!" "No," I've said, "you sabotage a piece of equipment and you have hurt one of your brothers who didn't know the equipment had been sabotaged."

Maybe I'm wrong. Maybe we ought to hit them from every angle we can...and quality is obviously a good one. We're recognized for quality. We've won again, for the seventh time in a row, the best retreadable truck tire in the States, our plant produces it. But I think the economic pressure of not getting the production that they need, hopefully, will be enough. That way we haven't tarnished our name with the public so that if the company does come around, we've lost so much ground that a shutdown will follow.

Surrender Risk. I explain to my people that management is coming down on them so hard and picking on them for every little nit-picky thing because they're trying to scare them and frighten them into going back to operating normally. I say "You should expect that. If they can intimidate and hammer you, and you go back to operating normally, just to get them off of your ass, who then has won here?! *They've* won! It's worked for them."

Union Strategy. I've told them if we are going to win, the battle is now going to be a longer battle. And the two key words will be *persistence* and *consistency.* We have got to be persistent and we have got to be consistent in what we do: We have to *never* let up! We've got to set our plan out: This is what we're going to do. This is how we're going to do it. And, *never* let up...if we are going to win.

They're going to try to scare us. Right now management is in its intimidation mode. They're watching everybody *real* closely. Any slight crossing of the line, you know, and they want to call you up, and discipline you, and the membership is pissed off as hell with this.

I tell management, "Look, you should expect that. You've got 1,200 pissed-off people in their plant." And I tell my members the thing I'm afraid of with this in-plant protest is you'll be gung-ho like hell for about a month, and then you'll let it peter out. And you'll go back to normal...and that is just what the company is counting on.

I explain that what we've got to do is outlast them. This is where the persistency comes in. We're going to have to know where we are within our rights. We're going to have to walk the edge. And we're going to have to *stay* on the edge: You can't let up.

What I'm hoping it will come to is some corporate leader will say, "Look guys, we're not scaring them back into work. So now, what are we gonna do? Its obvious they're in it for the long run. So what are we gonna do?"

Impact on the Local. There is more "unionism" going on now. We're putting out a lot of consistent literature. We've got our "Working Under Protest" buttons out in the plant. We'll probably follow them up with some black armbands: That's one thing the Japanese unions do - they show protest that way. Our union flag that was flying outside the plant in the row of six flags: We've taken it down so there is an empty flag pole. Almost anyway we can show forms of protest we use, almost anyway at all.

Impact on the International. Early in July of '92 we joined all the other locals of the Bridgestone chain, our old Firestone system, in a meeting with corporate management. Our international president was there. The local leaders had been hearing bits and pieces of our problem, so I filled them in on what had really happened. Our District Director also spoke, which helped, because our union president had initially been getting his information from the Bridgestone management and believing it.

When our President finally realized from his own guy - the District Director - that he was getting bullshit from the company, and what Dan was telling him was correct, he finally came around (I had not supported his recent candidacy, but had backed the incumbent, whom he defeated). When he got clear on the matter I started to get the support from the international I needed.

Some of the other ex-Firestone locals had been around sometime, and had previously had traditional adversarial relations. They were now actually commenting on how well things were going at their plants. They had not previously seen such good relationships. Things were getting done that needed to be done.

These local presidents told the Bridgestone managers point blank that "We used to scorn him [pointing at me] back in the early 1980s, when you guys first brought the Firestone plant in Tennessee, and were the only foreign-owned plant at that time." [I was going to meetings at that time and getting up and pointing to labor - management participation, and advocating that employee participation was not bad: You need to go in there, and try to control it, and try to get the benefits for your members, 'cause they *do* want a sayso in their destiny and what happens in their surrounding.]

The local presidents said "We used to argue a lot about this with him. And he used to stand up and always tell us we were wrong. And he would stand up and promote the approach of this company. So, for you guys to do this to *him*, it was him that was a major reason that we came around to helping and promoting the Employee Participation Program. If you're gonna stick that knife in *his* back, we'll tell you right now what we are gonna tell our membership when we go back."

They really drove the point home! This was not me telling it to the Bridgestone executives, but the presidents of other locals. The company people just sat there - and it seems like every time they opened their mouth to justify or rationalize anything they did in our situation, they just seemed to get in deeper.

It felt good to be in that room, 'cause all of us local presidents, we just fed off of each other. It was almost like every time the company tried to throw a punch, they were hit with seven solid shots on the chin...bam, bam, bam! We just beat up on them...though I don't think right now it has changed anything.

Impact on the Industry. Even the industry's trade magazine, *The Rubber and Plastics News* when we made our unconditional offer to return, they entitled their editorial on the subject "Cooperation." They basically said to Bridgestone management, "Look, if there was ever some seeds with which to build a good relationship, the local has made the first move!"

That is what we tried to tell them in negotiations: "Look, we've had a little rainy period for the last couple of weeks. But sometimes - and this is a Japanese saying - sometimes after the rain the ground gets harder. So let's springboard off of this situation, and let it enable us to move to another plateau of labor-management relations."

But the company's feelings were hurt, and this and that. In effect, they've lost face. The group that is now in charge believes the strike was strictly my call, not me following the wishes of my membership. They laid it straight on me. They can't believe I've had the *nerve* to strike them: We are the *first* local in the entire tire industry to take on a

Japanese company. Naturally, I've faxed letters to my contacts in the Japanese management. But the connections I had with them are no longer in any way controlling the situation.

So, to me, our partnership wasn't worth shit! When we had our first real problem one side just totally abandoned its principles.

Impact on the Inside Reformer. In a lot of ways our inside protest makes my job easy as hell! It was much tougher trying to explain and educate the membership as to why we needed to go in new directions, why we needed to work with the company and try and make their business operate better, and things like that. Now its just whatever the company says, I say the opposite. But it doesn't fit my grain.

Second Afterward: (February, 1993). We don't use the language "inside strike;" we call it a "protest." Very few people accept overtime and nobody puts out any extra effort, even though the company needs the overtime.

Its not really going as strong, however, as I wish with our transition of local officers which is going to take a little while to work out. We're going to try to be patient with them. But I think the people are getting to the point where they are pissed off. And they want the company to know they are pissed off. It's almost like "Well, we've got to live with it: So let's make the most of it... Make the best of it... Go about our business."

We have no shopfloor officers active now at all. We would normally elect 60 of them at this time, but not during this transition period.

Our plants are operating well; we're putting tires out. But not exactly what they'd like us to be putting out. And as time goes by people stay in touch with what went on, what caused us to strike in the first place. We have a lot of T-shirts, several basic types, one of which a lot of guys wear on a daily basis: It shows a mad dog giving the company the finger, and it says "Don't get the little fella mad!" We got another that uses the Ghostbuster emblem, and a third one alluding to Pearl Harbor with which I don't particularly agree. These are all to help the people remember what it is all about. The local is not issuing these T-shirts, or anything like that: It is a personal project of some of the guys...who resent working in "Firestone's prison."

When I was hired into the plant back in the '70s the company said "We're the boss; you're the worker," and "workers are all just a bunch of animals." It seems like we had gotten to be equals and we had anticipated things getting even better. But now we're back where we began in the '70's. You wouldn't think this could happen.

I wrote to the old man who ran Bridgeton at the takeover time. But he is no longer in control as he had once been, and is actually getting out. Its strange. The Japanese individuals calling the shots now, they don't make any bones about it: They say they don't give a shit about participation or equality. "We're strictly bottom-line guys."

And it shows in our operation. It filters all the way down to shopfloor level.

The first time I met the guy who took over from the old man I got the sense he was totally different. Now we're working in a totally different environment.

Some of the managers will tell us privately how bad they feel about what has happened, and how much they miss the time when were getting along. They tell me how much they admire that I stood up and tried to change things, tried to get us going in a better direction. They're dazed, and like me, a lot of them can't believe what has happened.

It's not only what has happened in the workplace, but also what has happened in the local. When I was promoting union-management cooperation I was bucking my International President. I did not support him; I backed the Secretary-Treasurer who ran against him. It was a strange circumstance, as I've known the president for years. He's an honest guy, and I like him, and he did a good job of organizing his campaign. He did as well as you can during our concessionary bargaining, as tough a job as you can ask for.

People got up at our recent Convention and said he was as the same good leader he had been in '81 and '87. I got up and said what was different now was how much more ambitious he had become! So I was on his shitlist from the git-go at the Convention. He's real smooth, and you get the impression he agrees with you, but you do not where he will wind up.

When it came down to our contract negotiations the International sent someone in to run our contract talks. This person had never been in tire contract talks before and we'd never seen him before. It was his first time! He was pretty much lost. And when it came down to crunch time, the International President met privately with Bridgeton executives to cut a deal.

I tried to get the International President to understand that if we didn't take a strong stand, right there and right them, the industry would run all over us. But he didn't want anything to run the show, and didn't want to put pressure on Bridgeton to change directions. He wanted us to accept the same master agreement he was getting for everyone.

Now, only now, other locals are realizing what a tough time the former Firestone plants are going to have...since they didn't back our strike, and this company is going for all it can get.

After we went back in I decided to run for re-election. But I really didn't campaign. It was a mixture of things. I certainly felt burned-out.

Since losing office I've felt better than I felt in a long time. People knew I had tried to go in and not be head-basher, tried to work things out. But the company had abandoned that approach. The company was now being run by a bunch of assholes. So my approach no longer fit...and my opposition looked liked they would argue with the company just for the sake of arguing.

My opposition had bird-dogged my administration from the start. If I said it was daylight, they said it was night. They won big, by two to one...led by the guy who had been past president. We had run against each other often, and it had always been very close, a difference of only 20 or so votes out of about 800 votes in our 1,300-member local. I was Secretary and he was President back in the adversary days with Firestone; people called us "Batman" and "Robin." Hell, the two of us organized this plant, so we go back. And I don't have any problem with his leading now for awhile, him and his whole slate (*all* of my people lost).

One of the new President's problems is that no one on his slate has had any experience running a local, none of them. His new Secretary-Treasurer, for example, has absolutely no experience dealing with a bank. He was only a shop steward. None of them realized how much work was entailed...like me, six years ago. Back then we had 700 or 800 members; today we're a 1,500- member local.

The President, shit, he's got too much pride to ask for help. But he needs backup. I've offered to explain why and how we did this or that...and I'm still waiting for a call.

As for the months ahead, I really don't know what is likely. I feel like I'm an observer of a bad movie, one I'm still watching and don't know how it will end.

There was some talk of our opposing the new President, and I told my guys "Do what you want to. But fighting him would be the worst possible thing!" None of us are doing that, none of us. As long as he is doing a decent job I'm very content to stay out on the sideline.

What have I learned from all of this? That until the participation thing is taught in Business Schools, until it is incorporated into contract language, no matter how progressive a management you are dealing with is your participation will only last as long as does the contract. That's the problem with American business! Until this participation things is recognized as *the* way to do business its real fragile. It can crack very easy. It is either going to take legislation, or its going to take a total rethinking of business to bring out the benefits of participation.

TQC - a Fresh Union Approach
Ike Gittlen
(USWA)

An impressive thinker and unusually far-sighted unionist, Ike Gittlen tells a remarkable tale of hope first raised and then dashed, of defeat snatched from the very jaws of victory, and of the inordinate influence of outside forces over the parties directly involved in a joint labor-management project. Careful attention should be paid to his insights into -

the strategic importance of having a plan, almost any plan;

the ways in which an assertive local can rebut downsizing maneuvers;

the inevitability of conflict among local union colleagues, and the need to roll with it;

the indispensability of democratic participation in critical decision-making;

the contribution membership surveys can make; and -

the ability of the rank-and-file to know the difference between those who did and really did not let them down.

Especially dismaying is recognition of how vulnerable and fragile are efforts to create labor-management cooperative efforts. Contrariwise, especially encouraging is confirmation of the enormous productivity gains that can be had from such projects, provided, that is, that both sides are pursuing the "win-win" possibilities inherent in the situation.

It all began in the early 1980's, when our International Union, the United Steelworkers of America, negotiated a Labor/management Participation Team (LMPT) section into the Master Steel Contract. It was a tightly structured program and the International compiled a set of guidelines that accompanied the contractual language. In addition, each "pilot" location was sent a bunch of consultants to shepherd their efforts.

Our local elected to become a "pilot" for the Bethlehem Steel program. Along with four other local officials, I was selected by our local union Executive Board to work with five management members on the actual implementation. Under the contract language that implementation would have been a relatively simple task of creating joint "teams" across the plant and conducting appropriate training and oversight. Apparently this "model" was not meeting expectations at other locations, and our consultants decided to free-wheel a bit. (We would find out later that they did not get approval from the international union or the corporation for this deviation).

The consultants urged us to convert our "implementation" committee into a "design" committee and tailor an entirely new participation process to the needs of our plant. We happily spent sixteen weeks traveling all over the country looking at other steel mills, labor/management programs, and new work arrangements. At the conclusion of this "data gathering" effort we tried to develop a program that included the best features of what we had seen.

While we were wandering the nation, we authorized the consultants to survey the supervision and rank and file employees of the plant. We developed a list of questions and they conducted extensive and representative small group interviews. They came back with so much data that we had to computerize it. The result was a telephone-size book of attitudes, complaints, and opinions that we felt a personal responsibility to address in our program. (We would realize later that the survey itself created a new level of expectations amongst both hourly and salaried employees at the plant).

Having done all of that, we got stuck. We had a full view of what existed out in the plant, and weren't too thrilled by it. Our plant had begun to lose money, and we started to feel pressure to change. We kept arguing back and forth, as to what we ought to be doing. Having got us to this point, the consultants suddenly insisted they had no role in helping forge a solution. We were hung up on how things were, as opposed to what we would like them to be.

There were all these arguments about who had to change first, and where to start changing. Naturally, we blamed management and insisted they take the first steps. In the spirit of "cooperation" they never voiced their belief that we should do the changing, but they didn't step forward with any great self sacrifice either. This went on for weeks and we were in danger of chucking the whole program.

Breaking the Impasse. The argument in the design team had been over where to start and what to do. I thought that if we could at least agree on a format, and some idea of where we ultimately wanted to get to, we might break our deadlock. I had been reading a good bit of the stuff that the UAW's Irving Bluestone had accomplished in the auto industry. Using those experiences, and ideas we had picked up from our road trips, I drafted an organizational structure. It was only meant to be a discussion piece.

When I presented it to the design team they unfortunately bought it hook, line, and sinker. There wasn't a hell of a lot of discussion, refinement, or argument about it. We were stuck, sixteen weeks of work were about ready to go down the drain, and this at least was a plan. Looking back it was a humorous document. The top level steering committee was called "The People First Committee."

There were a whole series of other committees for communications and the like. What it would have resulted in, had it ever had a chance, would have been an entirely new plant joint structure that would have largely replaced the current functions of labor and management. It included large shares of co-determination, joint decision-making, etc. Neither side, including me, had any idea of what it would take to get there. The plant wasn't ready for it, and didn't really want it.

We started down that road, and we did manage to do two projects. One dealt with proving we could be cost competitive with outside contractors on steel roll repairs, and the other was a white-collar project on non-duplication. The non-duplication project faded, but we eventually did prove we were lower cost on the rolls, and we do all that work today.

The Reality of Losing Money.   While we were creating our dream world, the real world plant was starting to lose serious money. Upper management decided that our 2,500 man workforce should be cut by 600. One of the things that really pissed us off was that while we were "designing," it was clear that another corporate group had been very busy developing a six-hundred job cut "black book". Apparently they had planned on coming to the LMPT to cooperatively cut these jobs. The Plant Manager was enough of a dreamer to believe we could eliminate a fifth of our workforce jointly. However, the Plant Labor Relations Chief had convinced the corporation that the Plant Manager was foolish: Even if it could be done it would take too long, and you shouldn't cut jobs cooperatively anyway.

At the same time, the consultants suddenly started pushing us to create shop floor teams. We then realized that officials in the corporation and union never did support an alternate design.

Cooling Cooperation.   When the 600 job cut idea became an official company demand, it was kind of a relief to us. We needed to know what water we were swimming in. We ended the LMPT process with a big to-do. (One top- level manager stood up at that meeting and denounced his other managers for double-facing the union. He was later forced to apologize to his fellow managers and eventually forced to retire.)   We had always talked about the LMPT as "experimental," "low likelihood of success," and other cautionary statements, so getting out was done without any political damage to local union officials.

The company had tied a major plant investment to the job cut demand and the local felt it could not ignore the situation. Prior to the LMPT the local would have assigned our two top officers to handle the job cut issue, and they would have negotiated a solution with the company labor relations staff. The experience of teamwork and the ideas of membership participation resulted in a very different approach. We authorized a five man "negotiating committee," of which I was a part, and decided to include the membership in the job cut review.

I had purchased an early model personal computer, and we brought it into the local union hall. A guy from an area computer center developed a specialized D-Base module for our project in exchange for a case of beer. We entered all the company justifications for each job cut, and then visited each job site and entered our members' comments regarding each of the 600 positions.

Division in the Ranks. The five man committee was not a particularly united group. The local President felt very sure that we had to cut the entire 600 jobs, and didn't understand why we were going through the extensive investigation process. He had become convinced, by company representatives, that if we didn't just roll over on the job cuts, the investment would not occur and the plant would be closed. There was a younger group that refused to be bullied by the company, and felt the decision was open for the workforce to make. We believed it was something we should carefully look at, but felt sure there was negotiating room. We did not believe that the corporation would shut us down if we refused to adopt their position entirely.

As the arguments raged within our five man committee, we stoically went through the job review process. Much to our surprise, the members were straight up with us. We got a solid feel for each job, where we could cut, and how to do it without hurting members' quality of work life or pay. In addition, we were able to negotiate a number of "early out" pension inducements. We captured 90 job cuts that had already been accomplished, so that when all the inducements were taken, we actually returned 90 members to work who would have otherwise been laid off. The final agreement called for the elimination of 170 currently active jobs, pension inducements for 260, a $32 million dollar plant investment, and the creation of a "Plant Waste and Cost" Committee.

Taking it to a Vote. Although the local had the authority to simply make the agreement, we insisted on a membership vote. The committee itself was split. At the ratification meeting committee mem-bers gave speeches both ways. I sided with the pro-ratification forces as did the majority of the committee. The membership, which had been kept up to date with our progress, and been involved in the development of the union's position, overwhelmingly approved the package.

Up to this time, the structure of Basic Steel Bargaining had left little room for local unions to bargain or have negotiating power. We tended to argue over local items, but never got involved in major job structure or pension issues. Those issues were all done by technicians in Pittsburgh, and then the presidents approved their work. For a local to put on the kind of effort we had was somewhat unusual. We had never done anything like it, and the company was startled by the thoroughness with which the job was done.

When we turned over our "computer book" that analyzed each job, they didn't put up much of a fight over our conclusions. If anything, we got grudging respect. We also negotiated an agreement to pay for the time and expenses of the committee effort. (We put that to a member vote as well.) I think the payment may have been a company guilt trip over the way they handled the LMPT process and a faint hope we could get back on that track once the job cut issue was behind us.

Another gain was that we got to see, for the first time, some important divisions on the management side of the table. The company labor relations chief became a hated individual. He ran their side of the bargaining committee, and it was clear that most of the management people didn't like him. They felt he was a constant impediment to their efforts to reach an agreement, and often times negotiated around him. This was our first opportunity to work under these kinds of bargaining conditions, and it built confidence that we could handle ourselves and deal competently for our members.

A Change of the Guard. All in all, the union came out in decent shape, considering that it was a concessionary agreement (the International Union had lost tremendous membership respect over the 1983 concessionary Master Agreement) The local president didn't fair as well, however. The local was divided on his performance, because he fell apart so completely and had offered so little leadership in the process. In the 1985 elections he was defeated and I became president.

The election was fought out against the backdrop of a new era in Steel. I argued that we needed a more professional and inclusive approach to local bargaining, a local that was more capable of dealing with company pressure, and a pro-active strategy to face the 1986 Basic Steel Negotiations, that promised (with Bethlehem near bankruptcy) to be concessionary.

Lynn Williams had become USW International President and he led the union to a much different bargaining style. He commissioned an independent study of the entire steel industry, and where it was headed. He called local officers together in Chicago, and shared it with us in a totally open approach. It was a pretty grim report.

At that time there was a big dissident movement in the Steelworkers, with which I had aligned myself. Forged during Ed Sadlowski's campaign for International President in the late 1970's, a loose group of local leaders continued to press for both workplace changes and structural change within the union itself. That group, along with everyone else, was sobered up very quickly by what the industry study reported. We had to confront the fact that we were in a different industry than the one we would like to have. Although we were not going to roll over, we had better find some innovative ways to deal with this, or we were going to get crushed. The old tactics of just saying "No" wouldn't work.

A Shift in Strategy. We didn't realize that Lynn Williams planned to change the ratification procedure and open bargaining up to local officials. In a major move toward the dissidents (and one calculated to restore membership faith in the International Union) Lynn pushed through membership ratification of the Master Agreement contracts in Steel. Prior to that, the vote of the local presidents was all it took to ratify a contract. This alone refocused the bargaining from satisfying the presidents to satisfying blocks of voting members. When the actual bar-gaining began, local officials were allowed to sit at the "table" with the technicians as they worked on the various key issues (i.e., seniority, benefits, safety, grievance procedure, etc.). While the top economic committee remained filled with International Officers and technicians, in the sense of inclusion, these were extremely successful negotiations.

The Union agreed to another concessionary contract, but one quite different from the 1983 pact. Instead of an across-the-board flat dollar amount, the 1986 wage concession was a percentage of earnings that was perceived to be fairer to individual members. In addition, there was an ESOP recoupment feature and profit sharing. The International was straight up about it, didn't promise any recoupment, but simply said it was there. In terms of presentation we could say it was an "investment" instead of a "concession." We also used the dire bargaining circumstances to negotiate a revolutionary protection against contracting out of our work. This section gave locals unprecedented power to bargain over and arbitrate, and it created a major new area of union work and power.

Voting No. I was pleased with the new contract, in terms of what had been accomplished. But I ended up campaigning and voting against it. I came to the conclusion that giving Bethlehem wage concessions was counter-productive. I thought they were becoming concession "junkies" and would do nothing to solve the operating problems our members were hollering about every day. They would just wait for the next opportunity to ask for money out of our wallets. Beyond that, I wanted a moratorium on job cuts. If we were going to give back wages, benefits, and jobs, it seemed the company had made a full raid without justifiable return in the Agreement.

It was a strange situation. It split our local politically because our Grievance Chairman (the other local official at negotiations) promoted the contract and openly curried favor with the International Union. As the ratification vote approached, deep rifts were created by the pro and anti-contract efforts each of us took part in.

The International Union was very concerned that the contract wouldn't pass, and was very disappointed with me. It wasn't until the last minute that I finally made my decision and I think they had counted me as a "yes." The top union officials made a tour around the country, and made a presentation at every single Bethlehem site, prior to the mail ballot vote. We had huge attendance at the two Steelton meetings, with hundreds of people at each one. In the true spirit of democracy, I spoke in opposition after five or six officials spoke in favor (including the Grievance Chairman). The membership gave me a warm ovation, which both shook and angered the International contingent. In the end, our local voted for the package 51% to 49%. The rest of the locals also voted for it by fairly thin margins and it passed with about 55% approval. I continued my "black sheep" status with the International.

Showdown Over Grievances. The ratification left the local badly split. The issues went beyond the contract and had to do with a whole attitude towards how we were progressing and what the local union's strategy ought to be. I led one faction, and the Grievance Chair led the other. Part of the rift had to do with my belief that the local was spending too much money on grievances (which hit directly at the Grievance Chairman's area of responsibility.) I had long discussions with him over the waste of talent in this area and how much else he should and could be applying energy and effort towards. In a less personal way, I insisted that our plant would not survive unless we directed money and resources toward operating issues. If we didn't play a role in fixing the problem, we wouldn't need a grievance procedure.

The Grievance Chairman, and many others who had dedicated themselves to this work, would not hear any of this. They loved the adversarial arena. Loved the rules, procedures, and all the paperwork in a pseudo-lawyer setting.

The International Union had a split personality on this issue. I believe that some officials were in tune with the kinds of thinking that I was going through. Some ideas were considered during the 1986 negotiations. However, the International Union knew that the locals historically had been a glorified grievance-processing mechanisms, and were concerned about a frontal assault on the strong hold grievers had in many locals. Many favored building and reforming the grievance procedure and its adherents...in effect, making it more efficient and effective, but preserving its central role in the locals.

In our local, it was clear that wasn't going to happen. The grievers didn't want anything to do with new approaches...they were driving to solidify their position. Unfortunately the argument became polarized so you were either pro-grievance people or you were anti: No middle ground existed for discussion of roles and relative importance.

Our membership, however, was increasingly aware of the difficulties we were entering and the need for change. They may not have recognized why, but they understood that the grievance procedure wasn't protecting them from what was happening on the shop floor.

The pro-cess of filing paper after paper after paper, in a procedure that was slow and had such low win rates, was not a solution. From the memberships' perspective, the company was flexing its muscles, violating more agreements, and finding loopholes in contract language on a daily basis, while the grievance procedure piled up thousands of cases in backlog.

Broadening the Mission. We began to promote the idea of a "full service" local. It became hard fought immediately. We argued for a completely new approach that brought efforts on legislation, in-plant problem-solving committees, safety and health, and political action on par with our grievance efforts. The grievers favored filing tons of cases in hopes of "breaking the company" by the shear weight of the backlog. While they waited for their mountain of paper to bring the company to a more reasonable relationship, they began to break the local financially.

The local became an armed camp. We pursued a number of the "full service local" ideas under the local presidents' constitutional authority. We used appointment powers and the authority to take committee actions to work at other efforts. We were also able to redirect local finances towards these efforts.

It finally came down to the 1988 local union elections where the membership wiped out the Grievance Chairman and fifteen top local officials. It was a stunning message from our members that served as a mandate to try new ideas, alter our direction, and most importantly, to end the civil war.

Exercising the Mandate. What followed was a three-year period where we ran the local "our way." We began by conducting a major grievance procedure review, and with the help of the International Union, eliminated the thousands of cases in backlog. We then did new joint labor/management grievance procedure training that focused on settlements in the lower steps of the procedure. We recast the grievers as resources to our shop-level people in their application of the contract. We also did a number of informal and formal membership surveys. Through these we tested ideas we had on how to improve plant operating problems and their reaction to higher degrees of involvement and problem-solving. The results were very supportive of the direction we had promoted during the election, and helped get company agreement to a number of new initiatives in the plant.

The plant economic condition had continued to deteriorate, and we knew management wanted to separate us from Master Agreement bargaining in 1989. We felt we had to be open with our membership regarding that danger, and develop pro-active strategies to prevent that kind of bargaining ouster. We developed a decent relationship with plant management by working slowly at successful efforts to include our members in operating issues.

We began with a safety program that had a major impact in the reduction of plant accidents. The grievance procedure cleanup

and training caused a huge reduction in the time and expense associated
with complaints, and then allowed consideration of new joint efforts to
affect the plants problems. We built credibility by involving rank
and file members in major problem-solving issues, and we proved we
had the political wherewithal to come up with results. That gave us an
edge.

Using Teams for the Union. The master agreement
prohibited the use of joint teams in the collective bargaining process
itself. We began to use on contractual issues mixed teams of local
officials and members who had no previous negotiating experience
Initially we tried this process in the conversion from "single-factor
productivity-based" incentive plans to broader "multi-factor gain
sharing" style plans. We also used them much more extensively in the
development and arbitration of grievances. We are now at a point where
there aren't many issues at our local where a mixed negotiating team is
not used.

I don't want to mislead anyone that these teams operate solely on
the basis of consensus, or have total autonomy. That is not the case.
We still reserve the final decision-making power for the union, and in a
number of instances our mixed committees could not come to agreement on an issue, and local officials ended up making a "command decision." But even in those cases, the product of the discussion was far
better and far more accepted by our members than had we not included
members in the process at all. In addition, our members have a far
broader understanding of how difficult collective bargaining is, and the
process the union must go through to gain a particular advance or
benefit.

As we began to get our act together, and put our political civil war
behind us, the International Union became more flexible about what we
were doing. They could come into the local without being forced to
"choose sides." Word began to get back to the International that the
work we were doing was paying off. That we had some control. That
we weren't a bunch of crazies. That maybe we had learned a little about
where we were headed, and it wasn't just fuzzy rhetoric anymore. This
new-found credibility for our local at the International Union level was
to become a key factor in the 1989 round of negotiations.

As 1989 approached it was clear the contract would be a non-
concessionary pact, the first in nine years. The Bethlehem local
unions have an internal caucus known as the Bethlehem Coordinating
Com-mittee (BCC). It met several times prior to the negotiations and
came to the conclusion that our number one agenda item had better be
reten-tion of Master Agreement status for all locals. Several local
unions were part of the Master Agreement, but they had agreed to
reduced wage scales to keep their plants open. Other locals (like
Steelton) knew that the company wanted us out of Master Agreement
bargaining.

Just prior to the opening of negotiations, all the locals signed a petition to the International Union that stated we would not vote on any Agreement that excluded locals, and that everyone had to be satisfied before any of us would ratify. It is difficult to tell what effect the petition had on International Union strategy, but it was received soberly, and the negotiators clearly spent a great deal of time identifying each local's key issues.

Close Call in '89. We weren't at the '89 contract negotiations (in Pitts-burgh) a week when the chief negotiator for the Union called us into a private meeting. He told us that the company had placed a demand on the table to take us out of the Master Agreement, cut our wages by five dollars, roll back benefits, and slash hundreds of jobs from the plant. He said he wasn't sure what he would do about it, and wanted to hear our thoughts on what should be done.

Much to his surprise, we laid out a complete plan of how we wanted to proceed. The elements of it essentially had us working on efficiency in exchange for staying within the Master Agreement. He expressed a willingness to move in our direction (along with some sane skepticism regarding the achievability of our plan), but told us we would have to convince the company that it would solve the plant loss problem. We laid out a number of pieces of information we wanted to get from the company on plant operations. We felt we could show them how to close the plant deficit without the severe wage, benefit, and job cuts that formed the heart of the company proposal.

The unions' chief negotiator arranged a meeting with company negotiators, reviewed the plant's condition, and then backed us in our information requests and our negotiating strategy. Bethlehem was negotiating for all its plants, and couldn't afford to screw up the discussions over Steelton alone. So a chagrined company pulled together our information request and began to explore our proposals.

We brought additional local union officials in and went through a whole bunch of financial information. We looked at the plant from every conceivable angle, and probed every possible cost-savings device. In the end, we showed that with some fairly minimal improvements in yield, productivity, purchasing practices, management reductions and change, alongwith efficiency efforts on our part, we could move the plant into the black. These estimates were built on modest market projections, without any tremendous increases in sales, profit margin, and the like. We maintained that it was the company's responsibility to match those efforts with capital investment and technology improvements that would move us into sustainable profitability.

The company insisted that our numbers couldn't work. That we should be thrown out of the Master Agreement. That we would never secure the savings we were claiming. They wanted the rollback. They wanted the immediate hit. They wanted to solve the problem quickly, by raiding our wallets. On the last day of negotiations, we were still not listed as part of the Master Agreement.

The International held out for us (and two other locations that the company wanted to separate) and finally reached a compromise agreement. The plant management and the local union would work on the local's ideas for the first eighteen months of the new agreement, and the results would then be reviewed by both the International and the corporate bigwigs. We would remain in the Master Agreement, but a dollar wage increase was contingent on how faithfully and productively we worked at our proposals.

"Constructive Conflict." We went to work. In the maintenance areas we put guys on committees and began to restructure seniority units, work rules, and assignment practices. We gave the company greater flexibility, while still protecting important seniority rights and increasing pay where members had more responsibility or were more productive. After three such "restructurings" we had completely overhauled the maintenance systems for our plant-wide crafts and repair shops. We created a host of Efficiency Committees in each Department, where shop floor workers looked at the Departments' books and operating procedures, and came up with all kinds of ideas on how to improve productivity and effectiveness.

We also developed a Member Orientation and Training Program (with help from the Labor Studies Center at Indiana University of Pennsylvania) that taught union history, our Constitution, and associated restrictions and guidelines we had to follow while working on our efforts.

The "Bootstrap Warriors." We developed a number of public relations kinds of presentations to help describe what we wanted and what we expected. We called the entire effort "Constructive Conflict." We wanted no illusions that we were in any honeymoon with the company, or that we had false expectations regarding the company's attitude toward the union or our members. This was an effort to preserve our plant and our standard of living. Not an effort to create any utopian relationship between management and labor.

We told members who were volunteering for work in the effort that they were "Bootstrap Warriors." We were "deputizing" them to act on behalf of our membership in the same way that the officers and shop stewards were "deputized" to administer the contract. We expected them to adhere to constitutional rules and act in a representative capacity. In addition we expected them both to insist on ever-widening circles of participation by their co-workers and to maintain union solidarity as a primary concern.

This kind of message and its associated training programs put a new perspective on the effort for our members. They seemed to understand that this wasn't a give-away program or a place to suck-up to the boss. That the union intended to achieve progress out of the effort and get a real handle on decision-making through it. In addition, we stressed that they would be supported in their work.

We made the elected Zone Grievance Committeemen responsible for their areas, so they felt part of the process. The election had settled the issue of expanding their role, and they were receptive to the new work we were proposing for them. We pressed the positive side of what we could accomplish and encouraged them to help build a new kind of local union through the effort.

Focusing the Committees. We dispensed with a lot of stuff associated with quality circles and labor/management teams (LMPT's). None of our committees were structured like that. Every committee was either a Contractual Committee working on direct contract language changes, or a Process Committee, whose responsibility was to find more effective ways to produce our products. We felt we had to fix the business. If the place continued to lose money, we were that much closer to a sale or shutdown. Our guys had always complained about the stupid stuff that management did, and wanted a shot at making it right. We put a system in place that said "put up" or "shut up," and our guys "put up!"

A Cheap Idea. Just to give you one example: We had a stockyard area with three overhead cranes that loaded steel scrap for the furnaces. It is like a cooking recipe; so much of this kind of scrap, so much iron, so much of that.

The problem was that the scrap came into the yard in long lines of railroad cars that required the cranes to run long distances to properly load the buckets. If you spent too much time traveling for scrap, you would never get a break (there were no defined lunch periods or break times; it was catch-as-catch-can.) The traditional way of handling this was to"substitute" heavier scrap, or scrap closer to the bucket. This cost hundreds of thousands of dollars in inventory adjustments as we used costlier scrap to get a break.

We sat down and talked about this. A guy said "Look, instead of bringing up a twelve-car draft, bring up nine cars. We'll move the draft around so that the scrap you want is always close to the bucket." It didn't cost the company a dime, our guys did it, and they save hundreds of thousands of dollars. That's the kinds of things we were getting done.

No Bowl of Cherries. We also had some difficulties. We wanted our guys to seriously comb financial sheets and look at the "books." We wanted to focus on less management decision-making. We wanted to review management's job duties. We wanted to hire consultants that would move us toward self-directed work teams. We wanted direct contact and discussion with the corporate officers and the Board of Directors. We wanted more say in business planning and capital spending. The company people couldn't talk fast enough to spit out the reasons for ignoring these proposals.

Yet every one of those issues came from complaints of our members...about limits that they had hit...issues they had failed to resolve...problems they needed support to handle. For example: A committee would be listening to a supervisor say "we can take guys out of this area by changing this, and this, and that"...and our guys would say "maybe we can do that, but we want to talk about taking supervisors out of that same area by changing this, and this, and that".... And they would report back that the management wouldn't allow that.

We had an incident where a group went out and actually looked at the purchasing that was being done on gloves and coats, and stuff like that for hot steel areas. They then went out and found cheaper suppliers. The company refused to discuss those purchasing arrangements.

Our guys were saying "Hey, if all the manual labor is going to slowly be phased out, we need to have some way to get at some of these other jobs" [management and white collar positions]. We had a real bad situation where a guy who was out on Workmen's Compensation went to college and got straight "A's" and an accounting degree. A job came up in the Accounting Department; it went to the future son-in-law of a personnel manager, and our guy stayed off on full Workers Compensation payments. And we said, "This is bullshit! We can't explain to our membership that we are really making systemic changes in the plant when this goes on."

Management, in it's rhetoric, was not opposed to the changes we wanted. In the 1989 negotiations they favored them. But when it came to practical application they blocked real change. They had themselves deceived to a certain extent about how much they were changing. They always accused us of wanting to go too fast.

Dollar Day. In spite of the differences, when the 18-month period ended, the effort had succeeded beyond our own expectations. We had involved over 500 of our members (about a third of our total membership) and had saved an estimated five to ten million dollars.

The problem was that other factors didn't stand still. The bottom fell out of our product markets, there were unexpected cost increases, and the company was no closer to capital investment that would have given us key product advantages. As the review (we called it "dollar day") came, the plant was still losing money.

To management's credit, and in spite of those issues they did not agree with us on, they had worked hard to make the effort a success. They spent considerable time, money, and resources over the period to support our direction. We were interested in quantifying the results. We didn't want a phony program.

When the tally was in on Dollar Day, the project hadn't pulled the plant into the black. We urged the company to give credit to the momentum we had built up, the startling savings that had been achieved over such a relatively short time period, and view the dollar wage increase as an investment on the road to eventual success. There was so much good stuff going on that it didn't make sense for them to oppose the wage increase and thus kill the project.

Both management and the local gave presentations to the Review Board established under the contract. Management opposed the wage increase primarily by bellyaching about the plant profit loss, but it couldn't argue that we had not done everything we set out to do. We put the Review Board through an extensive slideshow and testimonial presentation, and blew them away. Even the upper level management guys privately commented that they couldn't believe what they were seeing.

The contract language was written in a way that left the International Union with the final say over the wage increase. In spite of strident appeals by the plant manager, the International told the company we had held up our end of the bargain, and the wage increase was ours. Our plant manager went back to his office, and we later were told he broke down and cried. He was that bitterly opposed to the raise. Our members were elated, and felt justified in all the work they had put into the effort.

Taking Home His Marbles. The effort, however, went downhill. The plant manager just totally lost interest in cooperation. He didn't have the heart for it anymore. He couldn't put any more energy in it. All the steering committee meetings and most of the plant committees petered out. Everything we were doing kind of came to a slow stop. We cleaned up some loose ends, some departments tried to keep work moving, but it was over, and we knew it.

What Did We Learn. The union came away much stronger and more united. Our membership took great pride in what they had been able to do. We had tremendous participation...broad-based across the plant. We had reached a point where people were clamoring to get on committees and get items moving faster than we could train them and expand the effort. We had this huge momentum forward, and then this dead spot.

Alongwith a lot of our leadership I was were concerned it would look as if the union betrayed these people by taking them down this dead-end road. Instead the entire weight fell on the company. There didn't seem to be any question in our members' minds that we had done the right thing. That the local had provided the right leadership. And that it was the company that had bummed out.

We made up certificates for all members who had participated, and thanked them for their efforts. We made it clear through newsletters and meetings that they had produced real results, and were instrumental in achieving the wage increase. We had uncovered a number of key leaders through the process that we have come to rely on more in our everyday work.

The local has greater ability to act now, and closer ties to its members. There seems to be a greater membership understanding of the business we are in, and what the union is up against. Even within the plant management, certain communications and management practices continue to hold on.

Afterward. Since that time, our local has gone through a local union election, with the vast majority of the current officers and Grievance Committee people re-elected. We have had to contend with a proposal to make our plant part of a joint venture with British Steel, which failed. A new plant manager has been assigned.

We just recently concluded major negotiations that brought $80 million dollars of new equipment into our plant and launched us on a new round of joint work to make the plant highly competitive. At the same time, the company is trying to sell 25% of our plant to another entity.

Each of these challenges has stressed the local, destabilized our members, and forced us to rapidly respond to issues we had never dealt with before. So far we have dealt with those issues successfully. The local leadership has remained an effective force and retains membership support. Credit goes to a continued insistence that our members participate in all phases of what our local does, and keeping a strong stream of two-way communications going at all times.

Behind that is a continuing interest on the part of our members in using their solidarity and leadership to retain their jobs. And that, after all, is what brought people to the union movement in the first place.

TQC - Found Wanting
John Alexander
(URW)

An insightful and engaging talker, as are most inside reformers, John Alexander grew up influenced by a coal-miner world of pro-union story tellers. Unique among co-workers in his keen interest in the ideas of serious writers about work reforms, he grasped early on the strengths and weaknesses of the Deming Total Quality Control Program (TQC). Outraged by TQC mismanagement, he has never since stopped opposing corporate sabotage of its enormous potential.

Alone among all the other contributors to this volume, John Alexander does not serve as an *official* inside reformer, which is to say he does not represent his local in his role as a change agent. Quite the contrary. Precisely because the company hand-picked him, and put friendly pressure on him to join as an employee spokesman, John has a seat on a company-wide committee to promote a TQC program. Not withstanding this uncertain start, John has always seen his role as very union-related, since he firmly believes organized labor is *the* key to whether or not TQC can help revive productivity, enhance American competi-tiveness, and, most vital of all, give workers solid reasons to upgrade the value they place on organized labor.

Four questions addressed by the essay below shed fresh light on the uncertainties of TQC in union-management settings:

What's wrong with letting the company run its own TQC program?

Why should a local union insist on sharing in its operation?

How can a local union best counter corporate misuse of TQC?

How far might a really fine TQC program go in removing a superfluous layer of middle management?

Still persuaded TQC offers much that both labor and management can profit from, Alexander continues to fight for its realization...and uses his essay to offer sound advice to other inside reformers eager to do the same.

My father owned his own beer distributorship in Pennsylvania, and the majority of our customers were union coal miners. Riding on the beer truck with my dad I heard all the miners' stories. He felt unions were necessary, as did my grandfathers on both side. My grandfather on my mother's side was a member of the United Mine Workers for many years. While I'm the first person in my family to be a longtime union representative, my family has certainly been supportive of unions.

Total Quality Control Program (TQC). Two years ago I was invited to a large meeting at our Akron plant to learn about Goodyear's new TQC Program, a joint labor-management project.

Several hundred management people had been sent to Japan to study successful ventures there, all of which were based on Dr. Demming's theories, and understandings, and teachings. They returned enthusiastic, and were going to implement it now at Goodyear...where I've worked for the past 22 years.

The problem, right from the beginning, was that management and management alone was exposed to this program, even though we were told it required our participation. Union members were to merely go along and see how it transpired, with the idea that they could drop out at any time.

Listening to the speakers I became more and more troubled. I had previously read one of Dr. Demming's books and had seen several TV shows on him. So I had some idea of what this was all about. When the company finished the presentation and asked if there were any questions, I gave my opinion that it was a great idea to implement this program and I would certainly go along with it and help any way I could. But....

Revealing Start. I insisted Goodyear did *not* understand TQC because they had just finished laying off five carpenters, five members of our plant local. And they had hired non-union sub-contractors to do the work which our laid-off men would have normally performed, work that included fashioning and hanging a large Golden letter "Q" and building a the display case for TQC paraphernalia. I told everybody listening that TQC was intended to protect we workers, while what the company was doing was an insult! TQC said you are *not* supposed to lay our people off and replace them with outsiders!

Countering the Company. That sparked the company's interest in me. Which amazed me, as I'm pretty vocal. One of the company's speakers asked me some question. As a local rep for seven years, and the local's Safety Committee's Rep for the past 15 years, and not a shy person I let them have it!

But I always try to leave an avenue which can be addressed. I don't accuse them of being underhanded. In other words, I'll argue that their ignorance is what is screwing things up. There *is* always a way we can straighten things out! If you take the approach where you don't call them a whole big bunch of..., if you leave them a door open to come back, and if they're sincere, they'll do it.

If they're really sincere they'll come back and try to straighten out the problem. If they're not sincere, and are underhanded, then they'll try to persuade you over to their side. So one way or another they're going to address the issue.

But if you just put up a wall, and don't invite them in, then there is a good chance they won't come back in: They'll just label you as a "troublemaker," and they'll just discredit you. So, the best strategy is always leave the door open.

Signing Up-On My Own. When this original presentation was over (it lasted several hours) they had a large dinner. After I sat down I was approached by some of the management people who were trying to implement this program. They wanted my opinion and offered to put me on the Corporate Headquarters Steering Committee. I joined it.

I'm not really an official representative of my union in this capacity. I'm there as an employee. My union local did not send me, the company invited me. I went on my own. But what I've done ever since is try to explain the program to union officials, and try to get them to see it as the opportunity it is to revive labor, change management, help the people in the plant, and just maybe, rescue the entire nation.

Local and International Reaction. Most unionists I know don't believe the program is going to succeed. They *absolutely* do not believe it. And it won't, if it doesn't get the proper input from the proper people.

Certain key people in my local believe the program is just another way of management trying to take advantage of the people. If the union backs it, the union is selling out to the company. The union verbally said it would back it, but behind the scenes, it has taken a neutral position. In other words, the leaders protected their votes - and everybody got to hear what they wanted to hear. That way they didn't feel they had hurt their voting political position in any way, shape, or form.

The bottom line for our leaders is if they make a mistake they won't be voted back into office. They feel, at least I hope they feel, that they can do more good for the people by being in power: If they lose their position, there is no good they can do for the people. What they're doing is what is politically conducive to getting things done...and that is the way most politicians feel.

I felt the position the union leaders were taking was absolutely the worse that they could take, by sitting back and letting the company run with it. Because there would be a certain number of workers who would believe in the TQC program, because they want to see fewer people laid off, and whatever it takes to reach that end. As well, the news media support these programs. There have been successes in other industries with these programs. The company could just literally split the union right down the middle! They could abuse everybody! And the union would reel back and never know what hit it!

I felt the company had to be protected from itself, from the temptation it might feel to misuse TQC and hurt us all. I worried that Goodyear would take a sound idea, and transform it to serve only *their* short-term ends. Not maybe even because this was their original intent. But when they experienced a lot of control, with people controlling other people, they might not be able to resist. I thought this program could be a *great* program, and it could be used for the benefit of the people as well as the company. Or it could be used to abuse the people...and I felt I had to at least try and shape a desirable outcome.

Rough Going. The company tried to get 50/50 representation, but we were unable to hold onto this: Its probably about six or seven union people now, and eight or ten management people. We've had quite a few union people quit because they're disgusted. This has been two years in the making, and they haven't seen enough positive changes. They feel the company just doesn't want to "walk their talk."

The few of us who have hung in there have taken the position that if this program fails, it will not fail because of lack of our participation. It will fail because management refuses to do what it is supposed to do!

Report Card. We've actually made great progress. I feel that the program has a good possibility to succeed! I feel that we have stopped management's ability to use the program against the people, absolutely!

It hasn't been easy. The company has tried to discredit some of my ideas, saying they were "just your opinion." They tried to get us to go along with their version of how the program works! They're the experts! Management was sent to Japan!

I knew they were wrong. But, I could only take pieces of information I learned from TV or I read and attempt to tell them, because there was no book that I could find that states what ingredients are necessary for a successful program. I needed some kind of data to support what my theory was as to what was necessary. Even Demming, when he states what will work and won't, gives a list of generalities: He gives no specific list of ingredients, no formula! But, there *is* a formula!

Union "Cookbook." The Chairman of our committee agreed to let me put on a presentation to our group. It lasted three hours. I used for an analogy the ingredients one needs to bake an apple pie. There are certain ingredients needed, and there are certain benefits from an apple pie. If the apples are left out, you get a different result: You get a cinnamon roll. The same exact ingredients, minus the apples, is in fact a cinnamon roll! It is not without its benefits, but it is *not* an apple pie!

There is a basic set of ingredients necessary for a sound labor-management cooperative program. It has specific benefits, which are readily observed in the Japanese and in some of the German programs. But if the main ingredient is left out, you end up with a mere management productivity program. This is of course very different, as is an apple pie to a cinnamon roll.

This was what Goodyear's management was actually implementing. They were calling it a labor-management program (TQC), but, in fact it was a management productivity program. They wanted the benefits of a labor-management program, but in essence they were building something very different.

When I presented this information, I drew diagrams on a blackboard of a pie, a cinnamon roll, a labor-management program, and a management productivity program. I didn't disclose the main ingredient, which was missing in the labor-management program, until the presentation was nearly over.

This ingredient was brought up time and again previously by the unionists. We had been getting into heated discussions, even some name-calling by people on both sides. Some members left the committee. We wouldn't back down and they wouldn't either. While we had no data to support it, we would say it has *got* to be this way!

So, all in all it was good to have it out. This type of confrontation removed any fear of saying what one thought. Without the ability to speak openly, success would be beyond reach. I believe, at least for those who stuck it out, there is now a greater respect for one another.

The major ingredient missing, of course, is job *security*. And that's the one ingredient the companies always want to omit. They want to have the ability to replace you with temporary help. They want that *flexibility*. In contrast, we want them to retrain laid-off brothers and sisters to do any work the company is considering hiring temps to do.

Reaction to the Presentation. In response to what I had presented, the company requested data to support these ideas. So I phoned Dr. Higdon Roberts, Director of a Center for Labor Education and Research, and told him what I had done. Along with his resume he sent me a significant amount of research material and data supporting these ingredients. I copied all of it, and took it to our next meeting and gave copies to everybody. I went through it in detail, and there was no longer any way they could discredit this analogy.

They were still reluctant to concede the point. I stated if they could not give us data proving I was incorrect, then it was safe to assume I was correct!

Proof or Disproof. In an effort to either prove or disprove this analogy, the company brought in their national consultant. He was usually paid to come in and address large groups. It was unusual to have him come to our meeting of 15 or so.

Some of the management had really felt threatened by my presentation. I had basically told them - "If you don't implement these ingredients, then we should drop the program! If you're really not trying to implement a labor-management cooperative program, and you're trying to implement a management productivity program, we will *not* be a part of that!" Basically, we had uncovered an intentional or unintentional flaw, and we would only stand for a genuine cooperative program.

I looked over at the national consultant and realized I didn't know what position he was going to take. I didn't know the man. Goodyear was paying him a considerable amount of money for coming that day. There seemed a good possibility he was going to say what the company expected him to say: So I just sat back and listened and watched as the meeting progressed.

The consultant began by speaking and answering question in generalities. After about 45 minutes of listening, I felt the man was creditable. I started by explaining my previous presentation (I didn't know that a company team member had sent the consultant some of our previous proceedings, including my presentation to help prepare him). He knew right where I was coming from, and he basically backed me up 100%! In other words, the consultant's presentation and empathasis on job-security was just as good or better than the one I had given, and he supported these issues entirely!

"O.K.," I said, "then the issues as I've framed them are correct?!" "Yes," he said, "that's correct?" "Then how," I asked, "can we get management to believe it?! To believe that actually this program will benefit the company if they implement it in a correct way?!" He said (this was great!) that "the real problem here is this management [and they were right there in the room], doesn't have any balls! They *know* what is right, because you've told them. What you told them was right! I'd already told them the same, though in a different way. But, they don't have the balls to do it. Either the system doesn't allow it, or they are scared to lose their merit raise. But they just don't have the balls to do what is right!"

I said "I agree! They *don't* have the balls! I wouldn't have put it so blunt. I would have been a little more discreet. But you're right: That's a way of putting it! *Now*, how do we get them to do it anyhow?! Let's forget that, and let's progress."

The consultant replied - "What are you going to do? Sew balls on them?" He said "You are going to keep harping, like you are doing here, until somebody does something! You've got to find somebody in management who is man enough to go against the system!"

And that was how the meeting ended.

Continued Cowardice. Things calmed down after that. The company went back to the old ways of trying to discredit the issues, insisting that I was only voicing my own opinion. They even at one point tried to translate what the national consultant had said in their behalf! That was ridiculous, because he could not have been anymore plain.

As well, I've had several things done to me in a foolish attempt to shut my mouth. But, this always backfires! I got into an argument with one of the management in the room, and 45 minutes later he told me I was being sent to second shift. This manager assured me this had nothing to do with our argument. I only stayed on second shift for a short period of time. Some think this was due to some of my co-workers who perceived this as a repercussion to our argument and protested this punishment.

The way they did it was great! In one instance the manager who sent me to second shift was visiting a totally different department. A fork truck driver jumped from his truck and hustled to this manager. He said "Hello, Mr._. How are you?" And the boss said "Wow! What do I owe this to?" And the worker said "I don't want you to put *me* back on second shift!"

Another man got some shoe polish and went up to the same boss, in front of his manager and asked if he could shine his shoes. He said "Why are you doing this?" The worker replied, "I wouldn't want you to put *me* back on second shift!"

When upper management saw what was happening, coincidentally I was brought back to first shift. This boss was told he was not allowed to intimidate or mistreat me in any way. The best part of all of this, however, is that even though I was on second shift I kept coming to the meetings on first shift. I didn't care, as it was *very* important to me to help win this struggle!

Indispensability of a New Boss. Industry is "You do what I tell you to do! Right, wrong, or indifferent!" The worker knows what is wrong. He's the craftsman on the job. The man making the tires knows the best way to do it. He knows what is right or wrong more than anybody! He's the guy performing the job! The worker is really the expert, not management. They don't know the shortcuts. They don't know...but basically this is the way industry is in the U.S., and so we have a tremendous amount of waste!

What is needed is a change our work culture. In Japan the boss is not an omnipotent person. He asks his employees what they need to perform their job well, and he gets it for them, instead of saying "Go out there and do this!" I see the need to have the whole atmosphere of "Who's the boss?" change. Your boss should no longer be your boss: He should become your assistant, someone who facilitates the worker.

The change would allow the system to remove obstacles so that the worker uses his abilities to enhance, improve, or become a true asset to the company. Then, instead of wasting time, and of not caring what the cost is to the company, because the company doesn't care about them, one might feel that he *is* a part of the company, an integral part of it. The labor is what makes it *work*. The company will protect you for it. So, when the worker has a problem he works it out with management and corrects it

Its an entirely different attitude. Its motivation is for one to do his job as best as he can, in cooperation with a new type of boss who knows and values that opportunity.

Role for the Union Local. While I don't report on any of my participation committee work at meetings of my local, in my role as Safety Chairman I meet with our president every Monday, and we have discussed - step-by-step - what I am trying to accomplish.

I think the biggest difference this has made for my local so far is that the cooperative program has shown we can get benefits for employees *without* contract negotiations. If you can show it will benefit the company to give certain considerations to the people, rather than it coming through a negotiations' process, the company will be more willing to make the necessary changes to ensure the success of the program *outside* of collective-bargaining.

Second, if this program is implemented *correctly*, it *is* possible to address many of the problems that we have been unable to address successfully in collective-bargaining. For example, the security issue! It is not unusual for the company to use temporary people to replace our laid off members.

It has been repeatedly stated that our people should be cross-trained, consistent with TQC doctrine, to fill jobs the company is considering using outsiders to perform. We've identified many jobs our people could fill if they received some preparation. This would reduce the fear of layoffs and build trust between the company and labor. We have begun to move in this direction and it appears to some degree this issue will be addressed.

I can see the eventual success of our participation program affecting my local in two ways: First, by causing it to look differently at certain members. And second, by getting it to look differently at its adversarial relationship.

I was a district representative for seven years, and I represented people that I knew were reprehensible. But I felt it was my job to represent them. Out of 117 grievances I won 107 because I took my job seriously. I would tell the people what I *actually* thought of their behavior. But I would still vigorously defend all of them.

As everybody knows, there are certain people in the plant who just don't give a damn, no matter what, and are going to go sit in the corner every chance they get. The local may have to take a new position. One that encourages these workers to improve their performance, for the good of all concerned.

By this I certainly don't mean we forget our obligation to provide "fair representation." I just mean we take a new approach to the few people unwilling to do their part.

I'm convinced the local should keep its adversarial position on contractual items. You can't become buddy-buddy with the company when it comes to contractual issues. You still have to represent your people. You still have to enforce the contract. Because if the local doesn't do that, it will lose credibility with its membership.

At the same time, however, on issues such as productivity, where the local can help a man do his job better, it should work *with* the company. I think *the* big change when this participation program becomes successful will be that management will realize the importance of organized labor, and how labor ought to be a full and equal partner in the production process. We should be helping each other, rather than fighting one another over damn near any little thing.

Role for the International Union. All across the labor movement I see unions like my own sitting back and watching. If this is gonna be a winner, then they're going to jump on the bandwagon and *ride!* If its going to be a loser, they want to be able to disassociate.

The smartest position for the union to take, and we're getting closer to that point now, would be for it to jump in, and try to help make this program *more* successful by being part of it.

I feel the union officials are the ones who could make the program succeed. By them not getting involved, it actually hurts, because they seem to be the *key* people: Unions are the ideal tool with which to implement this kind of program! Working people would believe their unions more readily than they would ever believe their companies.

If unions implemented the program correctly, that is, convinced management to make the changes necessary for the program to be a success, the unions would become as attractive as participation consultants have become. Some companies, if the unions took up this wholly different role, might actually *want* the unions to be a part of their industry...so great are the likely gains in productivity!

On a Hopeful Note. What it all boils down to is this: I think we're going to succeed! To what degree, I don't know. We should succeed, however, because it is imperative that American unions help improve productivity, and to help keep industry here - and stop it from moving overseas, stop industry from going over there.

We're at a point now where this cooperation effort is either going to happen...or it is not, and at least I'll be able to say I gave the fight my very best.

Afterward (July, 1993). You want to know what's happened recently? The company decided that they would change the structure of what we had set up. They felt we could accomplish more if the group worked from the floor rather than from our Committee. The Committee decided to give it a try.

The first thing which was done awhile back - which was fine - was new committees were made up of like craftsmen. The pipefitters would have their own meeting with their supervisor. The repairmen did the same. The carpenters...and so forth and so on. This even included the janitors, who had their own private meeting.

Any problems labor had in those meetings they would pass on to our Committee. We would take it in, and as upper management was present, we would push the issues.

The one issue they wouldn't address was the security issue, naturally. At different points in time we made pretty good progress towards it, but it always reverted back. We heard all the reasons why they had to bring contractors in...for this reason or that. They couldn't give any guarantees of job security, and so forth and so on.

When I think they were finally convinced we were only getting gains for labor with our meetings, and they weren't willing to address the security issue the way it should be for that type of program, the suggestion was made that we would be better off if we worked from smaller groups of people right off of the floor. That was the company's suggestion...which I feel was an attempt to dissolve our immediate group.

We were told we could meet, but on a scheduled-as-needed basis. If there is a major problem, they told us, "We will just schedule a meeting and we discuss it." Yet, we have not had a committee meeting in months.

Actually, breaking down the committee to include all the floor-level people didn't really matter, because all the hourly are floor-level people. I think the company thought they could have a better influence on the smaller groups. But we informed fellow workers they should push their agendas in these meetings, whatever they are, and see what happens.

The pipefitters, for example, came up with some terrific ideas. Man-agement had come up with a special agenda that looked for ways to improve the shop and make the people look more professional.

The pipefitters jumped right on the bandwagon, and they said "We'd like to look more professional. We need to move our shop. It's in the wrong area. In order to thread pipe you have to carry it through a barrage of column posts. For a variety of reasons, it is dangerous, inefficient, and ergonomically incorrect. We've found the perfect area directly across from the pipe racks that can be turned into a new pipe shop."

Management said "You have to put this all on paper." So the pipefitters did, and did better than that. They acquired from engineering prints of the building, and inserted the proposed changes.

Then management said they didn't want just one group to move, because possibly another group might want to and all should be part of the changes. The company made no move to solicit these possible changes from the other groups. So we formed an hourly committee which spoke to each group individually. Suggested improvements were collected and placed on the print.

With the new layout we ended up with six extra bays. By rearranging storage, everyone's shop was larger. Everybody was put where they should be. No one was in front of the office to be watched, which is really how they had originally designed the shop about six to ten years ago.

Then we were stonewalled on actually implementing these changes...for all the reasons you can think of. Upper management said the move was a wonderful idea. Middle management didn't like it because it wasn't their idea. Consequently, nothing is happening.

On other issues we have been making progress. In at least one plant we have gotten the time clock removed. This was a monumental task and quite surprising when management finally agreed to it. We kept pounding that issue home...the fact that management didn't ring in or out, but the hourly people had to.

Management was preaching we were all the same. "Associates" is the new key word, rather than "employees." Well, if we're all the same, why aren't we treated the same? What you're telling the people is one thing, and what you're doing is something different. We finally got a change for a small bunch of the guys, and that was really encouraging. That was a "paradigm shift!" It had seemed like that would never change.

But it stopped right there. It hasn't spread to any other departments, including ours. This was supposed to be an experiment. If it worked well, then it would be adopted elsewhere. It went fine. The 35 or 40 men in that particular plant, out of a workforce of 1,400, thought it was great. It had no problem. There have been no reported complaints by management. Everyone seemed to like it...but it ended right there.

Now, at this point, labor is saying "O.K., you asked us for our opinion, and we gave it. Now nothing is happening." So everybody is saying "When you show us, we'll see what happens." Relations are *very* chilly.

As for me, my new Division Chairman, Gary, who won the recent election, had started to come to the Committee meetings. This was sorely needed. The Division Chairman should have been a part of the process from the beginning. But since management changed the structure of the committee meetings Gary has stopped coming. Gary did do a pretty good job when he attended. But many of his suggestions were met with comments by management like "Sorry, but we've already discussed it."

Middle management, openly, just comes up with pathetic excuses. I think the crux to the whole thing is they're threatened. If the TQC program was to work, there really wouldn't be any need for them. So its a matter of survival in their eyes. If you really get into the depths of TQC, the people begin to manage themselves. You don't need timeclocks. You don't need someone to discipline you and walk around and make sure you're producing eight hours a day. When the disciplinary actions or watchdog efforts are removed, the need for middle management is greatly reduced.

Now, there's always going to be work for first-line supervisors, even under a TQC program. They're there now to assist workers making the jobs easier in anyway they can. That is the structure of the program. They are not there to enforce rules and regulations.

We made the suggestion - of course, it was a dangerous one to make, but we wanted to make the point - we said "You know, we really don't need any management here. All we really need is just the upper management and the workers." Because the workers could take a turn being a supervisor in the office everyday, answer the phone, order materials, and do whatever needs to be done to help with the job.

Middle management, on hearing this, really felt threatened. Upper management, along with the TQC coordinator, suggested "Don't screw with these guys anymore. Don't go out there and look at them all day long. Let them alone! Let's see how this works!"

Actually, one of the management personnel, a foreman, retired. His primary job, as far as the workers were concerned, was to invoke disciplinary action. Many of the workers felt he created the problems he was known for solving. He has since retired and as yet has not been replaced. I might add, he was the primary stumbling block on many issues including the shop improvements.

I think TQC was always destined to go where it went. This is the position we took. We felt there was always hope it would work - and there still is - but without the company addressing the security issue for the workers there is no way TQC will achieve the desired results.

For example, we just laid off three more carpenters in our department. The company is now bringing in private contractors to do their work. How do you convince labor on the floor that their best interest is in TQC, when the company lays off men and brings in contractors to do their work? If you make sacrifices in order to increase productivity, you don't lose your job - that's the security that must go along with this program.

An example was given during the original presentation three years ago which illustrated it. The Japanese re-trained those who displaced themselves by increasing productivity. The programs which claim true success address this issue.

As for middle-management they've been told by upper management that attrition will be used to reduce their number. Some will also be assigned to different types of work than what they are now doing. But no one ever explained just exactly what that work was. It was pretty evident to them, no different from what it was evident to us, that if you don't address *our* issues, it isn't going to work.

Looking at TQC, then, from the point of view of middle management - it is perfectly understandable that they don't want it to work! It is not in their personal best interest.

To add to all of this mess, corporate headquarters has gone in with a chainsaw, and cut out salaried people like they were going out of style. There's a lot of discontent about this. Corporate types say "We don't need you anymore because of the new technologies." They do have more computers which are the biggest part of corporate headquarters. Entire divisions support computers for the entire world for Goodyear.

At the same time, however, that they're laying off long-time salaried people, they're turning around and hiring temporaries. These temporaries are working for $5 and $7 an hour. The previous employees were averaging $15 and $17 an hour. Top management replaced them, so to speak, with contractors, also. (Recently, an in-house lab laid off a salary hygienist. Several months have since past and three temporaries were hired to work in the same lab. One of the temporaries is a chemist).

So, there seems to be no reason for middle management to trust upper management. There's no reason for labor to trust middle or upper management. It is apparent they will cut anyones' throat. The program was to build trust. However without security this will never happen.

Recently we placed a lot of pressure on management concerning the shop move. We said "Look, if you can't make this move, and if you can't do what the people on the floor are asking, then you are giving evidence the program has failed."

Before we were passing along to the workforce all the excuses why it was taking so long for this improvement. Now we've informed management "You either make this move or you convince them you are only going to do what is in *your* benefit, and you couldn't care less about the workforce." We explained to them the longer you wait, the worse the situation is going to get...if they are to convince the people on the floor they really care about what they have to say.

The excuses management gives are pathetic. So everybody is saying "See, see, see! This is just what we said was going to happen." With a combined effort of the union members and a few upper management who really would like the program to succeed, the shop move finally took place. Overall, from the time of the original suggestion approximately one year had lapsed.

Security is still the major issue. However, management refuses to address it in a favorable fashion. All in all, things don't look too promising.

But, anything is possible. I still believe TQC *could* work. We did make some significant changes. If the company would just address some of the most important issues, the success of the program would be great. Even if middle management was not an obstacle, and played the part they should, without security TQC will never attain the desired rose-colored results.

TQC on Hold
Karen A. Hart
(CWA)

Born into a union household, Karen Hart was college age before she grasped the full significance of that for her politics and values, a realization she has ever since put into full-time practice. Currently the elected 1st Executive Vice-President of CWA's largest local in Northern California, Karen practices a brand of affable, attentive, and caring unionism that helps explain her rapid rise in CWA officialdom.

A close reading of Karen's story highlights the strategic value of the natural leader, the individual who cannot help trying to improve matters and who attracts the support of others for the effort. As well, her tale shed light on several major questions:

How can an inside reformer recover from a close defeat in a union election?

What use can labor make of Quality of Work Life projects?

How can labor respond to a major change in corporate culture, one largely detrimental to the union?

What can an inside reformer learn from a close reading of relevant union contracts?

Karen stands out in one additional way well worth highlighting: She scans highly esoteric literature in telecommunications and closely follows fast-breaking developments to keep her local and the CWA from being blindsided by rapid changes in cable TV, fiber optics, and so on. Intent on helping CWA members make a transition into high tech jobs, she models a distinct and very timely role for reformers.

I remember my dad when I think of my first contact with unions. He and mom met at Antioch after World War II, and he ended up working as a management administrative assistant to a vice-president type at an aerospace company. He subscribed to the newspaper of the state AFL-CIO and used to show me articles he liked. He died when I was only six. And years later when I got active in unionism I asked my mother why he bothered to subscribe: She said, "Well, he just cared about working people."

Due to bureaucracy the state AFL-CIO did not remove my father's name from its mailing list for 14 years after his death. So, as a kid in junior high and in high school I read his labor paper on and off, and could recite labor's "Don't Patronize!" boycott list.

Mom was a school teacher, and I can remember when her local of the California Teachers Association went out on strike for two weeks in the early 1970's. During my freshman year at college they had a second strike. I came home before it occurred and helped her move her personal materials out of her classroom, things the school district had not paid for. When I asked why we were doing this she said no scabs were ever going to use *her* teaching aids!

Thanks to dad's newspaper, which just kept coming in, I always knew what the important issues were to labor, issues I could never have known about from our local newspapers. And I also noticed when there would be a picket line in front of a workplace, and all that sort of thing.

I didn't know how pro-labor I had become until I took a class in auto mechanics while going to college. I remember listening to the instructor boast about how they had gotten rid of a union that represented workers in his shop, the UAW or the Machinists, and how one went about doing that sort of thing. I was silent, but I was also totally appalled...and I remember thinking, "God, I'm pro-union!"

Going to Work. Nothing really happened, however, until I left college at 19 and went to work for the telephone company. My instructor at school had warned me that sexism was always going to get in my way unless I got more than some "pieces of paper," some college diplomas or certifications behind me. Even though I was already doing the same or better work than guys, I was going to be discriminated against, no matter what the government said about affirmative action. And that was the whole "Catch-22!" Business didn't want any of us, and it was going to be hard for me to get the kind of equipment repair work I liked doing.

Standing and waiting on a long line for three hours one day in order to get telephone service installed in a new apartment of mine it occurred to me to ask if the phone company had thought of hiring any more pole-climbers and installers to speed this whole process up? The order clerk gave me a collect number to call, and they sent me an employment application. When I saw it was postage-paid I thought "Why not?," and I filled it out and sent it in.

Joining the Union. After I got hired my first shift kept me from going to CWA [Communication Workers of America] union meetings. Later when I could attend I did, because from my family background I learned to respect the difference between just belonging to something and being really *active* in it. Within six months of joining I was saying to others - "I haven't been on the job very long, only six months or so. But in that time I haven't seen you at a local union meeting. If you'll come I'll buy you a beer afterwards."

We soon had this little thing going whereby we had dinner, usually at a Chinese place, before the scheduled meeting of our local. And then afterwards we'd all go out together, whether for pizza or beer or whatever.

I remember one of the guys telling us about the 1947 strike, and how you couldn't get any time off of work unless you struck and won that right...things like that got talked about. I got the impression the union did some good things. While some of the guys might have been pissed at a current officer or even at the entire union at a point in time, overall, they seemed to think it was okay.

Moving Up and Learning More. About a year into it I became a job site steward almost by accident. As a phone repair technician-in-training I rode by chance with a guy who had been the Napa local's president and was now one of our stewards. While he wasn't very active he was trying to get CWA to co-sponsor some sort of rehab program to help alcoholics like himself.

Anyhow, one of the good things he did where I'm concerned was take me over for my first visit to our local's office. When you're an installer repairman you quickly get to value an available clean bathroom and free coffee, both of which the CWA local office offered us. As it was near the garage where we parked our repair trucks I liked getting to know about it. I met the office secretary, and she assured me if I ever had any questions about any union matters I should just phone her and I'd get attention.

Shortly after, when I got asked to run for a union office, I felt better about all of it because I had begun making calls to the local office and *had* gotten useful answers.

Without knowing I was one I became a natural leader in our workplace. I suppose it's not surprising since I came from a family that has always said - "You've got a problem? Well, fix it! Do what you can to fix it!"

You also have to remember guys kinda like to read pornography or whatever, but I don't read that stuff. So while we were on the road driving between phone repairs I read their copies of *Popular Mechanics*. And when I finished with those sort of magazines I'd read our CWA contract a lot. I got to know it clause by clause, page by page. I didn't know how to interpret many of the clauses, but when we got into a fight with the company over whether somebody would get paid for their absences, I would say "Well, you know, that's covered on p. 29" or some such page.

Hat in the Ring. Later, when I had moved three counties away, somebody in our local forgot to mail out ballots to a small group of voters, and we realized they also hadn't had a chance to nominate anyone. The officers got worried the Department of Labor might learn about it, and, over this neglect of a group of only about 10 in our local of maybe 2,000 people, the government might order a whole new election. One of the officers who had heard I knew the contract well asked me to help out by running for one of the open spots on the Executive Board.

I asked what I would be expected to do? The officer said "Well, your job will be to keep an eye on the other officers and make sure you're the voice of the people." I thought I could get behind that, so I ran. In my CWA local nobody really campaigned; you just expected everybody to know enough to vote for you.

I learned a valuable lesson from all of this as I wound up losing by one or two votes out of perhaps 200 cast. I learned that just because a lot of co-workers knew my face and liked me, many still did not know my name! I learned that just because you work hard doesn't mean the people necessarily know exactly who you are...and that cost me the election.

Fixing (Union) Things. My work location was 227 miles away from the local office of our union, and this isolation forced me to do a lot on my own. I went out, for example, to sign up non-members and was surprised when 15 or so said "If I have to fill out one more of those cards I'm going to barf! I just don't want to do it anymore, you know. Forget it! I filled out four of those cards in the last five years."

When I looked into this I found all of the officers had just been too busy and distracted to follow up. So I began to promise new members there *would* be follow-up! And I'd go to the local's secretary and say "I don't care if you mail them the last out-of-date local newspaper! Just mail them *something!*" So she finally was able to get the cards I got new members to sign into the International Union's computer in Washington, D.C., and they finally began to get the communications we should have been sending all along.

Our problems meanwhile increased with the phone company. People were being declared "surplus" without any advance notice, and being told they had been transferred to another worksite...overnight! Others were working 14 hours a day, as required by *mandatory* overtime, at least six days a week - and the company was considering forcing this for seven days a week! I was personally having trouble keeping up my part-time college work as the company didn't give a damn whether or not sudden changes in my work schedule kept me from taking mandatory course exams. I was learning a lot about how horrible things could get.

"Sticks and Stones...." When we were declared "surplus," meaning next to get laid off, I was told I could transfer out of the rural area I was in to a major city. I chose a phone company site in Berkeley, close to my mother's house and close to more evening college courses.

Just about the first day I was on the new job, however, I got called a "scab" by my new local's chief steward, and that *really* pissed me off. I was putting my lunch box in the company repair truck because I had to get used to a new routine. I put it in before start time so that I wouldn't forget it. At my previous location I had been leaving it behind in the company garage, and once you're out driving in the hills your sandwich is dead by the time you get back to it.

Without looking to see who it was or what I was doing the chief steward freaked out and started yelling about "God Damn scabs, who start before the shift actually begins..." He went through a whole tirade, and I was not amused one bit! Especially not being called a scab...since only a year or two earlier I had damn near killed myself keeping real scabs from undercutting a strike of ours.

In 1980 we ran a 30-hour strike in Northern California, and it nearly killed me. I didn't sleep the entire time, working as part of an informal strike committee based in the living room of a steward (the person who had promised use of their garage had gone away on vacation). Since ours was a rural environment which had been dealing with an economic depression for over 10 years we knew how to rely on groups in the United Way, in the local churches, and we knew how to survive...by sticking together.

I tried to bring some of these attitudes with me when I transferred to Berkeley. Within a month of arriving it became known I had been a steward up north and they asked me to sit in on grievance meetings. I wasn't even a steward in this local, and I wasn't sure I wanted to be this active so soon because I was still looking for housing. Most members watched TV and didn't read and didn't pay attention to things. It was an attitude of "I'm out here for me!" It wasn't the strong type of CWA local I had hoped for: It was more like "Oh God, what a mess!"

TQC/TQM. When the chief steward was transferred to another site I became a steward, largely because I wanted to involve the local with Quality of Work Life projects. I had attended the CWA California and Nevada Conference on a vacation day before I moved, and I had been impressed as hell by a union guy on the CWA staff who talked about how to use the QWL process to work out problems.

He was much too academic, however, and if this had been my only exposure to the idea I'm not sure I would have bought into it. Things, however, were getting so horrible with the company and there was so much at risk that I left the Conference thinking maybe we should give it a try; we didn't have much to lose.

I drove many, many miles...it was not just across California...but over the mountains and through the mud to get there...on my vacation time.

They talked about the whole QWL thing: What it was supposed to be able to do and what it wasn't. And I *liked* it...at least back in '81-'82, at the outset. Its strength was that it was a *bargaining* process. So if a workplace found a very productive *new* way to do things, a way to make the job more productive, but also a way that could have cost them that job, the bargaining process said - "If the idea came out of that unit, no one there will lose their job!" It would not trigger a layoff, a surplus, or downsizing, whatever word we're using this week to cover that.

From CWA's perspective, however, there was never enough follow-up to continue to let AT&T managers and supervisors know it was a *union*-reliant process. Instead, the quality groups typically got off and weren't supervised well. They typically ran rather quickly into frustrations and problems.

Shortly after the California/Nevada Conference I met my second-line manager to discuss something or other, and I asked him what *he* thought of QWL? He got all enthused and said, "Well, that's one of my second quarter goals. We're going to have a committee and we're going to...." I broke in and reminded him of something I had learned at the CWA Conference: "You *can't* have a QWL committee at a worksite *unless* the local union initiates it." He was not especially happy to get my message, as he was so new he hadn't known anything about it.

Experimenting with QWL. Once my manager had recovered from the shock of learning CWA counted in the QWL process we went along in setting up a trial committee, one of the first three or four in all of Northern California.

It had a lot of frustrations, I mean, *a lot*! You cannot just get a bunch of people together in a room and expect them to easily or neatly make a whole bunch of decisions. We had a lot of problems that proved too damn hard to fix, though overall, I think the experience was okay.

Score One for Us! I had a success here. One of my units was a construction garage. They figured out a way, as the contract allowed us to switch to ten-hour days, they figured a way to let their managers go on the 4-10; their engineers got to go; their clericals got to go. They figured out successfully how you can rotate such people off of long-standing tasks that have them supporting 5 day, 8-hour co-workers, so that it is not a "big deal." They made sure the change did not disrupt the entire group of which they were a small part. And they were very good at explaining the ground rules to new people when they came on, and they got them plugged into what had happened.

Once More With Vigor! The Quality of Worklife Committees kinda continued for awhile, even after divestiture and our big strike in 1983. But we did not have a "Memorandum of Agreement" with the new regional Bells on this after the '83 breakup.

In '85 the management that had made Pacific Bell a *very* innovative company, that had steered us successfully through divestiture, got really interested in reviving the whole quality idea, this time on its own, now that it was separate from AT&T. The top people wanted to figure out how to deal with the surplus and downsizing issue, one which had begun to drain too much energy from everyone.

Top management created teams of their principal officers, up to executive vice-presidents, which meet with our local union presidents. They made sure that once a year even the president of Pacific Bell met with all the presidents. A lotta work was done! And, in '85, they worked out an agreement with us that promised layoffs hereafter would be along seniority lines if your particular job was designated "surplus." You were only able to bump by seniority to grab hold of a new job within your own of four areas they carved out of all of California.

As someone who was "surplus" at the time in my area, I disagreed with the union's acceptance of this so-called "compromise." The guarantee had previously been that the company would *not* lay *anyone* off. But the new compromise took us into 1986 bargaining, and resulted for the first time in the history of negotiations between CWA and a Bell Systems company, in a settlement a week early!

The company at this time was talking about the virtues of a Business/Labor partnership. We created a Common Interest Forum to air our ideas, and even lower officers of the corporation began to get involved in cooperative efforts with grass-roots CWA people. We were able to accomplish *a lot* of things! A program the company bought into, one called "Leadership Development Systems" (or LDS), spread throughout, with its message that corporate officers had to learn how to work better together and develop a team concept. LDS promoters told everyone, "Well, we're going out from under the umbrella now, and down the road there's going to be *serious* competition! We have to get out there and stay ahead!"

Stirring Trouble...from Within. Unfortunately, a lot of corporate types had a lot of problems with the leadership development stuff. Like all giant bureau-cracies, what they do at the top, the little guys are also expected to do. Many not at the top resisted it as kinda invasive; it interfered with their "religion," *their* preferred way of managing.

What my role became - as a unionist - was to figure out what in hell they were saying?! I took this role on myself, and I went into it as if I was trying to make sense of a foreign language. As a person representing the workers I had to understand what the company was saying in order to figure out where they were going...in order to dodge the bullets and get to the other side.

Out of it, as a trade unionist, I got two things: One was a meeting for our LCIF sessions (I often chaired) which, for the first time, was incredibly detailed. Two was a Purpose Statement, a "So in a way...therefore" statement, one that focused on the management and on getting results from them out of our quality meetings: We were *not* just to meet to hold meetings!

I learned from an "insider" friend that the Purpose Statement was deliberately produced to spur the democratic processes: Anyone was free to get up and say "I *disagree* with that Purpose Statement! That's not why I came here today!" I took this seriously, and would often point out that the Statement had all kinda good stuff about the customers and the company. But it did not say anything about the union and the employees. So I would urge attention to them...and this would change the tone of the meeting, usually for the better...if the union people present were aggressive about it, knew why to support this quality of work process, and told management where we were coming from.

Sticking it to CWA. What really hurts is that the company used to be run by people who were sincere, or who at least were very convincing. They're all gone, and with them has gone much of the little good we briefly and painfully achieved in the QWL process...before divestiture, that is.

Early on, just like I had heard from the union speaker at the California/Nevada meeting, we learned we're more successful when we work together with management on solving problems than when we're fighting each other. We came to like some of the *joint* projects, like our Business/Labor partnership back in 1986, and some good things actually got accomplished.

They've since killed the attitude that makes cooperation possible. New management people have no experience at telecommunications. Or at fair dealing with labor. And all the good feelings QWL and pledges of job security once earned are gone. It's a damn shame, as we gave the concept a chance at the start. But the company keeps playing games and wound up screwing everything up.

Seachange Problems. From '85 until '88, when we continued to have management that, like us, had gone through divesture, and we all had a lot at risk and wanted to make things work, they were fine. We got a lot out of the quality process.

In '88 the company shuffled the deck. They switched key people around, and we got some new top people who, in our view, didn't have anything at risk anymore. They hadn't gone through what we had. So, we spent the next year dealing with new managers who hadn't bought into this process, and we had a lotta problems.

Many of our CWA local presidents had not gotten earlier pro-worker agreements put into writing...and this now gave us a lot of headaches. We had thought we could always do that later, but the tone changed drastically...so much so that in '89, we ended up in a strike.

Back in '86 we had had a *serious* 26-day strike against AT&T. Here in California we got some gains out of it, like the new Quality Process Agreement, and some more good stuff. But I was left wondering if we had done as well in '85/'86 bargaining as we should have?!

Measuring Up. So, in '89, when I got to attend my first CWA national convention, I spent a lot of time reading contracts. It was my first convention, and I hadn't realized CWA had a Contract Department. They had a lady there, and she had an exhibit table. I sat down and read layoff provision after provision, the first thing I ever read in a contract. I learned that our little 36-hour strike in '89 had earned us - and New York Telephone - the *best* contract layoff provisions! We went into divesture with the 2nd best contract (next only to New York) in the entire Bell system! I ended up much prouder of our California contract than before I sat down at the table.

Neglecting Basics. Our '86 contract, because it had all this business/labor partnership stuff, got a lot of pretty vague stuff in it: I'd always said you could drive a freight train through it. In contrast, our '89 contract had our CWA California people do an excellent job of mending the fences to plug a lot of those holes.

The '86 contract had been negotiated by top level people, who then passed it down to local bargaining committees for ratification: It was kind of a really abstract way to negotiate. As a result, the grievance and arbitration procedures were incredibly weak. On the bright side, we were able to get a lot of day-to-day issues settled at the time and on a daily basis. But we were weakened in protecting our people fired for "dumb things," as when the boss is just out to get somebody. So, many local union presidents lost their next election in '88 when people saw what the '86 contract *really* meant.

When I think back on that time I think in a lot of ways the union had gotten lazy. I don't think we spent enough time working together and planning for our part in the Leadership Development meetings. I know that for every day we met with them, management spent a whole day planning their part and working on their stuff. I suspect one of the reasons we did not do this is that it meant calling the company and asking the company if they would pay to have our secondary and tertiary leadership pulled off of their jobs for a pre-meeting planning session. The logic I heard was that we'd do our planning at our state convention. That was fine, but I didn't attend it..I wasn't a delegate, nor were most of the other CWA local union people I dealt with at our Leadership Development meetings.

So this was a major downfall of ours, kindof consistent with the suspicion some of us had had when it first came down the road. I collected all the quality of work charts that got turned out so I could translate them into English, so that we could keep our butts covered...but it wasn't anywhere near enough. We wound up giving it all up after '88, when corporate leadership hit the fan, and we got a ballot-box change in local union leadership in Northern California.

Seniority Haunts the Scene. In the '89 contract we saw to it there was no language about quality of worklife projects, or any such thing. I don't think there are now any committees, etc. The last of it died in connection with a clause that said the union had the prerogative to appoint the members of any worksite committee, even one that looked after coffee availability. That we had absolute control over who sat on those committees (non-members, scabs, challenged that in Merrysville, CA., and the NLRB ended up ruling in our favor, since even a coffee committee could end up discussing work conditions).

As we go forward into this new era where we don't have the Business/Labor partnership anymore, everything is unclear...except that the company says it now wants to declare entire departments surplus, rather than treat people by their seniority. Back in 1985, when I objected to this wholesale dismissal approach, I wasn't listened to - and yet now it more and more resembles the proverbial camel's nose under the tent. We've got a *real* problem with this one!

Management seems far more pleased than us: We wanted the company to get back to basics. To train recruits to do the job *well*. And to instill in them the importance of their work to the community. But the company has its sights elsewhere, as its heart was set on winning the famous Malcolm Baldridge Award for QWL.

Sticking it to AT&T. We recently turned this Baldrige obsession to our advantage, and they're still reeling from the shock. At the 1990 CWA convention in San Francisco our union passed a resolution blasting the lousy quality of AT&T management many members are suffering with - regardless of the company's QWL "happy talk." We told the AT&T Labor Relations managers present as observers that CWA, as the union on the property, would do everything in its power to keep the Baldrige Award from being mis-assigned to AT&T. No other union in the entire country had previously stood up as we did and promised to derail a prestigious national award a CEO has his heart set on - and this caused one helluva good stir! I loved it!

Back to School. Me, I've turned my attention nowadays to all the gee-whiz stuff my members are working on. I care about those weird technological things, and I've taken all the telecommunications courses I can at a nearby university: In addition to *wanting* to go myself, I didn't feel I could represent people if I didn't understand what they did. I keep trying to get a better understanding so that when we talk about workplace problems they are having, it isn't just a "blackbox."

The union is so busy dealing with downsizing and layoffs and other issues, it is distracted from the sort of stuff I'm now into...significantly *different* ways of doing communications technology. It's like the difference between the horse-and-buggy and a jet, a *big* jump like that. As it keeps rushing ahead, I go back to my members directly involved in it, and I say - "I don't understand...," and they help me catch up, again. Fiber optics uses, digital conversion technology, laser uses....

I get excited just talking about these technologies, because as I do, *new* ideas occur to me about why AT&T *may* be doing this or that, and, new products or services that *could* be developed. Now, as for what it means to my members, if they are still working on horse-and-buggy technology they cannot be flexible, and they may not make it to the year 2000 and be pension-eligible!

Getting Others Back to School. The company alleges my people can use the tuition-aid program, which paid for all the classes I took, and upgrade and transfer yourself to a better job. But people get frozen, and can't move around, or their job title is declared "surplus." People are frightened! They don't even want to touch the fax machine!

We, as the union, could help them understand how simple it is. Then we could go to an MS-DOS world, and show them how not so difficult that is (though I don't like it, because it's too cumbersome). Along with getting them to understand, we could explain this is why you need to brush up on your reading, your math, and go back and take some electronics-electricity classes...go back and re-learn some of that stuff in a new light.

I help people pass tests the company requires, barriers set to try and filter people out. I've updated training materials I developed years ago, and re-applied them to today's surplus environment.

People in the techno gee-whiz world do not always know how to communicate: They might be a computer-nerd kind of person, the kind that doesn't communicate very well with non-computer types. So, our

CWA local actually went out and found people who knew their stuff *and* had the ability to communicate with their peers, people we could urge to take and pass key tests.

Cable TV Companies - A New Frontier. I've also become co-chair for bargaining with TCI Cable Television's Bay Area unit...in five separate locations.

I quickly learned that certain TCI cable TV franchises with cities and counties in my area were expiring while our protracted bargaining with Pacific Bell was going on. But because we were so busy in changing local union administrations, and dealing with all sorts of other problems, like a company-initiated decert, we didn't immediately pick up on this expiration opportunity...so I helped change this.

When the franchise renewal hearings landed in front of our area supervisors, our very progressive Central Labor Council, after realizing we were tied up in negotiations, represented CWA's viewpoint. It explained to the supervisors that they should take notice of TCI's refusal to negotiate a contract with our CWA local, and should weigh other options to the cable company's request for "rubber-stamp" renewal, other options for better service for the community.

I got my local union president to dress up and go and testify directly. He asked the supervisors if they wanted to be known as elected officials who took their county into the 21st century - with a *backwards* TV system, as all around them better systems were going into place?! Systems with more community access to channels, better facilities, and other attractions, like a PBS channel...which TCI wanted to drop. He pointed out that CWA was a very community-minded union, one that genuinely cared about the quality of all community services.

In California the cable TV companies are regarded much as if they were a utility. So we had to figure out an angle where they were vulnerable. TCI, as the nation's largest cable TV company, could outspend us forever...and it does, sponsoring employer-initiated decerts of their locals from coast-to-coast, and nasty things like that.

With these franchise renewal hearings, however, we think we *have* found a vulnerability of theirs...and we're on the case! They may begin to rethink how they treat us, especially as we are tying up with dedicated consumer advocates, people who have long been a pain in the side to the phone company, the power companies, the water company...and now, the cable TV companies.

Like the union movement, the consumer movement attracts people with a lot of energy to burn, people willing to burn it on doing some good...and we're joining forces with the "Consumer Cable Cops"...to go to the cable TV regulators, and intervene in the franchise renewal process.

We intend to organize the 60% of cable TV employees in our area still outside of unions, and in the target companies we're going after everyone, "wall-to-wall." I've had my local union president go and meet with a Teamsters president who has some cable TV members, and

I'm talking with the relevant IBEW business agents about how all of us in this area can cooperate to win more for cable TV employees.

We sat down with the public officials and said - "You've got a serious problem for your community, as here is the trade record of these cable TV operatives in other areas, a record of *poor* service, poor resource allocation, etc., etc. It is not just our contract problem, but a whole lotta things that should have you supervisors concerned!" They heard us, TCI learned to take us seriously, and we'll be back...whenever a cable TV franchise renewal seems relevant to our trade union goals.

To me it was innovative to go to a regulatory body that had nothing to do with our union contract dispute, but was a place that was a public area where the cable TV company was vulnerable, and put the squeeze on. They know we'll be back next year, and every year when their contracts are up for renewal...so they'd be wise to start dealing. We told the supervisors TCI was denying us a contract, and thereby rejecting labor peace. And thereby threatening the quality of cable TV service available to the community. As our members lived in, and cared about this community, we wanted it to have only the *best* such cable TV franchise possible...and that required that we got our contract!

We *did* get it! And TCI was put off a year by the supervisors, who rejected the company's request for a 17-year franchise in favor of a one-year extension. We helped the public officials think in terms of a 5-year, instead of a 17-year renewal, and this is the first place in California where CWA and an area Labor Council together has achieved this - as we're the local people with the energy and motivation to do it!

Making Sense of It All. The role I've come to play, a job for the union that is not written anywhere but that I've come to take on, is saying - "Here's the global picture of what is going on...and we're in deep trouble if we don't figure out how to avoid the technological conflicts ahead!" I say - "Here's something coming down the road, some new piece of gee-whiz tech. I don't understand it. But my intuition says we've got trouble." I then devote time to trying to get some members to work with me on this. I want to continue to help our people still in the old technologies, the old world, learn how to get into the new world.

Now that I've been elected 1st Executive Vice-President of CWA's largest local in Northern California, one with a budget of over $1,000,000, I'm hoping to do a lot more with this "advance warning" interest of mine...and my knowledge base here has already expanded a hundred fold as I've set out to answer a thousand and more questions. CATV companies, especially those busy now installing a fiber optics network in every community possible, are going to blindside many "sleepy" phone companies at a great cost in jobs to our CWA members...unless we think *fast*, act *now*, and somehow get out *ahead* of all of this...or, at the very least, give it one helluva good try!

Part VII

Downsizing's Toll

"We must seek to make what happens, in substantial part,
a logical result of our having planned that it should happen."
Simon Ramo, *Century of Mismatch*; 1976; 204.

"It's a recession when your neighbor loses his job;
it's a depression when you lose your own."
Harry S. Truman

While decelerating somewhat, downsizing continues relentlessly, especially in the core sections of the economy where large employers are opting to focus on a fundamental competency and outsource all the rest. High wage manufacturing jobs continue to be lost, only to be replaced by lower-paying and often only part-time jobs in the services, the kind of jobs that keep people insecure and ratchet down the American standard of living.

Worried themselves about where their next paycheck may come from, inside reformers in shrinking workplaces are distracted by their role as confidant, supporter, adviser, and advocate for co-workers ahead of them on the dismissal list.

Certain of these union activists have been busy inventing new ways of striking back, new ways of conveying to corporate and union officialdom alike their resolve not to go quietly, but instead to rage against the dying of the dream. Long ago convinced they were as good as anyone else, and were therefore owed considerable care and respect, they damn well intend to secure both!

Substantial job loss is likely to persist throughout our chaotic transition to a post-industrial Information Age economy. Accordingly, the inordinate pain of unwelcomed unemployment will probably be with us for years to come. A careful reading of the case below by a feisty and creative inside reformer offers many leads to better-than-ever union counters to the unacceptable misbehavior of "killers of the [job] dream."

TQC - After the Work Runs Out
Rhonda Bailey Maddex
(CWA)

What happens to labor-management cooperation when the company begins massive job losses without end? A former local union president, Rhonda Bailey Maddex, now out earning a law degree, tackles four difficult questions:

> What alienates a local from initial support of a Total Quality Control/Total Quality Management program?

> How can a local profit from a mail poll of its own membership in difficult bargaining situations?

> What can union leadership do to lessen the pain of wholesale job loss?

> How can local union presidents help redirect their own international union?

Especially valuable is Rhonda's advocacy of "thinking outside the Box," a call for fresh and creative approaches consonant with the brightest potential of union reforms.

Given the strong likelihood that technological displacement, outsourcing, mis-management, and overseas competition will cost millions of American jobs for years to come, it is vital that union leaders plan as far ahead as possible and plausible. Creative use of newspaper ads, private home "picketing," calculated "potty break" lineups, and other ways to apply pressure are explained by Rhonda, albeit with a note of rue that such hard-boiled tactics must sometimes take the place of labor-management cooperation.

My father, who had a career as a phone company technician, used to tell me I had to carry my own weight; I couldn't expect anyone to do for me. This be-came a sort of sacred rule for me. So after I spent seven years as an officer in my CWA [Communication Workers of America] local, one that was 90% male, I won the presidency in '87 and I *really* began to shoulder some weight!

Trying Cooperation...All too Briefly. In the 1980s CWA and AT&T were active in joint participation at varying levels of the corporation. We enjoyed some success and experienced considerable evaluation in the way we worked. Although we worried abit about radical technological change we could see coming our way, union rank-and-filers felt they had a say in this process. Over and again we heard AT&T management saying "Our employees are our most valuable asset," and we almost came to believe them...almost.

Everything changed, and entirely for the worse, when Bob Allen took over as CEO in 1989. He warned that AT&T would now become "lean and mean," and he set about with a crew of "long knives" associates making good on this threat. He didn't take long driving out left-over executives who respected a negotiated agreement, valued customer service, and wanted to help preserve the dignity of people losing their jobs.

Somebody I know on the inside told me about a management meeting that early on showed Allen's influence. The people attending were told that if any were still inclined to favor customer satisfaction, something we had stood for as long as I can remember, they could just as well get up and leave! The new focus was going to be elsewhere; AT&T was going to go all out to increase dividends. Anyone still committed to customer satisfaction could just check right out of the meeting hotel and go home, as the new AT&T did not want to waste money paying for their room.

Poisoning the Well. It wasn't long before ordinary workers also got the word that the customer no longer came first: If we found customer service sud-denly at risk, "Tough! So be it!"

This new attitude hurt...and we didn't like it much at all. We saw AT&T as having only one purpose under Allen, as that was making profits, profits, and *more* profits. This undermined what was left of any confidence we had once had in the company's leadership, and we could no longer trust its commitment to us or to our value to AT&T.

Coupled with an unending stream of layoff lists, the company's "customer-be-damned!" attitude led to a lot of disgust, very low morale, and sharply reduced productivity.

Pursuing Quality...the Wrong Way. Sensing the mess it had made of em-ployee relations, AT&T moved overnight into a "Quality Process" approach, but it only managed to make an even worse mess of things! Their approach was a top-down, management-driven process, one which included CWA only as an after-thought, and then only in response to our *demand* that they wake up, get serious, and begin to pay attention to us!

It didn't take long to realize the whole thing was not so much about qual-ity, or us, or even about them, so much as it was about Allen's lust to win a Malcolm Balridge Award for the company. And to complete a *really* convincing award application Allen needed a rubber-stamp endorsement from CWA.

Striking Back. Seeing that the CEO suddenly needed something of value from us, or feedback on his way of running things, we decided to give it to him...*real* good!

Ignoring CWA in Washington, which has its own fish to fry, and has its own deals and dealings with AT&T, we set out - some of the more angry locals like my own - to document what the people in the front lines thought about the mess created by the new AT&T.

Conducting Our Own Poll. We learned we had about 107,000 members in the AT&T system, and we sent a mail-response questionnaire to about 4,000 of them. Since we had no funds to speak of, and were in a big hurry, we did the whole project quick and dirty.

One local wrote the questions, coordinated the mailing, and covered most of the expenses. Others pitched in anyway they could. In short order we got back about 500 responses, and they were hot!

Our members were angry, frustrated, and disappointed. Thousands were staring at the possibility of layoffs or technological displacement. While they told us of their anger over these threats, the majority were even more p.o.'d that they could no longer do the high quality work they had done before Allen abandoned the customer. They resented management roadblocks put up to keep them from servicing people like in the past. They knew Allen and his crowd were getting hefty raises while they were being kept from providing a quality product...and they were furious!

We tabulated our results, and mailed copies to CWA headquarters and to Bob Allen...with a separate and special package going directly to the judges for the Baldrige Award. We also gave out our findings at the last meeting scheduled of the joint AT&T-CWA Central Region Quality Process project. When the management people there learned we had already sent the survey data to Allen and the Baldrige judges, they were *very* upset: They had not expected such 'outrageous conduct!' I still smile when I remember that silent room of ashen faces...staring at the truth.

Pink Slips like Snowflakes. By late 1989 it was clear new joblessness in our industry was going to set all sorts of records. The year began with 13,500 technicians doing what I did, but we knew that when the digitalization conversion was completed in '93 our ranks would be down below 6,500. Over the two to three years after that even the 6,500 would probably be cut one-third or even one-half! Heck, the copper we worked with could only handle 90 circuits while our new light-guide fiber could transmit 24,000 circuits - so we knew we were finished.

My local of 260 members had once had about 63 doing my job, just in Des Moines, Ia. and the number had fallen to 18 when I finally got laid off in late 1990. I had had terrible moments of anxiety and fear at having no paycheck and no job. I found the possibility of losing economic control terrifying...so before it happened I focused on doing what I could for others I knew were even more frightened, more scared out of their wits.

CWA has done a good job in the last two contracts of winning considerable layoff improvements: We have substantial termination pay, surplus priority placement for transfers, money for moving, enhancement of retirement checks, paid retraining options, aid in job searches, aid in resume-writing, and aid in interviewing skills...but, even with all of this, it can hurt like hell.

Layoffs in the AT&T Personnel Department had left the few survivors there drowning in work they'd never catch up with...so I basically served as a stand-in. All day long and in the evening after dinner, I took calls from CWA members desperate to get answers and reassurance. I used a network of contacts I had made over the years, and I shared as much as I could learn from friends I had inside the company.

Things got so crazy that near the end I was faxing advice in every direc-tion, but the internal layoff process remained chaotic at its best. No amount of warning people prepared them for the reality...although I did as much preparation work with co-workers on company time as I could.

Lower-level managers simply did not get the straight story, so employees got screwed making life-shaping decisions based on bad information. I had seen it happen to systems technicians earlier all over the country, and I didn't want it to happen to my members. So I just took charge and started sharing "hot news" as soon as I got it. And pretty soon I had control of the information.

Managers began saying "Ask Rhonda, she'll know! We don't hear anything!" It bothered them a lot that their supervisors just left them hanging. It simply proved to me, however, what I had been coming to realize all along - "If you've got the information you've got the power!"

Power to the Locals! Which brings me to an effort some of us made, and some who are still in the industry continue to make, to exercise power from below, from outside of CWA headquarters.

Twenty or so, each of us a president of what was known before divestiture as an AT&T "Long Lines" local, agreed after bargaining ended in '86 that the situation had become intolerable. We vowed "Never again!" We learned that AT&T was planning to layoff thousands and thousands of us. After 1986 bargaining, we created a coalition of local presidents who just won't roll over and be nice. We meet once every quarter for a day to share ideas, and we deliberately stir trouble in the "trenches."

Now our CWA Vice President tells the company he is not in control of us - which he isn't - and the company had better think twice or the "wild people" out in the field - all of us - will *really* make trouble! We're betting this will work: They *need* our cooperation!

Our one-month strike in '86, a *very* bitter one, had earned us very little, except for a growing realization that high-tech was making our employer strike-proof! In defiance of a CWA ban against formation of a caucus confined only to our 'Long Lines' locals we created just such a group in late '86. CWA was afraid a 'civil war' would break out, pitting us against CWA locals at the regional Bell companies who also had AT&T union members. So we rushed to give headquarters assurances no such foolishness need develop...even while we tried to promote new militancy in our AT&T ranks.

Within a year we attracted about 15%, or about 53 of 476 eligible locals (including CWA locals of regional Bells) to our four-times-a-year meetings, and a lot of good contacts were made. Each local or state-wide caucus sent one formal representative, and generally covered only the barebone expenses entailed: People used their vacation time, gave up work time, and family time, as we met only on weekends at various locations across the country. We used all that QWL training to run intense and highly productive meetings. It felt *good* and it began to payoff!

Standing Up! We went to CWA's 1989 convention loaded for bear, and they soon knew we were there! After the '86 strike, our leaders had signed hundreds of stipulations altering the terms of our contract, hundreds! Our caucus went to the microphone and told the delegates that any stipulations CWA headquarters wanted to sign with AT&T between contracts should be reviewed beforehand by those members we had elected to our CWA Bargaining Committee.

Convention delegates were shocked to learn how many stipulations... hundreds of them...had been quietly agreed to by CWA's top leaders. To drive the point home we taped together xerox copies of the stipulations, the fliers stretched from one end of the Convention Hall to the other!

Sure enough, certain CWA leaders came to us to cut a deal: They wanted to avoid an embarrassing convention floor vote on our motion, and assured us we had already gotten our point across. We went ahead anyhow, just to drive it home, and when the votes of 2,000 delegates were counted, our amendment had won an overwhelming endorsement! This impacted all bargaining units, not just our AT&T one!

We were not opposing the signing of stipulations. Our beef concerned our fear that if only headquarters' types negotiated between-contract stipulations we'd be represented by people possibly too far removed from our shopfloor lives. We wanted the reality focus provided by our elected Bargaining Committee...especially as several of our caucus members sat on that committee. We were correct, and it was right that we won!

Gaining Significance. Our caucus, the "Ad Hoc" Committee, remains alive and well. We bring a lot of ideas into the deliberations of formal CWA committees and we've gained a lot of respect for this. We understand CWA is up against it in an industry hell-bent for downsizing, so we've actually set up a subcommittee to "think outside the box;" that is, to come up with creative ways of getting AT&T's attention, and maybe thereby win something for our people.

Our subcommittee recently got CWA to run an ad in the *New York Times* which targeted the investors AT&T relies on. Wow, was the company upset! It hit so hard that CWA agreed to pay for more such ads. The union also agreed to a $2 a year assessment for each member in an AT&T local...an amazing break-through earmarked to turn the heat up where AT&T is concerned! A rank-and-file committee on which our caucus naturally has representation will monitor this new fund, and see to it that we stick it to AT&T.

Our focus now is on running a corporate campaign against AT&T leaders, especially Allen, the CEO, who is beefing up profits by magnifying layoffs. He has taken technology plans that were not scheduled for implementation until '93 and rushed them along to occur in '90! He wants to replace high-seniority skilled workers with a new workforce of less skilled part-timers...and destroy our union incidentally along the way! We are his albatross.

Using Every Advantage. In 1988, CWA launched a "mobilization" program in an attempt to arouse grass roots awareness and action. Many locals, including some of the Ad Hoc members, were resistant to what appeared to be just another bureaucratic fad. Soon, however, other Ad Hoc members were participating as mobilization coordinators, and the program was turned into an avenue to run some of our best ideas - such as the *New York Times* ad, or gather proxy votes for the AT&T stockholder's meeting. In fact, it was an Ad Hoc member that proposed union representation on the Board of Directors at a 1992 stockholder meeting.

Our "Ad Hoc" Committee wants CWA to get tougher and harder than ever. We want Allen sent the message - "Dare try to screw us...and we'll screw back!" We're angry! We're smart! And we're finally united in a caucus of AT&T local union presidents intent on moving our union to a stronger and more rewarding course.

Leverage and Tactics. CWA's leaders should use our existence to everyone's advantage, everyone in our union, that is. We're a loose cannon on the deck, no doubt about it, and the union should warn AT&T they can't entirely control us...which is the truth! CWA could use this warning to urge management to weigh all the harm speeding up its schedule of layoffs is causing...and maybe, just maybe, get AT&T to slow the pace and spare the pain abit.

With this tactic and others our caucus may yet help CWA in ways barely glimpsed by any of us. We're kinda proud that the union's Executive Board already views us...a bunch of upstart mavericks, a bunch of loyal trouble-makers...as the single *most* influential grass-roots caucus of several in our union.

Afterword (July, 1992): I recently finished school, having used my CWA-bargained tuition benefits for laid-off workers. At the end of this month I'll graduate from the George Meany Labor Center with a B.S. in Labor Studies.

As I was finishing up, CWA and AT&T were in bargaining. The night of the contract deadline I got a call from Midge Slater, president of CWA 7102 in Des Moines. She had wanted me to know that the contract had been extended and that I should be down at the local hall with them! She invited me into the weekly conference calls that the bargaining committees were having with the locals. So, I went! It felt good to be back in a union hall!

Some of the "Ad Hoc" members were on the bargaining committee, others were "mobilization" contacts. Hearing the familiar voices of friends who had continued the battle, I felt such pride for how the group had evolved!

From the conference call I learned just how "thinking outside the box" had progressed; e.g., members were soliciting the public to change long distance carriers at numerous informational pickets across the country. This was a BIG step for many who had previously felt they would jeopardize their jobs by taking business away. Some members were even soliciting the customers they worked with and getting results!!!

Management was being driven crazy in many offices with prolonged "pencil tapping" sessions that created considerable noise. People were taking bathroom leave ("potty breaks") all at the same time. One office had fifty people lined-up waiting. Certain locals had scheduled "safety" days, which required time-consuming vehicle inspections and clean-ups. One technician said that his shop hadn't been that clean in twenty-five years and they were PROUD!

Drew Lewis, former Secretary of Transportation and a member of the AT&T board of directors, had become the first target in a corporate campaign plan. The fact that he lived in a town of over 10,000 steelworkers may have had some impact!!! Bob Allen's home had been picketed for the second time in two years.

And certain operators were spending a day processing all calls "manually", so customers got that old-fashioned personal touch for as long as they needed it. That killed management indices!

The list went on and on. Different units were "creative" on different days and the company could not keep up with the "action." In addition AT&T business unit managers had decided that they would take over bargaining this year and cut out most of the labor relations people. CWA negotiators quickly figured out that these people were there to advance their careers, and could have cared less about the employees or even the company as a whole! When the federal mediators finally stepped in, these guys bailed out in a hurry, and labor relations was allowed to step back in.

Even in the midst of this management bargaining fiasco, the company told CWA it plans to reduce the labor relations group from about 167 nationwide to 10. Our union will have its work cut out! LR can't even keep up with its work load today!

Well, CWA members kept up these actions for six weeks and finally got their contract without a strike. I knew that much of this grass roots militancy had its start in our Ad Hoc group, and it felt great to see that with unity this can really work!!!

It has not been difficult for me to leave AT&T, but I cannot leave the labor movement. I have been accepted at Drake Law School and will begin my first year in September, 1993. Convinced by my AT&T experience that "management is too important to leave to management," I want to help labor reach those in positions of power on behalf of those who cannot, in order to help balance corporate decisions that impact our lives.

More Potent Political Action

"What does labor want? We want more schoolhouses and less jails,
more books and less arsenals, more learning and less vice,
more constant work and less crime, more leisure and less greed,
more justice and less revenge."

Samuel Gompers, AFL President, 1881.

"What does labor want? We want...we do not know what we want.
But, at the very least, we want to be cut in on the deal."

Thomas Geoghegan. *Which Side are You On? Trying to be for
Labor When It's Flat on Its Back* (New York: Plume ed., 1992), 6.

Nearly three decades ago a leading labor intellectual, Gus Tyler, forecast the imminent arrival of a new era of "political unionism."[1] He envisioned a shift so dramatic and emphatic as to have labor appear "in coming decades to be more a political party than a bargaining agent, although, in fact, bargaining will be as intense as ever and the unions are unlikely to organize a labor party... The end product will probably be a realignment of national parties with labor as the mass base for the party of liberalism."[2]

To his credit, Tyler concluded that "because the labor vote is the product of cumulative education and effort, the era of political unionism will come upon the nation slowly... It will mark a revolution and, like so many other American revolutions, it will come piecemeal and silently."[3]

Two case studies below make clear the centrality of politics to American unionism. Both activists move on the stage of statewide electoral politics. Neither makes light of the difficulties they confront. While frank about limita-tions of resources, each nevertheless accents the positive. Both model the patience and perseverance required by any who would immerse themselves in labor's political "wars."

Especially intriguing about the case provided by James A. Teague is his account of personal growth from knowing little or nothing about politics at any level to reaching a point now where he is a self-made proponent of the use of the Constitution as a model for civic and organizational affairs. How he connects this evolution to his involvement in feisty acts and militant attitudes reveals much of value about this particular type of inside reformer.

Richard A. Finamore, in turn, offers an example of a tireless individual driven to give his all, and then some! Persuaded political contests and victories are of strategic importance to a social movement like organized labor, this inside reformer is the sort of stalwart on who much depends, regardless of how any particular race turn out.

Above all, the two activists make clear the linkage of their roles with "a transcendent meaning for all those workers - not only militant unionists - who are searching for leadership and social solidarity."[4]

References

[1] Gus Tyler. *The Labor Revolution: Trade Unions in a New America* (New York: Viking, 1967), 198.

[2] *Ibid.*

[3] *Ibid.*

[4] Nelson Lichtenstein. "What Happened to the Working Class?" *N.Y. Times* (September 7, 19920, 19.

Raising Political Consciousness
James A. Teague
(BMWE)

While a lot of media attention has been paid in recent years to *corporate* culture, far less has gone to *worksite* culture, or the remarkable "community" of attitudes, actions, and values that are created by co-workers in distinctive work settings. James A. Teague, an organizer when he wrote the following essay, and now the Acting State Legislative Director for his railroad workers' Brotherhood in Massachusetts, helps remedy this situation a bit with his evocative account below of rail work and rail union realities.

Witty and affable, Teague's material urges consideration of six important questions:

What are the sources of work pride that inside reformers should note and respect?

How can a wildcat strike be turned to reform advantage?

What sort of harassment should a reformer expect in a very conservative work setting?

What value has the U.S. Constitution to the reform cause?

What value has PC-utilization to the reform cause?

How can a local newsletter and letters-to-the-editor be used for reform gains?

Above all, can inside reformers earn more talk about union reforms and railroad innovations, like Mag-Lev systems overseas, than sports trivia and the weather?

I come out of a middle-class background. My dad, after leaving the seminary during the war, married and started out as a mail clerk for the railroad - though he also went to school nights at Boston College. Twelve of his 14 children survived, and my folks raised us all as decent clean-cut New England Catholics.

During his first ten years working for the railroad dad was a member of the Brotherhood of Rail and Allied Clerks (BRAC), back before it became TCU. He was a local grievance chairman, and was very successful at it. After he completed college, however, he started moving up in the company until, when he retired, he had been senior management for the past 20 years.

His politics as he went up the ladder did not change at all. He did his very best to represent the company, but by a *very* ethical code. I know for a fact that before the railroad industry was ready to even consider there might be an alcoholic problem dad was working with troubled individuals, from the ranks, in helping them through treatment...which at that time was just a psychiatric institution and a bunch of pills for awhile. He kept a sympathetic view toward labor, though individual leaders really aggravated him.

I consider my father and my grandfather to be probably the two finest men I've ever known. My grandfather worked in the mills around Lowell, Mass., all of his life - and that helped me grow up with a fascination about labor history.

I've always rooted for the underdog...maybe because I've always been a Red Sox fan. Some of this, of course, is from having been raised Roman Catholic. At school we studied the saints, the martyrs, and Christ and the Sermon on the Mount. I think a lot of that has stayed with me. Everybody in my family reads and still does, and we have always been encouraged to give a damn, to care and act on it.

A Chilling "Hello". When I was hired to build and maintain rails I found the line had a "closed shop" agreement and I had to join as a condition of employment. The full-time officers of my union, the Brotherhood of Maintanence-of-Way Employees (BMWE), and of my local, were all retirees. Rank-and-filers were so inactive that *anything* above zero attendance at a local meeting was judged a good turnout. But I already knew what unions could offer, and I also knew they called forth obligations.

The first communication I got from my union, the third largest of all in the rail industry, came after I passed my 60 day probation period. It explained that I now had to come up with three months dues and my initiation fees within 10 days or the company would be informed to terminate me. And that was all the letter said: It didn't say "Welcome to the Brotherhood," or anything.

A point of pride with me is that our union doesn't deal with those letters any more until you're well into the process. We greet members in our local personally. We try and get an officer to meet them. Or call them. Or try and get a correspondence going with them as soon as we learn they are on the property.

And, in fact, if they eventually don't join our union they eventually get the nasty letter, and we will follow through, but we try first to welcome them in.

Defining a Role. It was important for me not just to become a member, but also to keep my job. I had just left college. Nowadays I know that what I had done was drink myself out of a free ride to a conservative Catholic university in the South. I had spent a year there... matriculating or drinking, I'm not sure which...probably the latter.

So, at that time I got my first introduction to labor as a movement, as opposed to what had been in the books I had read...which was probably more reading than many people who had been in unions for years, just because I like to read.

I attended my first meeting eleven months after I joined the Brotherhood. We ran a few people for office and the power-holders kept rejecting them for having not met the dues requirement, 'cause the dues collection was lousy at the time. Hell, I went to meetings where if you had 3% attendance you were doing well. And that 3% was there because the local opened the bar immediately afterwards. Generally that was the second order of business - to table a motion to open the bar right then.

Nevertheless we did elect a new slate of officers, with the important exception of the two guys who actually controlled the power of our local. We didn't have the authority at that meeting to reach them, the Assistant General Chairman and the Secretary-Treasurer. This last guy had held the post for 30 years, and, as a retiree, he had no contact with us except for the local's meetings.

The post of Recording Secretary for the local came up, and nobody wanted it. I was kinda the new guy, but the guys knew me because most of us were from the same shop and the same crew. We knew something about one another, having worked together for almost a year now. So one of the guys who had been there about three years said "Let's elect fuckin' Teague fuckin' recordin' secretary. He's been to college, so he must know how to fuckin' write."

And basically, that's how I got started.

The Quiet Years. At that time in the 1970's, things were running pretty smooth. We were working for a bankrupt carrier and we didn't get our contracts on time. But as soon as our International settled the trustees kinda' swallowed it, even though we weren't part of those negotiations. We had to go through the motions for the bankruptcy court and such. Somebody would come up with our money.

We had work rules our people were fairly content with, and if a grievance happened, the Assistant General Chairman came in and tried to minimize the damage. (The way we had of settling disputes in the crew back then was to call a guy out into the bushes and just "duke it out.")

Job Satisfaction. There are times nowadays when I miss being with the B&M, as roadbed conditions are very different from when I started. I deal less often now with the major rail wrecks. And I used to love nothing better than to show up on a major disaster, where there was just a hole in the ground where a lot of piles of freight would have previously run every half hour.

All these reporters and TV cameras going out and showing just *massive* destruction...the only thing I can compare it with are pictures of an airline disaster. But 24 or 72 hours later...probably not having been home any time to sleep, and maybe getting just a sandwich or two right there, I watched a set of rail wheels go over that spot...almost like new!

When I worked for the Boston and Maine, which was a bankrupt railroad that didn't have a lot of money, and was trying to keep the wheels turning, I was in charge of the Boston section, which was the yards. They were absolutely falling apart.

So myself and my friend Vinnie, who ran the other crew, used to refer to what we did as "creative maintenance." We'd go out to the latest derailment and put together a piece of track that had been busted apart ten times in the past week. We put it together with the same materials. By shimming and wedging in place of spikes and ties, we'd get the next car or train delivered...and all the guys took a lot of pride in doing this.

When we worked as a surface crew we'd look back with pride when we did a mile or a mile and a half that day. A tie crew always talked about a 1,000-tie day, a particularly *good* day. If you get a 500-tie day many times that is the best day possible, in most circumstances...and you've worked *hard*! But every now and again you hit one of those days when everything goes right...when the track machinery is not breaking down, when you are not working in sludge...and you can push out 900 or 1,000 or 1,100 ties.

When I went to work on Amtrack I had never been involved in a joint-eliminator in-track welding operation. In my first year I learned Amtrack had an enormous set of standards as to how it was supposed to be done and such. The manufacturer said crews averaged between 15 and 25% defects: Amtrack had lowered that to 10% defects. In the first year not only did my crew surpass the record by over 200 welds, but we had a failure record of less than 2%.

By the time, a year later, when the company ran an independent test of our work, we were up to about .5%. That's about zero defect level compared to what had been expected!

Work Ethic and Leadership. My friends, *poorly* managed, are going to take advantage of every opportunity to kick back and relax. Certainly in the rail industry there are few incentives to perform well. Hell, I worked for three years, and the only time I saw a supervisor in the field was on one occasion. Their absence doesn't really mean that much, though, since the person who *really* counts is the foreman - a brother in our union - and whether or not the men will work depends on his relation with them, not on that of any supervisor.

Some of the best days I've had as a foreman have occurred when I've said - "Well, if we make six welds today, we'll go home." The Amtrack average in this corridor was three. Our average was about four and a half. And I knew that after a certain hour I was just not going to be able to accomplish anything; that's just how it is.

And I've had days where my approach has resulted in eight welds! Most of the productive success we've had has come directly from the employees: They *revel* in doing good work, and will...provided it makes sense to them.

Taking a Strike. In 1978-'79 we had a wildcat strike. A contractor has been called in to do some of our work. That had never happened before. When some of our members went to a supervisor and asked what were the new men were doing here they were told "It's none of your business!" We had members who were laid off at the time, so we said if you don't do something we're gonna call the union. And they said "Go ahead and call!" So we did, and got no response from our president - who had just not been put in the coffin yet.

Six guys decided to picket the location. And all of them were fired. What should have been something readily resolved left us instead out on our own hook to do something about it. Six guys walked out, struck, and got fired. Nobody would have paid attention to them for anything else; they were just a whole bunch of bullshit people, not our elected leaders. Well, we got them reinstated after our strike had lasted a week. Every craft on our line honored our picket line, and we shut down the line for an entire week.

We got major publicity within hours 'cause our strike also shut down a commuter rail system. Major pressure came from the courts and federal marshals right from the outset, but the fact is they didn't have any strike structure to go after. The situation was just completely and totally chaotic, at least from the company's standpoint.

It was a *great* strike, in that they were totally unprepared for it. We had 100% compliance. And there was nobody to say "O.K., guys, go back to work!," because we weren't listening to anybody.

Our General Chairman came up to Boston from New York to go into court and try and plea bargain. Even there six of our members were standing in front of the judge, all of them in handcuffs, telling the judge they couldn't tell the people to comply with the court's back-to-work order because the strikers didn't belong to them. The strikers were not following the officers of the local; they had no actual standing, and six of them had even been terminated by the company. They weren't picketing any more as they were under arrest. So the judge decided to order the company to reinstate the men and arbitrate the grievance.

Taking Charge. At the next meeting of our local we tossed out our 30-year Secretary-Treasurer and all the rest of the incumbents. I took a position as a grievance handler, and we signaled to the union's General Chairman that he was finished: It was a given; he was gonna' be gone!

True, we replaced him with someone equally ineffective, but that man soon dropped dead. His replacement had a better idea of how to play politics, and that was by doing something!

By that time four or five locals in the BMWE had radical reform caucuses, including my own. We have no formal name, and are best known for daring to send a challenger to the BMWE convention 'cause we were Goddamn sick of sending the same old delegates. Though we barely realized it at the time we had put together a reform movement... though not without taking a lot of shit. Reformers in our Brotherhood are still labeled "communist," and some of the guys still look cross-eyed at me and say - "Ask him! He'll show you his Party card!"

Even with this crap we managed to put some of our people on the Executive Board. We managed to change some of our bylaws. And we eventually got a couple of our people appointed as Assistant General Chairmen. We remain pretty loose, though we have a formal progressive caucus now within our union, and we kibbitz with similar guys who have won control of two other railroad brotherhoods. Although I don't personally adhere to all of the caucus positions, I am generally sympathetic to the idea.

We still have too much power in the hands of the Old Guard. I worry about it all the time. I hear talk that they want to force "retrenchment " on us and I know that really means falling back on the traditional rules, regulations, and bylaws, the Old Guard uses to shield themselves.

I prefer the U.S. Constitution as a model. God, but I love that document, because it is a living, breathing instrument. It allows you to read it; it allows you to interpret it. I think we should use that model to bring our Brotherhood into the 21st Century, to help it stay alive, stay relevant, and maybe even get out ahead.

Changes Coming. They've got technology coming along that will eliminate the need for more and more of our 47,000 people. Computers and sensors now ride over the tracks inspecting them, and I can see where a foreman will no longer sight track himself, but only watch out at gradecrossings that someone isn't coming his way. He'll be able to quicken the pace of his patrol, and soon be able to cover more and more sections that used to require other men.

My job as a track foreman has become more and more technical with every passing year. It gets farther and farther beyond the ability of laborers to move up and someday do my sort of work. I'm now required to learn stuff as complex as track-buckling countermeasures complete with mathematical formulas that vary with weather conditions. I now have to carry a pocket calculator, and I'm expected to become skilled. We're looking at rolling machines soon with the computer capability built in not only to detect problems, but also to *fix* track right on the spot. Everything is changing, and with computers getting smaller and smarter all the time, there's no end of change in sight.

I became a foreman with less than three years' experience on tracks. I had to sit down and qualify on the operating rules. They gave me an open book test. I had to write the book out and take an open book test at home. And then go in and take another open book test. And then I was qualified to do a foreman's job. Now you have to take that test, but it's not open book anymore. It is much more complicated.

Struggling to Stay Up! We know we've got to adapt, just like our work is changing, so we've begun to update our local, and none to soon!

What I'm proudest of is that our BMWE locals now handle their own first- and second-level grievances. When I first started with the BMWE, this was tightly held by the General Chairman and his assistants, all of whom were full-time union employees. Our locals, in contrast, were led by people who drove spikes for a living, and who did their local union work on their own time, by and large.

For the past four or five years my local union president - and I
assist him in this - has been able to draw 40 to 60% attendance to our
meetings, a point of real pride with us. It is an outstanding statistic!

Of course, they're coming out in large part because they're angry
over the concessions we took after our one-day strike in 1990. A few
days before the national strike the craft of our General Chairman and
other signed the terms offered, and that put maybe 25% of the rail
workforce under contract. And for the same terms they could have had
three years earlier! Our leadership didn't put it out to us, which was
fine with me. I figure that the way the Railway Labor Act works, if
it's that bad you might as well have it jammed down your throat then
acquiesce in it, then give some form of legitimacy to the document.

We ourselves were not *directly* involved, so I was never out on
strike. The crafts started off with striking just the major freight
carriers. Had they let the strike run its course, the plans were to put it
all down, the entire rail system, freight and commuter alike.

All the rail workers waited for what the rail union leadership had
promised: Either they would go to jail. Or the White House would try
and break us like it did PATCO. Or we would win a much improved
settlement. Our chairman had promised we would *not* go back without
one of these three resolutions: We would stay out as long as it took in
order to win!

Goddamn, the whole thing was ended by Congress in a day, and
we'll never get over our embarrassment. Everyone was left feeling
misled. Deceived. And thoroughly let down. Our world is one of
machoism, and the members have concluded the Chairman had no balls:
A drive to recall the bastard, or at least turn him out at the next
convention, gains more support every day.

With everyone still pissed over this embarrassing mess attendance
is up at all the local meetings: People really come out when they're
angry to see just what in hell we're doing to set things right again.
We're trying, at least they've got to say that! Most of our local
officers, while not computer-proficient, have an idea of how to work a
word processor and get a membership list and run a phone network...all
of which earns respect from guys who show up at the meetings.

We've been preparing for two years in advance for the next round of
negotiations, and have already assigned men for picket line duty and set
schedules. We've let the men know what is available to them and what
we require of them in picket duty, and what they'll gain for that.

Helping Members Keep Up. If I can take any personal pride
in anything that I've done with the union since I became one of the
brokers of the power structure, since I "assented" into the structure of
my local, it is that the membership has become better informed. More
active. And more aware. We've got a helluva long way to go, but at
least we're moving. Now they're not just waiting for us to give them
the information: They're asking questions. They're keeping up with
what is going on, as best they can.

You have to remember, we don't own NBC, so getting out the word isn't easy. I just initiated a newsletter on legislative matters in the state that may help. It's not a newsletter as such: The Constitution says whenever I spend any money I must make a report on it in writing to the National Legislation Director. And what I've begun to do is send copies to the local legislative reps, to help stir them to get on the agenda of their local meetings and make a legislative report - even if only to say they've got nothing to report. And I'm trying to get around to the various locals myself in the state.

I've done a letter-writing campaign to the newspapers, and I've had a number of them published. They're targeted at stirring up my own membership, though the general public also gets the message. I send copies to various locals to use over their own signature in area papers: I don't care whose signature appears at the bottom as long as the letter gets printed.

I've come to rely heavily on this tactic. We've only got 700 to 1,000 members, depending on the employment season, spread over the entire state of Massachusetts. With those kind of numbers I can't walk into a state legislator like Local 4 of the Operating Engineers can, and say "I've got 4,000 members living in Boston. Tell Billy Bulger I *want* this bill passed!" So what I've done is start a lot of letter-writing, and I've continued on with that.

Not always to applause, mind you. I wrote a letter over my own signature, *not* using my union identification, that expressed my sympathy for Anita Hill. My members, however, tended to side with Clarence Thomas - "Ah, she's just some bimbo tryin' to make a name for herself! How come she didn't say nuthin' for ten years?!" - all that kind of stuff.

But, for as much flack as I took for my letter in the newspaper, they all *read* it! They were all talking about it. And at a local meeting I used this to get them talking about the *union*. About its position in this matter. About Supreme Court decisions. Before this I don't think our membership had thought much about the Court, one way or the other, except when we had a case before it. So I've got no regrets: Hell, to hear the guys actually talking about unions and the Court was worth all the flack...and more!

In other letters I've tried to get some attention paid to stuff *real* close to us, stuff like Mag-Lev systems overseas. We'd have to completely retrain our people if the nation goes mag-lev, as we have no experience with it. We should make contact with the key engineering firms that design this stuff and study it, just to get some information that we could make available to the membership...information I'd write about.

When I'm not busy stirring the pot and agitating with my letters I stay busy talking up at every local meeting I can get to. I fill the brothers in on legislative matters, and try to get them to understand the importance of our PAC. As none of them have heard a word in the previous nine years from the Brotherhood's Legislative Department I get a fair hearing, if only the novelty of my message.

Tomorrow's Agenda. We've got to do more to consolidate the smaller crafts before some disappear altogether. We must win some reversal of the trend to contract out our work, one that may be costing 30% of our traditional jobs, and we've got to slow the hemorrhaging of jobs to new technology.

A key to all of this is achieving concerted action among the crafts. Far too much time is spent on relatively minor jurisdictional matters. In my department I see jobs unnecessarily lost just for a lack of knowledge among the crafts of the scope of our agreement with the rail company. Hell, a lot of our most active local members could not - on a bet - name the railroad crafts now under the umbrella of the Railroad Labor Executives Association.

We've got to do more on mergers. I've talked over and above and around this for about three months last Fall, and a recommendation came to the floor last December that we start contacting other locals to find out *their* feelings about this. If we don't start looking to some of the smaller crafts, with which we have much in common, (the shop crafts, the signalmen, the special and technical engineers), if we don't start talking with some of them we're going to find ourselves going hat-in-hand to the Clerks or the UTU. I think this is something I can pitch to our national leadership.

In the 1980s productivity in the rail industry increased as much as seven times the national average for all industry. We used to do plots by eye, and a guy could get a proud reputation from one end of the system to another for having a "true" eye, better than any surveyor's tool. Now a computer does our plots, and one man operating it does away with at least two traditional jobs. Right up front we should *demand* a fair share in the benefit that has accrued to the carriers from this increase.

Organizing has to be taken seriously, as it hasn't for the past 50 years. To survive we must attract new members, even in non-traditional settings. Why aren't we organizing some of the non-union contractors now stealing our jobs? Shouldn't we examine methods for unionizing "temp agencies" that now contract for work we used to do in-house? To do as little as we have been is to allow the stagnation that will lead to our demise.

Drawing It All Together. I went to a job interview recently to organize for another railroad craft, a *very* technical field. One of the gentlemen, in the course of the interview, asked me how, since I didn't know his field, I could possibly expect to speak to his members and expect to organize people in his field? I said the subjects we would talk about - the respect and dignity you should get in the workplace, a fair wage, the right to have grievances addressed - those things cut across the entire spectrum.

You don't have to have driven spikes for a living to know that its hard work. You don't need someone standing there cussin' you and calling you names while you're doing it - you don't have to have done that to know that that's wrong! And you may not know or recognize the specific dirty name the man was called to know that he was offended by that type of treatment...and it needs to be addressed! It needs to be corrected!

That was an eye-opener for my interviewer.

I've not yet been confronted with the classic old dilemma where I would have to decide whether or not I would blow up a railroad bridge - and I pretty well know where I'd come down on that. But I've never considered the stuff I do as either ethical *or* unethical: In an organizing campaign recently I used private confidential files someone had gotten for us from inside the company. I never really considered how the stuff had come to us; I just used it! I did not hesitate to do so for an instant!

I enjoy it now when I see members overhauling the BMWE structure because their issues are not being adequately addressed. I don't think that we're militant enough in labor, not by any stretch of the imagination! I wish we could enjoy some kind of peaceful co-existence with management. But I believe management has taken the opportunity granted it by the law and political climate to up the ante. To test the limits. I don't advocate violence, but I think it's going to happen.

Being through what we've been through in the last ten years in our industry I understand where a lot of the frustration of our people comes from.

I'll give you an example: I work with the train inspectors who are organized on the Mass Bay Transit Authority system (MBTA). They had a contract that was freely negotiated and granted them 100% employer-paid health care benefits. The legislature, however, just passed a law requiring them to pay 10%, and it is probably going up soon to 25%! They had a contract, freely negotiated, which said they would not: This wasn't even a matter which went to arbitration. So, these guys are now angry, very angry! And they believe themselves of a higher social sphere than my own track-repair members, and definitely better educated.

This sort of thing is what has me thinking the potential for violent rifts is out there, just under the surface, waiting for the right time to explode. Possibly things are so bad now...we've been hemorraging membership for 30 years, as have all the rail unions...that something is going to have to change.

We in the labor movement, most particularly at the lower levels of the power structure, have been forced to look at our future through the ravages of the present. I think we have the ability to look beyond the traditional course of our movement to the continued existence and growth of our organizations. I think the time is coming when the voices for change within the labor movement will become the dominant force. It's going to change, or we're not going to exist.

Pushing Politics and Safety
Richard A. Finamore
(UTU)

As if being a change-agent inside labor wasn't hard enough, imagine a situation where you have no paid time for your effort. No expense account. A membership not entirely convinced of the importance of your effort. And company officials unable to respond to you without clearing everything with distant higher-ups. Add to this responsibilities in not one, but two time-demanding and high stress union matters - campaign politics and workplace safety - and you begin to understand the remarkable situation of Rich Finamore, a Legislative Rep with UTU, a major railroad union.

At first glance his story would seem to entail little of the vigorous struggle to reform unionism from inside common elsewhere in this volume. On reflection, however, it becomes clear he models a life of political activism, an abiding faith in the power of the ballot box, that may force many to re-assess their cynicism and passivity where union political action is concerned.

A careful reading of this material can help answer such questions as -

What does a reformer do as a political activist?

How responsive are well-off unionists to calls for political involvement? Why? And what can an inside reformer do about this?

What are the wellsprings of motivation for a union political activist, and how deep do they course?

Especially inspiring is Finamore's sacrifice of earnings, family life, and personal time to the "Cause," a sacrifice many other inside reformers share in varying degree, and one which labor's opponents consistently underestimate in its frequency and undervalue in its significance. So long as unions can continue to earn and deserve this sort of allegience, the labor movement will continue to astonish its would-be pallbearers.

Basically what I am is a Legislative Rep for the United Transportation Union, a railroad labor union. I originally hired on 14 years ago in 1978 as a brakeman on the old "B & O" railroad, which, through mergers, became the CSX. Now I'm a locomotive engineer.

Background. What drew me to the labor movement was the fact that I came from a very, very poor family. My father and mother divorced when I was very young. There were four of us altogether, and we lived in a housing project in New Castle, PA., west of Pittsburgh. We lived 18 years on welfare, which was sort of like a slow defeat. It was *not* a union neighborhood: It was a welfare neighborhood: It was *tough!*

My grandmother on my wife's side (she's 85 years old, God Bless her! I love her to death; she's been like a mother to me), she always told me - "The labor unions built a machine in the 1950's, when you was a kid. It's because of them people that we have what we have - our pensions!" "Now," she says, "you have to fight everyday to keep what you have, 'cause somebody is out there who wants to take it away."

It really grates on me that my mother and grandmother (they are still alive today) have to spend half of their Social Security (no pension for my mother) on medication and the other half on rent and utilities. I mean, what kind of retirement is that?! It's crazy!

Inside Reformer Role. I have two responsibilities these past eight years as a Legislative Rep: I do everything in my power to get labor's friends elected, nudging railroaders to give a damn, and I also promote safety in our industry.

Just last year, for example, I took three months off as a volunteer, three months with no pay coming in, to help assure a win for a key state lawmaker. I ran phone banks in my part of the state. I delivered leaflets. I went door-to-door. I did anything asked of me, so important was the cause, though we eventually lost. But I won an internal victory within myself knowing that I can make a difference.

I take my own personal vacation days and days without pay to push for votes for labor candidates. I'm not paid for any of this, but I spend so many hours at it I might as well be paid. Any letters I put out, I absorb all the postage myself. The guys don't understand this. I do this on my own, I do it for nothing, because I believe we *need* labor in politics.

I also do it as part of my dedication to the labor movement: I live it. And dream it. And sleep it. And breathe it. Its hard to raise two boys when you are not paid for your time or expenses, but I do it anyhow...because that's what it means to me. I think my 18 years on welfare sort of inspired this.

Now, since I'm well-paid as an engineer, I can go back and hit it hard and make up some of the money it cost me to go out on unpaid leave for union work. We make a good living. But even if I couldn't, I would do it again, which is how vital I feel is this political work.

I go from one political race to another, working all out, and trying to get more railroaders to see it like I do. I work nights after I get in from a train run; I'll work til 2 o'clock in the morning, 3 o'clock in the morning, 6 o'clock in the morning...whatever it takes. I'm that determined, because I feel we *have* to turn this country around!

My voice now carries influence. Most of the men respect me (some think I'm crazy). They respect what I am trying to do for them and what I believe in. They feel that as long as I'm there fighting for them, they can depend on me: The honesty is there.

Reform Challenge. It is hard, however, to get railroaders involved in politics, like I struggle to do. They're basically content. It's me that is not at ease, that wants to see a better America.

When I got out of the Marine Corps after high school and hired out on the railroad I immediately felt an attraction to unionism. I saw how it could help improve our working conditions. Later, after I had moved from being a brakeman to being an engineer, after I had about six years in, I ran to become a UTU Legislative Rep. I've been elected twice since, most recently by acclamation (there are about 40 of us in my state).

If I ever got a union expense account, or actually got paid by the union for my time on union matters, I'd probably lose my marriage! It's gone 20 years, but my wife might not go for this. Because I'd immediately get active in politics full time! I'd be lobbying these guys every day. I'd be just going crazy! That's my ultimate dream: To be a full-time legislative rep for my union. But the UTU is cutting our posts, so it is a tough dream to ever realize. I've been offered two positions in management, but I know this is not right within me and so I've turned them down.

Reform Difficulties. It is a hard sell to the membership. Many do not actually believe in politics - which is in my blood, as I believe it is the *only* way to *really* change things. Lots of guys, however, are only concerned with getting that paycheck, period, nothing more, nothing less.

I don't want to say they never care. Some railroaders realize that the federal government and the Association of American Railroads create short-lines to circumvent labor agreements and to get away from unions altogether. That's something they realize, but they don't think it can happen to *the*...until it does, and then its too late.

When we have UTU lodge meetings I'm usually vocal and I tell it like it is. I file reports for the guys when I come back from meetings of our UTU State Boards, and I post them on our bulletin boards. I'm thinking now about expanding my outreach to include leaflets and political buttons to stir the guys.

I tell the guys to get out and register to vote. But a lot won't even do that 'cause they'll lose too much money if registering results in being called up for jury duty: That's the mentality I'm up against, you know. This is just a select few, now, don't get me wrong. I don't want to criticize the vast bulk of the membership: They are my friends and I love them dearly.

But I can't make no bones about it: Trying to get my brother railroaders politically active is a tough cookie to sell!

Safety Role. Closely related to my political activities is my second responsibility, that of creating a safe place in which to work for our members. If there is an unsafe condition I'm gonna have it fixed. Or I'm gonna bring in the Public Utilities Commission and they're gonna have it fixed. Safety is probably just as big a part of my job as politics.

I'm fighting now to protect a piece of legislation we have on the books, the Federal Employers Liability Act, that the employers are trying to get rid of. It gives us the right to sue if we're injured on the job, and it's a powerful tool.

The company doesn't like to clash with me on legislative matters, 'cause they know I'm conversant with the rules and I pose a real threat. Where safety is concerned, I do have to give the company credit, 'cause they do try and keep it a safe place to work...though I resent the effort railroad companies nationwide are making to take away our right to sue after accidents. Fortunately, they're finding it hard to convince Congress to throw us railroaders into a system as archaic as Workman's Compensation.

Summing It Up. The biggest satisfaction I've been able to take from eight years as a UTU Legislative Rep is knowing I can do something and get it done! So many times I've argued, argued, argued, only to see nothing gets done: It was that way for my first four years in this job. Then I started talking with other UTU Legislative Reps in the state, and with higher-ups in the union who were legislatively-inclined. And I found out what their secrets were. This enabled me to know what to say and what to do, and, all of a sudden, I began to get some respect.

My greatest frustration comes from my inability to get the company people I speak directly with to do the right thing. I'd would rather sit down with them, if they're the officer of the railroad company, and say, "Mr. Trainmaster, why *can't* we get these safety lights put in? Why *can't* we start cleaning up safety hazards? Why *can't* we get these engines cleaned up a little bit?" That's the way I'd rather have it, you know. But maybe they're just too scared at the local level to make decisions: Everything has to come from middle and upper management, so the local managers I deal with are powerless.

Back to the Ballot. I turn for guidance to my hero, Eugene V. Debs, a great labor leader, who wrote that the only way we can beat them - the corporations and elements of the federal government in collusion with each other - is with the ballot. That is the *only* way! We may not have any money, but we *do* have the ballot!

Part IX

Union Democracy at Bay

"Those who expect to reap the blessings of freedom must, like men, undergo the fatigue of supporting it."

Thomas Paine

"Unions need to rally their ranks, to bring their members into active participation in the lives of their unions...Internal democracy is no longer simply an ethical demand for more justice and better representation. It is a precondition for labor's survival."

Anon. "Organize!" *Labor Research Review,* Spring 1986; 2

Cynicism among certain union power-holders takes the form of defining a "good" rank-and-filer as one who never attends meetings, dutifully shows up at rallies, consents meekly to everything done and said by officialdom, walks the picket line when told to, and in every other way, toes the mark. Unlikely ever to come to the attention of higher-ups, this bare shadow of a member is relied upon by entrenched incumbents to preserve the (false) illusion that everything is just fine.

Quite different are proud rank-and-filers and inside reformers who make their presence known at all meetings. They question everything in a revealing way. They demand a satisfactory accounting for anything asked of them. They make their presence known when on a picket line. And in every other way, they make their mark, convinced as they are that things could be a hellova lot better.

Bad-mouthed by disdainful incumbents as malcontents, ball-busters, and radicals, the dust-stirrers seldom raise hell just for the hell of it. Rather, most owe allegiance to a self-generated, homespun notion of what a democratic and dynamic union should resemble, and most are outraged by the disparity between that model and what may actually exist.

All the more valuable, therefore, are two cases below that take a reader behind-the-scenes in "no-holds-barred" power struggles. Advocates of a participative model of what union governance is all about, the two inside reformers provide a template against which all locals could usefully measure themselves. While much of the pain attendant on their struggle is conveyed, so also is much good advice offered. Above all, a strong case is made by two resilient activists for the end soon of democracy denied.

Challenging Business as Usual
Paul Plaganis
(TCIU)

Choice of metaphor continues to reveal much of consequence about event-shaping unionists. It is not surprising to learn that inside reformer Paul Plaganis thinks of "family" when he thinks of union: "The personal aspect of how a union can touch someone's life and improve it on a personal level, that to me is what is really significant in union structure."

"Family," however, as applied to a local, can mean very different things to different people. Some unionists, for example, think of obedience, conformity, acquiescence, and docility, with younger members deferring to their elders, females to males, low wage-earners to high, and so on, in a traditional time-honored Old World Formula. Others, however, like former TCU chairman Plaganis, have a far more zesty culture in mind. They champion mutual respect, a tolerance of differences, and the creation of a safe haven within which searching questions can be raised and sensitively explored.

Four questions addressed by Paul highlight what unionism as a "progressive" family matter entails:

What is it that especially disappoints about a traditional business agent?

How can a proposed contract be effectively opposed, and what might such opposition cost reformers?

What difference can helping a troubled member make in the life of a caring reformer?

Above all, how does a reformer fight back after being purged? What is most helpful in a personal recovery process and in resolving to stay effective? How does one continue to promote overdue reforms on an unofficial level, keep up an indispensable sense of humor, and stay committed to a vision of still-better unionism?

I was born and raised in Highland Park, NJ, where I lived for the first 18 years of my life - and my mother and father, now divorced, still reside there. My father comes from a family of Greek immigrants who came here in 1915 or so. His father was a strong influence on me, a narrow-minded and prejudiced man...but, given his background and his life, its understandable...and forgivable. The wonderful smells that came from my grandmothers' kitchen still linger...a sweet woman.

My mother comes from Irish-German immigrant background. Her mother was German; her father had an Irish background...and I never knew him well.

Ours was not a "union family." Neither my father or mother worked in a union environment. We were union-neutral: Bad things were not said about unions; good things were not said. It wasn't a topic that was brought up.

My father, his father, and a couple of uncles ran a newsstand across the street from a major train station, one of those 24 hour-a-day deals, all weekend as well...they were self-employed types.

My impressions of labor as a child began very young, as strikes of newspaper people in New York City when I was about 10 cost our family our money for about two weeks, though my father was not bitter: He just waited it out. As a teenager in the '60's my image of labor became one of a construction worker, in his T-shirt, with his hard-hat, and his American sticker decal on the side of his helmet...somehow, I concluded, if you were in labor you were a pro-war hawk.

I came to find out later on in life that the AFL-CIO back then had been supporting the Vietnam War movement. When I think of war I think of worker killing worker...stupid! Labor, whose main job it is to promote...and to protect the workers that pay their dues...here they were promoting an opportunity for workers to get their ass shot off in a foreign jungle. I don't know...maybe someday I'll be able to figure that out.

Schooling and Neighborhood. When I look back now on my schooling I think, "God, was I cheated!" I went to the kind of high school that prided itself on sending 80 to 85% of its graduates onto college: I was not one of those. I think very, very early we are classified - as if we are put on the high road to the college courses, or the low road to the trade courses. I was placed in the trade courses...and I feel some resentment now that I was not pushed higher...by my parents and by myself.

I've taken it upon myself in my adult life to correct this. College had always seemed like a mystical place, a place where smart people went. I think different now that I'm part of the college-degree program at the Meany Center. It is a place where people go to learn...from each other.

I grew up in a working-class neighborhood made up of roofers, firemen, policemen, construction people, and a doctor. I thought the whole world was like that...or it should have been. It was a *fun* neighborhood, a never-ending holiday of every possible religious festival, filled with fun kids, understanding parents...it was really one "family." Every parent was *your* parent, and you didn't dare cross 'em. Unfortunately, we had to grow up.

Wanderlust. After high school, with the Vietnam War going on, I had a real definite choice to make: Either I could not go to college and risk getting my ass shot off, or go to college. So, being the survivor that I thought I should be at that time I enrolled in college...and lasted six weeks. I quickly realized college wasn't for me at that time.

After I left I sold my car, brought a plane ticket, and took off for the West Indies for six months. Spent my first winter out of college on the beaches of Barbados, basically living with local residents. After running out of money, and returning back to New Jersey, I still felt a need to see more...more people, more places.

So my sister and I spent the next summer in Alaska: A *real* nice time! Very rewarding! Camped for three months straight, out of a VW Beetle...God, but it was fun! Got to know my sister very well: Still have a book she wrote about our trip in Alaska...one of my prize possessions. Upon returning from Alaska we decided to stop in Oregon. I must have been 20 at the time. We liked it so much we both decided to stay.

Going to Work. I got a job working with my uncle, who was a master mechanic. We worked in a non-union sheet-metal shop, just the two of us, for a year, and I learned a lot of about sheet metal. Realized I didn't want to come to work hung over 'cause it was a *very* noisy place: 7AM in the morning you're banging sheet metal. It was *not* fun if you were not in a proper state of mind.

I was terminated after a complaint came in from a customer. I was wearing my hair at that time in a pony-tail, and it was almost down to my back. When I went out on a house call to fix some lady's furnace she called back to the office and told the boss she really did not want someone with long hair coming to her house. I got called into the office and told either I cut my hair or I was fired.

I got fired.

Probably one of the best moves I ever made. I came back east, and ran into one of my uncles who had worked his way up to Division Rules Examiner for a railroad. And he said, "Hey, you want to work on a railroad, kid?" And I said "Why not? What the hell!" They offered $2.57 an hour, and that was 50 cents more than I had been making. And after six months I'd get $1.50 raise, so I'd be making over $4 an hour, and that was big bucks in 1972 - so I took a job on the railroad.

I didn't know *anything* about railroads, but I learned. I qualified for different roles over six or seven months, and finally passed all of my exams.

Thinking Nothing of Unionism. In my high school we never studied unions. I cannot think of one time in all those years that we ever discussed unions or studied unions. It was just not a subject apparently of any great importance at the time. (I don't think that much has changed since in our elementary education, though its something that *should* change. And I think it *can* change!)

One of my earliest impressions of unions involves Jimmy Hoffa. He seemed to be an admired personality in the New York and New Jersey area. It seemed if you worked as a Teamster member or drove a truck you made good money. The equation boiled down to "Teamster=Money." The membership did not give much heart to the fact that their leadership might be somewhat corrupt: They were more concerned with the benefits this "corrupt" leadership was able to gain for them.

I've come to believe that to some degree members want a little bit of "radicalism" in their leadership: In the case of the Teamsters it was their connection to organized crime. I think we can do better in the future.

The focus point of my growing up - with respect to unions - somehow remains the murder of the Yablonskies. I vaguely, vaguely remember it. It was something you saw on the news, almost like a movie. It had no relevance to me. I did not know any miners. I did not know that unions could be corrupt. I did not know there was such a thing as a need for democracy in unions. Why the Yablonskies were killed I did not know...and I did not care. They were abstract persons in an abstract setting.

Unions just did not have any meaning for me, personally, as a child, a teenager, or a young adult...though my vague unease with the Yablonski murders stands out in my memory.

Going Union. It wasn't until I hired out with the Penn-Central Transportation Company in 1972 that I first became aware - vividly - about labor unions.

I remember the first Local Chairman I met, God, but he was powerful! He was so good at his job as Business Agent that for eight years at it he never lost a discipline case. And out of hundreds of claims that he submitted (we called them "penalty claims") he only lost one - and that's because the claimant gave him the wrong date on the alleged violation. A strong guy...a *strong* guy!

But he was definitely a traditional business agent. He was just concerned about making sure that we made money. There was no talk about union democracy. Or robust unionism. Or community involvement. Nothing! It was just - "Here's your job. Here's your working agreement. If they violate it we'll fuck 'em!" That's it: Plain and simple!

It pretty much stayed that way for quite a few years. It didn't really change until 1983 or 84...but I'm getting ahead of myself.

Working on the Railroad. We worked six, seven days a week, every day, month after month, back when I started...*a lot* of work in those days. I worked as a freight agent in the Boston area, and was basically in charge of all the freight operations in eight offices up and down the line.

To be honest, I didn't know shit about it! But, since it was a union position and it had to be filled by someone from my craft, I'd go there and play "boss." Basically I sit and read a newspaper. Everybody took care of their own jobs. We used to run little lottery pools. Go grocery shopping. Go to the bar drinking. It was sort of a loose place.

From there I held jobs working as a tower operator, a bridge operator, eventually winding up in the Chief Train Dispatcher's office, working as an operator clerk. Basically I was working right in the nerve center of the whole New England Division. It was good background information for how to become a *good* railroader. In time I was put in charge of two territories, and I directed all passenger and freight trains over these two locations. I ran the trains on signal indication through remote control signal switches: I had a lot of responsibility, and they worked me to the bone!

We were short of people, as we always seemed to be, and I can remember working stretches of 40 to 60 days in a row, without having a day off. Everybody I worked with was also working like that.

Butting (Union) Heads. It was during that time that I can remember having my first *negative* run in with the union hierarchy.

My lodge had been merged with a clerical lodge in the area, and since we were both in the same parent union there was no conflict...but I had a new union rep to rely on.

Sure enough, three or four of us, myself and my coworkers, were brought up on charges by management for some alleged violation of such and such a rule at such and such a time. We called the union rep up and asked him to come and defend us against these charges. We all attended the formal hearing, but the union rep did not show up. So we called him at his work location, and he said - "Oh yeah, I'll get right over. I forgot all about it." It sure made us feel good, when our jobs were on the line, to learn that he forgot.

He came over, and the investigation started. But he did not ask even one question of us or the company witnesses about the whole incident. When the investigation was over the Hearing Officer turned to him and said - "Do you have any comments or criticism about the way this investigation has been conducted?" I know I had a lot of them, but we had been instructed not to answer. He said he would reserve comment until he had reviewed the transcript.

I thought to myself - "What a shitty job he just did defending us!" My job could have been depending on that investigation...so, from that day on I wanted his job! I thought to myself "I can do a better job than this, and we deserved a better job than this."

Fortunately he was up for re-election the next year, and I knew I could get support from all the people on my craft, 30 of us. But he had about 250 in his craft, so it would be tough. I put some feelers out, and found he wasn't that well thought of, but no one wanted his job, so things just went rolling along.

Oddly enough he was very well-connected in the union, very highly thought of! I thought to myself - "Jesus Christ, they think highly of *this guy*?!" I don't think he knew how to write a decent claim, and he sure didn't know how to defend anybody in an industrial hearing...and they were as commonplace as showing up for work.

So I decided to run against him.

Running for Office. At a meeting for nominations a friend of mine nominated me. My sister, who was now living nearby, helped me get up a flyer and we took it to a union printer. We addressed 300 envelopes, I put on the stamps myself, and we sent out this little flyer.

I can still remember to this day when we had the election count at a union meeting two months later. I was sitting there when the vote finally came out, and I had beaten the incumbent two-to-one! It was a strange feeling: I was happy. I was excited. I was frightened! Now the responsibility of all of these members was on my shoulders. I felt like Atlas.

I can still remember walking home and finding my woman friend out, but having to tell somebody, so I phoned my mother, and my brothers, and I called friends of mine...I was just *so* happy!

Well, I have to admit, the jubilation wore off real quick.

Holding Office. Two weeks later I was officially sworn in, and I fell right into it. There were a lot of things that had to be taken care of. The company was right in the middle of bankruptcy. We were basically under government control. There were a lot of complicated legal things going on...and these members needed *good* union representation! They needed more than someone to just file a grievance. They needed information. They needed to be *involved*! They needed someone who was able to be a conduit between the company and them, and the company and the union. And I think I filled that void very well.

I had very good support from Steven Tolman, my immediate union supervisor. He was, and is, a *dedicated* trade unionist...really the only one I have met from my union so far, or at least out of my system board...they aren't trade unionists so much as they are old-fashioned business agents.

Steven and I became not only union brothers, but brothers in the true sense. We worked our asses off. We presented claims. We defended people. We gave them information. We wanted *them* to become active.

We traveled all over New England, our territory, in his station wagon, with all the dog hairs in the front seat...meeting members, attending grievance claims conferences, defending members, holding union meetings...and we talked on the phone at least three or four times a week (our phone bills were outrageous!). It was constant communication, constant talk about what to do, and what procedures to do, and what course to take, and how we could serve the members better.

The five years Steven and I worked together were the best five years of my union career...so far. I got to see the good, and I got to see the bad of my union structure, my System Board.

Doing For Yourself. I quickly learned the more things we could do on my level - without getting the hierarchy involved - the better we were off. And Steven realized that also. I thought to myself - "Are we the only two who want to see *robust* unionism? Are all these other people just business agents? Or are they involved in real unionism?!"

Well, I found out what they were involved in: They were involved in the status quo. The ways they had been taught by their mentors were how they were going to run things.

As Stephen and I became older in our union activities we were eventually isolated. It was like, well, they really didn't know if they could count on us to be team players anymore. There were a lot of spies out there, and of course, we had some in our midst.

Kiss of Death! The real break we had with our hierarchy came when, in '86, the union negotiating team sent the new contract out for national ratification...with their blessings. The contract was a piece of shit...absolute piece of shit! Once our signatures had gone on that contract it would have effectively wiped out our craft.

The union hierarchy thought it was a good deal. They failed to explain to the membership what some of the contract language meant. One phase would have permitted "electronic data interchange," and the union wanted to gloss that over. But I knew what *that* meant! It meant freight and railroad companies could use their clerical forces to produce shipping orders and way bills and all the assorted paperwork needed for freight shipment; the railroad could now tie directly into the shippers' computer. And the shipper's clerical people could input the information from their work location. They could bypass railroad clerks and go right into the railroad company's computers.

Kiss of death! Kiss of death if you were a clerical employee on the railroad.

Fighting Back! We just couldn't sell this shit to our members. We were opposed to it, and actively supported defeat of the proposed contract.

It was like being involved in the Watergate coverup, for Christ's Sake. We got phone calls, and were basically told - "You've *got* to be a team-player! And we've got to be able to count on you! We *need* this contract, guys."

I can still remember saying to Steven - "We just can't go with this contract. It just is not right. It will sell the membership down the tubes. In fact, we won't *have* any membership left if we go with this contract."

We got *a lot* of shit about it. Steven got more than I did, 'cause he was my boss...but it rolled down the hill and hit me. For many weeks we both campaigned against the contract. I can still remember members of the top leadership saying to us - "Don't let the membership know the *true* meaning of this contract. We want it ratified because the international president wants it ratified, and blah, blah, blah." Well, we did not go along with that approach.

Ever since that time we have been put in the "outsider" group, along with others who did not agree with the policy our System Board was taking with respect to the contract.

Biggest Mistake I Ever Made! Soon after that we were called into Philadelphia to attend a System Board meeting, about 60 of us.

The General Chairman at the time had this new proposal out. It was an interesting proposal, and being naive as I was of union activities I was intrigued.

The proposal pointed out we then had 60-some independent locals. His resolution wanted to change this into a district structure. All the finances would then be handled out of the System Board. The reasoning was not too many people attend local meetings anyhow. And some locals have a lot of money, and some don't have any money at all. To put the fire department where the fire was, we could better allocate our finances if this was all done from a central location. There would be no need for a local vice-president, and trustees, and sargent-at-arms, and recording secretary, and all the basic union positions that go along with the local union.

So, we agreed to it. It sounded like...well, we need money over here, and everything will be status quo. And we trusted the General Chairman. "Let's do it!"

We passed it! Biggest mistake I ever made! We quickly found out that before we got home from Philadelphia almost 20 letters had already been mailed out, abolishing 20 local union representatives...and merging their lodges into other lodges.

It didn't effect me, but I thought to myself: "This has got some *real* bad ramifications!"

So I started hearing stories about if you disagreed with the General Chairman, or if you were not "politically correct" and didn't go along with the Systems Board's policies, the General Chairman would recommend to the International President that your lodge be dissolved and merged into another one...and you were effectively thrown into the street without a lodge anymore.

It eventually happened to me.

Chilling Effect. If you did not go along with the official doctrine of the hierarchy, regardless of the fact that you were democratically elected by your members, the General Chairman could veto your members' wishes
...and fire you. Take your lodge members and throw them in a lodge that was a couple of hundred miles away, and effectively wipe you out.

They effectively wiped me out in January or December of 1989. I got one such letter of abolishment...thanking me for all of my support and hard work and dah, dah, dah. And now, "take a hike, Paul!"

I thought to myself, "This sucks!" My membership had just re-elected me, unanimously, a year before, and now the General Chairman, for "financial reasons," was abolishing my position...never asking my membership, never asking me, never asking my immediate supervisor...just arbitrarily deciding, "Well, we'll do away with *that* guy."

When I said to my General Chairman that I was willing to continue on and do the lodge work for nothing, he said that was "too expensive!" A sad, sad story. We were more concerned about finances than about representing the needs of our members.

Setting It Right. Today I put a lot of thought and energy into an agenda I'd like to see the union consider - things like continuing education. Time off from work or even sabbaticals from work to attend higher education or to increase your skill level. Greater participation in worker-management groups. And co-management and co-determination of workplace issues, instead of the adversarial relations many union people and management people still cling to in the railroad industry.

Those days are gone! You can only squeeze so much blood out of each other! It doesn't work anymore. We live in a competitive industry: The trucking industry is at our doorstep every day, trying to get as much of our business away as they can. Until labor and management realize they *have* to work together, I continue to see negative things in the future.

It is imperative that the membership soon realize there's life after the railroad! The industry is going to get rid of as many of us as they can. In '76, we had 110,000 employees; now, in '91, 30,000, and in the next three years, they plan to go down to 18,000 employees. Its phenomenal...and yet the union is *still* pressing for higher wages! Unbelievable! *Un*believable!

This is a tough nut to crack. The membership remains preoccupied with wages and benefits, short-term gains, instead of long-term rewards, instead of ways to boost job security.

Deskilling. As if things weren't bad enough, I'm now watching at first hand the steady deskilling of the clerical work we do in the rail industry...where we once had *proud* people, who were way bill clerks, or rate clerks, or stenographers, or a whole host of other office positions. Now they're basically doing computer input work. Everything is formatted for them. They're closely monitored. They're watched moment by moment, and there's no more "think process" in their work.

They've become a *disposable* workforce. If I can train somebody to be proficient at data input in two days, then how much will management care about the employees' concerns? If they don't like it, they can get out...and the company will hire some other 19-year old to take their place and train them in two days.

What's the difference, I wonder, between some of my people working on a computer, doing data input day after day, eight hours a day... and my grandmother, as a child, rolling cigars all day in a cigar factory? It's all production, production, production!! We've created a new kind of "sweat shop"! And we've *got* to do something about this!

Why Bother? When I get down and begin to wonder why I stick with it, why not just say "Fuck it!," I remember Ivy, and what she wound up saying to me.

I had a situation where one of my clerks, a 55-year old woman, turned out she was an alcoholic. We had a confrontation with her, the

Employee Counselor, her supervisor, and myself. I really wasn't comfortable in my role of advocating that Ivy admit her alcoholism in front of the carrier...because I wasn't really convinced she *was* an alcoholic. I had really no comprehensive training from my union or company to identify potential or actual drinking problems in employees...sad to say. (Personally, I think unions *should* have good training programs for their shop stewards to identify potential problems before they become big problems).

Well, anyhow, I was real leery about this. My close friend, an 88-year old retired Minister, convinced me it was worth a shot. You might save someone's life, or be part of saving someone's life. So, I went to the meeting, which lasted about an hour or so. It got *very* emotional. I had to say somethings that really weren't true to Ivy, about her rights under the collective-bargaining agreement. But in the back of my mind I was thinking we just had to push her to go and get some help for herself.

I left and stood outside the office in the doorway. It was a cold night, it was November, and it was raining. I was standing there with the Supervisor when Ivy came out...she was being escorted off of the property. She had reluctantly agreed to go to an alcohol treatment program somewhere. As she walked past me, she stopped, and said, in a *real* cynical voice: "*Thanks* a lot, Paul. I thought you were here to *help* me."

I'm telling you I felt lower than whale shit. I was really devastated. I questioned my role as a union official *and* as a person. Maybe I had been wrong?! Maybe this person did *not* have a drinking problem?! It had been a tough call.

Six months later I happened to see Ivy again. She had returned from the rehabilitation program, and she stopped me at a union meeting and said: "You know, thanks for your help six months ago. It might have saved my life."

To this day that remains the *most* significant chain-of-events that has effected me in a positive manner as a union official. That because of a chance I took, and because of *her* courage, a chance *she* took, she is now a *recovering* alcoholic. She is productive, and she is happy. The most successful and significant *personal* thing I've done so far has been to take part in the rehabilitation of one union member...just one.

I hope it is not my only one...as it gave me great, great satisfaction. To touch even just one life, just one person, has made my eight difficult years as a local union official worthwhile. To this day that one instance still stands out as *so* rewarding!

Figuring Out What Really Matters. I'm sure, to some people, it would be nice to win an election with a 1,000-member bargaining unit. Or to obtain a good contract. Or to find success in the mechanics of what union people do. But to me unionism is a *personal* thing...the interaction between the membership and yourself. They look to you for guidance. They look to you for direction and understanding, compassion...something I don't think "business agent" types can provide.

I look at myself as a psychiatrist, a social worker, a shoulder to cry on...the human element. When the membership suffers, I suffer. When a person was found guilty of a charge, I felt I was "convicted," also. Or I might have failed in some way.

It really is a *personal* business. And because it is, because I look at it as a personal undertaking, I get a lot of satisfaction on the personal level. I get *more* satisfaction out of helping my membership...not on matters of collective-bargaining or grievances or discipline hearings, things along those mechanical cut-and-dry aspects of unionism. But when they call me up and just want my advice about something, just want to bitch to me about things in general, or what they think about this or that, or how about this...things not really related to collective-bargaining...*those* are the things I get satisfaction from. I knew when they call, they trust me...that they trust me to give them advice, worth thinking about.

Reaching Out. As a union leader you're a cheerleader. You're the coach. You are always looking for a lot of assistant coaches. You always want to have more coaches on your side. You want more people to take an active role.

Personally, I believe unions should be more involved in people's *daily* lives, not just in their worklife. How can I, as a union official, and the union, influence or make a significant improvement or betterment in a member's personal life?! In their home situation? In their finances? In their healthcare? We have a whole myriad of services to offer that are not germane to collective-bargaining or to the contract: Those things *really* need accenting by organized labor!

Even though I had no formal guidance here from my International, those are the things that gravitated to me...Union is "family," and I mean that from the bottom of my heart. We're in this together....

When I get called and asked for advice, I feel members are saying they *trust* me...they trust my integrity, and trust I give them an unbiased opinion, give them both sides, and let them think about it the pros and cons. I extrapolate everything that can happen, and do *not* give them a "Yes" answer. Or a "union" answer. I let them look at all sides of the issue.

Looking Back. I really miss my membership...now that I've been forced out my steward's role. When it was stripped from me in '89 I felt I had lost my family. God, I *cared* for those people...and I still do! I think about them. And I have concern about them. I spent six or seven years building trust and faith and cooperation between my membership and myself...and I miss them. I miss them dearly! I just hope the best for them!

Its been tough. It's probably like when a parent has their child grow up and move on. I feel a certain amount of pain...and there is some bitterness. I feel I have so much to offer my organization...and they refuse the invitation. They're afraid, I think.

I don't understand why. I'm no threat to them. I don't want their jobs. It doesn't matter if you have an official title: If you can contribute to the Movement, or to your members, or to your fellow workers, *that's* what matters! We're all pushing for basically the same goals, though we may have different views on how to get there. We should be helping each other, and relying on each other's strengths.

I feel that my union really doesn't have time for this. My new local chairman is deathly afraid of me; I've known that for quite sometime now. He definitely keeps me at arm's length. He gets *very* upset when his membership calls me up for advice. I give it to them. At our meetings he presents a mechanical view of things, and I present a more humanistic approach: That's why I think he doesn't like me to attend anymore.

Looking Forward. There's got to be some other union somewhere which can appreciate the contributions I can give to their membership. I will have mixed emotions about leaving the railroad, but I will leave...and I've had two offers from other unions recently.

I desperately want to stay active in the labor movement and contribute to it. If I can't do it in the rail labor unions, which I don't think I can, I *will* do it in another union...one with the democratic structure of the Mine Workers, and a hunger to aggressively organize professional people, hospital workers, and the female, the Hispanic, and the black workers...everybody!

Nostalgia Time. I will look back on my years in rail labor and the rail industry with great fondness: It is a *fun* place to work! And the union, as much as I criticize certain things it does, it has been a good foundation...but only a foundation. It has a limitation, a narrow mentality about what unionism is and ought to be...a narrow focus for narrow lives, as if we lived in isolation...which we don't.

Union Reforms. I'm busy pushing a reform of our union by-laws that would re-establish locals, instead of districts, ultimately leading to the autonomy necessary for a local president to run his local with some degree of freedom of democracy and freedom of expression...without fear of retribution from a General Chairman.

Most people I speak to who are officers think there is nothing wrong with our by-laws. They do not want them reformed. They "yes" the General Chairman, who wines and dines them, and everything's hunky dory...Why rock the boat?

Local chairman who were not purged (20 of 75 went down like me) are well-connected. The membership is so spread apart it would be hard to run against some of them. They have funds with which to run around campaigning, though they call it "doing union business," so they're pretty well-entrenched...and most are not challenged.

I'm supporting a resolution to change our bylaws, and it will pass at our Systems Board meeting if it went to a secret ballot. But if the officers insist on a handvote, then "the Eyes of March" are upon you. The local chairmen know this is wrong, but they just can't take the risk of opposing the General Chairman...who can do away with the Lodge of anyone of them, just by writing a letter to them.

I can't blame the local guys and women: They're just looking out for their ass. You sure as hell can't serve your local if you don't have one anymore. So, I don't think the bylaw reform will pass anytime soon: The people who would have to support it are just too intimated to do that.

When I think of the hierarchy in the labor movement today, two things come to mind: One, they're temporary tenants. Right now they have the power, and the direction, and they're exercising it as they see fit...as they see fit. It's their shot...but they're only temporary. Second, someday we reformers will inherit the labor movement.

What shape the labor movement will be in when we get it is another question. But we will have our chance...there is *no* doubt in my mind.

Try, Try Again...in Other Ways. Having been branded a dissident, and assigned a seat in the back of the class, having been labeled a "radical" and put "off limits" to brothers and sisters who might otherwise talk with me, I continue to challenge the system that has made me an outcast.

I'm enjoying working now on an unofficial level. Without holding office I have much more flexibility and freedom of speech, and I don't have to answer to my General Chairman or get his "permission." I finding that most of the members respect me as before - since as I never lied to them - and they continue to call for advice...which I continue to share.

I have no official title at all now, and I'm really enjoying it. I'm working without the restraints I used to have, and I'm having quite abit of fun. Sometimes its easier to go around a big rock than over the top of it.

Offering a New Politics
John Murphy
(IBEW)

Energetic, engaging, and droll, John Murphy has taken more than his fair share of blows and setbacks over his decade-long struggle to renew his IBEW local. But, much as is true of all inside reformers, he has taken the count on one knee and come up off the canvas to go another round.

John believes deeply in the ability of the rank-and-file to make sound decisions when prepared with the facts, informed through honest debate, and protected in their right to privately decide as they might. His election campaign, as reported in colorful detail below, treated his local to the most thoughtful and far-ranging advocacy in its history...a compliment to the intelligence and maturity of those to whom it was addressed.

All the more valuable, therefore, is John's analysis of the strength and weaknesses of this "take-the-high-road" approach to union politics. Inside reformers weighing a direct election challenge to incumbents will find many applicable lessons in John's field-tested strategy, a politics of principle that shuns personality attacks, hyperbole, and promises of patronage rewards for the faithful. In their place John highlights a thoroughgoing, multi-phased plan for pragmatic reforms, one that can set his union brothers and sisters to thinking - "Damn, this just *might* work!"

I've spent the last 10 years trying to turn my IBEW local around because it hurts to know that in *my* local, which is like my home, the concept of brotherhood or solidarity is really gone. It's going to take time to rebuild. And without it, without our membership united, we can't effectively negotiate with the contractors. We can't effectively fight for improvements that less than half the people understand.

Our members, my brothers and sisters, are not in the right space. They all should *care* that some of us are out of work - that some of us are out of health insurance. Others are making $60,000 or $70,000 a year, with full medical benefits, but some of us have been out of work for 18 months with no medical benefits. And those well-off members don't care. So I say 'Shame on us!' The Business Manager, a man I've gone up against twice, he gets some of the blame. But shame on *us*, too! There are a few of us speaking up, and more and more are starting to, but we've got a long way to go.

Now, however, that our reform slate won four of the eight spots we fought for, including the presidency of our local, we've got the best chance we've ever had. But that's to get ahead of my story.

Try, Try Again. I was a three-time loser in local elections when in '92 I topped a ten-year-long campaign by running again for a top office. The first time I ran was in '83 when I tried to get elected Business Manager. I didn't have a clue as to what I was doing. I knew things were wrong. I knew some-one had to do something to change it. I got eight votes.

I was coach of the local's softball team at the time, and the joke was I couldn't even carry the team's votes! We were gonna get T-shirts that said 'I voted for Murphy,' but you had to order at least a dozen...so we couldn't do that.

In '86 I ran for treasurer, and I got up to double figures, about 96 votes out of 400 of our 596 members who vote. It was a three-way race, and I only lost by about 40 votes. Then, in '89 I ran for president of the local, and lost by 32 votes. There was nobody by then who didn't know something about me, whether it was true or not. I'd certainly gotten name recognition...and all as part of my ten-year-long plan to renew my local.

In '89 I actually won a post to everybody's surprise: Three guys, all incumbent officers whom I disagreed with, ran against me for delegate to the IBEW international convention: They split the vote and I got in and went to the Convention with my Business Manager (it was his worst nightmare, having me along!) It gave me a chance to meet with other brothers and sisters bucking incumbents in their locals, and we exchanged a lot of useful ideas.

Taking on the Seated Officers. A small group of us, brothers and sisters who had been talking and batting ideas back and forth for years, members I'd gotten to know and like in my earlier runs, got together and formed what we called a Rank and File Slate. We agreed to each try and raise $250 toward the election expenses, and we put seven names forward, with me a candidate for the second time for Business Manager.

From the start we organized our entire race around the local's job re-ferral system because people were getting screwed. I can tell you horror stories; local officers were getting preferential calls for job openings, while other people were out of work 16 months!

A vote for us would mean a vote for a new system that would give people the right of unlimited refusals off of a job referral list openly posted in our local's hiring hall. If the job offered wasn't what you had been waiting for, and you were #1 on the list, you wouldn't have to take it. You could let it roll. It went right by you to the next person, and you kept your spot on the list.

Naturally, some members were not sure about this idea. People had gotten used to the old way, with all of its cronyism and favoritism. People had gotten used to getting a phone call at night, and to hoping the Business Manager was their friend and they were going to get the "good" call. But it didn't always work out fairly. Guys who were well-connected, and had only been out of work two or three months were getting calls to go to work, while others as long as 16 months were not getting calls.

Our referral system reform was the cornerstone of what we were gonna win on. We had other good ideas, but the thing that was going to win for us was reforming the referral system...since it affects everyone.

Learning the Ropes. There are a lot of things to know about challenging an incumbent, and it's helpful if you learn them beforehand from some really experienced pro's. I was really lucky in this way.

In my hometown of Hartford a bunch of politically sophisticated street-smart activists in 1987 put together a third party they named "People for Change." It is basically built around a lot of community group support and labor unions. It's already been successful in knocking the Republicans off of the Hartford City Council. As for the oldline Democrats, we wiped them out working in coalition with progressive Democrats, because the oldtimers were not sensitive to working peoples' issues and to union issues.

This is where I really learned how to run a political campaign. I also got involved with a Connecticut group called L.E.A.P. (Legislative Electoral Action Program). It has 30 member organizations, including "People for Change," of which 17 or 18 are labor unions, with the rest made up of women's groups, environmental groups, the coalition for gay and lesbian civil rights, and other progressive organizations. These are people with a lot of common interests, but people who used to go up to the Legislature every year and get their brains beat in when they were working independently. Now, when they work together through L.E.A.P., they have some great new successes.

What I picked up from working with "People for Change" and L.E.A.P. were sophisticated systematic ways of figuring out how to do voter tracking, polling, and targeting voters. This information is *very* important! And I cannot encourage unionists enough to get involved in area elections and learn how to do run elections so they can implement this knowledge in their union campaigns.

Confronting Isolation. Our first move as a Rank and File Slate was to find out what people in the local *really* thought and felt about things. We had to do this because over the past 12 years our Business Manager had totally disconnected us from each other, as members, and from the labor movement: Nobody knew one another.

When our opponents ran the local meeting and controlled it nobody knew that the guy next to them had worked somewhere under a different and better job referral system, a system where they had a choice of jobs or a chance to refuse jobs. We found when we asked at the forums *we* ran that about one-third of the guys had had this sort of positive experience. But when they ran the official union meeting nobody got to know that anybody had been somewhere else.

Their standard response to everything I brought up was that it was illegal or couldn't be done. They relied on how few of our people had ever worked outside of Hartford: They had a Hartford-centric view of the universe. The sun rose and set on Hartford...and I kept saying it just ain't so!

There are a myriad of ways, a whole range of job referral systems out there. They're all different...but a lot of guys, if they haven't traveled, they don't know this. When a "suit-and-tie" stands on a stage and says "that's illegal, its against the law," they think the "suit-and-tie" never lies. The guy standing next to me on the floor may lie, but not the guy on the stage.

There is such a powerful dynamic at work. Whoever is up on stage is *the* authority, whether they are right or wrong. I mean, members just trust 'em. They intimidate members. They're like a vulture hanging over a cow.

When the rank-and-file slate did our open meetings we took the podium and tables down off of the stage, where they were up about 3 1/2 feet above the floor, and we put everything at floor level. It was amazing the change in people, just the dynamic of that. It really evened us out a lot.

Reaching Out. We held two open forums and two Candidate Nights, all of which was new to our members. While only about 35 members actually attended, hundreds learned within days what had gone on, and we got *a lot* of attention in spite of the fear and intimidation.

At our first open meeting people did a lot of venting. We used large flip charts and wrote down everybody's ideas. The members, however, did not grasp what a "platform" from an opposition slate could amount to. They were not connected to the idea: "What do you want to mess around with that for?" we got asked. We said we wanted to see change! We asked them, "Do you want a *fair* referral system?" "Yeah!, I want that! How do we get it?" And then the ideas just went up...boom, boom, one after another, and I filled sheet after sheet after sheet.

At the second meeting we also had some guys who were puzzled by the idea we were gonna build a reform platform. We explained that "It's what we all believe in. It's what we sit around and talk about at coffee breaks, at lunch, and at the bar afterwards." Immediately some guy said "What about the referral system?!" We ended up filling up about six pages of ideas at both meeting places: It was amazing that even though they were geographically at opposite ends of the state, the ideas were all the same! It was all stuff we had previously come up with at coffee breaks, ideas people felt deeply about!

Hearing from the Opposition. Our incumbent Business Manager got up at the next meeting of our local and devoted his report to the referral system: "I run an *honest* referral system!" Of course he had spies at our two meetings. But the beauty of our reform movement is that was all in the open and they couldn't attack it! Because it was all based on *ideas*! If you read through our literature there was not one slam at the incumbent.

And that's an important part of trying to do this kind of campaign. Because we've all got the horror stories. Everyone knows what they are. In fact, when people come together they all talk to each other about it. But if you are going to win, I really believe you've got to stay as positive as possible.

Candidate Night (Scheduled and Unscheduled). Our rank-and-file caucus sponsored two Candidate Forums. We invited all the incumbents and anyone else who wanted to run for office to come and answer a set of questions. And then field questions from members in an open forum.

Even before they were held the Business Manager went nuts. He screamed at us that he would never go to one of the forums. He said people could ask questions of him right there, at the local's regular meeting. So members got up and started asking questions, and I felt like it was eight or ten years of good hard work finally paying off.

The Business Manager challenged and mocked everyone who asked him questions. Many people flatly dug in their heels and said "No, that's not what you told me prior. What about this...or that...." It was really good to see!

Incumbent Surprise. Sometimes people were afraid to come to our meetings. At our second meeting four of the incumbents chose to show up. All four stood out in front of the gate staring at the people driving in. One was probably about 6'5" or 6'6", and people told me later when I called them, "I saw this *big* guy, and I drove right by. I didn't want him to know I was coming to your meeting."

If I was them, and I was in their mode, I would have done it a long time ago. They thought this thing was not going to go anywhere. They were shocked when they found out we had 110 people at our first two meetings at two different geographic sites. They thought this challenge was nothing, and they never treated it seriously...till the end.

Building a List. I spent six weeks on the phone, every day and night, building our address list of people, calling members and asking them to empty out their address book. All the law requires is that when you bring your mailing in to the local union, they will send it out for you, but the local is not required to give you a copy of the membership list. You build it yourself, the hard way. And the incumbent officers can decide when to send out your mailings when the 30-day election period starts if you let them. I wanted to get mail out on *my* schedule before 30 days, and not on theirs, so I built my own list.

(We weren't even allowed to be in the same room when we had the local mail out literature for us. We had to sit 40 or 50 ft. away from where the envelopes were being labeled for mailing and look through a doorway).

You need to find a way to communicate without counting on the official lists of addresses and phone numbers because incumbent officers can always count on the enormous power of the incumbency. They know who everybody is; we still don't know. (They have access to telephone numbers. They insist they don't campaign with the job referral list and the calls they make, but they do. And this allows them to campaign during the day.)

By the time I got done building my list I probably had about 450 out of 551 eligible voters: We did an O.K. job on this. Every name you get is a victory, when the incumbent is so closed about handing out a list of names and addresses. To me, this matter of building a *big* list was a victory.

We used it, of course, for more than mailings alone. You've got to call and engage people in issues. Many do not read the literature you send them. We used only members of our slate in our phone bank, as they knew the issues and could talk to them. We reached about 280 out of 551 with our evening phonecalls, and as 198 pledged to vote for us, it was another "victory" of sorts!

Finding Out What Members Want. It was important to use a survey early on to find where we did *not* have a lot of consensus, so as to leave those things out of the platform we were creating. We tried not to censure questions suggested by members for our survey, but we did not include all the items raised by the questions in our platform. We included 67 questions in all.

When I first proposed the survey, I had no one on my side. People said it was stupid, a waste of time. No one would take it seriously. We sent it out with stamped return envelopes addressed to my house: All people had to do was fill it out.

A lot of my own people were skeptical about whether or not members would go for this, but we got back over 32% of our mailing list! Anybody who does polling will tell you when you've never done a group before, eight to 12% is about average...and with 136 back from 420 mailed we got *much* more!

We mailed these surveys to all the incumbents as well, the Business Manager and the officer slate, because we were interested in what they thought, even though they were not interested in what we were thinking. Even some we thought were schmucks took time to answer the survey: It was really great!

As a result of survey feedback we changed a lot of things in our platform. Like when we asked about a range of things we were looking for, the ranking we got back helped us narrow the range we later supported. We also learned when not to use a specific proposal, but to substitute instead a broader idea, because people were all over the board concerning the specific we had posed in our survey.

Reacting to Racism. We had to censor a couple of questions put up for use in our questionnaire, as they were the very antithesis of being union. One asked "Do you believe American citizens should go to work first, even if the non-citizens are our members?" We did draw on a different mix of people, but never excluded anyone. When we knew a question was racist, and was directed toward some Jamaican and West Indian people we have as members, we ignored it.

I explained ours was a movement of inclusion, rather than excluding people. And that was when I first started seeing people on my slate stand up and agree with me. They said, "Hey, if they're a union member, and their dues are paid up, they have a right to be on the job referral list!" I was pleased to find I was not alone, and that others would stand up and say this racism was *not* what we're about!

Hearing More from the Opposition. The Business Manager got up at the next meeting, and spent 30 seconds explaining that work was slow. Then went on to take 20 minutes to rebut our survey item-by-item: It was great, that the incumbents had studied it at their Executive Meeting a little earlier. They had really read it and I appreciated that, because we had put a lot of work into the whole thing.

Drawing People In. What we did was repeat over and again that we wanted input and we wanted ideas. We sent our platform piece on the referral system out to all the members, complete with model language in it designed just for Local 35. It is the first piece of mailing the members got from our slate, and it was the cornerstone of our campaign.

This was how we thought we could get people to begin to think differently. What we had always run into whenever we tried to suggest changes at contract time was the "suit-and-tie" up on the stage saying "Oh, that stuff is great, but its illegal. You can't do that. You can't do that." We were gonna fight the "suit-and-tie" who stood up on the stage as rock-throwers from the back of the hall; only this time we were going to use our platform as a new type of "rock."

Finalizing Our Platform. Reaction to our platform was very enthusiastic. The fact that we took a majority of the Executive Board really speaks to that. To write the final draft I drew on our first two discussion meetings with 110 brothers and sisters, and then the results of the survey we put out, and then some follow-up meetings where we sat down and shaped the actual language.

I don't think there was anything in it really new. It was a compilation of reforms that I took from my Meany Center work, my ongoing work with the Association for Union Democracy, and from my brothers and sisters in local 35 and others from IBEW locals around the country.

Some friends told me it was too wordy. It wasn't standard sort of campaign literature. I said these people had been starved for information. They hadn't had a newsletter in five years, and before that it had been very sporadic. They didn't get union information. There was no discussion of ideas. People for the most part, I said, would eat this up - and I was right! It was the right thing for the right time.

Platform Controversies. Our proposal to reduce the salary of the Business Manager, or me, if I won, was a bombshell! People were shocked to learn he made as much as he did. One of the biggest fights we wound up having was over his salary. Some felt you had to allow him to make so much more so that people could respect him as a powerful leader. "No," I said, "you respect a person as a worker...in terms of his work, his deeds, and his actions." I wanted to get rid of the current 150% over-the-average figure for a general foreman, and we're still studying different ways to do this, but we haven't reached consensus yet.

We also fought over setting a two-term limit on how often a person could serve as Business Manager. I wanted to oppose the mentality that you should be a union officer for life. I wanted two terms-and-out, but my slate opposed putting this in our platform. I personally was committed to it even though the Platform Committee left it out of the final platform. We fought like the dickens over this one. They felt I was taking away their right to perpetuate someone they supported, like me, if I proved to be a good leader. I didn't agree, but I went along, since sentiment was overwhelmingly against my position. Leadership development was a key component of our rank-and-file movement.

We also argued a bit over my idea that we should require people to come down to the Hall to get a job: Nobody should get a job-referral call over the phone. I explained that we needed to build solidarity, and that required people being in that union hall talking to each other, and doing that everyday. Most of all, members could see that they were being treated fairly and honestly.

Additional Printed "Weapons." To the considerable annoyance of the incumbents we offered all the members a copy of the local's contract and its bylaws. These you are supposed to easily get by asking at the union office, except that when you do you're told "They're at the printer. What do you really need them for?! *We* can help you. We're here to help you! What do you need to know, and why do you need to know?"

So, people have been afraid to ask for these documents, as the business agent can affect their livelihood: They'll be in trouble. Its a pretty sad comment on how things have been.

Opposition Tactics. My opponent made a lot of positions I had taken, especially those from a 2 1/2" pile of newspaper clippings he kept in his top desk drawer. He had me speaking in support of gay rights and in support of People for Change's South Africa initiatives. And all the other things I had done. I didn't shy away from any of it, although I know it hurt me with some of the members. I have tried to consistently link the struggles of all people. None of us can persevere on our own.

A rumor was spread near the end of the election to the effect that I was getting money from two lawyers representing the largest non-union builder in our area. This rumor confused the two with two other lawyers I had asked for advice about our credit union. I got slammed a lot about this alleged involvement.

The political party I chaired from 1989-1991, "People for Change," (PFC), was blamed for blocking three building projects downtown which would have meant a lot of jobs for our members. This was put in a mailing attacking me.

It was not true. Basically, all of these projects ran out of money. PFC slowed down all three projects to extract more concessions for the community, like promises of jobs for people who lived in the city of Hartford. There was no basis for the charge of our being anti-union, but they really did try to go after me on this.

As for red-baiting me, incumbent officers had done it in the past. This election was no exception. I got knocked for my ties to other unionists, like hospital workers: "They don't care about construction workers!" I would respond - "How do you know? Have you ever talked to one? Don't you think union people should work together?" "Oh, yeah." Most members would begin to see how silly this all was once you started to look into it.

In the long run I suspect my involvement in third-party politics was a slight negative in the minds of Local 35 members. People saw I got a lot of good qualities and experience from it, built some leadership skills, and was able to bring together some fresh groups...but some of the guys still remained suspicious of it. I will always be proud of my involvement in People for Change.

Why are people afraid of me? I've always been outspoken on the job. And I did have a reputation as a partier back 10 or 12 years ago. I cleaned up that act, so all my opponents could attack was the fact that I had brought the Business Manager up on charges twice, because of failing to do certain things. I've had him before the NLRB. I haven't been afraid to take him on when he's been wrong.

That's been part of the problem he had with his own negative stuff. He always said Murphy was doing this because he hates me and was out to destroy Local 35. Instead the issue was a local union president who, as a project manager, negotiated away our 36-hour workweek and our double-time...a clear conflict-of-interest. And the president completed his sellout of the membership when he took a job as president of a local electrical corporation after he delivered our most valuable contract language to the contractors. This is what it was about, *not* Murphy versus the Business Manager!

That is how they win - by taking an issue-based campaign and turning it into a personal vendetta. That is what they excel at, and that's why the key to winning is not to get into a pissing contest with them. If you stick to your ideas, and don't get into "Oh, you screwed me here!" and "You're a liar," you're better off. The other stuff doesn't prove anything, and only threatened to get us away from the *real* issue, which was the referral system. The other stuff muddies things up, which is why we stayed away from it. There may be a time and place for it, but this was not it!

What Not to do! I found it really worked *not* to get into an attack and not get into what the other people were doing wrong. But instead, to focus on what *we* wanted to do that was *right!* It kind of made people who really read our literature ask "Now aren't we doin' something like this now?" It made them make-up their own negative piece.

Before I started writing my campaign literature I got samples from other IBEW guys from around the country who had run races. One guy who had lost had been incredibly negative in his attacks. Everything was poison and sarcasm. I felt people did not want to see that. They wanted change, but not through negativism.

I tried to impress on people that warts and all, we had a platform! If we got tied up in the personality stuff we were doomed to fail. If we stuck to our document we could de-personalize the contest, and stick to ideas and issues, and get a lot further.

It's vital to just keep talking about ideas, and stay as positive as possible without taking a shot. Union politics are *not* like normal politics: It is foreign and different! Union campaigns almost always involve an incumbent, and rarely is there an open seat. So it's usually an attack versus defending-your-record type of thing.

I didn't see where resort to personal attacks or a more militant stand would have helped me. Everything is predicated from the past elections and upon what has happened. We're into like the ninth or tenth year of trying to change this local. We tried militancy in '86 when we kept hammering away with questions: "Why is this happening? Why is that happening?" And we got really slammed in the final vote. And I was brought up on charges and suspended for six months and fined... and subsequently won my appeal.

It gave the opposition room to continue to charge that whatever I seemed to be doing I was actually trying to destroy the union. So I resisted using negative material, and I insisted that anybody who thought our '92 literature was negative had to explain that to me. I *never* took a shot at anybody!

Instead we offered some real clear choices. In places where there was nothing now, we wanted to institute something, like appoint a second business agent to service a distant part of the state. And where there *was* a job referral system we talked about the need for a complete overhaul of it, in order to take away a lot of the Business Manager's direct power over people's lives. By dismantling the current referral system, long-term power is amassed by the local union as a whole, and short term power by the Business Manager is diminished.

Why Did I Lose? When all was said and done, I lost my bid for Business Manager by 82 votes out of 416 cast. I got 167 to the incumbent's 249. The members wanted change, but they were not ready to go to the whole distance. They were not ready for all the change we represented, all the change we put before them.

I tried to get some sleep the day after, but it was impossible. The phone kept ringing with people calling to say how sorry they were. I told them we won four of the seven executive board slots, including the president, so we actually had won...even if I didn't make it.

Our slate is terrific, and it *will* hold together. The guys on it said they didn't know how they could manage without me as their Business Manager. And I said I had tried to get them to understand that *they* had *all* it took, and that *they* could do the job, with or without me.

The International will probably rush in to remind us we cannot interfere with a duly-elected Business Manager, but our local president alone gets to create and appoint committees...and I'll stay active in that way.

Three years from now we'll challenge again, and by that time more of our message will have gotten over. In the meantime, as I'm #245 on the laid-off list, I've got to start looking for a job. I've gotten a few calls to do political work for state reps and state senators, and I expect other jobs will open up.

My best friend was in tears when the vote became known, but I told him to focus on our 4-in-7 win: In two weeks we gonna have one helluva victory party...and then we'll start earning an even bigger victory three years from now.

Three Weeks Later. I think what happened with me is that people wanted change, but they were afraid of *total* change. They think they can accomplish enough through the structure they have now, through our new reform-oriented E-board.

We had a victory party last week. We drew about 80 or 85, of whom 30 or so were from other unions. Attendance was a bit low, as people are still a bit afraid to be associated with us...but, it was a start.

It's almost like the Munchkins after the house drops in "The Wizard of Oz.": "Come out, come out,!" "Is it really okay?" And that's where everyone is at: They're really waiting to see how this new structure, our slate and the old business manager, is going to work.

If we hadn't won any positions at all, I'd have to take a hard look at what we did. But winning president, vice-president, recording secretary, and one of the three executive board seats is pretty good (we lost treasurer by eight votes, and another E-board seat by 23 votes, having put up for it the first African-American ever to run for office in our local). Our ideas were there...they were just not ready for me. The members think they can get all this without me there, and that will be tested over the next three years.

I would have been far happier had I won. I'm not trying to deny that. But the fact that four of our slate did gives us an opportunity to effect policy changes, and to change the course of the local, and to fight the International to redefine local rights. We want the power of the Business Manager scaled back, and that of the president expanded, just as called for in the IBEW Constitution.

Where Now? We're trying to set up expanded committees because there is so much work that needs to be done. You can spend time trying to figure out ways to save money on health costs. Or time on pension fund investments, and how to avoid people who are blatantly anti-union or antagonistic toward us and will not hire us to build their buildings. We need to spend more time working with our investment counselors and trustees to figure out where our money is going.

We intend to interview all the incumbents, all the guys already sitting on various committees. We'll ask them if they've read our platform positions. "Do you see where we'd like to take some of the funds? Do you have a prob-lem with this? Do you intend to stick out our term? If you are going to retire soon, would you be willing to train your replacement for six months or so ahead of time?"

We'll use a group process approach. We'll sit down and a group of us will interview everyone. The president, one of our slate, will have the ultimate decision, but we'll offer advice. That way we can buffer him from some of the pressure he is feeling from personal friends who'd like him to appoint them to this or that committee: He can defer to our group process. He can explain there is only so much to go around, but if they accept another assignment and work on a group they didn't ask about, it will help prepare them more for four, five, eight, or ten years down the road.

We intend to foster a lot more open discussion and give-and-take than we've ever had, since we will have a president running the meeting now who understands what we're all about.

We haven't had an active Political Action Committee in years, so we intend to get that off the ground. Its a presidential year, and there are a lot of political races we could be involved in locally.

The president of the Greater Hartford Labor Council, seeing as he is a carpenter, was *extremely* annoyed that our opposition said that Local 35 was not affiliated because the Council doesn't care about the needs and concerns of the construction worker. He said "What the hell am I?!" The officers invited him to come and explain the Council to our E-board. I made a motion two years ago that our local rejoin, but I was told then I was out-of-order: It was a decision only of the Executive Board! It really isn't, but I let the battle go on for another day. Now we control the Board, and I expect we'll say we want to do this...as it *is* finally "another day!"

I'm really pushing the E-board and the trustees to serve as a model. We'll do more surveys of our membership. We'll ask if any care to serve on committees or trusteeships, so that no one will feel they are left out or are out of the loop, because no one asked them. I'd like to see our Health and Welfare trustees do an extensive survey of health, and where we are going with our health insurance. They need to be putting a whole lot of time into this. Pension trustees, annuity trustees, health and welfare trustees...all should use surveys, and find out more and more.

When someone says "We should be doing something about this," we'll say "O.K., we'll form a committee. Would you like to work on it?" One of two things will happen: Either someone will lose their bluster and not want to do anything, but just throw a snowball. Or, they'll care about the issue and want to get involved. We'll create a mechanism, and a vehicle for them to start compiling information on this and bring it to the trustees. We'll give members a new chance to participate...something to shoot for...as part of a leadership development track.

Making Everyone Count. The other night, at our victory party, a member came forward with his wife and said "No one has ever asked me about my opinion. No one has ever asked me to be involved. But you guys, you actually want me to be here!" And I said, "Yeah, we all need to take a piece of this! No one can do it all." So, I have a few people in mind to do a newsletter. And a couple I want to get involved in the Meany Center pro-gram.

Networking Reform. We'll reach out to similar reform groups in the IBEW, like the Oracle Club in Local 134 in Chicago, which just won a clean sweep in June. Some of them first started running for office in over twenty-seven years ago, and never won an elected office. One of their founding members was about to retire, but said he would see this through, and won! A wonderful story, and a wonderful group of people...in an 18,000-member local.

There's the beginning of pulling some of this reform stuff together. There's the "Spirit of 58," Local 58 in Detroit. They were able to elect the president, but nobody else. He's kind of getting whipsawed by his members and the people that are in power. The members want total change yesterday, and he doesn't even have a majority on the policy board, like we do.

We need to do more phone-calling and networking back and forth among our reform groups, so that we can do some things to improve the IBEW. We have the start of something good here, and a bunch of us met in St. Louis at our International Union convention in October 1991. It was a great feeling to get together, especially as we actually won a couple of issues at the Convention.

Where Next? To a Committee on the Future. I promised to set up something to look far out beyond today, and I'm functioning now as a committee of one. A whole new wave of technology is coming: We're not going to have magnetic motor control, which has been the mainstay for the last 20 years. It will be a thing of the past in the next 10 years. There is a whole new wave of technology coming to do this stuff. More fiber optics, more electronics...and understanding how a magnetic control item works will be passé. The wave of the future in the electrical business is moving faster and faster.

Now that we've won a majority of the E-board, it *will* happen: A Committee on the Future will be created!

Where to Next?   To Redefining the "Enemy." I kept saying the contractors were not our enemy. They are at times, but generally what do they want to do? They want to make money. They're in business. Some of them have stockholders and even when privately owned, they like to make money. They don't employ us because they're humanitarians; they hire us to help them make money. So they'll want to work with us when they see we're really committed to re-educating our workforce...to re-dedicating ourselves to being the absolute best we can be.

I think some of this is already occurring as at least one major contractor has approached an elected member of our slate and said "Hey, we really want to sit down and talk with you guys about ways we can work together to get more work." It's fantastic, since our guys have not even been sworn in yet! So I think there is a lot of potential for doing good things with progressive contractors.

Grand Strategy?! We'll not try to implement our platform all at once. We'll develop instead a long-range plan that will accomplish that over time...one I'm busy working on now. Almost every month a piece of the platform will be discussed in front of the Business Manager at the Executive Board meetings, with just the officers present, and we'll ask him if he supports it? Or not? And we'll take it from there.

We hope to win our issues, which will be great, because that's what it is really all about, not who delivers on them. We want to provide an *honest* referral system for the members. I don't really care who implements it: If it gets done, *that's* the important thing. That we win the issue!

If the Business Manager turns us down, we'll have a detailed record of when our reform ideas were floated in front of him and when and why he refused to implement them. The strategy then is we'll explain three years from now in 1995 that we were able to accomplish only "X'"amount. We want to move up to "Y" amount, but we can't do that without changing the Business Manager: "You elected us to do certain things; we could only get this far. Now its time for the next step!"

Part X

Unionists at Bay

"Cave canem" (Beware of the dog)

Latin Proverb

"Every man's life, liberty, and property are in danger when
the Legislature is in session."

Daniel Webster

Both cases below are by inside reformers forced out of office by
governmental officials convinced the continuance of each was not in the
best interests of organized labor. The two targets of this grim accusation
emphatically deny any guilt, and in rebuttal raise substantial questions
about ways with which the government now polices unions.

A careful reading of these troubling cases should help raise useful
questions about the correct use of the RICO tool, and the correct approach to
the fiduciary responsibilities of unionists involved as trustees for jointly-
managed pension funds.

There is no gainsaying the fact that very serious charges, including
allegations of Mafia linkages, were made against the first writer. And
comparably serious charges, including endangerment of millions of dollars
looked to by several thousand pensioners, were leveled against the second
contributor. None of these matters is resolved, of course, by the
presentation here alone of an account prepared at my invitation by the
defendant.

Rather, the point-of-view of the target of government monitoring
helps highlight relatively new sources of labor pain. This should give a
reader an opportunity to tentatively assess RICO and DoL tactics in
consequential matters like this.

As the government is likely to make more and more use of such new
tools, it is important that inside reformers and others in and outside of labor
- *after* seeking out and assessing the government's side of the case - take
and act on a thoughtful position of their own in these controversial matters.

RICO and a Target's Response
Roy Silbert
(HERE)

Alone among the contributors to this volume Roy Silbert has the dubious distinction of being barred for the next ten years from any involvement in the local he headed between 1985 and 1992. As he explains in a fascinating rebuttal he rues the day the Justice Department concluded he and his entire slate of officers were Mafia-dominated and had to go, an allegation he strenuously denies, as it led to an outcome he bitterly resents.

A careful reading of Roy's case highlights five of labor's rarely discussed, but increasingly significant problems:

1) How much trust can a leader place in each and everyone of his staffers? How attentive should he or she remain to the affiliations and values of these staffers?

2) How fair is the federal government's use of its RICO powers against local union leaders?

3) How adequate are union constitution provisions for helping local union officers defend themselves against RICO allegations?

4) How reasonable is it to purge an entire local's union slate for the alleged crimes of a few?

5) What is the role of the rank-and-file when a local's officers are accused of RICO-related offenses?

Roy appreciates the skepticism with which his answers are likely to be greeted, given the stigma he bears, and he asks only an open-minded and fair hearing for *his* side of the matter.

His case, of course, is not included to exonerate him. Nor is it here to permit a judicious weighing of this highly controversial matter, as no representation is included of the government's successful case against the Silbert leadership of Local 54, H.E.R.E.

Rather, Roy's case is included to underline an aspect of labor pains all-too-rarely discussed in public - the use of RICO as a tool against union office-holders - except as part of a union-bashing approach by anti-labor media. Roy Silbert, unapologetic and unbowed, a man still serving labor as an international union staffer, focuses below on what he has learned from the worst experience of his life, the better to help others avoid following after down a RICO-shadowed path.

In retrospect, I am sure there are many reasons and forces that led to the eventual dismantling of the prior leadership of Local 54, which is affiliated with the Hotel and Restaurant Employees International Union, and represents over 20,000 such employees living and working in

South Jersey. Local 54 had four offices that enabled us to represent over 60,000 participants in such funds as Health and Welfare, Pension, and Severance.

One conclusion I draw from the local's current difficulties is that all of the above translated into *power*. And this was too much for some government agencies, individuals, and employers to tolerate. I believe the two most damaging tendencies were greed and jealousy, both internal and external. I do not claim to be naive about these matters as I put in 15 long years of service to Local 54.

Background. I began as a shop steward bartender in an after-hours club in Atlantic City. I had tendered bar most of my life, while either going to college or supporting myself and my family at the time. I began my union career as a full-time organizer, became a business agent, and created the new position of Grievance and Arbitration Officer, along with the parameters of that office.

I was elected Vice-President, and in 1984, was elected President when the incumbent, Frank Gerace, stepped down because of government agency pressures (the Casino Control Commission and Division of Gaming Enforcement made public allegations that Gerace was associated with organized crime).

During my tenure at Local 54 I earned a Bachelor of Science Degree in Labor Studies from the George Meany Center, and a Master of Arts Degree in Labor Policies from Empire State College, State University of New York.

The Hammer Falls. All of which explains why I do not claim naiveté, as I knew about my union's business from the streets on through academia. What I did not realize, however, was the extent of the jealousy, greed, and determination of some of the employees and agents of the Local…certain casino owners and elected politicians…a cabal! I never realized the extent of the jealousy and determination the government had to drive its effort to dismantle the leadership of Local 54.

The difficulty of understanding the government's purpose beneath the vendetta from a labor perspective is what did the government, or the membership the government alleged to have been mistreated, have to gain by filing a federal civil RICO suit against seven officers and agents of Local 54? In addition, civil charges were filed against 40 to 50 individuals, including the General President of the International Union, Ed Hanley.

Some of the alleged mob figures cited had been jailed for 10 years! Or were dead at the time that the civil suit was charged! The obvious answer to the question of gain is not only the publicity afforded elected officials, but to place in positions of importance in Local 54 their political hacks…positions that would reward them or their law firms lucratively.

I realize that the publicity that the federal prosecutor had intended to achieve was enticing, to say the least. (This includes the then Attorney

General, Richard Thornberg, who stood before national cameras and announced the filing of the civil RICO charge against Local 54 officers, although Thornberg, I'm sure, had no idea who or what Local 54 was or stood for).

For the Defense. I am positive that no one in the Justice Department who participated in this suit had ever taken into consideration the accomplishments of those local union leaders involved.

For example, during my seven-year term we purchased a new building, renovated it, and more than tripled the office space. We provided meeting space that allowed some income as we rented it out to other locals for meetings. We also purchased the abandoned building next door, which was renovated to provide office space to our Health and Welfare Department. This enabled our members to do any business they had with our local all in one stop. Downstairs was to be converted into a Training and Orientation Division which would allow us, in coordination with employers, to conduct a training program for those just entering the industry.

As well, we created a Members' Assistance Program on site so that members would have the use of the psychological, drug, marital, and alcohol assistance, if needed, in addition to the benefit provided.

A fully computerized development of the grievance and arbitration process was created, so that all or any of the 3,500 grievances and 335 arbitrations that were filed each year could be called up at any time, and categorized for analytical use.

A Spanish Department was created, with three employees, to better serve the needs of the Hispanic community, including health and welfare, or any other dispute that had to be settles (as in the dispatching of jobs).

Also, a Scholarship Fund was created, and utilized by members and their children to assist with a college education relevant to the hotel or culinary industry.

I also created a PAC and a Strike Fund, so that the Local could become even stronger politically and could encourage its members, if necessary, to conduct a strike to improve their bargaining position.

We also developed so many social activities in any community in which the Local had an office. For example, we had professional basketball players offer clinics for the children of our members. We formed softball, bowling, and basketball teams so that the membership, as part of the community, could participate and feel more at ease during their off hours.

The Case Against Us. On December 19, 1990, all of the energies that the leadership of Local 54 had put forth came to a screeching halt. A civil RICO suit was filed by the federal government and by the Casino Control Commission against Edward T. Hanley, the President of the H.E.R.E. International Union, and Local 54. The hook, of course, in the media headlines was the word "Mafia," which encouraged readers to buy papers, and increased the profile of those filing the charges.

A portion of the case was based on an informant's taped conversation with two current business agents of the Local. Their attitude was that they were entitled to more than they were currently receiving in both delegated respect and income. They decided they would take the opportunity to run against me in an upcoming election, and boasted in the tape of their connections with Philadelphia Mafia members. The tapes, which were used by the government, had many false allegations and statements that ultimately helped the government appoint a monitor to take over Local 54 and force me out.

Refuting the Charges. The irony is that the lawsuit stated that the incidence that began this investigation occurred in 1973...when none of the current officers involved were even employees! Or in some cases, not even members of Local 54! In my case, not even living in New Jersey at the time!

The suit goes on to allege that throughout the 70's and 80's the membership of Local 54 was threatened, coerced, and intimidated into abiding with the wishes of its local officers. And were terrified of running as opposition during a union election.

It should be pointed out that not *one* witness from the membership came forward and supported that statement. The only witnesses the government utilized were convicted racketeers who agreed to testify on condition that their sentences were reduced.

The difficulties in defending against a civil RICO case is that the standard of evidence is reduced to a point where double and triple hearsay is admissible. It is simply impossible to rebut to a judge or jury's satisfaction that the preponderance of hearsay evidence is not an indication of some type of guilt.

It was nauseating to sit in a federal courtroom and listen to the prosecutor ramble on about murder and mayhem that had occurred in Local 54 over the years. Even the media that I had become relatively cordial with looked over with glances that certainly didn't comprehend what the prosecution had to say.

The government alleged that the Mafia controlled Local 54 primarily through its benefit funds. For example, two allegations made in the civil RICO charge were that the Mafia misdirected funds intended for the Health and Welfare and Pension Fund. Also, that the Mafia misdirected dues monies coming directly from the membership.

It was not until after the Consent Decree was signed that the government discovered that all money contributed on behalf of the membership through a collective-bargaining agreement is sent directly by check to the administrators of all three funds. Also, they discovered - after the signing of the Consent Decree - that all dues money is sent by checkoff, by check, from the employers directly to the Local's bank. No cash changes hand, other than a small amount that comes across the dues counter and is collected and receipted by clerks.

Lessons? In hindsight, I have learned it is important for labor leaders to know and sense immediately the difference between a disgruntled employee and one who is so all-obsessed with greed for more money and power that he no longer is concerned with either the local's reputation or potential destruction, but simply with their own self-serving egos. A leader should immediately confront the dissension and flush it out and correct it by rapidly dismissing such an employee.

It may sound absurd to other labor leaders, that they should not treat their employees with respect, and not assume that they are adults, and that they will conduct themselves as such. It seems that one should be able to be treated responsibly and maturely, and not have to be concerned that an employee does not care about the welfare of the local, but only with his or her *own* welfare.

It is unfortunate that the misdirected energy of one or two agents, or employees, can help the government force a union into an untenable position.

Striking Hard. The external greed and jealousy I had mentioned is reflected in the advice I got from a friend and attorney running for the office of U.S. Congressman in southern New Jersey. At a 1986 rally just before the expiration of a collective-bargaining agreement between Local 54 and the casino industry, we were able to draw almost 7,000 members onto the boardwalk in front of Convention Hall for a Labor Day and Support-of-Local 54 Rally. At that time he told me I had just sealed my own death warrant. Because immediately every power-broker and politician in town now knew I had the power of the people and of the membership to achieve a better collective-bargaining agreement. In other words, the perception of a power-broker's fear of another's power is enough to set off a chain of events that sometimes cannot be reversed.

The external jealousy and greed of the Casino industry was indicated by their reaction to the strike that followed this rally of Local 54, the most effective and the most threatening to those in the casino industry and those in power in the community. Fifteen thousand workers walked out at midnight, September 15, 1986. And for all practical purposes, they shut Atlantic City down.

For the next 72 hours, until a federal judge declared that the strike had become too violent, and ordered the picket lines taken down, the industry realized the frustration of those who put in many, many hours a week to help the casino industry generate the profits that it does...only to be offered concessions and 25 percent cutbacks in wages and benefits. On the other hand, it forced the power brokers to set in motion an effort by all of those involved, either directly or indirectly, to be sure that the leadership of Local 54 did not continue to have the type of power that it had in the fall of 1986.

In retrospect, there is nothing I would do to change the rhetoric that was used prior to or after the strike to energize the membership, and then defend and deflate that energy after the strike was ended. Those in a leadership role fully understand their obligation to lower the expectations of their members, and at the same time, encourage them to move forward with work stoppage activity, if necessary.

Why Sign a Consent Order? Once it was fully determined that none of the seven respondents had the financial means to continue through a six-week trial, which would have cost approximately $200,000 more per person, the union and its officers settled with the federal government. I personally spent all of my family's savings, cashed in bonds, and took out loans until it was obvious (the trial had not yet begun) that this case would financially destroy my family.

In addition to the appointment of a monitor to run Local 54, the Consent Decree stated A) That I resign, with no implication or admission of guilt; B) I can work for any local or international union (I am currently with H.E.R.E. as an international auditor); C) I am barred for 10 years from office with Local 54, but this is subject to being opened by either party at anytime to reduce the time barrier; D) no fines were levied; and E) all pension and severance benefits were retained.

Lessons Learned? Unfortunately, the type of scenario I have described is simply beyond the control of any one group of union leaders once the government has determined it will go forward with a civil or perhaps a criminal RICO suit, as it has in the case of other unions in this country. I don't know if there is any precaution that can be taken once the government has determined that a local union is a target and sets the legal system in motion to take control of that local.

In retrospect, the best advice I can offer is to eliminate internal and external dissension and jealousy by immediately confronting it. Listen to advice, but make your own decision, based on a gut feeling and your own knowledge of your local union and its membership. Do not let lawyers dictate the selection of other lawyers, particularly on a political basis. And instruct the lawyers of *your* intentions, rather than what their agenda may be.

Above all, do not be afraid to take risks. Do the best job you can for your membership, and hope that your local or international union continues to operate without the type of interference that has occurred in many, many locals and international unions in this country during the past ten years.

DOL and a Target's Response
Dennis Walton
(IOUE)

Few local union leaders are as well-known, or as controversial, inside organized labor as is Dennis Walton, former Business Manager of a South Florida local of the Operating Engineers Union. Dennis first came to fame in the early 1980s when he pioneered in investing jointly-managed union pension funds in real estate development projects, an option previously thought prohibited by the law's requirement that trustees safeguard the funds in very conservative ways. When Dennis, in a major court case, defeated the government's indictment of his real estate ventures, he was invited coast-to-coast to lecture to other unionists eager to boost the returns on their pension funds.

More recently, however, as Dennis explains fully in the case below, fate has turned against him. The recession saw the Florida real estate bubble burst, and a relentless government pursuit has forced Dennis to step down as an officer of his local, even as it has endangered $42 million in pension funds of his local.

A careful reading of this unusual case sheds light on five of labor's major problems in this complicated matter:

1) How can returns on pension fund investments reach desirable levels and the funds be leveraged to promote employment for unionists?

2) What are reasonable standards to allow risk-taking, and yet keep such funds safe from major losses?

3) When is government policing of union pension investments reasonable or not?

4) When should an international union rescue the pension fund of an ailing local? When not?

Above all, how can organized labor begin to use the potential clout of its billions of dollars of pension money in far more rewarding ways than at present? How can those who would learn from Walton's lessons (and his plight) turn this option to newfound advantage?

Again, as in the case of Roy Silbert immediately before this one, the Walton case is not included to exonerate him or even permit a judicious weighing of the matter, as no representation is included of the government's case against his approach to pension investment. Rather, it is included to air certain stressors too rarely discussed outside labor's confines, the better to enlarge the circle of knowledgeable and concerned parties.

(It should be known, however, that thanks in part to Walton's daring-do the first and only such mutual fund was established in 1994 to invest union pension funds exclusively in the stocks of companies friendly to organized labor. As a members of the Union Standard Fund's Labor Advisory Board I know the criteria for eligibility for investment include a company's labor relations history, the regard in which it is currently held by relevant locals, and so forth.

Dennis Walton, unapologetic and unbowed, a man still serving his local as an activist and adviser, focuses below on what he has learned despite enormous pain, the better to help guide progressive pension fund investment by fellow unionists.

How do I feel now? My stress level has come down substantially as is my work load, but for about a year or so I was on anti-depression medication, sleeping pills and blood pressure medication continuously. Some days I did not know if I was coming or going, I was in court so often. After all, it is not everyday that a local union and its pension fund loses $40 million due to a vicious legal assault by our own government!

If I had not personally lived through this nightmare, I would not believe it. It hit me hard. It really hurt my family and it hurt the union membership. I survived. Our union has survived. A lot of people supported me against all odds which means more to me than anyone will ever know.

I will never forget it. We have been attempting to get a Congressional investigation into the Department of Labor and the various receivers involved in our case. I have contacted Congressman Larry Smith and Congressman Johnston. I contacted Senator Bob Graham. Hell, I've even written to "60 Minutes" urging them to tell the whole nation what happened to my local.

What the Department of Labor did to us is a disgrace. It was targeted genocide. They embarked upon a course of action to intimidate and eliminate an outspoken labor leader. They cared not a single bit about how many other lives were crushed in the process. It was *wrong*, and I'm working now to see it never happens again!

Background. As I explained to you in our first interview for *Robust Unionism*, I got started in '73 when I was appointed a business agent for local 675, International Union of Operating Engineers (IUOE), in Pompano Beach, Florida.

Our co-managed pension fund back then was run by six non-salaried trustees, three from our local, three from our contractors. It took in about $1 million a year in employer contributions we had earned in bargaining. And, along with deferred wages and interest earned on fund investments, it provided for the retirement needs of our members in a quiet and unexceptional way.

Unfortunately, the fund was kinda careless where it invested our money, and when we discovered we were actually lending to vicious non-union builders, we were furious! Goddamn, it was just one week after I became the local's Business Manager that a picket alongside of me protesting at a nonunion building site pointed to a sign identifying the big money backers of the project and said - 'Ain't that a bitch! We just handed these same insurance companies ten million dollars of our money!' I decided on the spot to try and stop this sort of crap!

Knowing I had to learn a hellova a lot more about the entire matter I started in a labor studies program at Florida International University and by '84 had earned a Bachelors.

When all of us trustees met in '78 to rubber-stamp the advice of our paid consultants, like we had done for years earlier, like a zillion other union-management trustees were doing all over the country, I blasted the whole fuckin' arrangement. So, we swept the money-changers from the Temple, fired the consultants, and dared to take charge of our fund investments ourselves!

That's when the fun began...though the Department of Labor soon took all of the fun out of it, and then some!

For the most part, the union movement across the country was simply handing over billions of dollars of pension fund capital to these huge insurance companies, investment firms and banks without any regard to how these huge sums of money were being invested.

I wrote a letter to Bob Georgine, President of the AFL-CIO Building Trades, and to the Board of Directors of Union Labor Life Insurance Company, all of whom are General Presidents of the various International Unions, asking them to take a stand on this very issue. I began asking a lot of questions and I was not getting the right answers.

It seemed to me that organized labor and the government was perfectly willing to have trustees "rubber stamp" whatever action or investment decisions were made by these so-called investment professionals. I asked myself, "Who were these princes of privileges in three piece suits? Have they ever walked a picket line? Have they ever seen the sorrow of unemployment when a family loses its home, its car? Have they ever felt this type of grief?" I seriously doubted it.

Our Trustees embarked upon a new course of action, one that would ensure our dollars were invested in the best interests of our membership. They decided to invest in commercial real estate, in projects that insisted on "union" construction when they were built. Real estate was performing very well in the early 1980's and the market returns were excellent.

The Trustees rolled up their sleeves and jumped in feet first. We decided to leverage our pension fund money to get us some new work, as we were hurting real bad. We used to have 90% of commercial construction, but many contractors had gone "double-breasted" on us, and we had very few jobs for our people.

We also decided to go after *real* returns on our investments. Hell, when the pro's were "advising" us we only earned 1.8%, and other funds were just as bad, pulling in only 3.2% in the '67-'77 period. I *knew* we could do better! And when I learned our Fund had lost over $1.8 million in the last three years because of the poor performance of our bond portfolio, I knew working people had to seize their *own* destiny!

We hired a full time Employment Retirement Security Act (ERISA) attorney, an economist, a financial officer, and a Staff Engineer. In the very first year, we made an astounding 78% on our investments. The best part of these types of investments was that we were creating jobs for our people. Our membership's morale went up. Organizing activity was increasing. Even though we were in a battle with the Department of Labor over our Home Loan Mortgage Program, things were going great.

Five years later we got $174,000 per acre back on 80 acres we had bought in '80 for $25,000 per. While our yield on stocks and bonds was far lower, we still earned 14.25% overall, a hellova sight better than the 1.8% the pros were killing us with.

Naturally, word spread. I soon got speaking invitations from across the country. I testified before the Presidential Commission on Pension Policy. I threw down a gauntlet at that hearing and advised them that "We will be exploited no longer with our own funds, nor will we stay baffled and apathetic due to nebulous interpretations of ambiguous regulations."

I insisted that organized labor could fully meet the legal requirements of the ERISA Prudent Man Rule while still honoring social criteria in creating jobs for our members. I felt with all my heart that the rest if the union movement would join us because it was right and it was a natural course for organized labor to take.

Government Opposition. A lot of friends and business associates had continually warned me that the government would never leave me alone. Trouble came soon enough. The Labor Department filed suit in 1981 charging that the Trustees had violated the Prudent Man Rule as set forth in ERISA..

The government bureaucrats in their complaint stated that our Trustees had paid too much in labor costs for construction on the land we had purchased. They also alleged that in our Administrative Service Contract between the Pension Fund and the local union, the local was not paying enough rent to the Pension Fund on the space the local occupied in the Pension Fund building. In general, the lawsuit alleged we had not acted in the best interests of the plan participants and beneficiaries. The charges were bullshit, but we had to defend ourselves anyway.

I recall the Labor Department actually taping me at seminars where I spoke. At one such meeting, I made the following statement:

>"I found after waking up to my real fiduciary duties that
>incredibly the Department of Labor was suing the Trustees
>for breaching them. Could it be that the Republican

Administration, the aggressive defenders of the status quo, have the best interests of the multi-national corporations foremost on their agenda over that of the plan participants and beneficiaries?"

We won this lengthy battle in 1985 after which I was continually asked to speak to various labor organizations. I carried the message coast to coast that Union Pension *Power* had arrived, and it was time to make the most of it!

Exoneration. I will never forget how relived I was following an eight day trial in 1985 when Federal Judge Jose Gonzalez ruled entirely in the Trustees' favor right from the bench. The tension was so great that I broke down after his decision. I was absolutely convinced that with this decision, the tide had turned for organized labor. Our Trustees had been diligent in doing their homework before ever investing a dime. We were thorough. We hired the best professionals and they performed all the necessary studies. The Judge chastised the Department of Labor for bringing the lawsuit. He actually complimented the Trustees for the innovative use of pension fund capital.

It was a great satisfying victory. I was so glad it was over. I had had seven years of war...but we had been right. They had been wrong. It was a matter of principle.

It was my understanding at the time that our case was the only reported case wherein the Trustees of a Pension Fund had actually beat the Department of Labor. I should have known that they had no inten- tion of continuing to allow me to espouse a Pension Fund Revolution.

Continued Opposition. I knew I had made a lot of enemies in the government and the labor movement, as well. I criticized a lot of International Unions for investing pension fund dollars in nonunion projects, including my own International. Prior to the victory with the Department of Labor, a lot of people were convinced that because I had dared to challenge the system, we were wrong and the Trustees had to be guilty.

I guess it did not help matters by speaking my mind and not mincing my words. My message was often given to union and management trustees, as well as attorneys and Fund professionals. I stated: "We as union trustees have in the past committed misfeasance, malfeasance, and nonfeasance. We have been bogged down in the muck of indifference and ignorance. We have in the past done a great disservice to our people by being apathetic." Unfortunately, a lot of guys took my criticism personally.

It took a lot to get them to grasp my real point...that pension power was the most effective single tool that labor movement possessed. We had to use it. We were not winning on the picket lines. We were not winning in the courtroom, and we were certainly not making any headway in the political arena. The National Right to Work Committee was creating political chaos about our pension fund investments, insisting it was illegal to preclude nonunion contractors from bidding on projects funded with union pension funds.

I remember clearly a statement made by the President of the Associated Builders & Contractors ("ABC") to the newspapers. He stated, "Unless I could convince other union leaders and trustees to follow suit in a large way, one Union standing alone does not have much of a chance to change things." In hindsight, it looks like his point was very real.

I guess what hurt me the most was the refusal of our own International and the AFL-CIO to join in our battle. People say that we are "organized labor." But the truth is that we are probably the most disorganized group on the planet. Other labor leaders made statements that I was a loose cannon on the deck. I do not deny that. I was my own man. I catered to no one and I touched some sore spots when I called some leaders in the labor movement apathetic. Our program was a sound one in spite of what the mental midgets of big government and big business had to say.

Ahead of the Game. With the court victory behind us, we continued our investment philosophy diligently. Between 1978 and 1985, we placed a substantial portion of our Pension Fund portfolio into real estate investments. Our portfolio was diversified both geographically and product-wise.

Our Pension Fund Investment Policy Statement was drafted by professionals and submitted to the Department of Labor for their review. We had acquired millions of dollars worth of real estate that to our best estimate would generate over $300 million dollars worth of construction work for members of the building trades unions.

Spreading the Word. I went coast to coast telling any audience that would listen that if we all joined together and created a huge pool of capital, we could wipe out unemployment in the building trades over night. If all of the General Presidents of the International Unions ever got in the same room on the same day and decided on a strategy of job creating investments, big government and big business would get a message they could not ignore. They would know that the labor movement was alive; we had a voice and we would be heard.

Government Does Not Forget or Forgive. During the time I carried this message, the Department of Labor was fuming over their loss to us in the court. So it came as no surprise when they came after me and the local 675 Trustees a second time with a vengeance. We were dragged back into court in 1990 for an alleged lack of diversification, which they had brought to the Trustees' attention in 1983 but had never acted upon.

At the onset, I was confident we would prevail. Every action taken by the Trustees was done so with professional advice and total compliance with our Investment Policy Statement and all applicable ERISA laws. What we had achieved was significant. No union had ever dared to attempt what we had done. We had changed things and hopefully started a movement.

However, during the Reagan Administration, the Republicans enacted a Tax Recovery Act in the early 1980's which provided for great incentives for investment in real estate. Then the Reagan Administration deregulated the savings and loan institutions. They soon realized their tax law was a horrible disaster, and they repealed the Tax Recovery Act in 1986. Our Trustees found themselves with far more real estate than we could absorb as properties were turned back over to us, one after another, as a result of Congress' abrupt change in tax law and deregulation of the savings and loan institutions.

At the same time, the Pension Fund was required to carry its real estate assets at fair market value. The Plan Consultant and Actuary nevertheless advised the Trustees that we had to raise the level of the pension benefit to retirees, even though we were experiencing cash flow problems.

By this time, the Department of Labor had filed a lawsuit for lack of diversification and engaging in a prohibited transaction. They claimed that because the local union loaned $2.5 million dollars to the Inverry Hotel Corporation (a subsidiary corporation of the Pension Fund) this was an illegal transaction. The reason the Trustees felt they had to make the loan was because the original lender had gone belly up, along with several other thousand others when Congress changed the rules.

Our local had to make the loan if we were going to save our hotel. We discovered this was a prohibited transaction, but we still had to act in the best interests of the plan participants. So we made the loan any-way, and prepared to have another war with the Department of Labor.

We were receiving conflicting advice from different law firms. One law firm, Feder & Associates, advised us not to file for a prohibited transaction with ERISA regulators. Another law firm advised us to file. We listened to the Washington law firm, Feder & Associates, who were the original attorneys who won the first lawsuit against the Department of Labor for us. They were wrong, and we were attacked by the DOL for not filing.

In retrospect, I realize we should have filed, as was advised by the law firm of Sugarman & Susskind of Miami, Florida, even if we were turned down by the DOL. At least, the local would have the $2.5 million. To this date, the Pension Fund has lost the hotel and the local union was not repaid its $2.5 million dollar loan.

Even while we were holding our breath and praying the hotel would stay afloat the economy nose-dived deeper and deeper into trouble, and our clients leasing and renting on our properties went under. We began to get properties turned back at the same time that our liquidity was being eaten up trying to service the hotel. Worse of all, everybody stopped building, and there was no longer any work for our members.

The real rotten fact is that if the Department of Labor had cooperated with us in attempting to help us with the workouts on the real estate assets, we could have saved the assets. We had financing in place with The Equitable on the hotel. We had Prudential negotiating a major joint venture with us. We had workouts structured on our other real estate ventures.

Everyone begged the Department of Labor not to file the lawsuit, but they were hell bent for revenge. They cared not for the retirees and our members. They were simply determined to crush Operating Engineers local 675 and Dennis Walton. It was not much of a surprise to find our joint venture partners abandoning the ship once the Department of Labor pursued the lawsuit. The bastards in the Department of Labor brought everything crashing down. They did it with malicious intent. Their timing killed us. I will never forgive them.

Betrayal. As I mentioned before, the law firm of Feder & Associates worked on the Brock v. Walton case in 1981. We trusted Feder & Associates at that time, but the Department of Labor got to him. He turned against us. We found out that he had agreed to recommend to a Consent Decree without the Trustees' approval. They immediately fired him.

By then, however, the damage had been done. We retained another law firm, Groom & Nordberg, of Washington, D.C. The government then sought an order to terminate the ability of the Trustees to pay for their legal counsel from the Fund assets.

At the end of a long running battle of legal maneuvers, the government was victorious. The Trustees lost the right to use Fund resources to defend themselves, a horrible decision.

Now, the Trustees were faced with an injunction and two Receivers (both attorneys) for the Pension Fund. In February, 1990, the nightmare moved into full bloom. It was unbelievable. Each of these attorneys hired accountants, investment experts, tax experts, and real estate experts. All of them duplicated the work previously performed. Our pension dollars were required to pay for this re-invention of the wheel. Our Pension Fund was being raped and the government stood by and did nothing.

To make matters even worse, this case went through three Federal Judges (Thomas Scott, Norman Ryskamp, and Stanley Marcus). Each time we had to start all over again.

If I thought that matters could not have gotten any worse, I was wrong. I was finally so exasperated by the way things were going, I made a deal with the devil, the Department of Labor. I agreed to step down as Chairman of the Board if they agreed to a joint stipulation to appoint our past Consultant to the Pension Fund, Jere T. Brassell of Southern Benefit Administrators, Inc., as Receiver and replace the court-appointed receiver who was doing nothing.

I should have known better when the government agreed to my proposal. Our attorneys recommended against it, but I had known Brassell for fifteen years. I trusted him explicitly. I felt sure he would work with the Trustees to save the Fund.

I was wrong. He had developed an alliance with Feder & Associates and we also found out that he was on the payroll of the Department of Labor as an expert witness. He soon made us aware that he would not jeopardize his relationship with the Department of Labor and he turned against the Trustees. He hired all new professionals, and just at the time when we were making a proposal to the Central Pension Fund of the IOUE to merge into it. He ordered new actuarial studies, new audits, etc. At the end of the day instead of negotiating workouts with our assets, he deeded all the properties back to lenders and led other assets into foreclosures.

Brassell settled lawsuits at extreme disadvantage to the Pension Fund and basically wiped out every dollar worth of equity, while at the same time, Brassell and Feder were drawing thousands of dollars a month in fees.

The Trustees were infuriated. Our local union membership was horrified at the actions taken by the government to wipe us out.

Hanging in There. Things were looking very gloomy. Our attorneys were gone. We had no right to utilize Fund assets for defense. The Pension Fund was getting raped, with pensions slashed from $1,000 a month down to only $200. It was disgraceful.

In August, 1991, I came up for election. At the same time, Brassell & Feder in conjunction with the Department of Labor, attempted to charge me and the Trustees in contempt of court because our retirees had received a full pension check prior to Feder & Brassell receiving their fees. We were in court again with the Department trying to intimidate us with this Contempt of Court charge.

The Fund Consultant even got involved in the union election by sending out derogatory propaganda about me and the Trustees. He cut the Health and Welfare benefits, cut the pension benefits to the retirees, and increased his monthly compensation. The Department of Labor did nothing. His position was that he had to have ample funds to pay himself and the attorneys he had hired prior to paying any retirees their full pension.

I pray if there is any justice in this world that this man receives his due for the pain he has caused many innocent union members.

I was desperate for help from our International or other labor unions, but it was to no avail. The only response I got was from the General President Carlough of the Sheet Metal Workers International Association. He was very sympathetic. He sent an investment team to Florida to evaluate our real estate transactions. In the end, however, we could not do the joint venture with the Sheet Metal Workers. He is a man I will always admire and I thank him for his effort.

I went to our own International and begged them to help us legally and any way possible. General President Frank Hanley is someone with whom I had previous differences of opinion. He advised me that if I wanted help, I would have to step down as Business Manager even though I had just won the election. President Hanley committed the entire resources of his office to help save the pensions of our members if I resigned, settled the lawsuit, and allowed another election to be held. It was the hardest decision I ever made. But I love my union.

However, there was much more at stake than my own position as Business Manager. The real issue was the attempt by the government to squash any interest a local union might ever have in trying to be creative with its own pension fund dollars. What was at stake was whether or not "social investment" criteria, like leveraging our funds to get contractors to build union, would stay alive as an idea worth pursuing.

Hanley told me that I was a real thorn to the Department of Labor. I agreed to resign and appointed a true loyal friend and Assistant as Business Manager, Joe Gagne. Within weeks after my resignation the Department of Labor submitted a new Consent Decree which the Trustees signed: We pled *nolo contendre*, and they agreed we were now judgment proof and would not be prosecuted. We admitted our real estate ventures had lost value, and, because of all of this real estate, our Pension Fund had lost money.

Our new Business Manager held another election which he won easily.

Current Troubles. Our Pension Fund is still being raped. We hope to get rid of Jere T. Brassell soon and begin rebuilding. We hope to resubmit our proposal to the Central Pension Fund, I.O.U.E., for reconsideration of a merger to restore our benefit level to retirees and future retirees.

You would think after this two year legal battle and the lawsuit settled, the government would stop. They have now commenced a grand jury investigation of our local Union and Pension Fund again and are carting truck loads of records and trying to tie up our staff. It appears they are determined to create a circumstance or situation to even further destroy this little local union. The Department of Labor has now stated they want another election. It is outrageous, but it is happening.

Learning the Hard Way. What I have come to realize is that the Department of Labor consists of human beings, men who carry grudges. They have unlimited resources. The plan participants are the last priority on the government's list. What is sadly ironic is that not once during this entire ordeal could we ever establish who the person was that made the final decision in the Department of Labor?

I am now on staff acting as a business representative working with Business Manager Gagne. I am hopeful that the Trustees of the Central Pension Fund will consider the merger once the government's puppets are removed by the court. Our local will rebuild. We can rise and fight again.

If there is a message in this terrible tragedy it is that no one union can do it alone. It takes the power of many unions working together to fight an onslaught such as local 675 has experienced.

Another chapter has turned in my life. The experience has been horrific. I intend to learn from it.

Part XI
More Unionism

"A strong commitment to democracy need not rest on any simple-minded 'rank-and-filism;' it need not depend on the assumption that the members are always wise and virtuous, or the results of democratic procedure always good...but it seems the essence of the matter is that with democracy improvement and growth remain possible; without it, not."

Irving Howe. "The Workers and Their Unions."
Dissent (Autumn, 1959), 445.

Over a hundred years ago pioneering political scientists Gaetano Mosca and Robert Michels wrote about unions turning into bureaucracies, and warned even then about the related peril of entrenched leaders losing touch with core values. Nearly 50 years ago, in 1958, the warning was repeated in an overlooked gem of analysis, *As Unions Mature*, by labor economist Richard A. Lester. He ranked high among the other costs of "hardening of the organizational arteries" a growing aloofness of entrenched leaders from the legitimate needs of those on the bureaucracy's payroll.

Today, labor's well-kept secret concerns the ironic opposition of many union presidents to the unionization of those on the union's payroll. Facile arguments are made that business agents and IU representatives are actually management types, and therefor neither qualify for or need union protection. Similarly, office personnel are characterized as too knowledgeable about the union's finances and other delicate matter to allow them to be represented for bargaining purposes by another union. Much to the glee of labor's most rabid critics the NLRB has often found unions guilty of unfair labor practices in opposing unionization drives or in dealing with a staff union.

Happily, the three cases below give reason for cautious hope the past here is no longer prologue.

Diane De Young Rau explains the need she felt for union representation as a key staffer with an unusual local made up of university graduate students. Frank in sharing the awkwardness entailed at time of collective-bargaining, she goes to explain why, on margin, staff unionism amount to a "win-win" situation.

John Scally tells of the contribution made by a virile staff union he heads to one of the nation's major international unions. A man of strongly-help opinions, he lambastes those in labor's officialdom who fail to grasp the legitimate needs staffers have for all the rewards of unionization they laud throughout the organizing drives they give so much of themselves to... rewards like respect, appreciation, grievance machinery, and bargaining power.

Paul Anderson, an officer of the same union as John Scally, rounds out the matter with his far-sighted espousement of modern personnel practices for labor, a progressive reform by no means at odds with staff unionization (the two go better together!). One of only two contributors to have earned an MBA degree (Wendell Young, Sr., being the other such unionist), he outlines a series of administrative improvements overdue throughout organized labor.

While the case against staff unionization commands the respect of far too many higher-ups who should know better, the three cases below remind us bureaucracies of every stripe are prone to mismanagement and to moral perplexities that explain the *indispensability* of unionization as both buffer and advocate.

Health Insurance and Staff Unionism
Diane De Young Rau
(AFT)

A major contribution many inside reformers make takes the
form of something as straight-forward as perseverance.
Committed to staying the course almost regardless of how tough it
gets, they can help a local struggle through its awkward infancy,
survive a commonly stormy adolescence, and mature into a
coherent and commendable organization.   Much of this
progression is artfully conveyed below, and the value of longterm
mentoring by an inside reformer is made clear.

Several questions are raised , each of wide relevance:

What special challenges, if any, are posed for internal union
reforms by a membership with higher-than-average
educational attainment and lower-than-average union
consciousness?

What are the responsibilities of an inside reformer in helping
new officers get up to speed?

How can major medical insurance coverage be turned to reform
advantage?

How can handling grievances for non-members be turned to
reform advantage?

Finally, of what significance is the ability of the change-agent to
feel he or she is having fun (albeit along with a reasonable amount
of job stress and frustrations)? How vital is it that the change-
agent earn a decent wage? And how critical is it that the change
agent be in a union so as to help assure a high quality of work life
for that individual?

Finding myself with two elementary school age children to support
after my marriage ended in 1987, I went to work part-time at $5 per
hour at a rural golf course club house arranging tee off times and selling
beer and snacks.

I needed more hours than were available at the golf course, so I
answered an advertisement for a $5 per hour part-time clerical assistant.
It turned out that this job was offered by an AFL-CIO union of graduate
students employed as part-time teachers or in other education support
capacities at the University of Oregon. The Graduate Teaching Fellows
Federation Local 3544 was one of only three such unions in the country
at that time.

I have worked for this local of the American Federation of Teachers
(AFT) ever since, and I currently serve as their Union Representative.
I'm also earning more than $5 an hour, thanks to a contract which my
co-worker and I negotiated with our employer. But, I'm getting ahead
of my story here...one that I enjoy sharing about growing in my work,

about feeling like a Den Mother sometimes, but mostly about how privileged I feel to do work which I find fulfilling.

Union Family. Sometimes I think my attachment to labor may be a genetic thing, or something close to it. My dad, for example, was the president of his Sheetmetal Workers local for a long time, perhaps close to 20 years, through the 1950's and 60's. So, I grew up with unionism at the dinner table: The labor press was right there with other newspapers in our house. My mother was a Roosevelt Democrat, as politically active as she could be...later, a Stevenson supporter and an ardent Wayne Morse fan.

I think it fair to say, that, in the context of the times and like his contemporaries, dad saw unionism as a means to increase the size of his paycheck and to insure financial security for his family, while mother saw it as that and more...a way to achieve fairness at work and to improve standards for human beings in general.

So I grew up with multiple views of unionism: My dad was proud of the financial gains which unionism brought to our family and my mother focused on a softer side, a more idealistic and decent side. She could be a critic of unions, too, and she did not hide the disappointment and danger she felt when she saw evidence of racist attitudes among unionists. Mother told me a great deal about the social and economic conditions in which she grew up, her experiences as a legal secretary (no union) during the Great Depression and on into the 1940s. Their influence on the attitudes I hold today is broad and deep.

AFT Local 3544. We have the voluntary membership of about 600 of 1,000 graduate students who work as teaching and research assistants, a group whose average age is 30 to 32, half of them married, and half of them, including many singles, still raising young children. Many are international students and some, especially from the European countries with strong union traditions, are among the most militant in spirit.

Teaching assistants come and go all the time, and so our ranks are always changing and we always seem to be organizing and reorganizing. Their politics, their attitudes, their values...are all pretty diverse, and they divide into roughly three types - those eager to get out and work in business or start businesses of their own, those hoping to stay forever as teachers on a college campus, and those preparing for careers as professionals - chemists, engineers, lawyers, etc.

My job has been to help AFT Local 3544 do the best possible job it can for these rather unique dues-payers, a bloc of articulate, independent-minded adults whose familiarity with unionism is generally very limited...speaking, that is, of the vast majority who are native-born Americans.

My work is fun, though not without its stress and frustrations. I wish, for instance, that organized labor would pay more attention to the needs of groups like this, for they are near a jumping-off place. They will leave their universities and spend their lives mixing with and shaping the ideas of millions of others. We ought to be sending them off with a good, solid feeling that they are especially fortunate for having had a union to represent them. I'm not sure that labor, for all its promotion of labor education, understands this.

Getting the Job Done. My day at our two-person local office begins with my brief scanning of the newspapers to learn what sorts of events have occurred relative to higher education in our state, to labor, etc., keeping in touch with what happens when the State Legislature is in session with regard to higher education budgeting.

I handle all the accounting and bookkeeping functions for the local. We have had such tremendous turnover in treasurers (seven in three years!) that it became necessary to have one person handle the financial stuff, especially in light of the requirements unions must meet these days.

Nearly every hour finds me fielding calls from graduate employees wanting information about our union and about their employee rights in the workplace, which is probably the second most-common type of call I receive (the first is about our union's medical insurance plan). People often want to know if they are being paid in accordance with the salary schedule set forth in our collective bargaining agreement with the university, and I calculate that for them. Then I turn to the mail and try to deal with the daily correspondence (which is quite heavy sometimes) in between phone calls and drop-in visitors.

We have a clerical assistant in the office who is generally charged with the responsibility of keeping t he membership list updated. Our membership changes constantly, so the updating is an endless task. I used to perform that function and I find that I miss it, as working with the list helped me learn many names. It pleases people when you recognize their names or you can spell their names. I still like to work on the updates sometimes, just to keep in touch and learn the names.

Jennifer, our clerical assistant, joins me in producing the newsletter each month. Jennifer is a part-time typographer for a local newspaper, and we've had excellently produced newsletters, thanks to her. Generally, news-letter contributions come from one or two union officers and from me.

Top Leadership. The officers, of course, drop by, though right now, out of eight executive board positions, only three are filled. That's terrible; its pathetic! And what makes it even worse is that we've had 20 different officers filling an 8-member board over the past three years!

Our last president, however, was wonderfully faithful! She showed up or called in every day! In fact, it was rare that she didn't come to the office to see what was going on. She was only 23, very young, and she knew she needed more information and education about labor. So she took advantage of the opportunities offered by the AFT Oregon

Federation of Teachers, Education & Health Professionals, to learn more about the union work she was doing.

Our new local president, a young male international student from Japan and a student of sociology, has excellent instincts, and is very progressive, very quick to spot needs and urge us to move forward.

Local Autonomy...and Naivete. Being part of a federation, the AFT Oregon Federation, is different for us, I think, than it is for some of the other union locals which are under much more control from their internationals. We are very independent, and sometimes that is a cause of frustration for me...because with each successive local executive board, or group of new leaders new to the labor movement, it feels like I have to reinvent the wheel.

I educate them to their responsibilities, to the needs of our organization, to be accountable to our members in lots of different ways. Sometimes I end up in what seems to be endless, exhausting explanations of why the law requires some kinds of union business to be conducted in certain ways. This reminds me that, generally, we receive very little in the way of education about the role and function of organized labor.

Coming Together. Our general membership meetings are once a month, and the Executive Board meets usually once a week, or once every two weeks during the academic year. I have to admit its unusual to have more than one or two people, other than the Executive Board officers, show up at a general membership meeting. The attendance is very, very low...unless there is a crisis looming, or a contract upon which to vote.

If I depended upon the attendance figures from general membership meetings to tell me about the state of our union, I'd say we were dead. But I know we're not. We must be providing valuable service because I am busy all the time! I never sit idle. There are always phone calls to return and questions to answer for members of our bargaining unit who are contacting us wanting information about their rights, benefits, etc.

But there is so little participation from any of these people when it comes to meetings and decision-making. I wonder, honestly, why that is? Whether they don't feel a part of the decision-making process? We get very few complaints from those we represent, so they must not disapprove of us entirely.

Rattling the Saber! Not that we don't have some serious differences of opinion dividing us about policy, something that just goes naturally with these curious and sometimes skeptical folk. One bloc, for example, would like us to stand up more firmly to our critics in the faculty, while we prefer diplomacy to dynamite.

Some of the faculty, I have to admit, however, can be quite difficult. They have no union protection themselves (a fact which makes our mission more challenging). Faculty opposition ranges from pleading ignorance of our union's existence to outright defiance of us.

Some believe we have no place on a university campus, that teaching assistants have no business being organized and no right to a union or to the protection of a union because they are essentially students. Usually we hear this reaction when a question has come up about how a faculty member is treating his or her graduate assistants. They get very upset sometimes, but we try to remain civilized and dignified in our approach, as low-key as possible, but firm.

Some of our members call for more militancy, while others think raising an issue about working conditions is almost too confrontational in the first place.

In the last two or three years, we have noticed the emergence of a subtle new style of university administrator. There is a sharper business edge to some of these people. Sometimes they seem bloodless and cold, definitely not a group of "Mr. Chips" types. Like it or not, higher education, especially in a climate which does not support education for its own sake, is a business. Departments which attract money will thrive; those which do not will always be hungry and may not survive.

Showing Our Strength. It was a terrible time for us in 1989, when a takeback was proposed during bargaining. We held a rally and then we marched, carrying signs, right through the office of the president of the university. We made a whole lot of noise!

Some of our American members disapproved of the fuss we caused, even though they wanted the same things as we all did. They just hated to see our untidy and upsetting behavior. It was like a fight at home, I guess, a domestic argument that gets the family all upset. At the same time, however, some of our international graduate student members thought our militancy was just great!

And I have to say, the ultimate result was favorable. I doubt that we would have won our contract terms if we had not done it. We know the university president has remained concerned ever since that we can show up to protest at any function, any university ceremony, and sorely embarrass him in that way...a concern of his we turn to our advantage in negotiations with management.

Why Join? When outsiders ask me how we've attracted 60% of those eligible into membership, given how very, very few graduate employee unions there are in this country, I have to give a lot of credit to the fact that the union took the initiative to secure a health insurance plan for our bargaining unit...even though the administration of it produces a great deal of extra work for the union office.

Our major medical insurance coverage looks very good in contrast to the plan available through the university. It is still, however, an insurance plan for which people must apply and pass a health screen...so it is not a "good" plan or a real substitute for national health care. As well, I'm not particularly happy about dealing quite so much with insurance, although I'm quite happy to do that if that is what members of the local need and want me to do. I just wish it was a better plan on which I spend about an hour of my workday everyday.

Going Union. Some years ago a fragile unaffiliated staff union was formed by my predecessor. It was not popular with all the officers on the executive board at that time, and I guess it is safe to say that it was one of the big reasons she was forced to quit. Happily, we've come a long way! The office clerical assistant has joined me in reviving this staff union, and in '91 we successfully negotiated our first contract with the local. There were some rough moments, but on the whole it went well. We came out - both sides - relieved to get past it and fairly happy with the results.

Most of us would agree that, in a perfect world, a union would be more than a service to which its rank and file subscribe. Among other things it would be a shining example of an ideal workplace, carefully managed and nurtured to preserve those illusive qualities of justice and decency to which it aspires. In order to secure solid and lasting improvements, unions must become more improved in their own role as manager than the employers whom they seek to improve.

Finding a Source of Income. Before we negotiated, I calculated how much it was costing our local to have the two of us put in approximately one hour per day handling the medical insurance plan. When the time came to renew our agreement with our insurance company, and to ask them for some changes, we asked them to reimburse us for the time we spent taking applications and answering insurance questions, and they agreed to do just that. We then turned a new administrative fee provided by the insurance company into the salary increases we were seeking for union staffers.

I still have concerns about having done this: Does it fall into the category of a "kickback?" Everyone on the Executive Board with whom I've discussed this concern said "Oh, it sounds like a fine idea!" We would not have gone along had the insurance company proposed raising premiums. Indeed, premiums have not increased in four years. Or if they had refused to increase the annual maximum benefit, which was low. So, for right now, it feels OK, but I think it is the sort of arrangement which bears careful watching by the local's executive board.

Part of the dilemma here was that my salary was very low, less than $20,000 a year, and even with child support, it was very hard to get by on that amount (especially as I had children who needed violin lessons, singing lessons, and demands of that nature...and I wanted to do all those things for them).

So, this is working - and I think the local can be proud of the fact that for its size it's doing its part to set a good example in the way it pays and treats its own staff (something that has not always been the case.)

Enrollment Mistake. Nobody has to be a full member of our union to qualify for the health insurance plan, and this was dumb of us! In fact, if there were things I could change about how decisions were made in the last few years, that would be one. The board made the open eligibility decision out of a very serious concern that access to medical insurance was just not going to be there at all for some people, so they decided that fair share fee payers would be able to buy it too. When this happened it was a very tense, emotional time.

Of the 400 in our bargaining unit who choose not to join 600 others in our local as members, I'd guess only about 10 to 20% take advantage of our medical insurance offer. Lots who come to get information about it say very apologetically to me, "Now, I'm not a member yet...," and I immediately make sure that they get a form. And they often later file both a membership form and an application for insurance together...so it's turned out to be a great organizing tool!

Helping When It Hurts. I also notice that when we handle grievances for people and are successful, as we usually are, those are people who will also step forward and say "Well, you know, I wasn't a member, but now..." We are winning perhaps 85 to 90% of the grievances, many of which deal with work load (being asked to teach more hours than their FTE). To that end, when we publish our little academic calendar, which we give away free, we have a place on each page to record the number of hours spent by each employee doing different parts of the job each week. If they get into the habit of recording their time, it makes wonderful evidence to produce in that kind of grievance.

Another common complaint involves failure to be reappointed. And a third type, supposedly headed for arbitration, deals with layoffs. Just after the university announced in Winter term '91 that it would be cutting programs, and there would be a loss of between 100 and 150 positions, including graduate employees, we said "Gee, you know, you need to provide these people with layoff notices, because that is really essentially what you are doing. Make sure they get put on a priority re-appointment list so that they get similar jobs, perhaps in other subject areas in which they might also be qualified by virtue of the interdisciplinary nature of their studies."

The university would not do this. They indicated that they didn't believe it was a layoff that was taking place. They considered it a "failure to reappoint."

In many of these cases, however, people had made major changes in their lives, such as moving across country with their families, because the university had told them "You can expect three years' worth of graduate teaching fellowship assignments to pay your tuition and to support you.'" When the teaching position is taken away, the tuition costs become a tremendous burden.

So we're backing all of the people involved, whether they are members or not: It makes no difference to us.

Where Next? I still have hope that our local will somehow get involved soon in the matter of child care. About a year ago, I started doing a bit of research on the subject, and I've been checking ever since to see if there is a need that isn't being met, such as latchkey or some other form of child care for our group. There are a lot of single parents in our local, but, curiously, I didn't find a whole lot of enthusiasm for this on the part of those around me in the local. Most of these people, however, are single and childless.

It is hard to locate members who are single parents because they, above all others, don't come to our meetings. They just don't have time to even make a phone call. Even if things are going wrong, there has to be something that is really wrong and really a problem before they will come forward, because their lives are driven by the clock, the schedule, and the twenty-four hour demands of responsible parenting.

So, I thought one way to approach this would be to check with the university and find out what they have got in place, and find out what they see as an unmet need. What I found in their reception to me, which was not very overt, was sort of a territorial ownership kind-of-thing about child care. I found an attitude that I interpreted as reluctance to see an outside organization play in the game.

Since the top two issues in a recent membership survey of ours were health care and child care, we expect the latter to become an increasingly critical issue. There is a tendency on the part of the university to want to raise the minimum FTE size of appointment. Previously there were lots of 8-hour per week appointments - with a full tuition waiver included. Now it looks like they'll make half as many 16-hour appointments as the 8-hour type, which will mean only half as many tuition waivers. Making single parents move from 8 to 16 hours will be more of a pinch for them. And I suspect we'll be hearing more about the impact on child care.

We may have been a bit premature in beginning our child care inquiries last year. Maybe in a year of so we'll be able to do more.

Holding the Line. I try to get our Executive Board and members alike to understand the AFT is working for them off this campus as well as through our local I remind them that student workers at public universities still enjoy an exclusion from any Social Security contribution requirement. I remind them that President Bush in 1990 called for the inclusion of student workers in this requirement. AFT's lobbying efforts, in alliance with those of the progressive congressmen we support, warded off any new obligation of our members to pay into Social Security from their very meager earnings.

Unless we take the AFT's political advice on this issue to heart, we're going to lose this fight...and many other Washington-based struggles like it! We've got to hold the line, and get more politically involved!

Spreading the Word. We were asked recently by the National Association of Graduate and Professional Students to participate as a union in a workshop about graduate employee unions at one of their conferences. This sounded like a good opportunity to make contact with people who might be interested in organizing. I asked AFT about funding for someone to attend and make a presentation at this conference, but the funding was not forthcoming: There were apparently other organizing priorities.

Naturally, I was disappointed about that. I know there are obstacles to organizing graduate employees and that the union's organizing effort has to be continuous and ongoing even after certification, because of the transient nature of these bargaining units. Plus there is always the debate over student status vs. employee status; the employer can be counted upon to assert that graduate employees are students enjoying the university's benevolence in granting them fellowships and, as such, are not a group entitled to bargain collectively...even though we know graduate employees often teach 40% or more of undergraduate introductory classes and provide a critical source of inexpensive labor to our universities.

I receive calls with increasing frequency from official and unofficial graduate employee groups asking about our experience in forming a union and asking for names and phone numbers of those who might help them. Sometimes they are people who have left this university to pursue Ph.D.'s somewhere else, and they are disappointed to find out that their pay is lower than here, plus there are only weak or vague (or no) limits on workload. They really want to know "How do we get a union here?" I give them the appropriate AFT names and phone numbers.

Summary. This is a fertile field to cultivate, this matter of graduate student unionization. Because it is an opportunity to influence a group of people who are headed out into academe or management (into whatever!... a million different occupations!). This is a chance to influence them before they leave the university, to teach them how important and valuable are labor organizations, how important is collective action.

My experience is that many graduate students who didn't know what to expect from us, because they didn't know about labor organizations, are pleasantly surprised when they find out what things we have to offer them, what we can do to help them understand their workplace and their work environment, and what we might be able to do to improve things in the future.

True, the per capita that will come from groups like ours will not be as great as from a unit of full-time workers. But ignoring able-minded, potential supporters with potential influence in diverse areas the world over is a damn shame, especially since the long-range gains of organizing these groups, attempting to meet their needs, and cultivating their friendship can really pay off.

Afterword (July, 1992): We're headed for a new academic year amid the usual ups and downs. We've added vision care to our major medical plan and we're working on a dental care provision. Some departments in which we were heavily organized (teacher education, school and community health) were eliminated by the Winter 1991 budget cuts (which came about as a result of taxpayer revolt) so, we're faced with even bigger organizing challenges. This budget problem is due to become much more extreme in '92-'93 if the voters of the state don't agree to some form of revenue replacement.

The layoff grievance which we thought would wind up in arbitration didn't. Although some graduate employees were "displaced" by the university's cutbacks of Winter 1991, there actually were more graduate teaching fellows in Fall 1991 than there had been in Fall 1990...more proof, I guess that this inexpensive labor source will be there to shut out the lights in the unhappy event that the need would arise.

Winning Through Staff Unionism
John T. Scally
(CWA)

A long-time CWA staffer and a founding member in 1990 of the International Congress of Staff Unions, John T. Scally serves as both a CWA rep and the head of a union of CWA employees. Buoyant and witty, he is preoccupied with his dual role of both improving the work lives of those he represents outside of CWA headquarters (rank-and-filers) and also those others he represents, wearing his union leader hat, inside headquarters.

Second to none in his deep-in-the-bones commitment to organized labor, John is troubled nevertheless by an ironic record of often bitter opposition by elected union leaders to the unionization of their office workers and the union's field representatives. His material raises four especially vexing questions:

How can a union expect the most from those on its payroll when many resent feeling undervalued and taken-for-granted?

How can a union expect the solving of personnel problems without the intervention of a staff union?

How can a union treat its staff union any different from how it hopes to be treated by employers with which it negotiates?

Above all, how can a *labor* movement harbor opposition to the desirability of any to profit from trade unionism? How long must it be before union bureaucracies appreciate the distinct contribution unions of staffers can make to an organization's productivity? How much longer must John and others argue what should be self-evident, namely, unions are better-off unionized than not!

My father died in 1946, when I was 17. He was a very distant and private man, one I'll always regret never having gotten to know. He had worked in the mines as a child, and a coal mine fire in Maryland when he was 12 left him scarred for life, his face splotched and his body raw with scar tissue. After the fire his father moved the family north to Detroit...anything to get them away from the mines.

With little schooling my father judged himself quite fortunate to get a job as a policeman in Detroit. At our supper table he would occasionally talk about breaking heads of pickets or bashing strikers or laying into union marchers...and he never gave any of this a second thought. During the race riots in 1940 he shared many bloody tales of beatings he gave the "niggers, spicks, and others," a brutal liturgy that frightened and fascinated all five of us Scally children around the dinner table.

A bigoted and very lonely man, he was a *mean* policeman, the type that never takes his badge off, even when away from his job. I've lived my entire life in opposition to his. I've spent a lifetime thinking and feeling completely opposite. And he would turn in his grave knowing I've been active all these years in the union.

My mother was *so* different, a kind, a *very* kind person. A saint, the only woman who ever truly loved me. She was always helping somebody. And she never got anything material out of it. She'd bake things for the neighbors. She would crochet, knit, and tat. That's all she did while my father was alive. She would sit quietly in a corner, mending clothes or darning socks...and helping somebody.

My mother shied away from trouble, unlike my father who never held back. Occasionally she would get long-distance calls charged to our house bill, even though she never made a long-distance call in her life. I would urge her not to pay for them. And when I asked why she quietly did, she would explain - "I don't want to cause any trouble."

Going to Work. Everything changed in '46 when mom was left to shoulder the burdens of widowhood. She got her first outside job. And all of us - the five kids and her - unexpectedly discovered a positive side to trade unionism.

My mother scrubbed pots and pans in the kitchen of a public school, a job I called "permanent K.P.," and one I couldn't see anybody doing. But she never complained. And she took special pleasure in attending the monthly meetings of an AFSCME local that covered all such school system people. She had to take two buses to get there. And once there, she never said a word, not even a peep. But afterwards she couldn't wait to tell me every last thing that had occurred, every last word that had been uttered. She loved it! She was *so* proud to be part of it!

And when I asked her, "Mom, why don't you speak up? Why don't you say anything?," she would reply, "I don't want to cause any trouble."

Nowadays, when somebody is bad-mouthing the Movement, I ask myself - "Who else is gonna' represent my mother?!" People try to stick it to me by insisting we represent some bad apples, some drunks and the like. Sure, we do. We have to. But we *also* represent my mother. And people like her *need* us to speak for them.

Going to Work. After I graduated from high-school in '46 I became an assembly-line worker at the Hudson Motor Co. plant. I spent all day, every day, day-after-day, installing a left rear door on every third car body moving by the line. Holy Christ! I can't believe I actually did that, day-after-day.

Looking around I noticed one guy who did not do line work. And I found out he was the UAW steward. He kind of became like a big brother. When the whistle blew and we got a break he'd come over and sit with me. I'd ask him questions, like "what does the UAW negotiate?," and "how did the UAW get started?" I only worked there a couple of months, so I never got to a UAW local meeting. But I remember thinking how *powerful* the union was! It had gotten me my coffee breaks, and I was damn appreciative of all of that stuff.

Joining the Phone Company. Two of my high-school buddies got me to tag along one day while they went to a Detroit office of the phone company and took an employment test. Since I was there anyhow I decided on a whim to sit alongside of them in the test room. I fed them a whole bunch of correct answers for awhile, and filled out a test sheet for myself. Boy, were they ticked when I outscored them both! A little while later my two friends were notified through the mail they had jobs. But I was turned down!

Mad as hell, I went down to the Phone Company employment office and argued them into a change of mind. My feelings had been really hurt, you know. I was only 18 years old, and their letter really crushed me. Because they hurt my feelings, that's why I insisted on working there. I hadn't really wanted to beforehand, but I didn't like being rejected.

Going Union. Except for two years out with the Army Signal Corps ('52-'54), I spent the next 25 years ('47-'72) working as a telephone installer-repairman...and getting more and more involved with the union.

I still remember the first union meeting I ever went to. The chief steward in the shop said to me, "Hey, kid, we're goin' to a union meeting tomorrow night." And not knowing any reason to say no, I said "O.K." He took me to an old UAW hall, smoky as hell, I'll never forget that.

Up on the stage a little short guy was ranting and raving and raising hell about this and that. And he was saying "We're *not* gonna' stand for it!" I didn't know what "it" was, but I was sure as hell impressed by the way the crowd applauded him. He was tough! And what he said made sense. He showed a lot of courage, I'll never forget that. Now, over 40 years later, I can still remember the exact location...it sure lit a spark!

Turning to Activism. I became a shop steward, and when the independent phone unions, like the Michigan outfit I belonged to, joined in 1950 to create the Communication Workers of America (CWA), I was really tickled.

Myself, however, I was busy with non-union interests. At that time I was into church work quite a bit. One course the church offered, the "Christopher Course" in public speaking, really interested me 'cause I was shy about gettin' involved in my CWA local. It taught us that if we were *really* religious we could go into the marketplace and help change it. We could take our Christian values and change the market-place. I thought about it, and said "O.K."

And that's what started me getting *really* involved in my local union. I began attending every meeting...reading, talking, and thinking union. And it wasn't long before I got my dander up.

Making Trouble. A friend of mine decided to run for secretary-treasurer of our CWA local. As he was the guy who had made me go to my first phone union meeting (even before we created CWA), I decided to help him out. I saw they were going to count the ballots down at the local's headquarters. So I asked, "Larry, aren't you gonna' have an observer? I see on the union bulletin board that each candidate is allowed to have an observer to watch 'em count the ballots." He replied "No, there are so many candidates there will be plenty of people watchin'. They're not gonna' pull any funny stuff." I kind of agreed, but I also insisted that going over would lend a bit of class to Larry's campaign.

So I did, and I found it unbelievable, what the officers tried to get away with. They messed around with the tally. Larry lost, as did all the other challengers but one. The next day, however, the officers announced they had "found" a misplaced bag of ballots, and even that one guy was declared a loser. They succeeded in dumping a guy, an opposition guy, who had actually won the vice-presidency.

I was so angry with this highway robbery, so furious with what I had seen with my own eyes, that I decided to run for chairman of the local's Election Committee...and I won.

Trying to Secede. I knew even this win would not be enough, as the entire local was in the grip of inside workers, people who did not do the kind of work my buddies and me liked out-of-doors. We decided we wanted our own local, that we wanted to split off from the old one. I started a petition to this effect, and decided to make a show of our feelings at the next meeting. I chartered two buses and set out to fill them with technicians and splicers, my crowd.

Although I had always thought of myself as a kind of quiet and timid person, maybe stubborn, I really went all out. I stacked the aisles of the two buses with beer, and charged only a dollar a piece for the ride. So they got free beer back and forth for only a buck - and I got two full busloads.

Naturally, we overwhelmed the meeting. When we walked in everybody knew we had stacked the show. So as to be fair about it all, I asked for passage of our motion that there be a referendum within 60 days on whether or not to split up the local. I felt 60 days would give both sides plenty of time to handbill and get out their story. We agreed that, if we won, the local's assets would be divided up equally, even though we were entitled to 60%. The members listened carefully, and they agreed with us that we were *not* trying to railroad anything. So our motion passed.

Fighting Back. Well, lo and behold, the local's Executive Board over-ruled our motion. I insisted they had no authority to do this, that the membership was the governing body. It could overrule the Board, but the Board could not overrule the membership. I decided to take the Board to court. I got a hearing in a Common Pleas Court, where I tried to get an injunction to force the "old pols" to hold a referendum on splitting up. But since I could have appealed the E-Board decision higher up in the CWA, the judge threw out my case.

Now it was their turn, and they came after me. Officers of the local brought me up on charges before a union trial court. They accused me of ignoring a clause in the CWA Constitution that says you can't take anything into court without first exhausting all the procedures available within the union.

Everybody kept tellin' me, "Hang in there, John! You're right!" But, you know, I had six children to raise, and fighting meant a lot of expenses. The court case alone had already cost me $1,500 out of my own pocket, and in those days that was *a lot* of money. Still, I was too stubborn to back down. I spoke up for myself this time, instead of letting a lawyer do all of my talking, as in the Circuit Court. I was pleased when three of the five trial court members lined up with me.

But when they tried to reassure me by saying they'd find me innocent, I insisted that was *not* the point - since I *knew* I was innocent! When they later voted 5 to zero in my favor I thought I had helped keep 'em honest.

Pushing for Resolution. As soon as the dust settled, like the following year, I ran for office as part of an opposition slate. True to form the "old pols" found a technicality with which to defeat us, and I knew we had to resolve this one way or another: It could not go on. I insisted the local hold a special meetin' just to discuss a split-up. The "old pols'"agreed.

Once again I charted buses, though this time without any beer. And once again we packed the meeting. We had a real donnybrook! I challenged them to put us back on the ballot, regardless of the technicality - and vote us up or down. Well, they agreed to that, and we ran and we lost - but not fair and square! Some say we lost 'cause we were troublemakers. But to this day I suspect the count was rigged and we were robbed: I think we had lost before the first ballot was cast!

Splitting Off. The man who was making all the trouble for us had been local president for 15 to 20 years, and he had gotten ambitious. The UAW had "reached" him, and he began to agitate for disaffiliation with the CWA and affiliation with the Auto Union.

I got some of my buddies to secretly tape him telling local members the CWA was no good, and we ought to go UAW. Then I rented mail boxes around Detroit and began circulating cards that asked members to sign if they supported our wish to create a separate local for us outside men. When I had over 50% of the local in cards mailed to my boxes I presented the whole matter to the regional CWA Board. Since they knew by this time that the old president was a traitor they were ready to "O.K." my split-away motion and we finally got our own local.

Taking Charge. The men elected me president, and my problems *really* began! A lot of things all began to happen at once. I was threatened. My family got threatening phone calls. My wife got nasty calls, all that kinda stuff. I suspect they came from business agents who were afraid the split would cost them their jobs, but I didn't care. Other officers of the new local were shook, but not me.

I fought back! With a few dollars I got hold of a hand-cranked mimeograph machine and I set it up in my basement. Then I began to write leaflets exposing the enemy, the guys who ran the largest locals, and their cronies, certain full-time business agents intent on staying on the CWA payroll, no matter what. I said the most important thing on their agenda was taking care of #1, not what happens to Labor or to their CWA members. After I circulated some of this material the phone calls stopped.

Making a Model Local. We were excited to finally have our *own* local, and we set out to prove ourselves. We worked hard. And I learned that things are not always as easy as you thought they would be - but that's part of the learning experience.

First thing we did was rent a ratty old storefront and rehabilitate it, top to bottom, every square inch! Holy Christ, but that was a lot of work! Before a meeting of our new stewards I'd go to a store and buy out day-old rolls on sale. And all that kind of stuff. I took an old refrigerator to the place so we could have cokes and beers, anything to make it friendly.

I wanted to work on local problems full-time, but we just didn't have the treasury for it. So I had to stay a company worker, and the local only paid for my time when I took off from my phone repair job to do something for it. If I had left the company I'd lost my health benefits, and with six kids, I knew I couldn't do that. I wound up working for the company one day a week, and for the local the rest of the time.

"Missing in Action." I do mean - "the rest of the time!" I began sleeping in the back of the local office and spending weekends there. What with trying to prevent or end wildcats, or leading official strikes I was gone from my family all the time.

In fact, it got so bad that one time, during a strike, I came home after sleeping on a couch in the office for about four days. And I found out two of my daughters had gone off three days earlier to help out in a summer camp for crippled kids, and I hadn't known anything about it. Pitiful! Another time one of my daughters ran away from home, and I didn't learn about it for almost a week! That's really pitiful!

I made a trade. I traded my family for my local. And I know now it was my fault. I'm an adult, and I'll take full responsibility for it. I came to where I wanted to give unionism my life, and I've been doing that.

Joining the Staff...and Staying in Trouble. After four years as president of our local of outside men I accepted a position in 1972 as a full-time CWA Representative, a job I've held right up to the present.

Almost from the outset I got into hot water over my way of doing things...over my disregard for "standard operating procedure."

In 1975, for example, I tried to help a bunch of hospital employees unionize one of the first hospitals CWA ever went after. They had come to us with a lot of pain and a lot of problems. But there were no helpful laws covering this sort of union campaign, and the hospital hired union-avoidance consultants. Those S.O.B.'s put a display case in the lobby with $1,000,000 spread throughout, and a sign on the case read - "This is how much you will lose if you vote for the union." So we lost, 360 to 48.

Those workers were *really* fine human beings: I mean, they would not even consider striking to help unionize the place if that meant any possible harm to *their* patients. I wound up admiring them so much that I sat down after we lost and wrote a personal letter to all 450 or so eligible voters. I thanked each and everyone for having given me the opportunity to help them improve their worklives. I told them how much I admired their dedication to the sick and infirm. And I wished them all well.

Almost immediately I was called on the carpet and read the Riot Act! My regional director was furious that any of his reps would waste their time on a bunch of ingrates, a pack of losers. And when he figured out that I had used union funds to cover 450 or so postage stamps he was doubly furious! I argued with him, of course, and we agreed we just saw unionism *very* differently.

Grass-Roots Rewards. Soon after I was sent as a kind of punishment to bargain CWA contracts in a distant corner of southeastern Ohio, somewhere out in the middle of nowhere. A local of about 30 guys out there had some tough grievances. I called and said, "Since I'm coming over three hours to drive to hear your grievances, let's have a membership meeting. Let's talk."

Well, out of those 30 or so guys, about 23 actually showed up. Some came alone, and drove upwards of two and a half hours! Can you believe that! I was getting paid to be there; it was my job. But they came on their own time, and never complained. We sat around on old car seats torn out of junkers, and we talked. We talked about all kinds of things. About their grievances. About life. About God. And we talked long past midnight...and I thought "*This* is the grass-roots; *this* is what unionism is all about,"...and I loved it!

Making the Grade. Another time, in '83 in Indianapolis, I had one of the nicest experiences of my life - though a lot of "pork-choppers" would not understand.

I got there three weeks before they were going out on strike, and quickly got to know everybody. I decided to help out in the local's hall. So I scrubbed and mopped the bathrooms every night 'cause they'd get sloppy, what with all the extra coming and going. I also helped clean up the soup kitchen we ran daily for the strikers. I repainted the fading lines in the union parking lot, and just went from one of those kinda things to another.

One day when I was walking the picket line I overheard some of the strikers ahead of me say - "You know, the Goddamn union staff people, you don't see any of them out here with us!" And someone else shot back - "Oh yeah?! That's a staff guy right there behind us!"

It felt good to hear that, *real* good...especially when two other staffers pulled up in their union car, rolled down the window, talked briefly with some strikers, and drove away. I thought to myself, "That's what's wrong with unionism! You've got to be out here, on the line, *with* the people! You can't just urge them to sacrifice; you've got to sacrifice along with them!"

Hell, when I was assigned to Ohio I promised my 28 far-flung locals I'd attend at least one monthly meeting of each of them every year...and in my first year I actually got to 24. I'd drive three hours, attend from beginning to end, and not get home before 3AM. Before the meeting ended damn near everyone who had showed up came over to shake my hand, as I was the first staffer they had known to go out of his way to attend their meeting.

The Boss's Revenge. Things never got any better between my regional director and me. We used to fight all the time, and it got so bad he assigned me to my home. He ordered me not to make any contact with the locals I had been servicing, and he took my name off of the CWA mailing list, so I was really isolated. He made it clear he would never let me do any real work any longer in his region so I accepted a reassignment to CWA headquarters in Washington, D.C.

This meant a demotion. And I lost a lotta pay. And it was hard, very hard, on my wife and daughters. While my girls were raised in a truly union household, one which did them some good, and no special harm, this moving around from city to city was painful.

What especially bothered me was that many people in the union, especially cronies of the regional director, defended him and stopped talking to me. I was chastised...excommunicated, so to speak. And he was treated fine, 'cause the people on top kind of protect one another.

I remember how mad I got about this at one of our staff gatherings. I told them - "Not one of you fuckers have ever apologized to me for backing him against me. And that's okay. I can live with that. But I think you oughta look in the mirror someday soon, and admit you were wrong!"

Since the guy was convicted for misappropriating union funds more and more people have come around to seeing my side of the fight, but this has come years after the harm they let him do to me. Everyone is now more vicious toward him than I ever was, but I don't take any comfort from this: I feel sorry for him.

Setting Our House in Order. Back in 1962, ten years before I joined the CWA staff, a small group of staffers, people I call *heroes*, made CWA history. They were having some bad experiences with certain newly-elected officers whose election they had opposed. So they formed a union of CWA staffers. They felt they should have some sort of protection. They knew it was not exactly a popular move at that time in CWA headquarters.

To his credit, however, our president, Joe Bierne, took it very well. Jesus, he was a *good* man, a smart man...he knew the right course to take and he took it.

CWA agreed to waive their right to have an NLRB election test whether or not the staff really wanted to unionize, and president Bierne granted the new union full recognition. Perhaps he realized that certain recently elected officers would prove outstanding, while others would not. They're all human, after all. Joe was *very* good at knowing human strengths and weaknesses.

Thanks to this cordial kind of start, the relationship stayed calm for many years. Only *one* case had to go to arbitration. We had a staff person they wouldn't let transfer to the West Coast. They insisted on its being arbitrated. And we won. And she got her transfer.

Over the years, however, we began to get people elected with power over the staff who didn't have Joe Bierne's touch. The sad thing is that a CWA vice-president, when he gets elected, he finds he's stuck with a staff put together by his predecessor, a staff protected from firing by our staff union. He doesn't get to put a whole bunch of his people in.

Sometimes the new man can trust the staff he inherits: sometimes he cannot...or he feels he can't...and sometimes this could be justified. So, some new officers wind up not being very good to their staff.

They become vindictive, and they harrass some of their people. Naturally, we fight back...and urge that we quit fighting within.

Running a Staff Union. The Executive Board members of our staff union who get to the annual CWA Convention arrive two days before it opens, and, on our own time, we meet to see where things are. Since I became president we've gotten *real* militant about a lot of it.

When CWA, on the day before the Convention opens, calls a morning meeting to present its side of our current relationships, I get my members together that very same day - later in the afternoon - to discuss how we want to respond. First I make a report on the grievances of the past year. Then, on any arbitrations we may have gone to. Then, on any changes we might want to make in our bylaws. And I also get into other things I want them to discuss...with a lot of time reserved for "good and welfare."

I'm proud we have 100% enrollment, on a voluntary basis, from all 150 of the staff - a pretty damn good record! With dues at only $30 a month it is a hellova good buy!

It's because we're their shield. Everything is political in a labor union. And this is *the* problem with the union establishment today! If a staffer doesn't make his boss look good the boss is going to want someone else in the job. And if you don't give him all the support he expects he's going to be on your case. And if he comes to suspect you're cozy with his opposition, his political enemies, watch out! You're going to have a lot of trouble from him. You're going to be punished...even if none of it is true!

We fight back against all this sort of shit.

Hell, they're askin' us to cut down on our expenses, 'cause we're steadily losing CWA membership. Christ, we know that!

But we feel the burden should be shared *equally*. It should not be placed all on the staff. This is a *major* complaint of some of my people. It's a *very* sensitive issue with us: We believe in the concept - "All boats rise or fall *together!*"

To make matters even worse, some of the union's top officers will piss away thousands of CWA dollars on some junket of their own, and then dare to nitpick over the expense account of a staffer. They'll actually deny a fifty-cent parking ticket! Christ, cut me a break!

When CWA recently sent out a morale survey it's no wonder my people complained of being treated like second-class citizens. Like they're not being appreciated for what they're doing.

It Isn't the Money. I know our finances are bad, and we've got to reduce expenses. But my retort is, "As long as I see top officers going overseas on junkets, don't tell me any of that stuff! You've got to cut *everywhere* if we have trouble."

We've got our wage re-opener operating right now. Two years ago when we signed this agreement CWA's finances were in pretty bad shape. I was in favor of getting a three-year contract without a wage reopener. Just getting a built-in increase. But back then there was some thought about maybe things would soon get better. I knew they would not 'cause we're slowly going down. So that's why we're in that type of bargaining today.

They gave us a "song-and-dance" about the finances of the union, and about how we're in bad shape, and all this sort of stuff. And so, two years ago, we settled for a 3% wage increase. And then they turned around a month later and gave all the administrative staff a 4 1/2 to 5% wage increase!

That was horrible! They were already making a lot more than we were making, and some of the administrative assistants only do what some of our staff do. I thought that was kind of acting in bad faith.

Our people are actually out doing the work, and they don't get treated properly. They don't show enough respect to them. I finally told one of the vice-presidents: "It isn't the money! It's the insult! It's what you're doing to us! You don't give a damn about the staff!"

Point of View. In front of me some of the officers will actually say about someone on the staff - "Hell, he was *never* any good." I say - "Wait a minute! He's good as far as I'm concerned!" They reply - "He was always a complainer." And I shoot back - "Wait a minute! I tell you the same thing I'd tell a company: Why did you keep him for 20 or 30 years?! He's put in a lot of years. That's a lot of time, sitting in airports. That's a lot of time away from home, by yourself. That's a lot of years wasted. That's the course of your life. You just can't toss a man out like he was nothing! "

Source of the Problem. I appear before the CWA Executive Board from time to time, and I keep bringing up the same thing: That we've got to quit fighting *within*! We've got to quit punishing people because they supported the wrong candidate - which is really why they were going after the guy they said was a "complainer." When are we going to get over this?!

One of the top people likes to say - "You pick your side, and you take your punishment." More recently he told me, "Well, I believe in an eye for an eye. That's an old saying." And I replied, "Yeah, there's an old Irish song that says 'An eye for an eye...until everybody's blind.' The sad thing is that when that happens we can't see what we are doing to ourselves; we've lost our eyesight."

Reason to Care. You know, our staff people are out there by themselves. If you don't treat them fairly they can sell the union...or *not* sell the union. They can go out there and do a job with enthusiasm...or *without* enthusiasm.

When I try to make this clear I'm told the people at the top *do* understand. Recently I was told they were actually about to do something to "enhance" our job, kind of as proof. When I asked what it was they said we'd be taken out of the grievance procedure. Yeah, I said, but we'll be asked instead to handle arbitration cases, and do that to save on legal fees. They're not kidding anybody! Legal fees are going through the roof!

They then said - "Any monies that are saved will be turned back to the staff!" And I said - "I've been doing arbitrations now for the past two years, and I've not gotten a penny! No staff has! Or even a decent increase." They insisted either no savings had been realized yet. Or had possibly had gone into other things.

Playing Games. We've got an opening in one of the more desirable cities. And we've got a guy that used to live there, as a local officer. When he went on staff he got assigned to California. Now he's bid back.

We've got a staff union contract with posting and bidding. The only way they can stop a staff person is through an override, as for a female or a minority, or if there has not been any opportunities for a local person recently to be promoted in that area. They must send a letter to the president of the staff union - that's me - when they want to enforce an override.

They've got to send it *before* the bid closes - that's my ruling - so that they can't play games and see who they're going to get in a staff person response. And then say, "Now we're going to override!"

But they didn't do this in the new case. One person bid on it and he's a qualified staff person. They now say they're going to promote someone from the local. I said - "No, you're not!" They came to me and asked how I was going to help them out. I said, "I'm going to take you to arbitration!"

My God! A qualified staff person bid for the job! A lotta people don't like him. I don't even know the guy, and anyhow, that's beside the point. The point is he is *entitled* to that job. And I'm going to take them to arbitration if they try to fill it otherwise. We've got a contract...and they've got to honor it.'

There's ways to take care of inequities. They just have to write me a letter. They've done it several times before. All I'm saying is - if we have a staff union contract, wouldn't you expect them to *respect* it?!

Take My Car? Hell, No! They tried to take our cars away from us. We had to go to arbitration to win that one. The 15 "Wise Men" (and Women), our Executive Board...I just have a hard time contemplating people doing this...they just sat around a table and said "Our finances are in tough shape. We've gotta' do something. We'll get rid of all the automobiles for all the staff...except for us 15."

Can you believe this?! We won the arbitration case in part because this is a "condition of employment," and it's covered under our contract: They can't unilaterally change it!

After we won the arbitration case they told me I wasn't going to be assigned one of the newer cars. They had to be nasty. I said, "O.K., I don't care. You pay the maintenance, the expenses, all the gas and oil. What do I care! If it breaks down I'll either rent a car or sit in a hotel until you come and get me. I'll do my job whenever I have to do it."

They'll *never* let me get a new car. The one I have now is a 1984, with a lotta miles on it. We have to pay for any use we make of our CWA car for personal travel. It's like a benefit, so they charge us as if we were leasing the car from them. I always write a note every year when I pay the union's leasing rate saying that I cannot imagine anyone leasing a car that is eight years old. I mean, can you imagine me walking into a leasing company and saying, "Show me something snappy in an '84!"

Paying "Dues." I would *never* do anything as president of the staff union that would hurt CWA, 'cause it is *my* union. As long, however, as there are bosses who are unfair, and we've got our share...workers *need* a union! After all, we're dealing with people, and they come with weaknesses, as well as with strengths.

Hell, since I agreed in '89 to be president I've been a target of the weaknesses of some CWA leaders who should know better. It started in '84 when I decided I didn't like the way things were going for CWA staffers like me, so I ran for secretary-treasurer of our staff union. When it came time for the vice-presidents to pick which of their staff would get to accompany them to the CWA Convention - and thereby to our annual staff union membership meeting - I was told I hadn't been picked.

Christ, I was pissed! I realized for the first time that since the vice-presidents had this power to pick and choose among us, they controlled the outcome of our staff union membership meeting - since we voted there on our policies. Our bosses decided who went to vote - and I was determined to oppose this!

I ran and won on a platform that called for a switch over to mail referendums on really important matters. That way those members of the staff union not picked by the vice-presidents to come to the CWA Convention can at least vote through the mail on matters we'll be considering at our membership meeting.

After this win in '84, I got re-elected as secretary-treasurer in '86, and president (no one else would take it!) since '89. Nobody ran against me. I actually got a standing ovation, and it meant a lot to me, 'cause it was from my peers. It was from staff people from all over the country.

Christ, but I've paid heavy. As president of the staff union I'll never go anywhere in CWA. A lot of my members, they sure as hell like the fact we have an aggressive staff union. But they won't come out in the open and say it, 'cause they know it would hurt their chances of being promoted. Me, I've always been considered the "radical," the "bad boy" on the staff. Hell, they used to punish me by moving me so much that I never had a personal doctor or dentist. I'd just use whoever was closest to the place I was renting.

I've no regrets, though. Our staff union has made CWA a *better* organization, a *better* union. In the past 13 months alone, we've handled eight arbitrations, settled five, and only had to go to hearings in three. For four years previous we had only one case. So, without this militancy of ours, all hell would be breaking lose. People would be fired, and would not be able to bid on job openings. Lots would be abused on the day-to-day job, a whole host of problems that our staff union prevents. We've made CWA respect our contract with them, and it is a helluva better union for that!

Talking Back. At the same time I have no problem raising hell when one of my people is not playing fair with our union.

We had a staff meeting this week and got into a little dispute. We were talking about our internal procedures in our office, and what we are doing right and wrong. I said, "I don't know who is handling the scheduling of the secretaries, but if one of them goes to lunch, they must be staggered, 'cause there are six of them in our group, so there must be someone on the phones." I had to get an answer for a local recently when I was on the road. I called in from an airport, and the phone rang six or eight times, and was finally answered by a secretary from another group. So I said, "O.K., I'll call back." And I did, an hour later, from another airport, and the same thing happened. Three hours later I was at the San Francisco airport, and the *same* thing happened.

One of the people sitting there, one of my staff people, sarcastically responded, "Gee, Mr. *Union* Man!!" She was *very* nasty. So I said, "Wait a minute! I think I'm a *good* union man! I work hard at my job 'cause we're tryin' to service members out there. And I expect the secretaries to do the *same* thing! And if we don't handle the calls from these locals that need help, or from our members that need help, we're not doing what we're supposed to do!"

I had *no* problem raising hell about that! I wasn't coming down on any individual: I was coming down on the system, on *lousy* scheduling...and our staff union can help straighten that sort of mess out.

Reaching Out. In '87 I attended the first meeting of the Congress of Staff Unions. Seven outfits like ours each sent two delegates. None of the 14 delegates knew any of the others, and somebody raised doubts about whether we were too few and too small to make a go of it. So I said - "I know of one group that was started by only twelve. And it has lasted almost 2000 years. I think we can start with 14, and still make something good of it!"

Sure enough, the word spread, and in '88 we had 30 attend; in '90, 40 or more. We now have delegates from staff unions in the auto workers, chemical workers, flight attendants, paper workers, rubber workers, operating engineers, service employees, school teachers, and many others. I'm helping out by serving as secretary-treasurer, and boy, is it a headache!

We now call ourselves the International Congress of Staff Unions (ICSU). While we haven't changed the world yet, we *are* exchanging contracts and ideas among ourselves, and that helps! We run workshops that explain new tax regulations that bear on staffer expense accounts. We discuss strategies for helping staffs unionize. And we lift our spirit, we boost our own morale.

Unions, you know, are the worst employers around. Sorry about that! I've negotiated with many, many employers, and I have never met one as bad as the one I work for! Everybody in the Congress, but the paper makers unions, tells the same story.

While ICSU is not growing as fast as many of us charter members would like, a spark *has* been struck...and it should soon grow into a flame. I'm really excited about it.

Just Keep Going. When things start to get to me, I just remember what I was told by a wonderful union guy who's going to be 82, an old-timer. I love this man. Never said a nice word to me in his life, but I love him so much. He's such a *neat* guy! He's who he is, and never tries to be anybody else.

Some years ago, talking about the Bell System, he said to me - "John, you can't beat the elephant! You can't beat it. But you can keep on kicking it. And kicking it. That way you might move it a little bit to the left. A little to the right. A little bit back. And you keep on kicking it. You *never* stop. Don't *ever* stop kickin' it." And that's become my theory of life. I don't think I'll ever change people's ways. But I'm going to make them stop.

When I think back on how I got into this to begin with, it was my mother and the nuns in my Catholic School. Both of them talked about the need to help people. And the need for kindness. And they didn't differentiate among people.

My greatest contribution to society, at least the most rewarding, was working as a volunteer at "Luther Place," a shelter for homeless women in Washington, D.C. I spent weekends feeding them and caring for their needs. The bag ladies are abusive, self-centered, and difficult, but also lovely in a tough sort of way. I would leave the shelter on an emotional high after sharing our lives with each other. I recommend everyone share in such an experience.

I was once called "crazy" by a union official for spending my weekends at the shelter. Shame on her!

I'm not as courageous as I appear to be...perhaps stubborn. But I care about helping the "little" people. It *is* what life is all about, corney as it may sound.

I think of my mother when people nowadays badmouth my union work. They say, "Hell, John, you spend all your time on the grievances of drunks and misfits." And I shoot back - "No, I spend far more time helping people like my mother!"

Since my open-heart surgery in '77 I know I've been living on borrowed time. I'll just keep plugging away, confident that the good in unionism will win out. After all, the 100 Year War, another terrible time, eventually came to an end. It took 116 years, to be sure, but it did end. We'll come out fine, though it will take time.

Winning Mutual Respect through Personnel Relations
Paul Anderson
(CWA)

Thoughtful and well-spoken, Paul Anderson has come a long way since his boyhood on a small and struggling family dairy farm. As a high-level career staffer with the Communication Workers of America (CWA), the nation's premier union in telecommunications, Paul was responsible for the CWA's personnel management function when he wrote the material below, a role that had him sit opposite John Scally (author of the previous case) in labor-management negotiations.

Paul is quite unusual among the book's inside reformers as he alone has worn a "management" hat, albeit he did so as a thoroughgoing trade unionist second to none in his allegiance to labor's ideals. All the more valuable, therefore, are his insights into -

the normal state-of-affairs in a union bureaucracy;

the value of modern personnel relations approaches to labor union bureaucracies;

the motives of middle management in unions;

the strengths and weaknesses of union staffers; and -

the contribution outside experts can made to internal union reformers.

Especially helpful is Paul's conviction that union bureaucracies need not mirror the worst aspects of business bureaucracies with which labor regularly butts heads: Rather, Paul's field-tested approach encourages those who (like John Scally and other staff union leaders) believe organized labor can soon model superior bureaucracies for all to emulate.

My background is definitely grass-roots. I was born in rural Minnesota in 1941 to a farm family. We were small farmers...small to the extent that our type of farm, principally a family dairy farm, is almost extinct today. By any measure of the government we were probably poor. But I never really thought of us...my sisters and me (I was the last born)...as being poor. We ate very well. We slaughtered our own cattle and some chickens. We raised a big garden. I always had warm clothes on my back, and I had a bicycle. We were *very* basic. We didn't have very much money, but we didn't want for many things, either.

I attended a typical one-room schoolhouse which served 15 to 20 of us, depending on the year. It closed about three years after I went on to high school. The building is still there, and my kids think it's funny as hell. As I revisit the quality of education I received I'm sure by today's standards it would be looked at as not very well-rounded. But the teachers that we had were extremely dedicated and committed to making sure the students understood the curriculum. And if that required a rap upside the head, standing in the corner, or having your butt kicked, all us kids accepted it as part of the process. So I can't say I felt educationally deprived by spending eight years in that setting.

My family life revolved around the church: It was a *strong* social influence on my family. The Evangelical Free Church, a country church, served 35 to 40 families in the community. Ministers would come and go. It didn't pay very well, so the preachers generally were either just starting out in the ministry or semi-retired. The ministers looked for a place in a country setting where they were comfortable preaching'.

The church had a *very* strict doctrine. To be a member you had to publicly testify that you were a born-again Christian. No smoking or drinking; we weren't allowed to go to movies. So I spent a lot of years hearing "Thou Shalt Nots."

It didn't all make sense to me, but what I was taught became deeply embedded. And I believe to this day that many of my values are based on, and my actions are a result of the strong influence of the Church.

While the values of my religion stick with me, my youthful commitment to the church is not one I've maintained. I don't dedicate the kind of time to religion that the church expects, because at this time I have the desire. Maybe some day that will change.

I went into the Navy for three and one half years when I was 17. And during that time my dad sold the farm. My mother had passed away when I was 16, and dad decided to give up farming after I left. So upon leaving the Navy there really was no option to return to the farm.

Going Union. While I was in the service I met my first wife. So when the Navy released me I moved to Milwaukee, her hometown, and went to work for Westinghouse Electric.

This was my first exposure to a union. I can't recall unions ever being discussed in my family. We were what I would call a pretty staunch Republican family. My dad, at least, was quite vocal. I remember he didn't have any use for FDR. And I remember him making some disparaging remarks about Truman. And I don't believe to this day - and my dad is 94 - that he ever voted for anyone who wasn't on the Republican side of the ticket ... this includes any type of independent race. Although Dad's politics are Republican, age has mellowed some of his staunch right wing opinions.

I can never recall Dad having any strong feelings one way or another about unions. We had a couple of small industries in town, boat works and paper mills, and I can remember there were some strikes. But other than what we read in the newspapers, the strikes never became a topic of conversation.

First Impressions. At Westinghouse we were a total union shop, an apparatus repair shop, with 30 or 40 of us workers. I had performed that kind of work in the Navy, so I had no problem getting hired. After I had been there a certain number of days I had to join the IBEW. They gave me my card, and I started paying' dues.

I attended one union meeting, because I had to get sworn in, so I went but I wasn't really impressed. There was a whole bunch of people yelling and screaming about electrical construction worker problems. And a bunch of people screaming about Allis-Chalmers, and some other plants. It was obvious the local was really amalgamated. It had construction electricians, but it also represented a number of major manufacturing plants and their workers. So our 35-to-40 member shop was a small group within the local. After about an hour and a half, I became tired of their bitching. I left the meeting and went down the street and had a couple of brews.

Steward as Wimp. My next involvement with IBEW came about 15 days before I was going on my honeymoon.

When I had hired on at the plant I had told the person that hired me I was getting married in November and that I wanted the following week off. And he said "No problem.'" A couple of weeks before my wedding I reminded him I'd be gone for a week, and he said he couldn't let me off.

So I said, "What do you mean you can't let me off?!" And he said, "No, I've got a job for you up in Upper Michigan. I want you to go and help out the journeyman electrician repair a generator that was hit by lightning." And I said, "Well, I ain't going!" And he said, "You'll go! Or you're fired!" I told him, "You made a promise to me, that I could have the time off, and you're reneging. I don't know if I *want* to work for you!" And I stomped off.

One of my fellow workers had overheard. And he said, "Go see the union steward." I went and talked to Al, the union steward. I told him my plight. And he said, "Look kid, there ain't much you can do about it." I said, "Well, aren't you even gonna talk to him?" And he said, "Now, there ain't nutting you can do about it." So I thought that's damn dumb!

Well the way it turned out, the boss had second thoughts. And he said that, by the grace of God, he'd let me get off. I found out about two weeks later the job had been delayed because of lack of equipment. What a jerk!

Union Usefulness. About two weeks after I got back from my honeymoon there was an election for union steward. And Al was giving his little talk at a gathering we held at night after work. And he was saying he'd like another term, and he was "interested in representin'...," a whole bunch of bullshit! And I finally said, "You're full of shit, Al! You didn't do jack-shit for me." And of course, that

got some of the other guys to raise their eyes, and say "Who the hell is
a new man, talkin' like that to the union steward?!" But a couple of
them smiled.

So what happened was the election was three or four days later.
And some guy said "Are you serious about what you said about Al?"
And I said "Yeah, he didn't take care of my problem." And so one of the
other guys decided to run against him. And I campaigned for him. And
he was elected over Al.

Bell Calls. Working as a union electrician kind of got my
appetite a little stirred. So I went to a couple more of the union
meetings. And about a year later, all three applications I had filed for
apprenticeships with the electrical union, the electric company, and the
telephone company - came available at the same time. After looking
the three over I decided to go with the telephone company.

The environment that I walked into there - as far as the CWA
(Communications Workers of America) union - was quite different. I
was there about three/four days (I started off in the mailroom) and I was
approached by a guy who said he was a union steward from the floor
above. And he said he wanted me to join the union. And I said "O.K."
At that time we were an open shop, so I said "I was union at my last
place. I don't have any problem with that." "Good!" he says, "You
have union experience so now you're a steward!"

CWA Calls. So, that started me on my CWA career. A
few months later the local put me through some steward schools. It
was a pretty good bunch of guys that I worked with. And most of
them joined the union. As I moved to different jobs, the stewardship
kind of followed along with me. I became more active. I served as
an Election Committee chair. Suddenly the union was an important part
of my life.

Source of Appeal. I find it difficult to identify any one thing
that drew me to the labor movement. I think about the injustice I saw
when I worked at Westinghouse. I felt there should be some way
workers should.... even if their views or point didn't prevail....be able
to explain *their* side of the story. And it gets back to being fair: The
boss at Westinghouse had told me he'd do something for me, and then
he didn't do it! Well, there ought be some recourse to that! And I
think that drew me to unionism, to a certain extent.

Since I was in my twenties I think also I was lookin' for a way,
an avenue, or a vehicle to raise hell with management! I think I har-
bored some anti-establishment feelings, and I can't say I didn't enjoy
givin' hell to management once in while and puttin' them on the
spot.

But again, as I matured, (for lack of a better word), and accepted
more responsibility in the labor movement, it was obvious to me
that my desire to raise hell was not the focal point of my
involvement. I found as I went on that I could effectively represent
people and sort things out, help my fellow workers, and try to bring

about some meaningful changes. My success and the ongoing need to make sure workers were treated fairly was what kept me in the labor movement.

Union Career. In 1968 my involvement in CWA went from being a sideline to being my career. I went from being a telephone technician to becoming a union activist. I found my "calling," so to speak and my job as a technician at the telephone company became secondary.

At that time, the local I belonged to was, and still is, extremely active. Back in '68 there were a number of us who had recently become active and we got together. We were younger than the majority of people who were leading the union, were feeling' our oats a little bit, and thought it was time to make some leadership changes in our local.

It started out sorta small. But as it came time to nominate and elect, our group had grown. We ended running someone for nearly every office, and we ran as a slate. We didn't run against the president, which was a smart move on our part. None of us had the experience and the maturity then to handle the job. At that time the local had about 1200 or 1300' members, was politically active not only in the city, but in the state, and in international union affairs.

So, anyhow, we were successful in our campaign. It got a little nasty - we had a couple of challenges to our election wins - but it was also very exciting! And we won!

Winning Office. I ran for treasurer against a guy that had been around since dirt. A decent guy, but he had really gotten pretty comfortable in his 20 years as a local officer. I won't say he was taking advantage of the position. But he wasn't doing anything to set the world on fire either. And once the books were turned over to me I found he was doing what was just barely necessary, instead of trying to better the financial position of the union and its members.

I served as treasurer for one term. And about that time our president went on national union staff, and the vice-president moved up to become president. I ran for and won the vice-president's position. This gave me the opportunity to deal in all areas of our local.

Going After Members. We were in the midst of organizing campaigns at that time, not only units within the Bell company, but we also started organizing other companies We organized a machine shop, and an automobile service company. Then we started organizing what we called the interconnect industry, those companies that came along as a result of the Carterphone decision, which allowed non-Bell companies to sell telephone and other communications equipment.

So, we ended up having seven or eight of these external units that were not part of the Bell System, and they required a local officer to service their members..As Vice-President a lot of that became my responsibility. I enjoyed it and I met a lot of good people. Met some tough ones, too!

I can remember one guy: We organized a machine shop, and the owner did everything in his power to keep us out. But we won the election! When I went in to bargain the contract that same owner taught me a lot of valuable lessons because he put me through hell! We ultimately lost the unit. The owner was successful in firing some people. And even though we got them settlements some years later, he was able to use the stalling tactics that the NLRB allowed through their lengthy appeal procedure to ultimately discourage those that were still in the plant.

Through some legal maneuvers I delayed the decert for about two years, but it still happened. It was interesting: I didn't think I had more than one or two workers who would still vote CWA at that time. But after all was said and done we still had about 40% of them in our corner. That was a pleasant surprise! It was disheartening that we lost it but at least we didn't go down without making a statement.

Taking Over. About four or five years later the local president also went on CWA staff as an assistant to VP. That left his job open and I was elected without opposition.

As president I felt one of my main responsibilities was to develop others for leadership roles. The local had a strong commitment to leadership education. I've always tried to remember the advice given to me by one of the local's elder statesmen: "You're not immortal: By the Grace of God you're here today, but you may be gone tomorrow. And as an elected leader you have the responsibility to make sure the organization is protected and can go forward without you!"

Unfortunately then and also today, I find not everyone shares this philosophy. There are leaders among us, and not just in CWA, but elsewhere in the labor movement, who would never subscribe to such a theory because it would be a personal threat to them. (That's another subject, I guess..., egos that get in the way of labor's growth.)

Finding Talent. I can't say as local president I presided over a time that the local rose to any prominence, other than that we grew in numbers. Part of that resulted from growth in the industry, but we also did some merging, and organizing.

We were very successful in organizing part of our commercial and marketing group and brought in 300 or 400 members through our efforts. We found them rich in talent - especially the computer people and service reps. Quick minds! Quick to learn! Very disciplined! We convinced some to take on local leadership roles and some are still around! That was rewarding to me - putting an educational system in place that could involve more people.

I did some innovative things: I took the whole Executive Board on retreats. And sent them to the Meany Center for week-long conferences to broaden their perspective. And I encouraged them to enroll in courses and seminars in universities around the country. Our education budget was significant, but, in the long term, it paid off very well!

Joining the Staff. In 1982 I was offered and accepted a position as a CWA Representative, which is a full-time staff position. I hadn't been actively seeking such a position, but I looked at it as another step to promote the kind of philosophy I felt was necessary for CWA to grow and continue to be a viable organization.

As a local officer I had attended all the conventions and had been very interested in union finances. I appeared before a number of convention committees and asked a lot of questions, I believe, in a constructive way. But some people felt *any* questioning or criticizing or challenging was *not* what was expected of a good local officer. So I was held in disfavor by some, but that didn't bother me.

It did cause one interesting situation. At that time a candidate for staff had to be recommended by a CWA geographic vice-president and appear before the CWA national executive officers for an interview. If they felt you were okay you were put on staff.

Nearly all the officers were well-aware of my talents, or lack thereof, and one in particular knew about my long-standing interest in CWA finances. During the interview they asked me different questions about my family, what my goals were, and how I felt about the union's programs. One officer got a quizzical look on his face and said - "Paul, if you're staff, you realize that you can't do what you're used to doing at convention. You can't get on the floor and take the mike. You've got to keep your mouth shut. You can't take an active part in the debate." And he asks, "How you gonna do that?" And I said, "It might be a little tough. But I wouldn't be wasting your time here today - indi-cating my desire to be a rep - if I didn't think I couldn't handle that."

It was a pretty good answer, I guess. They continued their questioning for about a half hour or 45 minutes, I guess. And as we were ready to wrap up they asked if anybody had any further comments. And that same quizzical officer said, "Yeah, I got another one: Paul, are you *sure* about that situation at convention? Are you *sure* you can stay away from the microphone during the Finance Committee report?" I laughed. I didn't know whether I was being put on or not: I found out later I was.

At the next convention, just a few months after they hired me, when they announced the Finance Committee was ready to give its report, I just happened to walk up towards the stage, caught the eye of the officer who had put me on, and told him I was just leaving for awhile, *not* going to the mike. It was one of the few times in my life I ever saw that officer double over in laughter. While some of my colleagues thought it was luck that got me on staff, most were very supportive. (I have always subscribed to the theory that luck is the result when opportunity and preparation meet!)

CWA Rep. As a rep my main responsibilities were grievances and bargaining. And I tried to lead locals and help them handle internal and external problems. I knew nearly all of the officers of the locals that I serviced, at least when I started out, because my assignment covered about three-quarters of the State of Wisconsin, and I had been there as an active unionist in the state for about 15 years. I knew most of the people as friends, and they knew me, so there weren't a lot of surprises.

It was a different level of responsibility than that of a local President, but coming from the largest local in the district we had assumed some of the staff Reps responsibilities over a period of time. So there was really nothing new, other than now having direct responsibility and, in most cases, dealing with a different level of management.

Divestiture. Major changes started in 1984 when Judge Greene split up the Bell system, as this drastically changed our union's focus and our *modus operandi*. Divestiture caused my own assignment to broaden.

In addition to the locals I took care of in Wisconsin, I was assigned to take care of several AT&T contracts covering 10 states. The new assignment allowed me to interface with CWA leadership that didn't know me. However, this didn't cause a problem, dealing with AT&T caused a problem!

Playing Fair. I'll have to say it was very rare in my career as a rep or local officer that I didn't develop rapport with management. This helped me to sense where they were coming from and where they were heading. And I had a reputation of dealing fairly and honestly with management. I believed this allowed me to better service our members.... I saw some union people use strong challenging adversarial styles, and I didn't believe their ability to resolve things was nearly as good as mine.

Just to touch on that further: I remember once as a local steward on a grievance where I had the company right where it hurt. And I said "I can get 'em good this time," but one of my mentors frowned. When I asked what was his problem he said "You'd better choose your words cautiously. 'Cause you may have all the cards this time, Paul. But you'll find as your career goes on that you're going to be handling cases where you'll have to go in begging on bended knee with your ass in your hand. And if you acted like a jerk when you had the upper hand, chances are they're going to remember that and make you eat your lunch when you don't have the upper hand. So I suggest that when you go in tomorrow you handle your win with the same kind of dignity you would show if you were losing heavy."

I never forgot that. And I used this story whenever I trained new stewards and officers. It continues to be valuable to me now, though I wear a different hat. I try to instill that attitude in the people I deal with on my side of the table and the people I'm across from. One should remember we're all human beings, and we should treat each other with dignity and respect. We're there to resolve a problem, *not* there to beat the hell out of each other!

CWA Change. In 1984 the CWA Executive Board decided we ought to do some restructuring to deal with the results of divestiture. We redistricted and merged some districts together. This created two national executive board jobs that hadn't been there before - the Vice-President of AT & T technologies, and Vice-President of AT & T Communications. There were no incumbents and I thought I could do some good. So I ran for the AT & T Technologies post - the first time I had run for anything since being local union president, the first time I ran for *anything* on the national CWA scene.

There were four of us in the campaign, all staff people, which eliminated some problems. We didn't have the situation that develops in some of our campaigns where you have CWA staff versus local officers. Two candidates were CWA veterans, one from New Jersey; the other, from North Carolina. The third candidate was a fairly new staff person, from Missouri.

I was bucking odds, as I was the least known of the four, but it was a good campaign. I learned a lot and again I got to know a lot of good people. I ran hard, but I still came in fourth! I can't say my ego didn't take a bruise or two but I had really felt from the gitgo it would be difficult for me to win, so I wasn't crushed.

The years following the election brought massive layoffs and downsizing at AT&T. I recognize now that my inexperience in dealing with an employer that size would have buried me. It's *still* a bitch of a job today, regardless of who holds the position.

But anyhow, I can laugh about the campaign now: As it turned out, by *not* winning I really won!

Post-Election Development. After the election only one thing changed in my job; I had some national recognition. It is doubtful if I could have gained this in a short time period through any other method than running for national office.

In early '85 the CWA president and secretary-treasurer announced their retirement. Elections were held at the July convention. Because other elected officers ran for these positions it opened up several posts, and I got involved in the campaigns. There was no opposition to the candidates for president and sec-treasurer. Other offices, however, had challenges, and I worked hard because I wanted capable leaders to be elected.

My candidates won, and the evening of election day I got a phone call from Jim Booe, the new Secretary-Treasurer, and he said he wanted me to consider becoming one of his assistants.

I can't say that it came as a complete surprise, because the district vice-president I was then working for was quite a promoter of my abilities. Jim had evidently questioned him about me, and my vice president had given a high recommendation.

At the time Booe called me, I was ready to leave Wisconsin. I had been divorced for a few years. My son was in college and my daughter was a year away from getting out of high school. My plans were - Well, I liked Wisconsin and its people, but I was ready to broaden my background. Outside of my time in the Navy, my life had been spent in the mid-west. Nothing wrong with that, other than I knew I wanted to check out the other parts of the country! I was planning to look for a CWA rep's job elsewhere when my daughter graduated and had dealt with my family regarding that decision. My kids understood when I ran for office in '84, that if I had been elected, I'd have had to move us to Washington, D.C. or New Jersey.

So I accepted the job from Jim and a couple of months later reported to CWA headquarters in Washington, D.C.

Serving at Headquarters. I was the newest one to come into the assistant's job. While there were four of us, I knew the other three assistants were probably going to retire within a few years. Jim asked me to start getting as familiar as practicable with *all* the responsibilities in the office, especially the financial ones, as soon as possible. He wanted me up and running when the other assistants started retiring.

One of the responsibilities Jim gave me was personnel. As an Assistant to the Secretary-Treasurer I exchanged my "rep" hat for a management hat, and there was no question I was going to find out what it was like to be a manager *within* a labor union.

Life on the Other Side. I settled into my office, and got set up, and started doing some of the preliminary things one needs to do to get acquainted with a new office, a new building and new people. I was humored by some of the individuals who would stop in to see me and share little tidbits of gossip: I reckon that was because I was in charge of Personnel and that promotions and other such things went through that Department. They may have been trying to influence something to happen for them in the future, and felt if they gave me some inside info it would help. Anyhow, I found out who was gay. And who was lesbian. And who was sleeping with whom. They told me who owed money to whom. And who was doing... whatever to whomever. What had happened in the last ten years ... and all that sort of stuff.

Finally, in the most diplomatic way I knew I informed those people that I really didn't give a shit about such things! I really didn't care what people did on their own time as long as they were responsible employees.

My reluctance to care about their inside scoop was met with some surprise and dismay. I was to find out that the entire building was one gigantic rumor mill. I recalled that in the telephone company, the greatest rumor spreaders were the people who didn't have enough work to keep them busy. I pondered if the same was true at CWA.

Is Anyone in Charge? As I settled into the job I began to look at where we were with our employees and the things that were going on. I had inherited some arbitration cases and grievances that our local of the Office and Professional Employees Union (OPEIU) had filed. And as I looked at these I started to see some things that bothered me: It appeared that we were having serious problems with promotions. We had denied some because of poor work performance yet promoted others who also had lousy work performance records. In addition I found a lot of inconsistencies and neglect regarding employee matters. It was unbelievable what kind of a poor management job we were doing! There appeared to be workers showing up when they felt like it, working when they felt like it. I wondered "How the hell did it get like this?!"

After some review, I thought it would be good idea to get together with the supervisors and coordinators in the Secretary-Treasurer's office. At that time they numbered about 20 and were responsible for managing our departments' 120- plus employees. I thought I'd try to get to know them a little, and see what they had to say about some of these problems.

I asked one of the supervisors if they had a meeting coming up in the near future where I could have couple of minutes to speak. I got a quizzical look that said - "Well, no, not really." I should have read that sign that something was not quite the way I thought it was, but I pressed on.

"Attention Please!" I said, "Well, let's call a meeting!'" The supervisors and coordinators that showed up kind of nervously looked at each other. I introduced myself, and asked them to introduce themselves to me.

I started talking about some of the concerns I had after reading grievances, attendance sheets, and job performance reports, etc. I asked them some questions. There was dead silence. And it got quieter! There was nothing going on; "Porch light on; nobody home!'" They seemed relieved when I said I was calling an end to the meeting, and they didn't waste any time getting out of there.

Later in the day I met with one of the supervisors on another issue. I asked him, "Is this typical, what happened in there today at your meeting? Or was this a reaction because I was new? Or was it because of the subject I was talking about?" And the supervisor kind of hemmed and hawed a bit. And I said, "Come on! Tell me straight! I can take it! What is it?" And he says, "Well, we never had a meeting before." And I said, "You've got to be shittin' me!"

But I found there hadn't been any kind of a structure for supervisors. And furthermore I found it was a rare occasion when supervisors ever sat with their people, whether formally or informally, to talk about problems or offer recommendations. There was very *little* communication of this sort.

Turning Things Around. So, after my initial shock I set about to try and change that. I thought, well, we need some management training. Prior to coming to Washington I had spent a considerable amount of time at the Meany Center. I had gone through three months of staff training there, and had also attended a number of courses as a local officer. I had built up some rapport with a couple of the Centers' administrators. We set up a meeting, and I said "Hey, CWA has this problem...," and they were receptive to helping me solve it.

However, teaching "management" isn't something offered on their normal agenda. So we had to work through some administrative problems. I also evaluated a couple of management consulting firms' programs and discussed some of our problems with them. But I found they generally lacked the sensitivity and experience to deal with the union as employer, because we are a different beast.

There is no question that the employees of a labor union expect their employer to "walk their talk" when talking about treating workers better than the industries treat our members. And that can be a real issue...we union managers don't always remember what it's like to be a worker!

Educational Aid. I asked the Meany Center to try and put together some training that would focus on treating our people as human beings, while also developing accountability staying within that realm of sensitivity we were expected to demonstrate as a *union* employer.

It worked out well. The two Meany staffers who did the training came to our building and met with our supervisors who started to loosen up a little bit after a few meetings. The staffers asked me to give them examples of some of the problems experienced by the supervisors. So I related some of the attendance problems, performance problems, attitude problems...and whatever other personnel problems had come to my attention.

The training took place about a year after I arrived. By this time there was some water over the dam, and we had started to handle some of the tougher people problems so the training provided an opportune setting for the supervisors to deal with their specific problems. We did a lot of role-playing to bring out tough examples, and we discussed "how do you handle this one?"

It got *really* interesting, 'cause while the Meany staff disguised the issues somewhat, once they got working on it everyone would say - "Someone else has *that* problem?" And what happened - because the supervisors didn't know each other very well - it helped them find other people had problems just as they did!

Some of them openly shared their feelings and as time went by they became less hesitant about bringing up a problem. There was less fear they would be held in disfavor if they admitted they could use some help with a problem.

Through the training it became clear to the supervisors that some of these problems were beyond an easy fix. They threw a little humor into it and started to joke about it. They started working as a group and by the time we finished that first three day session they were having some fun, starting to get to know each other....and we went on from there.

Reaching Beyond the Work Role. As the supervisors started to counsel people and develop standards for accountability, we found that some of our people had *lots* of problems.

We got together with our union representatives, (locals of OPEIU, the staff union, the Newspaper Guild, and the Operating Engineers) - and talked about developing an employee assistance program (EAP). It was apparent we had employees with substance abuse problems. There were also family problems and troublesome situations as a result of employees being single parents, spousal dependency problems, and financial problems.

I thought an EAP Program would be very valuable, from my experience with assistance programs in the field when I was a rep, and from working with some employers setting them up. I felt an EAP would prove a *very* valuable tool for CWA and our employees.

The union reps and CWA management met two or three times to develop the program. And boy, did I meet with a lot of skepticism! It was my first realization of how untrusting some of the union representatives were of CWA management, especially the staff union - there was a *real* lack of trust and communication between it and some CWA administrators. There was also lack of trust from some of the OPEIU representatives who accused me of trying to put together something to monitor people and find out what kind of problems they really had, so CWA could fire them!

No matter how much I said, "Hey, the purpose of the program is to *help* people, not to build a record on them," I couldn't cut through the suspicion without outside help. So we engaged the D.C. United Way to send us some staff from the agency that handled abuse problems. To make a long story short, we finally put it all together. But not without a lot of difficulty and a few setbacks along the way.

My experience developing the EAP program proves that a labor union is not immune from the same kind of employer-employee problems with trust that exist in the "outside world."

Clarifying Roles. One of the problems of great concern was many of our employees didn't know what was expected of them. While some job descriptions existed there was a lack of clarity regarding what the employees' functions really were. Since we had been lax in dealing with problems in performance, the workers really didn't know what was and what was not acceptable and expected.

We had operated with a very low level of accountability. I found people making mistakes that caused our members and people in the field to file improper reports or receive the wrong amount of money, or be mailed the wrong records. As we examined some of these problems we found human errors. But there was not a systematic way to ensure a long term fix. Some workers were not being held accountable for their mistakes even when they knew better...when they knew what was expected of them. We had purposely chosen not to give people constructive feedback. Also, we were not recognizing the efforts of workers who were doing a good job...there was no reinforcement for them to continue to do well. We were not communicating.

Providing Feedback. One of the things I found earlier in my career to be a valuable tool was an annual employee review: The Bell System had always been very sticky about giving reviews but I felt that - while some people pooh-poohed it - it was a way that at least once a year one had the opportunity to talk with one's supervisor. Sometimes you didn't agree with what was put on the paper, but there was an option to write down what you thought - and go from there.

My fellow assistants and I discussed implementing evaluations with the Secretary-Treasurer. We recognized that evaluations were generally considered a nasty word in labor union dictionaries. So I said, "Well, let's call it a 'progress review.'" We agreed, and this meant that at least once a year all supervisors would meet with each of their people.

Since the supervisors were not trained in evaluating I again turned to the Meany Center. We put together a two-day session focused on how to evaluate and how to counsel people, and how to complete reviews. When we instituted this program we found the good workers enjoyed being reviewed. The ones who weren't such good workers had their problems brought to their attention and at least were told what was expected of them. Some of them even said "It's about time you talked to me I've tried to talk to you a couple of times, and you just don't seem to listen to me."

The review process requires our supervisors to meet with workers and give them the kind of feedback necessary for a work group to function.

Bargaining with CWA's Staffers. In negotiations with our local of the Office and Professional Employees Union (OPEIU) in 1986 and 1989 we made some significant changes in the contract regarding promotions. Prior to 1986 CWA, as an employer, was required to promote the most senior employee that bid on a job - regardless of their performance record: This was not only causing us problems as an employer, but demoralized the hell out of some of our very qualified workers who could not realistically compete for promotions.

I remember when I arrived at headquarters we had just promoted someone who had averaged being off the job over 80 days per year for three straight years. And we had just promoted the person to more responsibility! Of course with her past record she was in no position to handle it. But under the OPEIU labor agreement she had the right to get the job, and her union had to fight for her. She ultimately failed in her new position and we had to send her back. She arbitrated the case.

Supposedly, we "won" when the case was ruled in favor of the employer - but, we really didn't win; everyone lost! We had to start training another employee, the workers who were not selected were disgusted, and the grievant felt screwed.

We had a lot of people who were very well qualified and capable of doing the job. Yet they had to lose out to someone who was not capable or qualified.

So, we changed our contract with our OPEIU local. We had some pain doing it. But, knowing from the other side of the table what it takes to get something done, I presented the changes over a period of time so there were not any surprises to our employees or their union. And it has worked out to our advantage...for both, union management *and* union employees.

To ease the blow a little bit we put together a tuition reimbursement plan for the people so they can be looking to update their skills and became better qualified for potential openings. Occasionally we bring in some trainers to do some specific training at the worksite. I'd like to expand on this more as we go forward. Time and money are the only thing that are stopping us. I am disappointed that not more people take advantage of tuition reimbursement, but it has picked up some support as locals of CWA employees become more supportive of education.

As a labor union, I believe we've given some of our people a false sense of security over the years because we've always tried to accommodate them, no matter what the impact may be to our organization. As our resources as an employer become more and more limited, however, we too have to make sure that our membership's dollars are spent wisely. This is not being a chicken shit union employer. This is dealing with reality.

I find myself constantly reminding some of my fellow workers that the union is *not* in existence to benefit its employees: Our reason for being here is to service our members! And sometimes that means we get into tough choices where, unless the person is doing something very positive about preparing themselves for the future, unfortunately, they are going to be caught in the same kind of squeeze many of our members face with continuing technological advances. So I never pass up an opportunity to chide'em, to try and convince our people of the importance of *education*!

Looking Ahead. I don't want to leave the impression that all CWA's problems have been resolved. It's a long, slow laborious process. Supervisors and managers who have had many, many years with us find it very difficult to adapt to new ways. Sometimes it's two steps forward, two steps back. Some still find it very uncomfortable to meet with their people because they never had to do that before. Some still find it very difficult to be critical of poor performance and are reluctant to make their workers reach higher standards.

But, little by little it's moving along. And we recognize that we have to provide on-going reinforcement. So we use a combination of the Meany Center and management consultants, which helps reinforce our long term goals.

We are currently going through a study in CWA about our overall effectiveness and where we go in the future. Part of the feedback the officers are getting from the consulting firm is we don't involve our staff in a lot of the decisions we make. We don't make them feel like they are part of the team.

Envisioning a Finer Union. It's interesting: We've recently had a national staff meeting in Las Vegas. It was our *first* get together for this purpose in modern times. We were fortunate to have Ray Marshall, former Secretary of Labor, act as a facilitator and a number of other labor educators from around the country served as facilitators for our break out sessions. What we did was try to identify what a world-class labor organization in the 21st Century would look like. Then we broke into groups and talked about what it would take for CWA to be that world-class organization. After meeting, the groups came back and reported to the full group.

Of course, there was a lot of animosity voiced. There were a lot of issues raised, charges that CWA was not "walking their talk," doing the kind of things internally for their own people that they claim they want done for their members. In my opinion, some of it was bullshit. But overall, it was a good exercise!

And the last portion of the meeting was structured for us to explain and share with each other what we envision as our role in making CWA a world-class organization. The majority of the suggestions centered around more training. And better managerial skills for those of us that manage. Treating people better, being more sensitive to people, less politics and less political influence in making day-to-day decisions were all highlights.

The thrust of the suggestions reinforced my belief that if some of the managerial training we instituted in the Secretary-Treasurer's Office over the last three/four years had been expanded to *all* areas of our organization, we would have experienced fewer problems than were voiced at that meeting.

Employees as Resources. One thing I found very interesting that was brought out time and time again in Las Vegas was the desire for our staff people to have *meaningful* input into the organization...as far as making decisions and being more involved in initial stages of planning programs and policies. Basically, what they were talking is along the lines of quality circles and quality work life (QWL).

The reason I found it very interesting is that I worked with a number of the staff who were calling for activity such as QWL. Back in the early '80's, the Bell System and AT & T were promoting these programs, and we negotiated the process into our contracts on behalf of our members. When we set up arrangements for QWL training however, I recall some CWA staff people were very, very critical about us getting involved in any kind of participatory management program. It amazed me that some of the CWA staff are now looking for that kind of arrangement...with their employer, CWA!

So, being the inquisitive person that I am, I had to get a couple of them aside and ask, "Hey, you didn't used to believe this was the way to go, you used to really bad mouth QWL. Are you saying you've changed your mind?" And one kind of smiled, and said, "Yeah, I guess maybe I've grown up and see it in a different light." And the other guy said something mean about my mother...that was *not* true at all!

It does reinforce what I believe we now know as a labor organization, and what we are trying to accomplish with the employers that employ our people. And that is - "Make sure the workers have a say in their day-to-day work operations! They want to have a voice! And they want to be empowered - like most of our members."

This philosophy demands that the union administrators in the future must have sensitivity training, be more knowledgeable about managerial procedures, have a broader overall perspective of what *management* is all about. And learn how to listen!

I believe labor unions have operated from the premise that if you can win an election, or if you were a good union rep, you have the makings of a good manager of people. In my opinion this is *not* a given: A good labor leader and a good manager do *not* automatically have interchangeable abilities!. Consequently, within the political framework of our labor organization we have to find new ways to effectively manage our human resources. Our greatest resources of course, are our people.

Getting "Real." Three years ago we formed a Union Administrators Group in the Washington, D.C. area. It's made up of people who have responsibilities like mine; e.g. assistants, executive assistants who deal with personnel...those of us who, while not elected, have the higher management roles in labor unions.

We try to get together once a quarter for a dinner and talk about issues of common interest. We held one three-day retreat at the Meany Center and plan another one this year. We might be diverse organizations within organized labor, but there are a lot of common threads that run through all of our different unions.

Through this group we are finding ways to deal with some problems we all find very, very difficult...like what do you do when a union staffer gets burned out. What do you do when somebody has given you 25 years of good loyal service as union representative, busting their buns day after day, but are now just plain burned out? What do you do?

We're discussing the possibility of some personnel exchange programs between unions and some exchange programs with academia. Of course, we're miles away from making any of this happen, but we're

talking about it! We see a *real* positive mood and I'm really excited
about this group!

It's kind of ironic that administrators from rival unions like
AFSCME and SEIU sitting down, and working toward a common goal.
IBEW and CWA, also had many bitter fights, but now we're all
looking at ways that we can collectively affect the future of the labor
movement.

Some old-timers find our group really puzzling. One asked me
"Why do you think this sort of cooperation can happen?" I explained
the combination of situations that to my mind allow the group to exist
at this time. First of all, labor as a whole recognizes we can no longer
fight each other, although we will occasionally continue to be on
different sides in jurisdictional disputes. It doesn't mean we've got to
tear each other apart: We have identified the enemy, and it is *not*
ourselves!

Secondly, union resources are becoming more limited, and we have
to find creative and innovative ways to use our resources. And if it's
collectively working within the whole labor family to promote *all*
workers, that's what we ought to be doing!

Third, we've had a changing of some of the Old Guard with
turnover in several top union leadership positions. Situations that
caused some former leaders to hate each other's guts have diminished in
importance. New leaders recognize nothing is gained through reliving
the past and keeping alive formal adversarial relationships.

So as we go forward there is a real need for unions to pool our
talents and do things in a cooperative manner. I believe this will flow
over into our unions' educational programs and our political efforts.
There's no end of possibilities that can be accomplished by a labor
movement that's closely united.

Labor Administrators Tomorrow. I believe those who will
occupy positions like mine in the future will have an increased need for
education. An undergraduate degree will be mandatory, and a graduate
degree will be very desirable. Managing is a complex situation and it is
no easier *inside* a labor movement than it is outside. I think those who
are going to be able to put programs and plans together for a labor
organization...who assure it is managed in an efficient manner...are
going to be those who have a background that includes formal
managerial training.

In July I had the good fortune to complete my studies for a
Bachelor of Arts Degree. Through the Meany College program I
discovered one needs to have a broad educational background to deal
with complex problems and issues. The insight afforded me through
courses in science, psychology, and sociology will assist me as greatly
as the technical ones.   Hopefully I can find time to continue my
education and take graduate courses. I walk my talk!

The labor movement becomes more international every day. We're
headed for a total global economy, and if labor is going to survive it's

got to know how to be an international player. I look for future union administrators to be multi-lingual. As they'll have to be able to communicate effectively to work with our brothers and sisters worldwide. I think labor can set some real diplomatic standards for relations among the whole world's work forces as we go forward.

We'll have to continue to be politically active, and make sure we elect our friends and punish our enemies.

Overall, the role of the union administrator will be to keep the union going...to make sure the policies are well guided: to make sure internal union politics and personal egos do *not* alter our reasons for being an institution. To be damned sure to have somebody's ear and be able to promote a positive direction.

Closing Thoughts. I feel positive about things! There is no institution I see that is going to replace the labor movement. Labor furnishes a check-and-balance on the power of industrial might. I believe it is in the interest of everyone - whether they are part of or outside of the labor movement - that this balance be maintained. If other institutions, like religion or governments, could maintain this balance then there might not be such a convincing need for unions. But at this time I don't see *any* other institution in a position to take care of this job of checks-and-balances.

So, we will look a lot different in the 21st century, with more women and minorities as union administrators. Unions will continue to be *the* social conscience. I believe our charge will carry us well into the 21st century, 'cause there's nobody around who can protect people and be the social conscience any better. "Labor as an institution ain't broke, but it can use some fixin'!"

I predict 100 years from today, somebody - in some form of communication - will be saying the *same* damn things I have! And hopefully, when that person looks back, he or she will say that I made the job a little *easier* for them. If I have, then I will have accomplished what I expected to when I became active as a unionist nearly 30 years ago.

Afterword (July, 1993). A couple of years have passed since my first writing of this chapter. As with the rapid changes experienced by CWA's membership, my career changed also. My former boss retired and the incoming CWA Secretary-Treasurer saw fit to name someone else as her Executive Assistant. I was assured there wasn't a problem with my skills or performance; the politics weren't right.

Can't say I felt ecstatic about it, but someone once told me "don't spend anytime trying to lap up spilled milk. All you'll do is get your tongue dirty!" Years ago in both my personal and professional life I adopted the philosophy that when one door slams another opens. My job changes as a result of a new CWA Secretary-Treasurer has not proved an exception to my theory.

I now serve CWA as their Administrator of Finance, taking care of investments, pension and 401k plans, and property management. I overlook budgeting and other financial affairs.

The change also freed up some time to pursue an MBA degree. I am halfway through the George Washington University Executive MBA Program, affording me the opportunity to interface with academic and business leaders in a different environment. I believe my participation provides them with some in-depth insight organized labor that, in most cases, I find lacking in academia and the business community. Their views also help me realize the major work facing labor leaders as we all try to cope with the endless change facing American businesses and their workers.

Since my first writing, CWA also entered into new co-determination arrangements with a number of employers. A Democrat now occupies the White House for the first time in many years. Some of organized labor's leadership think happy days are here again. I think Bill Clinton will level the playing field somewhat. However, any significant gains by organized labor will have to be earned the same way our previous leaders won them, by making sacrifices and hard work. Management and politicians will not do the job for us.

Epilogue:
Transferable Lessons

"More than a torch has been passed to this new generation of leaders:
what they have is a clearer vision of a better world,
more productive tools with which to fashion it,
and the will and determination to settle for nothing less."

Victor G. Reuther.*The Brothers Reuther and the
Story of the UAW/A Memoir* (Boston: Houghton
Mifflin, 1979), 475.

Certain pundits write labor's obituary over and over again.[1] In sharp contrast, certain labor leaders insist they have everything under control. Unlike them both, labor's inside reformers - as represented by the 28 in this volume - reject the obituaries as premature and the assurances as false. They seek to replace all in the movement "who have been plied with the security of routine and soaked with the fear of action..."[2] They strive to ensure no further marginalization of organized labor, and strain through the darkness to see ahead.

Charge Strategies. Inside reformers understand strategy and structure are not separable. Accordingly, while recognizing the necessity of a good leader , they emphasize the indispensability of *structural* change, of re-writing a local or international union's constitution, bylaws, and other determinants of organizational reality to ensure long-lasting reform long after a particularly good leader has gone.

Similarly, inside reformers appreciate the need to employ strategic planning skills to systematize the pain-relieving process. They understand how vital it is to create rewards (performance-based raises, promotions, etc.) to induce innovation. They promote information flows. They work hard at reducing the risks of innovations. And they try to make constructive change, not paralyzing rigidity, the normal course of events.

Inside reformers believe unionism survives because it helps satisfy a need members have for moral status in a "family" they value. Accordingly, they take a pragmatic, rather than a doctrinaire approach to resolving problems. They look far and wide for advice and field-tested remedies. They harbor doubts, but are also capable of resolve. They take their own re-election seriously, but want to earn it in a fair and honest contest. Above all, they consider an empowered rank-and-file *the* highest source of authority.

Intent on achieving fundamental improvements, and aware as only participants can be of the complexity of the task, inside reformers identify personally with labor's well-being and its prospects. Challenged by its mix of both appealing goals and appalling performance, they insist recovery first and foremost requires *internal* self-examination and overhaul.

Recruitment Terms. Any reader drawn to "enlist" should recognize the importance of seven qualifications underlined by the volume's 28 cases, each a source of strength, and yet also a stressor in its own way.

1.) For openers, there is the indispensability of camaraderie. Single authorship of each case in this volume may create a false impression of impresario-like behavior. Quite the contrary! A careful re-reading will point up the great value placed on membership in a small, select, and informal circle of kindred spirits, of like-minded friends with a shared commitment to still-finer unionism. Mature enough to want constructive criticism from one another, group members help each other process fast-breaking events, refine strategy, bind up wounds, and rekindle enthusiasm.

2.) Would-be insider reformers will want to get familiar with scores of reform ideas waiting for custom-tailored adaptation to distinct situations. Field-tested ideas throughout the volume's cases barely scratch the surface. Books and journals offer still more reform options, of which there is happily no end - provided you know where to look and/or ask, and continuously do so.[3]

3.) The cases teach the indispensability of pragmatism, of taking a very practical approach that "requires us to reflect on our values and then test them out through practice, modifying them if they prove confused, meaningless, or lead to results contrary to our intentions."[4] Inside reformers prefer open-minded field tests to ideologically-prescribed "cookbook recipes." Honest and unsparing in assessing their own reform efforts, they know how to admit mistakes, correct the problem, and persist with a pragmatic campaign.

4.) Recruits should understand this is not a matter for dabblers or dilettantes. Those who set out to master a new idea or situation have to become obsessed with it: Not irrationally obsessed, but happily head-over-heels fascinated.

The exhilaration that can accompany rehabilitation of a local generally whets the appetite for still-more such gains. No role for those unwilling to give a lot of themselves, certainly for years, it should be chosen only by clear-eyed adults of steely resolve (preferably those already strong in the love and support of significant others, for as an Ibo proverb explains, "Where something stands, something else stands beside it.").

5.) The pressure is considerable to go where unionists have seldom been in search of still-better reform aids. Recognizing how much alike are the problems of all bureaucracies, inside reformers seek help from such (non-union) sources as organizational development (OD), human resource management, advanced personnel relations, and so on. Refusing to be put off by obfuscating jargon ("business-speak") and woolly-headed claptrap, labor's change-agents search for useful insights from focus groups, outcomes-based education, cultural diversity management, team-building exercises, and the trendy (if also short-lived) like.

6.) Inside reformers own up to considerable vulnerability, for as writer Gerald Sykes explains, it is "the beginning of wisdom and of knowledge with grace."[5] An inside reformer is "willing to be wounded, or to be temporarily ineffective and insecure."[6] Many feel they have not made the most yet of what is in them. Vulnerable to setbacks, they are also uniquely resilient and alive to hope.

7.) Finally, it is vital to underline a paradox at the heart of the internal reform effort: Namely, successful change-agents are comfortable being overlooked. A critical difference between certain outmoded union leaders and inside reformers involves the value each places on prominence: The former commonly love the spotlight, like to get flattering credit, and enjoy pulling strings in private, while the latter do not. An inside reformer seeks to release the "smarts" and energy commonly left ignored and untapped in the membership: Success comes when many energized dues-payers feel a victory is *theirs*, rather than owed to a larger-than-life "leader."

Summary. Until recently far too few unions put any systematic effort into securing feedback from the front lines of the organization. Or into attracting the ablest candidates to office or staff positions. Or into creatively adapting the organization's structure to new problems or opportunities.

In the last ten years, however, according to labor relations expert John T. Dunlop, "the difficult environment that has confronted American unions...has stimulated considerable study, review, and experimentation in new methods of management and administration... [methods that] are a substantial improvement over those in use a generation ago."[7]

All of which helps explain why many inside reformers like the 28 you met in this volume expect overdue changes soon in line with their renewal efforts. If labor revives in the second half of the 1990's, much credit will be owed grass-roots change-agents who continue to promote a finer-than-ever vision for the American labor movement....and for all of American society.

References

1 "Labor's obituary has been written at least once in every one of the 105 years of our existence, and nearly that many causes of death have been diagnosed...it seems we must be forever perishing so that others may be forever publishing." Lane Kirkland. "It Has All Been Said Before..." In Seymour Martin Lipset, *ed.* *Unions in Transition: Entering the Second Century* (San Francisco, CA: Institute for Contemporary Studies, 1986) 393.

2 C. Wright Mills, *The New Men of Power: America's Labor Leaders* (New York: Harcourt Brace and World, 1948), 290.

3 See in this connection, Arthur B. Shostak. *Robust Unionism: Innovations in the Labor Movement* (Ithaca, NY: ILR Press, 1991).

4 Michael Maccoby, *ed. Sweden at the Edge: Lessons for American and Swedish Managers* (Philadelphia: University of Pennsylvania Press, 1991), 300.

5 Gerald Sykes. *The Hidden Remnant.* (New York: Harper and Brothers, 1962),

6 *Ibid.*

7 John T. Dunlop. *The Management of Labor Unions: Decision Making with Historical Constraints* (Lexington, MASS: D. C. Heath, 1990), 7.

Acknowledgments and Apology

My greatest debt is to the 28 men and women who made this book possible: Without their candor, courage, and intellect, there would be nothing worth sharing...and little reason to expect more soon of organized labor.

As often before, my primary employer, Drexel University, was generous in its support through released time for research and the backup resource of a fine university library. Richard Binder, a specialist in social science literature, was of particular help, as with many earlier books of mine.

Julia Southard, my typist, kept up my often-faltering belief that this project would ever reach completion. Her forbearance, affability, and craft continue to make an invaluable difference, especially when the going got tough. Her cheerful promise, "You've got it!," in response to my request for last-minute, tight deadline work, proved a wonderful balm. Paul Southard, Julia's husband proved to be instrumental in helping this project come to its completion, with his "babysitting" duties and assitance in indexing.

Lynn Seng, my wife, showed me how to rein in my "busy-ness" long enough to draw this project to a satisfying close. As often before, she listened and helped resolve the project's many quandaries. This time for the first time in our long collaboration she undertook to tutor me in the arcane art of Apple MAC word-processing, a most trying task as I am not the easiest student with which to work. Fortunately she demonstrated here as elsewhere in our life together the patience, love, and empathy I have come to deeply appreciate .

While many friends read some part of the manuscript and offered constructive criticisms, none was as helpful as Joyce Kornbluh, a colleague at the AFL-CIO George Meany Center. She helped me secure several female contributors, and joins me in resolving to secure many more should this book soon earn a second new edition.

Thanks are also owed to Ike Gittlen, one of the volume's contributors, who secured a critical pre-publication order from Robert Pleasure, Director of the George Meany Center. Another Antioch-Meany Center student, Robert E. Peterson, helped with several cover design ideas (as did Christopher Gibson, Director of IMS at Drexel University). Similarly, Michelle Harris and Helen Hudson of University Press of America made certain the volume met the high standards we all share.

As for the apology promised at the outset I deeply regret my inability to secure a union "bug" from a unionized printer for this volume. Unfortunately, this has become more and more difficult to arrange in the publication industry, though if labor's inside reformers have the impact they promote this may soon change for the better: I certainly hope so!

Guide to Union Abbreviations

AFA	Association of Flight Attendants
AFT	American Federation of Teachers
ATU	Amalgamated Transit Union
BMWE	Brotherhood of Maintenance of Way Employees
CWA	Communication Workers of America
HERE	Hotel Employees and Restaurant Employees Union
IAM	International Association of Machinists
IBEW	International Brotherhood of Electrical Workers
IBPAT	International Brotherhood of Painters and Allied Trades
IUE	International Union of Electricians
IUOE	International Union of Operating Engineers
SEIU	Service Employees International Union
TCIU	Transportation Communications International Union
UAW	United Autoworkers Union
UFCW	United Food and Commercial Workers
UMWA	United Mineworkers of America
URW	United Rubber Workers
USWA	United Steelworkers Union
UTU	United Transportation Union
UURW&A	United Union of Roofers, Waterproofers and Allied Workers

Notes on the Editor

In keeping with his B.S. degree in Industrial and Labor Relations from Cornell University (1954-58), Professor Shostak has served since 1975 as an Adjunct Sociologist with the Antioch College degree program at the AFL-CIO George Meany Center for Labor Studies (Silver Spring, MD). He has also taught for or consulted with the Steelworkers Union, the Postal Workers Union, the IBEW, and many others.

An applied sociologist since earning his Ph.D. in 1961 at Princeton University, he has taught at Drexel University since 1967. Prior to that he was on the faculty at Wharton School of Finance and Commerce, University of Pennsylvania (1961-67). His courses at Drexel include industrial sociology, management and technology, futuristics, race and ethnic relations, social implications of 20th century technology, urban sociology, social change and social planning, and introduction to sociology.

Professor Shostak is the sole author of *Robust Unionism* (1991), *Blue Collar Stress* (1980), *Modern Social Reforms* (1974), *Blue-Collar Life* (1968), and *American's Forgotten Labor Organization* (1962); co-author of *The Air Controllers' Controversy* (1986) and *Men and Abortion* (1984); editor of *Guidelines from Gomberg* (1992), *Our Sociological Eye* (1977), *Putting Sociology to Work* (1974), *Sociology and Student Life* (1972), and *Sociology in Action* (1962); and co-editor of *Privilege in America* (1974) *New Perspectives on Poverty* (1965), and *Blue Collar World* (1964).

In 1987 Professor Shostak received the "Distinguished Scholarship" award of the Pennsylvania Sociological Society, the "Distinguished Practitioner" Award of the Section on Sociological Practice of the American Sociological Association, and the "Outstanding Practitioner" Award of the Clinical Sociological Society. In 1990 he was designated the Lester F. Ward Distinguished Sociologist by the Society for Applied Sociology. In 1992 he was awarded a study grant by the Swedish-American Bicentennial Fund that enabled him to explore with Swedish labor leaders the role of inside reformers in the world's strongest labor movement. In 1994 he assumed the presidency of the Philadelphia chapter of the Industrial Relations Research Association, the second-largest chapter in the country.